SOUTHERN FOOTPRINTS

A DAN JOSSELYN MEMORIAL PUBLICATION

SOUTHERN FOOTPRINTS
EXPLORING GULF COAST ARCHAEOLOGY

GREGORY A. WASELKOV and PHILIP J. CARR
Foreword by FRYE GAILLARD

THE UNIVERSITY OF ALABAMA PRESS | TUSCALOOSA

The University of Alabama Press
Tuscaloosa, Alabama 35487-0380
uapress.ua.edu

Copyright © 2024 by the University of Alabama Press
All rights reserved.

Inquiries about reproducing material from this work should
be addressed to the University of Alabama Press.

Typeface: Scala Pro

Cover images: (*above*; detail) *A Plan of Part of the Rivers Tombecbe, Alabama, Tensa, Perdido, & Scambia in the Province of West Florida, 1771*, by David Taitt, courtesy of Library of Congress; (*below; left to right*) Mississippian anthropomorphic head effigy, Bottle Creek; Ashley Dumas troweling, Spanish Fort; English wine bottle, Port Dauphin village, courtesy of the Center for Archaeological Studies, University of South Alabama

Cover design: Lori Lynch

Cataloging-in-Publication data is available from the Library of Congress.
ISBN: 978-0-8173-2205-2 (cloth)
ISBN: 978-0-8173-6153-2 (paper)
EISBN: 978-0-8173-9523-0

FOR LIN AND NICOLE

Contents

Foreword by Frye Gaillard xi

Acknowledgments xv

An Introduction to the Archaeology of South Alabama
and the Central Gulf Coast 1

PART I. SOUTH ALABAMA

1. The Archaeology Museum at the University of South Alabama . . . 11
2. Greater Mobile-Tensaw River Area 17

PART II. SITE DISCOVERY

3. Coastal Surveys 23
4. Surveys of the Mobile-Tensaw Delta and Mobile Bay 29
5. National Forest Surveys 36

PART III. ARCHAIC PERIOD (9500–1000 BC)

6. John Forrest Site 43
7. Lincoln County Mound 49
8. Silver Run 53

PART IV. WOODLAND PERIOD (1000 BC–AD 1150)

9. Gulf Shores Canoe Canal 61
10. Bayou St. John 68

11. Clarke County 73

PART V. MISSISSIPPIAN PERIOD (AD 1150–1700)

12. Bottle Creek Mounds 83
13. Dauphin Island Shell Mounds 90
14. McInnis Site 97
15. Dugout Canoes 107

PART VI. FRENCH COLONIAL PERIOD (1699–1763)

16. Old Mobile 115
17. Port Dauphin 124
18. Fort Condé 129

PART VII. COLONIAL PLANTATIONS

19. La Pointe-Krebs Plantation 137
20. Bon Secour River Sites 144
21. Rivière aux Chiens Plantation 149
22. Augustin Rochon Plantation 156
23. Lisloy Plantation 160
24. The Village 164
25. Water Street, Mobile 171

PART VIII. LATE COLONIAL/EARLY FEDERAL PERIOD (1764–1859)

26. The Southeast in 1773 181
27. Exploreum Science Center and History Museum of Mobile . . . 186
28. Historic Blakeley Park 193
29. Fort Mims 199
30. Ekvncakv/Holy Ground 208
31. Old St. Stephens 214

PART IX. CIVIL WAR ERA (1860–1868)

32. Africatown Visitor Center 225
33. Camp Withers 232

34. Spanish Fort 236

35. 1865 Ordnance Explosion 243

PART X. LATE NINETEENTH CENTURY

36. Spring Hill College 253

37. Eastern Shore Potteries 260

38. Mount Vernon 266

39. Lucrecia Perryman's Well 273

PART XI. MODERN TIMES (1900–PRESENT)

40. Bayou La Batre 281

41. I-10 Mobile River Bridge 286

Epilogue 289

Notes 301

Bibliography 335

Index 369

Foreword

This book by two of the nation's most accomplished archaeologists tells two stories. The first is a saga, recounted in accessible vignettes, of human habitation along the Gulf Coast. The second is a story of archaeology itself—a meticulous attempt to uncover and preserve a history stretching back across twelve thousand years.

Gregory A. Waselkov and Philip J. Carr have both spent a major part of their careers working as archaeologists at the University of South Alabama. In that capacity, they have wandered the hills and forests, the delta swamplands, and the streets of cities like Mobile, searching for bits and pieces of the past. It is tedious, often frustrating work. At times, in fact, it can even be dangerous, for human beings have long shared this place with snakes and alligators and swarms of yellow jackets and mosquitos. But the authors will tell you the discoveries are worth it.

Working with colleagues at other institutions and building on the effort of their predecessors and hundreds of volunteers with an interest in the past, Waselkov and Carr have put together a fascinating tale. As a reader, you can open the book and dip into its pages wherever you choose. Each short chapter is self-contained. But here are a few of the highlights.

Approximately seven thousand years ago, as South Alabama researchers have confirmed, Indigenous people from what has been called the Middle Archaic period of ancient American history were busy making art. Specifically, these artisans left evidence of intricate beadwork, fashioned from pebbles gathered from surrounding stream beds. Some beads were tubular; others were zoomorphic, or animal shaped. All of them were carved and polished, and the holes through which the beads could be strung were drilled with bits of stone no bigger than a grain of rice.

Like much of modern archaeology, these discoveries in what is now southwest Mississippi refute past stereotypes of ancient people—images of savages, noble or not, whose lives were circumscribed by the daily search for food. Instead, write Carr and Waselkov, the archaeological record from the Gulf Coast reveals a story of "inventiveness, keen observation of the environment, and artistic accomplishment."

As early as five thousand years ago, these Native people were beginning the practice of building mounds, and over the millennia other engineering feats would follow. Sometime around AD 600, Indigenous residents built an intricate canal, deep enough for their dugout canoes, across the Fort Morgan peninsula on the eastern side of Mobile Bay. South Alabama archaeologists suspect the builders of "the Indian ditch," as it was known to locals in the twentieth century, came from a permanent village near the mouth of Bon Secour River. The mile-long canal enabled residents to broaden their diet from nearby oyster-rich resources to the more diverse fisheries of Little Lagoon—and just beyond it, the Gulf of Mexico.

As year-round villages began to dot the coastal landscape and with the beginnings of agriculture—the adoption of domesticated maize, dating back to AD 900—the area experienced a major migration. Mississippians from the Black Warrior River, near what is now Tuscaloosa, began moving south toward the Gulf. By AD 1100, they were cultivating maize in the rich bottomlands on the edges of the delta. Sometime around AD 1250, on an island hidden away in the swamp, they began to construct sacred mounds similar to those they had built farther north. Around the same time on Dauphin Island, using oyster shells instead of dirt, they built what Waselkov and Carr call "a comparable townscape crafted from shells, at the edge of the southern sea."

A few centuries later, almost from the moment they arrived, Europeans began to desecrate these sites. In a journal entry on March 4, 1702, Pierre Le Moyne d'Iberville, leader of a French expedition, wrote about an Indian man who took Iberville's brother, Jean Baptiste Le Moyne de Bienville, to "the place where their gods are." From a temple at the top of a mound in the delta, Bienville promptly stole five statues: "A man, a woman, a child, a bear, and an owl."[1]

In 1702, the French under Iberville built an outpost on a river bluff twenty-seven miles north of Mobile Bay. Years of archaeological research directed by Waselkov helped pinpoint the sites of more than fifty French-made structures scattered across eighty acres. In 1711, the French settlers moved to the current site of Mobile. Along with Spanish Pensacola, founded in 1698, these rustic towns helped usher in a bloody struggle to control the northern rim of the Gulf. The French, British, Spanish, Native Americans, and the newly created Americans all asserted their claims to the land.

During the Revolutionary War, Gulf Coast battles were fought by proxy—Spanish troops allied with the United States battling Choctaw forces allied with the British. In 1813, as the War of 1812 raged farther north, a deadly attack on Fort Mims triggered a war in which American troops under Andrew Jackson broke the back of the militant Redstick faction of the Creek Nation. When the American Civil War followed less than fifty years later, bringing with it a massive loss of life, the greatest casualties in the port of Mobile came not from the battles of Mobile Bay, or nearby Fort Blakeley, but from a random explosion near the waterfront.

As Waselkov and Carr write, "on Thursday, May 25, 1865, at half past two in the afternoon, a vast stockpile of Confederate munitions blew up, killing hundreds and destroying much of the city's port district." The massive blast came as a work detail of African American volunteers—soldiers in the Union Army—were unloading captured Confederate artillery shells. There were reports of the blast being heard in Meridian, Mississippi, 140 miles away. Thirty-four city blocks were destroyed.

These are only a few of the stories documented in these pages. And the work of archaeology has continued. In 1993, the city of Mobile began renovating a playground known as Crawford Park. As luck would have it, one of the subcontractors, George Shorter, was a graduate student in anthropology at Louisiana State University (LSU) and a man with a long-standing interest in the past. When he discovered the remnants of an old well on the property, Shorter and PhD candidate Laurie Wilkie, also from LSU, began a careful excavation of the site. They uncovered an inspirational story.

The land had once belonged to Marshall and Lucrecia Perryman, an African American couple born into slavery. When freedom came at the end of the Civil War, Marshall bought three tracts of land in Mobile, a place where he and his extended family could live and build their lives. Over time, his wife, Lucrecia, became a nurse midwife, one of the leading practitioners of that vocation in southern Alabama. Scattered near her abandoned well were dozens of bottles that once contained medicine that she had given her patients. A moving exhibit at the Archaeology Museum at the University of South Alabama recounts her story today. She and her family now personify a legacy of aspiration that runs through the very heart of Black history.

Other discoveries have revealed a darker side of our history. In 2015, Waselkov and colleague Bonnie Gums led a team that located an Apache village site near the town of Mount Vernon in northern Mobile County. From 1887 to 1894, the site was home to Apache prisoners of war, including the legendary Geronimo and his followers. The Apaches—accustomed to vast, open skies and desert mountains where they could see for miles—hated it here. "There was no place to climb to pray," remembered Eugene Chihuahua, a small boy at the time of his family's incarceration. "If we wanted to see the sky we had to climb a tall pine."[2]

In 1902, eight years after the Apache prisoners were moved to Oklahoma, the Mount Vernon Insane Hospital, a segregated facility for Black mental patients, opened at the same site. Almost immediately, it was hit by an outbreak of pellagra, a nutritional disease causing skin lesions, weakness, diarrhea, and sometimes dementia. The hospital was desegregated in 1969. It closed its doors in 2012. Little has been done to maintain the historic nature of the site, painful though that history may be.

Today, scholars at the University of South Alabama continue to play a major role in preserving stories of the Africatown community, where captives from the slave ship *Clotilda* began to build new lives as soon as they were free. Other researchers have conducted interviews in the Alabama fishing village of Bayou La Batre, where residents—Black, white, and Asian—struggle to maintain their way of life in the wake of natural and humanmade disasters. And, finally, in the largest project ever undertaken by University of South Alabama archaeologists, Carr and his team are excavating fifteen sites, multicultural in nature, in the path of a bridge soon to be built across Mobile Bay.

In this accessible account of their work, Waselkov and Carr have given us a far-ranging history of human habitation on the Gulf of Mexico and of the attempt, equally fascinating, by hundreds of colleagues, students, and volunteers to put the pieces of that history together. It is, in the end, the story of who we are and how we got here. No matter our ethnicity or backgrounds, no matter when our families came to these shores, it is a story that belongs to us all.

FRYE GAILLARD
WRITER IN RESIDENCE, UNIVERSITY OF SOUTH ALABAMA

Acknowledgments

For this overview of more than fifty years of archaeology at the University of South Alabama, we have drawn on project reports written by former Center for Archaeological Studies staff, including Bonnie Gums, George Shorter, Sarah Price, Sarah Mattics, Diane Silvia, Richard Fuller, Noel Read Stowe, Rebecca Lumpkin Stowe, Raven Christopher, Tara Potts, Ashley Dumas, Ginny Newberry, Ray Keene, Amy Carruth, Warren Carruth, Michael Stieber, and Harriet Richardson Seacat. Philip J. Carr was lead author on chapters 5–8, 11, 32, and 41; Gregory A. Waselkov took the lead on all of the others. Judith Bense and John Blitz offered encouragement and suggestions that improved the final text, and Joan De-Jean translated several key passages from French and Italian.

Sarah Mattics, Raven Christopher, and Sarah Price created many of the project graphics that illustrate these essays. (Some maps in this book were created using ArcGIS software by Esri. ArcGIS and ArcMap, the intellectual property of Esri, are used herein under license, copyright © Esri.)

Volunteerism has always been a mainstay of American archaeology, and that has certainly been true in south Alabama. From the earliest days, Noel Read Stowe encouraged the participation of talented volunteers such as Dan Jenkins, Michael Poe, and David Smithweck, to name just a few. Some of our most important research has depended heavily on volunteers, including fieldwork at Old Mobile, Bayou St. John, La Pointe-Krebs, Ekvncakv/Holy Ground, Old St. Stephens, and Spanish Fort. Two important projects—investigations at the Gulf Shores Canoe Canal and McInnis sites—were accomplished almost entirely with volunteer expertise and labor. Among the several hundred individuals who have helped us in the field and lab, we especially thank those who have been dedicated supporters for many years (listed roughly in chronological order of participation):

Traci Cunningham, Jackie McConaha, Donnie and Lottie Barrett, Dennis Guy, Tom McCaskey, John Ellis, Gerry Ollhoft, Shawn Holland, Patrick Johnson, Barbara Hester, Jimmy Fox, Carey Geiger, Louis Scott, Brad Eklund, Kate Waselkov, Peter Waselkov, Nick Waselkov, Lori Sawyer, Glenn Thrower, Rick Fuller, Frank Vogtner, Lee Swetman, Curry Weber, Fred Van Cor, and Karrie Lovins.

Our research projects discussed here have benefited from support from many quarters. Our colleague Bernard Diamond (professor of French at the University of South Alabama) masterminded a sister city agreement between Mobile and Québec City that led to a fruitful and ongoing engagement with archaeologists at Université Laval, especially with Marcel Moussette, Canada's premier historical archaeologist, and to numerous student exchanges between our universities. At the local, state, and federal levels, officials with the city of Mobile, the city of Spanish Fort, the city of Gulf Shores, the Mobile County Commission, the Alabama State legislature and state agencies, and Alabama's congressional members and staff have all contributed in numerous constructive ways to the furtherance of our teaching, research goals, and efforts at site interpretation and preservation.

Alabama Historical Commission staff, in particular, have supported us in myriad ways but perhaps most effectively with funding for archaeological surveys and excavations from the Alabama Cultural Resources Preservation Trust Fund. From 1995 to 2010, the $8.5 million trust fund generated $700,000 annually for the state's preservation needs. The principal came from a fine levied by the Federal Energy Regulatory Commission against the Transcontinental Gas Pipeline Company (TRANSCO) for constructing a 125-mile pipeline through ten Alabama counties without regard for archaeological sites destroyed in the process. Until the trust fund was reallocated to other purposes in 2011, center staff competed for matching grants that allowed us to search for pottery kilns threatened by development on the Eastern Shore of Mobile Bay, to carry out emergency excavations at Port Dauphin, to offer public archaeology programs at Old St. Stephens, and many other worthwhile projects.

Over the years we have always found strong support in the community for our research. Some individuals, however, proved to be exceptionally dedicated allies, always supportive but also invariably urging us to do more to protect and interpret the most important sites. These archaeology stalwarts include Davida Hastie (Bottle Creek); James "Buddy" Parnell and Joy Klotz (Old Mobile); cousins Davis Smith and Leslie Smith (Fort Mims); Jo Ann Flirt and Mike Bunn (Blakeley); Jim Long and George Shorter (Old St. Stephens); Robert Thrower, Lori Sawyer, and Jessica Crawford (Ekvncakv/Holy Ground); and Harry King (Gulf Shores Canoe Canal).

Research at the Archaeological Research Laboratory (1971–91) and the Center for Archaeological Studies (1992 to present) has benefited from the unwavering backing and encouragement of administrators at the University of South Alabama, particularly all four of the university's presidents, as well as provosts and vice presidents, college deans, our department's chairs, staff at Sponsored Programs and Contracts and Grants Accounting, and the University of South Alabama Foundation. Many of these administrators were also instrumental in the university's creation of the Archaeology Museum. David Johnson deserves special acknowledgment for his leadership, as dean of the College of Arts and Sciences, then vice president for Academic Affairs, and finally university provost.

A number of university administrators and programs provided financial support for this publication: the Center for Archaeological Studies; the Center for Archaeological Studies Endowment; Kara Burns, director, and Jennifer Knutson, assistant director, Archaeology Museum; Native American Studies Program; Roma S. Hanks, chair, Department of Sociology, Anthropology, and Social Work; Andrzej Wierzbicki, dean, College of Arts and Sciences; Harold Pardue, dean, Graduate School; Nick Lawkis, executive director, Office of Governmental Relations; Lynne Chronister, vice president for Research and Economic Development; and Andrea Kent, executive vice president and provost.

To all the students, staff, volunteers, professional colleagues, university administrators, government officials, grant agencies, and private individuals who have supported the University of South Alabama's archaeological endeavors over the last half century, thank you!

SOUTHERN FOOTPRINTS

An Introduction to the Archaeology of South Alabama and the Central Gulf Coast

History is written in books, in people's memories, and in the detritus of our lives. To an observant archaeologist, the impressions we leave on the landscape and in the ground—our footprints, real and metaphorical—betray all manner of truths about the human endeavor, our accomplishments and our failures, across innumerable generations of existence on this planet.

Our scope in this volume is far more modest. With this collection of essays, we sample the archaeology of the central Gulf Coast, mostly in and around Mobile in southwest Alabama, with occasional forays farther afield, as revealed since 1970 by researchers based at the University of South Alabama. Our title, *Southern Footprints*, reflects our narrowed focus, although "southerners" subsumes a remarkably diverse cast of characters—longtime Natives as well as relative newcomers—who have trod this landscape over the considerable span of more than twelve thousand years.

Coastal Alabama and its hinterland are justly famous for exceptional ecological abundance and diversity. Mobile Bay and its associated estuaries are nourished by downstream flows from the immense marshes and swamps of the renowned Mobile-Tensaw delta, all bordered by Red Hills blanketed with longleaf pine forests and their boggy understory of pitcher plants. A powerhouse of biological productivity, this region has been appreciated as such by human residents for millennia. Little wonder, then, that the archaeological record left here by human residents rivals in complexity the environmental marvel that has long sustained them.

Since the end of the Pleistocene Ice Age, steadily rising sea level has slowly but inexorably pushed the Gulf of Mexico coastline northward, inundating earlier barrier islands and gradually creating something like the current coastal landscape around four thousand years ago. Archaeological signs of coastal occupation by Native Americans are increasingly abundant from that point forward. The density of ancient habitation sites testifies to large coastal and riverine populations, physical remains that echo in the deep oral histories maintained to this day by Choctaw, Muscogee, and other descendent Native communities. In later centuries, newcomers from Europe and Africa, and most recently from every corner of the world, have added their imprints to this region's archaeological record. South Alabama's archaeology encompasses the rich histories of all its occupants.

We are two archaeologists who have had the immense privilege to practice our craft in this extraordinary place. Our book passes along some of the archaeological stories we have learned about south Alabama's human past, about the origins of our present society, and how our region and society might change in the future. We also hope that you, the readers, will share our enthusiasm for the process of archaeological inquiry. How do we solve historical puzzles from the bits of pottery, oyster shells, broken stones, discarded bottles, and other physical accumulations of past lives? And, in the end, we invite you to join us in helping to preserve critically important archaeological sites for those who come after us.

Although south Alabama's archaeological record stretches back thousands of years, the research that has revealed so much of this region's archaeology is a fairly recent endeavor. Here is our story.

Between 1970 and 2022, University of South Alabama archaeologists—faculty, staff, students, and volunteers—carried out nearly 1,300 research projects in and around southwest Alabama. Some of these projects contributed profoundly to our understanding of life in this region from ancient times to the present. To celebrate more than fifty years of archaeology at the University of South Alabama, we wrote this collection of essays about those research projects we consider our "Greatest Hits," the ones that have proved to be the most enlightening or influential in reshaping our understanding of this region's history.

These essays cover a range of projects, from reconnaissance surveys where we searched for previously undiscovered archaeological sites, to indepth excavations, to the archival and laboratory studies that always accompany fieldwork. Students have been involved in every step of this research. They are the reason we do archaeology at the University of South Alabama. Hundreds of undergraduates enrolled in field methods courses have gained firsthand experience at some of the most significant archaeological sites in the Gulf Coast region. A select few of these students, the ones most serious about a career in archaeology, have written senior theses on research topics supervised by faculty mentors.

To augment formal classroom training, faculty at the University of South Alabama have always offered paid assistantships to motivated students who can participate in a variety of research activities. This aspect of student training began quite intentionally. When Noel Read Stowe arrived in Mobile in 1970 to direct the University of Alabama's excavations at the site of Fort Condé, he hired students for his field crew from the local college, the University of South Alabama. Student involvement in a high-profile scientific dig in downtown Mobile suggested to administrators at the University of South Alabama, which had opened in Mobile a few years earlier, that archaeology courses ought to be added to the undergraduate curriculum. Soon afterward, Stowe was hired there as an instructor in what was then the Department of Sociology (now the Department of Sociology, Anthropology, and Social Work), a position he held for twenty-nine years.

Impending destruction of the site of Fort Condé, which lay in the path of Interstate 10 highway construction, had prompted the first cultural resource management (CRM) archaeology project in Alabama. CRM regulations now require federally funded or federally permitted developers to consider the impacts of their actions on archaeological sites and to mitigate those impacts if the archaeological sites are considered significant. That federal initiative has saved thousands of archaeological sites across the nation from destruction through avoidance, by rerouting construction when possible. In cases where avoidance is considered unfeasible, federal rules can require scientific excavation, which has happened in thousands more cases since passage of the National Historic Preservation Act in 1966. Once Stowe arrived at the University of South Alabama, he established the Archaeological Research Laboratory so the university could apply for CRM contract funds, which enabled him to hire professional staff and student assistants. Among those first fulltime staff were Richard Fuller and Diane Silvia, who contributed immensely to our knowledge of the region's archaeology, while also serving as mentors to student assistants who gained invaluable practical training.

In 1987 the university created an undergraduate major in anthropology (the traditional academic home of archaeology in the United States), followed one year later by the hire of a second faculty archaeologist, Gregory A. Waselkov, as an assistant professor. When the university established the Center for Archaeological Studies in 1992, Waselkov became director and continued the university's engagement with CRM archaeology. He also began to compete for grant funding from federal and state agencies such as the National Science Foundation, the National Endowment for the Humanities, the National Park Service, and the Alabama Historical Commission.

Over the next three decades, many talented archaeologists—Bonnie Gums, George Shorter, Sarah Mattics, Ashley Dumas, Sarah Price, Raven Christopher, Harriet Richardson Seacat, Ginny Newberry, and others—have worked as senior staff at the center on contract and grant projects. Their contributions to south Alabama's archaeology are highlighted throughout this volume. Several hundred student assistants gained field and laboratory experience working alongside center staff and faculty, and more than a few have since gone on to productive and fulfilling careers in CRM archaeology, which now employs most of the professional archaeologists in the United States. Others hold appointments with museums and government agencies, and several are now tenured university professors.

Since Waselkov's retirement as emeritus professor in 2017, the Center for Archaeological Studies has continued to engage in CRM and grant research under the direction of Prof. Philip J. Carr (who had served as associate director since 1999). Some important research projects have been made possible in other ways, such as by contracts between the university and the Poarch Band of Creek Indians, by gifts from charitable foundations, and by donations from private individuals. Other projects have depended entirely on talent and labor donated by dedicated volunteers. The center's roughly 1,300 projects, accomplished by these various means, have touched thousands of people in our community and our state. For decades the Center for Archaeological Studies has been a principal avenue of community engagement for the University of South Alabama.

The extraordinary results of more than fifty years of archaeological research in south Alabama and adjacent areas have transformed our knowledge of human history on the Gulf Coast. Of course, others preceded us in this endeavor, and we have benefited immensely from the pioneering efforts of scholars such as Peter Hamilton, Emma Langdon Roche, Paul Boudousquie, Jay Higginbotham, Walter B. Jones, E. Bruce Trickey, and Steve Wimberly, whose accomplishments laid the groundwork for much of our research. But so much still remains to be done. We have been especially mindful of the potential for archaeology to provide insights about the lives of people who have been underrepresented or, in some cases, entirely overlooked in written histories—women, children, the poor, the illiterate, the enslaved, and the countless generations of Indigenous peoples who have occupied this land from the Ice Age until today. Our most rewarding projects have illuminated the lives of some remarkably accomplished but long neglected people, such as the brilliant Native American engineers who designed and constructed a canal for dugout canoes to cross Fort Morgan peninsula around AD 600 and Lucrecia Perryman, an African American midwife renowned in late nineteenth-century Mobile but largely forgotten until her homesite turned up in a city park during sports facilities renovation. Many such stories have been revealed by the archaeologist's trowel over the last half century.

Likewise, hundreds of previously unknown sites have been discovered, documented, and investigated, with some of the most significant now preserved for the future. Many of our region's state parks have been explored and their sites interpreted with input from center archaeologists. In the long run, the extensive artifact collections from these sites, now permanently curated at the University of South Alabama, offer nearly endless possibilities for future research and public education.

Our research findings are available to the public in published and online formats and through educational exhibits and programming at the Archaeology Museum, which opened in 2012 on the University of South Alabama's main campus in Mobile. As we enter our sixth decade, archaeology at the University of South Alabama continues to raise public awareness and appreciation of this region's rich archaeological heritage and the information it can provide about life in this landscape over the last several thousand years. The future promises many more discoveries.

Finally, a few words about this book's organization. The first two essays introduce readers to our topic and location, with a look at the University of South Alabama's Archaeology Museum and a geographical overview of this coastal region. The next two essays discuss archaeological surveys, the methods we use to find sites, and a sampling of the diversity of archaeological sites found in this region. The rest of the book, organized chronologically (more or less), begins with some of the oldest archaeological sites in this part of the country and ends in our own era. ("More or less" because people, having found some places more attractive than others, have occupied desirable spots repeatedly through the centuries, a fact that complicates a neat chronological ordering of our topic.) Consequently, these essays, taken together, do not form a sequential narrative of human existence in this region. Instead, we have written about how various past peoples have lived in this remarkably diverse part of the world.

Some of the places discussed here are publicly accessible (fig. I.1). We encourage you to visit them. These include the Museum of Alabama at the Alabama Department of Archives and History in Montgomery; Bottle Creek site on Mound Island in the Mobile-Tensaw delta; Shell Mound Park on Dauphin Island; La Pointe-Krebs house in Pascagoula; Lisloy on the grounds of Bellingrath Gardens and Home in Theodore; the city of

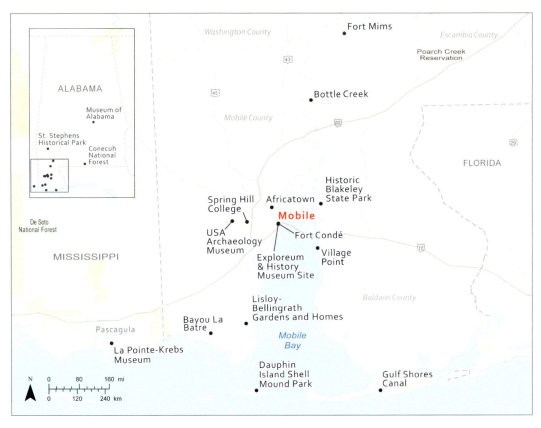

I.1. Publicly accessible museums, historic sites, and archaeological sites discussed in this book. (Base map sources: Esri, DeLorme; graphic by Raven Christopher, Center for Archaeological Studies, University of South Alabama.)

Bayou La Batre; Village Point Preserve in Daphne; Historic Blakeley State Park outside of the city of Spanish Fort; Fort Mims Park in Tensaw; Old St. Stephens Park in Washington County; and Fort Condé, the Exploreum Science Center, Spring Hill College, the History Museum of Mobile, and the University of South Alabama's Archaeology Museum, all in the city of Mobile. The rest unfortunately are not open to the public for a variety of reasons, most because they are on private land.

South Alabama still has many extant archaeological sites, an enviable situation due almost entirely to the foresight of our predecessors, the considerate landowners and land stewards who valued these remnants of the past and protected them from thoughtless damage or destruction. For example, for more than a century the McMillan family prohibited unauthorized digging while they farmed the Bottle Creek site on Mound Island, which helped preserve those mounds in their nearly pristine condition.

Enforcement officers with the Alabama Department of Conservation and Natural Resources now patrol that state-owned site to ensure its continued preservation. We hope you will draw inspiration, as we have, from the preservation ethic demonstrated by the McMillan family and so many others who have left us a wonderful archaeological legacy.

Please feel free to dip into this book wherever a topic piques your interest. We have intentionally kept our essays brief. Endnotes provide key references (cited in full in the bibliography) for readers who may wish to look further into a subject. Some are technical reports intended for serious researchers and are not publicly accessible in most cases. Many of the references written by Waselkov and Carr can be found online at two websites, Academia.com and ResearchGate.

PART I

SOUTH ALABAMA

CHAPTER 1

The Archaeology Museum at the University of South Alabama

... where visitors, young and old, can see results of fifty years of research, engage with professional archaeologists, and participate in educational events.

After decades of archaeological research in the Mobile region, the University of South Alabama's collections of excavated artifacts had become voluminous and their proper care increasingly challenging. A dedicated curation facility could solve those problems and ensure the collections would be preserved for future use and enjoyment. Members of the public also wondered, with justification, when they would see some of the artifacts uncovered by all this digging. Faculty and staff at the Center for Archaeological Studies, who were frequently called on to talk at schools and other public venues about our findings, began lobbying for an on-campus museum that would meet curation and public education needs.

In 2005, University of South Alabama's President Gordon Moulton, Dean of the College of Arts and Sciences David Johnson, and other administrators developed a plan to build a permanent campus home for archaeology. This new facility, the Alfred and Lucille Delchamps Archaeology Building (fig. 1.1), would provide a secure and environmentally stable space that meets federal requirements for curation of archaeological collections. Above the ground-level curation area, a three-thousand-square-foot exhibit space and a smaller temporary gallery would be devoted to community outreach and education (fig. 1.2). Building construction was completed by 2007, made possible by a federal grant and donations from the Delchamps family and the university's National Alumni Association.

1.1. Alfred and Lucille Delchamps Archaeology Building at the University of South Alabama. (Photograph by Dave Snyder, Center for Archaeological Studies, University of South Alabama.)

    Exhibit design and fabrication, however, would take another five years. Contributions from local foundations (Sybil H. Smith Charitable Trust, Crampton Trust, Hearin-Chandler Foundation, J. L. Bedsole Foundation, and Daniel Foundation of Alabama), as well as the College of Arts and Sciences; the Department of Sociology, Anthropology, and Social Work; and the Center for Archaeological Studies enabled the creation of first-rate exhibits built almost entirely inhouse by a large team spearheaded by Greg Waselkov, George Shorter, Sarah Mattics, Barbara Fillion, and Nick Waselkov. A video of flintknapper Andrew Bradbury fashioning a stone tool adds to the visitor's experience, as do paintings by artists Jason Guynes, Dean Mosher, and Sheila Nguyen Overstreet. Textile artist Mary Spanos applied her expertise in replicating ancient fabrics to clothe realistic human figures fashioned especially for our exhibit from live models by StudioEIS in Brooklyn, New York (fig. 1.3). Cherokee artists Mary Thompson, Sarah Thompson, and Geraldine Walkingstick (three generations of a basketweaving family) and Jim Long wove rivercane baskets and mats, and Kevin Welch carved a log corn-grinding mortar, all historically accurate furnishings for a replicated Native American house from eight hundred years ago. Other friends of the museum donated important artifacts

1.2. Museum visitors interact with the stratigraphy wall, October 2012. (Center for Archaeological Studies, University of South Alabama.)

and contributed additional content (fig. 1.4), such as Sid Hite's generous gift of Paleoindian and Archaic period stone tools. At a grand opening on October 16, 2012, we finally shared our archaeological discoveries with the public.

Because few people ever visit the most impressive archaeological site in the region—Bottle Creek on Mound Island in the middle of the Mobile-Tensaw delta—we decided to incorporate a bit of the Bottle Creek experience into our museum. The exhibit floor of our building was designed with a twenty-foot-deep chasm that gives museum visitors the impression of standing at a mound-top vantage point to view a panorama of the Mississippian town as it looked around AD 1250. University art students spent several semesters on scaffolds painting this mural, under the supervision of Jason Guynes, chair of the Department of Visual Arts. Other immersive

1.3. Mississippian chief (ca. AD 1350) at Bottle Creek, from exhibit at the Archaeology Museum. (Photograph by Dave Snyder, Center for Archaeological Studies, University of South Alabama.)

elements of the exhibit include a furnished replica of a French colonial Gulf Coast house, based on excavated remains of early eighteenth-century structures; the 1900-era front porch of African American midwife Lucrecia Perryman; and a forty-foot-long by thirteen-foot-high stratigraphic profile inspired by deep archaeological deposits excavated along Mobile's original waterfront, where the Exploreum Science Center now stands.

1.4. Late Mississippian pot replicas made by ceramicist Tammy Beane. (Photograph by Dave Snyder, Center for Archaeological Studies, University of South Alabama.)

The University of South Alabama's Archaeology Museum (Kara Burns, director; Jennifer Knutson, assistant director) typically hosts six thousand to seven thousand visitors per year, along with several lecture series, online and family-day programs, and other special events. Class field trips from area grade schools introduce busloads of children from every corner of southwest Alabama to their region's rich archaeological past, while acquainting them with the beautiful University of South Alabama campus (fig. 1.5). The Archaeology Museum, it turns out, is an attractive feature for young students weighing their higher-education options.

Students and faculty at this university, as well as researchers from

1.5. Center staff member Sonja Axsmith and Clarke County Public School students in Grove Hill, 2005. (Center for Archaeological Studies, University of South Alabama.)

elsewhere, actively study the collections curated in the Delchamps Building's ground floor. The sites highlighted in this book will continue to contribute to our knowledge of the past, as future archaeologists ask new questions and apply innovative analytical methods to artifacts recovered during the first half century of archaeology at the University of South Alabama.

CHAPTER 2

Greater Mobile-Tensaw River Area

... the environmentally diverse heart of south Alabama.

Few travelers approaching Mobile, Alabama, from the north on Interstate 65 realize the flooded forest they cross is the Mobile-Tensaw delta (fig. 2.1), one of the largest and most important wetlands in the nation. Thanks to effective conservation advocacy nearly fifty years ago by vocal champions such as Mary Ivy Burks of the Alabama Conservancy, Verda Horne of the Alabama League of Women Voters, and Auburn University zoology professor Robert Mount, the US Department of the Interior formally designated the Mobile-Tensaw delta a National Natural Landmark in 1974. The Greater Mobile-Tensaw River area encompasses the Mobile-Tensaw delta's entire watershed.[1]

2.1. Tupelo and cypress swamp in the Mobile-Tensaw delta. (Courtesy of Hunter Nichols.)

In 2016 the National Park Service partnered with the University of South Alabama and the University of Alabama, through the Gulf Coast Cooperative Ecosystem Studies Unit, to survey the state of our modern knowledge of the natural, cultural, and economic resources of the Greater Mobile-Tensaw River Area. In a resulting book, *A State of Knowledge of the Natural, Cultural, and Economic Resources of the Greater Mobile-Tensaw River Area*, editors Gregory A. Waselkov (director of the Center for Archaeological Studies), Fred Andrus (associate professor of geology, University of Alabama), and Glenn Plumb (chief wildlife biologist, National Park Service), with help from naturalist Bill Finch, assembled thirty-five specialists who know their corners of the delta better than anyone else. They contributed twenty-three chapters, written in plain English for nonspecialists, on such topics as geology, hydrology, paleoclimate, insects, mollusks, fishes, birds, reptiles, mammals, archaeology, and modern cultures of the delta.[2]

The volume (freely accessible online from the National Park Service's Natural Resource Report Series list for 2016) highlights the history of the delta and surrounding uplands, from their geological origins through changes in land use by humans, from earliest to modern times. America's preeminent biologist E. O. Wilson, who passed away in 2020, considered the Greater Mobile-Tensaw River Area a national treasure, with fauna and flora that "may well be most diverse of comparable geographical areas in North America."[3] Indeed, the Greater Mobile-Tensaw River Area has been called America's Amazon because of its biological complexity, with tree species diversity ranking among the highest in North America, a diverse assemblage of freshwater crustaceans, over two hundred species of birds, and likely the greatest turtle diversity in the world.

People's lives have long been interwoven with the dynamic rhythms of this remarkable area's lands and waters. A chapter by archaeologist David Morgan, with the National Park Service, reviews the archaeological evidence of ancient human history in the region (fig. 2.2). The oldest known sites, dating to twelve thousand years ago, are found in the uplands lining the delta, but in the delta itself such sites are deeply buried beneath millennia of accumulated flood-deposited silt. Eroding remnants of ancient shell middens up to four thousand years old can occasionally be seen during droughty periods of low water levels in the cut banks of the delta's many rivers, such as at Upper Bryant's Landing on the Tensaw. At the famous Mississippian period site of Bottle Creek, on Mound Island in the heart of the delta, yearly spring floods must have routinely caused occupants to move to upland habitations. Yet those same seasonal floods that annually inconvenienced Bottle Creek residents provided the large Mississippian population with abundant crops of maize, thanks to deposits of

2.2. Small Weeden Island culture pot, dating to AD 650–900, excavated from the Seymour's Bluff site (1BA72) by the Alabama Museum of Natural History in 1937. (University of Alabama Museums, Tuscaloosa.)

nutrient rich silts that regularly rejuvenated agricultural fields planted in clearings on riverbank levees.[4]

The period from AD 1550 to 1950, covered in Waselkov's chapter, encompasses the arrival of European colonizers and enslaved Africans in the Greater Mobile-Tensaw River Area, impacts of colonialism on Native peoples (many of whom were eventually forcibly removed from the region), effects of the Civil War, and the long-term importance of the logging industry that transformed the delta by selective cypress harvesting. These historical processes are all reflected in a rich archaeological record—from the sites of multiethnic towns, such as colonial-era Old Mobile, to plantations around the bay and delta, salt-processing sites (fig. 2.3) in the upper delta and lower bay, Redstick War and Civil War battlefields at Fort Mims and Blakeley, and traces of turpentine and charcoal production throughout the uplands.[5]

Environmental writer Ben Raines contributed a chapter on the culture

2.3. Salt-processing furnace made from a steamship boiler, Civil War era, Upper Salt Works, Clarke County. (Courtesy of Ashley Dumas.)

of modern people who still maintain close ties to the delta. Historic preservationist David Schneider led a team effort to document the current state of National Historic Landmarks in the region. These include Bottle Creek archaeological site, Fort Morgan, Government Street Presbyterian Church and Mobile City Hall (both in Mobile), and the USS *Alabama* and USS *Drum* at Battleship Alabama Memorial Park—an eclectic group of landmarks that well exemplifies the varied history of the Greater Mobile-Tensaw River Area.[6]

PART II

SITE DISCOVERY

CHAPTER 3

Coastal Surveys

> ... systematic searches for archaeological sites along the estuaries of coastal Alabama reveal abundant evidence of Native American fishing and shellfishing at sites threatened by modern development, environmental pollution, and rising sea level.

Residents of the Gulf Coast are all too familiar with the impacts of a hurricane's intense winds and storm surge (fig. 3.1), but new perils to life in the coastal region have emerged in recent years. On April 20, 2010, an explosion at British Petroleum's Deepwater Horizon drilling rig off the coast of Louisiana created the largest oil spill in US history. Over the course of 87 days, 210 million gallons of oil leaked into the Gulf of Mexico. That industrial accident threatened coastal and estuarine archaeological sites with lasting damage from oil contamination and from efforts to remediate the spill. Within weeks, University of South Alabama archaeologists Greg Waselkov and Philip Carr obtained an emergency grant from the Alabama Historical Commission (AHC) that enabled Center for Archaeological Studies staff to respond by locating and assessing as many of Alabama's threatened coastal sites as possible.[1]

Center personnel, assisted by a dozen volunteers, endeavored to reach coastal sites before surface oil and tar balls floated ashore (fig. 3.2). Three staff archaeologists, in particular—Cameron Gill, Robert Taylor, and Erin Stacey—shouldered most of the work. These three accomplished much of their survey by water in a variety of crafts: Boston Whaler, jon boat, kayak, and canoe. In the aftermath of the spill, Federal Emergency Management Agency (FEMA) personnel deployed miles of floating containment booms to retard movement of oil into Mobile Bay and coastal marshes. Our survey team found ways to access sites behind the booms, particularly in Grand Bay National Wildlife Refuge adjacent to the Mississippi state line,

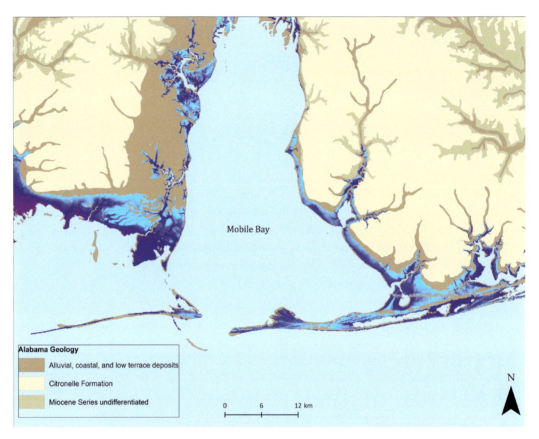

3.1. Alluvial, coastal, and low terrace landforms in the Mobile Bay area, with areas susceptible to category 5 hurricane storm surge inundation (in blue gradient). (Base map sources: Esri, USGS; maximum high storm surge inundation scenario sources: Scott C. Hagen and Matthew V. Bilskie [Louisiana State University, Center for Coastal Resiliency] and David Kidwell, Christine Buckel, and Ginny Crothers [NOAA/NOS/National Centers for Coastal Ocean Science]; graphic by Sarah Price, Center for Archaeological Studies, University of South Alabama.)

where US Fish and Wildlife Service personnel issued an Archeological Resource Protection Act (ARPA) permit for survey purposes.

For an archaeological survey of all sites potentially impacted along the northern Gulf Coast, from Louisiana to Florida, FEMA soon contracted with HDR, a nationwide engineering and environmental services firm based in Denver. Coincidentally, grants from the Mississippi Department of Archives and History to several universities had called for fieldwork that spring and summer at several of that state's most important coastal sites, including Graveline Mound, La Pointe-Krebs Plantation, and the Grand Bay shell middens. This sudden surge of interest in Alabama and

Mississippi coastal sites contrasted markedly with the inadequate attention paid them during the preceding seventy-five years.[2]

From 1933 to 1935, state geologist Walter B. Jones had conducted the only previous largescale archaeological survey of Alabama's coastline for the Alabama Museum of Natural History. According to archaeological lore, Jones spent his winters in the mid-1930s duck hunting along the Alabama coast and only incidentally reporting high-visibility shell middens to the newly created state site file. In fact, though, Jones conducted his site survey in partial fulfillment of a federal grant intended to support the museum at the height of the Great Depression. We owe a debt to Jones for recording over two hundred coastal sites.[3]

However, seventy-five years had been too long an interval between assessments of Alabama's coastal archaeological resources. When Jones carried out his pioneering survey in the 1930s, Alabama's coastline was essentially undeveloped. He documented an extraordinary number of pristine sites that, in the interim, have been destroyed or seriously impacted by natural or human forces. While indebted to Jones for his efforts, we should also understand how standards for archaeological survey have progressed since his day. He noted locations of sites, especially the highly visible shell middens, but retrieved few artifacts, presumably because he thought that recording a site's presence in the state site file would lead to its subsequent scientific study. Between 1940 and early 1942, archaeological excavation did occur at several sites, including the immense Andrews

3.2. Oil spill cleanup on Dauphin Island, July 2, 2010. (Center for Archaeological Studies, University of South Alabama.)

3.3. Cameron Gill wading through salt marsh toward an oak hammock, 2010. (Center for Archaeological Studies, University of South Alabama.)

3.4. Erin Stacey and Robert Taylor surveying a Grand Bay shell midden, 2010. (Center for Archaeological Studies, University of South Alabama.)

Place shell mound (1MB1) in Coden and at Strong's Bayou (1BA81) on Fort Morgan peninsula. But federal support for archaeology evaporated at the start of World War II, and little professional activity occurred on the coast until a resurgence of interest in the 1970s.[4]

In the aftermath of the Deepwater Horizon disaster, the center's survey team made a start toward a modern comprehensive survey of the Alabama coastline by revisiting seventy-three known archaeological sites and identifying twenty-three previously unrecorded sites (figs. 3.3 and 3.4). Of those sites, forty-three had been occupied in the Woodland period and thirty during the Mississippian period. Ten had colonial or nineteenth-century occupations, mostly Confederate salt-processing ovens on oak hammocks in the coastal marshes.[5]

Test unit excavation at one of the newly recorded sites, 1MB480, retrieved samples before that midden could be contaminated with oil. Tree tip-ups had churned much of the meter-deep oyster shell midden at this bluff-edge site, located near the southern mouth of Fowl River. One unit profile revealed undisturbed stratigraphy from Middle Woodland to Late Mississippian times, which we sampled for curation and future analysis.

The Deepwater Horizon oil spill revealed a poorly understood new risk to the archaeological record: the potential damage that crude oil (and the chemical dispersants used to clean up the spill) could cause to coastal archaeological deposits. Modern scientific archaeologists have only recently begun to contemplate and gather data about past diet, habitat, and climate obtainable from organic animal and plant remains, just the sorts of evidence most threatened by oil contamination. Consider a few examples of the sorts of information potentially lost to future oil spills. We can now analyze chemical residues of food embedded in the porous bits of pottery found in archaeological middens. Radiocarbon dating, our principal method of determining a site's age, depends on the recovery of uncontaminated organics. And bitumen (naturally occurring tar balls) collected and used by ancient coastal dwellers as an adhesive can inform us about natural oil seeps in the Gulf predating oil drilling during the modern industrialized era. Chemical contamination from a major oil spill washing ashore onto coastal middens would make all these innovative analyses impossible.

Our emergency grant from AHC of course did not permit the scale of survey required for a comprehensive database of coastal archaeological resources. Even the much larger HDR survey could not accomplish that ambitious goal, as we all necessarily focused on sites fronting the Gulf and adjacent estuaries. The even more numerous sites lining the estuaries of Mobile Bay and the Mobile-Tensaw delta, areas less exposed to the Deepwater Horizon oil spill, were not targeted during disaster response.

In the decade following that calamity, however, we have come to realize the universal threat to coastal archaeological sites posed by rising sea levels due to global warming. In Alabama's two coastal counties, nearly half of all recorded archaeological sites—over six hundred sites—are known to be at risk of inundation and erosion. Our survey documented how many coastal sites, even those not threatened by development, are rapidly disappearing through erosion. We have been shocked by the scope of site damage and loss that has occurred since Jones's survey in the early twentieth century. Waiting to reassess sites until a natural or humanmade catastrophe threatens is an unwise strategy. Simply plotting a site's location on a map is an important first step, but it needs to be followed by effective preservation or scientific study. This most recent disaster will have had at least a small beneficial effect if it spurs us to take proactive measures to counter this loss to the archaeological record, a nonrenewable resource from which we all benefit. It is high time we acted.[6]

Center archaeologists responded to the Deepwater Horizon event with a program of volunteer weekend digs that have systematically tested coastal sites vulnerable to damage or destruction due to cultural or natural threats. By retrieving and curating samples of mollusk shells, animal bones, pottery, and stone tools for future study, we are trying to ensure that future generations will have some information about ancient sites that otherwise will certainly be lost. The Native people who have lived here for thousands of years have also left behind traces of their finely tuned relationships with the environment, knowledge that we should appreciate and can learn from. We have a limited amount of time before the lessons of the ancients disappear forever.

CHAPTER 4

Surveys of the Mobile-Tensaw Delta and Mobile Bay

> . . . have painstakingly identified more than two thousand archaeological sites, many on land, some submerged, still others buried beneath flood deposits in the gradually subsiding delta.

Archaeological survey—the systematic search for sites of former human activity—is the starting point for most archaeological research. On occasion, someone will report the discovery of an important artifact or other tangible bit of the past found while walking a beach or clearing vegetation from property or metal detecting (with the landowner's permission, of course). But systematic survey yields the preponderance of finds by putting professional archaeologists on the ground and in the landscape with shovels, screens, and notebooks in hand. In unforested parts of the world, where artifacts and building ruins are evident on the ground surface, archaeologists can survey the landscape by simply walking and noting where finds occur. In places with dense forest cover, such as the southeastern United States, where the ground surface is largely obscured by undergrowth, the tried-and-true method of survey is shovel testing—systematically digging a series of holes in the ground and screening the soil to retrieve whatever artifacts might lay buried at those spots (fig. 4.1). By digging shovel tests spaced at standard intervals across the landscape and mapping their finds, archaeologists can piece together a story of that land's use through time.

In recent years, remote sensing and geophysical survey techniques increasingly complement the shovel-testing process. Aerial photography, satellite imaging, and LiDAR can now routinely reveal human alterations to land surfaces. For instance, LiDAR imagery showed us the feint trace

4.1. Sangita Shrestha and Raven Christopher shovel testing at the site of John Weatherford's plantation, 1MN112, Claiborne, Monroe County, in 2011. (Center for Archaeological Studies, University of South Alabama.)

of an ancient canoe canal across Fort Morgan peninsula in Gulf Shores, Alabama. Underwater sites, such as the recently located wreck of the slaving ship *Clotilda*, of course require specialized geophysical search methods, such as the use of side-scan sonar and subbottom profiling. Still, despite decades of shovel-testing surveys and impressive technological advances, most of south Alabama (and, indeed, most of the world) remains unsurveyed for archaeological sites. Much remains for archaeologists to find, study, and preserve.[1]

Modern systematic surveys for ancient sites began in south Alabama in 1933–34 when Walter B. Jones, director of the Alabama Museum of Natural History, obtained a modest federal grant to search that winter for coastal sites. This was also, coincidentally, duck-hunting season, which afforded Jones many a tasty meal during his survey, if we can trust archaeological folklore! Jones recorded 185 sites in Baldwin County alone, many of them important mounds and village sites subsequently destroyed by development and coastal erosion. His artifact collections and field records are all that remain of too many sites now lost.[2]

Soon after Noel Read Stowe arrived in Mobile in 1970 to direct the final phase of excavations at the Fort Condé site in downtown Mobile, he found employment as an instructor of anthropology at the University of South Alabama and immediately initiated a long-term research program resulting in six regional surveys. Supported by grants from the National Park Service and the Alabama Historical Commission, those field projects all focused on the Mobile-Tensaw delta: South Alabama Site Survey (1971), Clarke County Site Survey (1974), Mobile-Tensaw Bottomlands Survey: Phase I (1978), Mobile Delta Survey (1979), Mobile-Tensaw Bottomlands Survey: Phase II (1981), and the Forks Project (1984).[3]

Richard Fuller (fig. 4.2) and Diane Silvia contributed substantially to the Forks Project by clarifying the delta's cultural chronology and placing Alabama coastal archaeology into a broader northern Gulf Coast context. Those

4.2. Richard S. Fuller, on survey for the Alabama Museum of Natural History in 1998, next to the eroding riverbank at Bryant's Landing 4 site (1BA175), where stratified layers of marsh clam shells date as early as the Late Archaic period, around 2100 BC. (Courtesy of David W. Morgan.)

projects led to important excavations at the sixteenth- and seventeenth-century Pine Log Creek and Ginhouse Island sites in the 1980s. They also inspired surveys of Mound Island and Clarke County in the 1990s by Ian Brown and Richard Fuller with the Alabama Museum of Natural History at the University of Alabama.[4]

Although all of the archaeologists working at the University of South Alabama have been, by both training and inclination, "dry land" terrestrial focused, we have substantial interest in the "nonterrestrial" underwater archaeological potential of Mobile Bay and the rivers that flow into it. The bay itself began to form about 8,200 years ago, during a period of rising sea level, and the bay and delta assumed their modern appearance around 4,000 years ago. Every year, throughout that long time span, eroded sediments carried downstream by floodwaters of the Alabama and Tombigbee Rivers were deposited atop older land surfaces in the delta and bay, covering sites once occupied by Native peoples. One exceptionally early example is the View Point site (1BA281), a midden preserved by a layer of peat in the shallow waters of Bon Secour Bay, where local residents Doris Allegri, Michael Poe, and David Smithweck collected Late Archaic fiber-tempered pottery and stone tools. Much more recent are several Confederate batteries built to defend Mobile, still visible at times of low water in the marshes at the head of the bay. Sites like these, from two chronological extremes, hint at the vast number of submerged ancient sites that now lie deeply buried beneath meters of sediment, effectively out of reach of archaeologists, at least for the time being.[5]

Submerged shipwrecks are a different matter. Since the first Spanish caravel sailed into Mobile Bay in 1519 (or perhaps earlier), at least 282 sailing vessels, steamboats, ironclads, submarines, packet boats, tugboats, launches, freighters, and barges have been lost by wrecking or abandonment in the waters of the bay and adjacent rivers. Ongoing effort by the state of Alabama to excavate and perhaps even retrieve remains of the infamous slaving ship *Clotilda* is just the most recent underwater project in Mobile area waters.[6]

In 1967–68 a team from the Smithsonian Institution located and dove on the USS *Tecumseh*, a turreted Union ironclad warship sunk by a Confederate torpedo in the mouth of the bay, immediately off Fort Morgan, during the Battle of Mobile Bay on August 5, 1864. Initial interest in raising the well-preserved ship for museum display faded in the face of a $4 million cost estimate for conservation. Subsequent surveys since 1968 have monitored and documented serious deterioration of the shipwreck, apparently accelerated by unauthorized holes cut into the iron hull plates.[7]

In 1983 and 1985, Noel Read Stowe participated in searches for two

Confederate ironclad warships, the CSS *Huntsville* and the CSS *Tuscaloosa*, both scuttled at the head of the Spanish River by their crews on April 12, 1865, coinciding with the surrender of the city of Mobile to federal forces. The 1985 search, carried out by a self-funded team of local avocational and professional archaeologists—Sidney Schell, Allen Saltus, David Smithweck, William Armistead, Jack Friend, Stowe, and others—succeeded in locating both wrecks (fig. 4.3). One of the most intriguing shipwrecks perhaps awaiting discovery in Mobile waters is the Confederate submarine *American Diver*, also known as *Pioneer II*, a precursor to the H. L. *Hunley*, the first submarine to sink a warship. Both innovative submarines were privately built in Mobile. The *Hunley* was discovered in 1995

4.3. David Smithweck, Doug Shaw, Mike Poe, and Noel Read Stowe (*left to right*) at the University of South Alabama's Archaeology Research Laboratory at Brookley Campus, Mobile, 1984. (Center for Archaeological Studies, University of South Alabama.)

in Charleston Harbor, South Carolina, raised in 2000, and is currently on display there while undergoing decades of conservation treatment. *American Diver* foundered during an aborted attack on the federal blockading squadron in February 1863 and is thought to have sunk near the mouth of Mobile Bay.[8]

Even terrestrial surveying in the Mobile-Tensaw delta poses formidable challenges (fig. 4.4). Boats are essential for survey in this swampy, cottonmouth-infested, bottomland forest, which routinely floods every spring. In the remotest areas without cell phone service, getting lost is practically a rite of passage for archaeologists navigating the delta's maze of waterways or struggling to maintain straight survey lines through dense understory of head-high palmettos. Despite the exertions of two generations of archaeologists, the delta still holds most of its archaeological secrets. Although many of the 2,031 sites reported as of December 2021 from Baldwin (715 sites), Clarke (416), Mobile (595), and Washington (305) Counties are located in the Mobile-Tensaw delta, they certainly comprise only the most visible and easily accessible portion of the true number.[9]

Despite the formidable environmental challenges to archaeological survey in the Mobile-Tensaw delta, there are certain kinds of sites likely to be found only there. One rare but elusive sort of site we know once existed in the delta is the maroon settlement, a village created by refugees from slavery, so called from the Spanish *cimarrón* (wild). Today's delta is virtually devoid of permanent residents. Changes wrought by modern logging, eradication of the largest canebrakes, and the appearance of outboard motors make it hard for us to appreciate the sense of remoteness and impenetrability once associated with this watery landscape. The proximity of an enormous hardwood swamp—fourth largest in the country, after the Atchafalaya, Okefenokee, and Great Dismal—adjacent to a substantial enslaved population must have offered hope of a haven to those bold enough to attempt self-emancipation.[10]

A few terse historical sources mention maroon settlements in the Mobile-Tensaw delta. For example, in February 1789 Vincente Folch, colonial governor of Spanish West Florida, informed officials in Spain he had destroyed a camp of Black maroons on the Tensaw River and recaptured fourteen. The best-documented maroon settlement in the delta was located on Hal's Lake in the forks between the Tombigbee and Alabama Rivers, the southern extremity of modern-day Clarke County. Hal and fifteen companions, including a married couple and their children, had lived in two cabins on the lake for several years. From here, a place "very difficult of access," they used six dugout canoes to raid nearby farms, taking weapons and corn and killing cattle for meat and hides. Their discovery, in June

1827, by white hunters led to the capture of six, who said they were planning to build a stockade and expected others to join them in the depths of the delta.[11]

In 2003, Daniel Sayers, an archaeologist at American University, tracked down the site of a maroon camp on an island in Virginia's Great Dismal Swamp. After years of excavation, Sayers identified the locations of seven log cabins from a very small assemblage of artifacts that reflected the isolated and materially impoverished condition of the occupants. Discovery of Hal's maroon village site, which would be a difficult task, given the vague description of its location and the likelihood of finding few artifacts, could provide a fuller understanding of the lives of Africans who escaped enslavement and made homes for themselves, for a time, in one of the few places where freedom was possible for them in the antebellum South. The allure of finding such sites to add to our knowledge leads us to survey such remote and beautiful places.[12]

4.4. Aerial view of Larry Island on the Tensaw River, about two miles east of the Bottle Creek site in the Mobile-Tensaw delta. (Courtesy of Hunter Nichols.)

SURVEYS OF THE MOBILE-TENSAW DELTA AND MOBILE BAY   35

CHAPTER 5

National Forest Surveys

> . . . identify and preserve sites threatened by timber cutting and reforestation, encourage partnerships with federally recognized tribes, and illuminate overlooked aspects of our cultural landscape.

The US Forest Service manages 193 million acres of forest land in the country. Since 2013, the Center for Archaeological Studies has partnered with the US Forest Service to survey for archaeological sites in two of the nation's most important longleaf pine forest habitats. Efforts by the US Forest Service to restore the once-common longleaf pine has resulted in largescale timbering of other pine species and reforestation with longleaf seedlings, using a planting method that involves deep chisel plowing. Because both of those activities can seriously damage archaeological sites, steps are taken to identify sites and other cultural features before timber is harvested.

Because the US Forest Service is a federal agency responsible for cultural resources on its lands, archaeology in the national forests follows an assessment process set out in the National Historic Preservation Act of 1966. This calls for identification (referred to as Phase I survey), evaluation (Phase II testing), and preservation or mitigation (Phase III site investigation) of cultural resources. These three phases of archaeology comprise much of the work of the cultural resource management (CRM) industry that employs 70–80 percent of all archaeologists in the United States.

Faculty, staff, and students with the Center for Archaeological Studies have conducted many Phase I surveys across thousands of acres in Conecuh National Forest (which has 84,000 acres in southcentral Alabama) and the De Soto National Forest (518,587 acres in southeastern Mississippi). During our surveys, we have discovered over one hundred previously unknown archaeological sites and revisited many others already recorded.

Most archaeologists would agree with the quip that "a hard day in the field is better than a good day in the office." Shoveling on survey is hard work, and the weather can make a day in the field downright unpleasant. But, for those who enjoy the challenge, there is a lot of job satisfaction in exploring and reading an unfamiliar landscape, shovel at the ready, with dirt in the screen, and sometimes artifacts in hand.

Before fieldwork begins, however, Phase I surveys start in the office by checking for previously reported sites documented in the National Register of Historic Places, in the state's archaeological site file, and in other resources. Archaeological reports, county soil surveys, and published sources on the environment and history of the area are consulted to build background knowledge about a survey tract. Fieldwork usually begins with a walkover that allows the crew to identify aboveground features such as deteriorated or standing structures, examine areas bare of vegetation for surface artifacts, and familiarize everyone with the landscape. Crew members are spaced thirty meters apart for systematic shovel testing at that interval, and sites are defined by recovery of artifacts from clusters of nearby shovel tests.

Once a cultural resource is identified, an archaeologist evaluates its "significance" based on four criteria, one of which, Criterion D, refers specifically to archaeological sites: to be considered significant, a "property" or site must "have yielded, or may be likely to yield, information important in prehistory or history."[1] The capacity of a site to add important new information about the past depends on the archaeologist posing research questions that are appropriate to that site. What would we like to know about the past that this site can address? And does the site have "integrity"? Are deposits and features sufficiently intact to permit gathering of useful data? Phase II testing typically involves excavation of rectangular test units to understand the context and range of artifacts present. If a site is deemed significant, and it cannot be avoided during proposed tree harvesting and planting (or other potentially damaging activity) and preserved in place, then Phase III excavation takes place to answer the research questions posed during Phase II.

This federally mandated process has resulted in the investigation of thousands of archaeological sites in the United States and added immeasurably to our knowledge of the country's past. Over the years since enactment of the National Historic Preservation Act (NHPA) in 1966, archaeologists have dug many thousands, perhaps millions, of shovel tests for Phase I surveys. The vast majority yielded no artifacts, and that, of course, is what forest managers (or contractors or others who propose ground-disturbing activities) hope to hear. If nothing is found, and all other environmental concerns are addressed, then work may proceed. If something is found, then the CRM process moves forward through Phase II and possibly into Phase III. The prominent archaeologist David Hurst Thomas is said to have once summed up our principal objective in this way: "It is not what you find, it is what you find out." We always hope to learn more about our collective past and not lose the chance to do so because a site was overlooked in advance of destructive activities.[2]

In 2013 University of South Alabama archaeologist Phil Carr initiated a partnership between the university and the US Forest Service. Students enrolled in an archaeological survey methods course worked closely with Robert Reams, De Soto National Forest archaeologist, to gain practical experience with Phase I survey methods. Our students benefited from his deep knowledge of the natural and cultural landscape and came to appreciate his dry wit as an asset during long hot days in the pine forest. One center staff member who participated in that original project, Ginny Newberry, continues the partnership with Reams, conducting Phase I surveys and laboratory analyses.

Our work with the US Forest Service has focused on Phase I surveys, but in 2019, the Center for Archaeological Studies participated in that agency's Tribal Relations Program (figs. 5.1 and 5.2). In collaboration with the Poarch Band of Creek Indians' Museum (Kerretv Cuko, Building of Learning) and Tribal Historic Preservation Office, the center developed a Phase II archaeological test of site 1CV312 in the Covington County portion of Conecuh National Forest. Our Phase I survey in 2017 had identified 1CV312 on an upland ridge near a tributary of the Blackwater River, based on recovery of artifacts from sixty-two shovel tests. This collaboration between a university, a federal agency, and a federally recognized tribe allowed for Phase II testing, something that is not typically done, since potentially significant sites on US Forest Service land are routinely avoided during tree harvests and preserved in place.

Because forests have long been one of America's most important natural resources, archaeology in national forests has revealed some fascinating aspects of our country's economic history. Researchers in Michigan's Hiawatha National Forest have discovered maple syrup processing camps dating to the eighteenth and nineteenth centuries. Abundant evidence of charcoal production, turpentine collection, and tar making has been found in many national forests in eastern states. Spur rail lines and logging camps from the nineteenth and early twentieth centuries are routinely encountered in De Soto and Conecuh National Forests.[3]

5.1. Macie Chunn, a member of the Poarch Band of Creek Indians, excavates a Phase II test unit at site 1CV312, Conecuh National Forest, in 2019. (University of South Alabama, Center for Archaeological Studies.)

There is also great potential for innovative archaeology at Native American sites in national forests. Rock art of many sorts is known from numerous sites in national forests, including the now famous Red Bird River Shelter in Daniel Boone National Forest in Kentucky, where Cherokee syllabary writing is incised on the walls of the rockshelter. Native

5.2. Staff and participants in the 2019 collaborative project at site 1CV312 between the University of South Alabama, Conecuh District of the US Forest Service, and the Poarch Band of Creek Indians Museum. (Kerretv Cuko, Building of Learning) and Tribal Historic Preservation Office. (Courtesy of the Poarch Band of Creek Indians.)

Americans' millennia-long experience with fire ecology has prompted US Forest Service fire managers to collaborate with tribal experts and archaeologists to study the histories and consequences of anthropogenic fires in North American forests. In Alabama's Talladega National Forest, archaeologists have drawn on years of survey results to establish a fine-grained cultural sequence for that little-studied part of the state and to explore puzzling rock mounds and stone alignments that may have Native American origins. Archaeology done in advance of timber sales on US Forest Service land is illuminating many overlooked parts of our nation's cultural heritage.[4]

PART III

ARCHAIC PERIOD (9500–1000 BC)

CHAPTER 6

John Forrest Site

. . . where tiny, laboriously crafted stone beads challenge our preconceptions of life in the distant Middle Archaic past.

Imagine you lived in the South seven thousand years ago, during the Middle Archaic period. How would you have gone about transforming an ordinary pebble into a beautiful bead? The Indigenous people living on either side of the lower Mississippi River, in parts of modern-day Louisiana and Mississippi, developed an effective way to accomplish that challenging task. Using stone-on-stone percussion and grinding to shape locally available chert pebbles and the simple technologies of the hand pump or bow drill to perforate the rock, a meticulous process that took many hours, their skill and patience resulted in brilliantly executed beads, some tubular and some zoomorphic (in a variety of animal forms). Their feat of drilling through a chert pebble with a drill made of the same material is even more impressive if we consider the size of the resultant beads—most are less than an inch long—perforated with drill bits the approximate size of a rice grain. Some archaeologists refer to Middle Archaic stone bead working as a "lapidary" technology, invoking the term applied to precision cutting, engraving, and polishing of gemstones.[1]

Traditional views of ancient peoples who lived by fishing, gathering, and hunting often tend toward one of two extremes. The seventeenth-century political theorist Thomas Hobbes imagined our preagricultural ancestors must have endured lives that were "solitary, poore, nasty, brutish, and short," when each person vied against every other for survival in a state of savagery. At the other extreme, the eighteenth-century philosopher Jean-Jacques Rousseau thought ancient foragers lived together peacefully in small egalitarian bands, with few differences separating individuals in terms of power, wealth, or prestige, a state others characterized as that of the "noble savage." Early notions of human origins, such as these, invariably classified our predecessors as savages of one sort or another, a condition from which our ancestors only gradually emerged, according to these philosophers, thanks to technological advances in a march toward civilization.[2]

Modern archaeologists long ago left behind such caricatures. In their place, the archaeological record documents a wide range of ancient societies that depended to varying degrees on fishing, gathering, and hunting for sustenance, societies that varied in their economies, political structures, and beliefs. Instead of the unremitting savagery envisaged by early natural scientists, archaeologists find evidence for inventiveness, keen observation of the environment, and artistic accomplishment in every ancient society. The remarkable chert beads of the Middle Archaic provide just that sort of insight into life in southeastern North America seven thousand years ago.[3]

The landform known as the John Forrest site (22CB623), located in southwest Mississippi, appealed to many people over the centuries as a good place to live. Middle Archaic occupations there are recognized by evidence of chert bead manufacture, as well as the presence of a characteristic style of hafted stone biface, called a Sykes point by archaeologists. They are "bifaces" because the original stone pebble was flaked on both sides or "faces" to create sharp edges around the periphery and shape the final product. A short stem at the base of these tools allowed them to be "hafted," attached by means of adhesive and sinew lashing to a wooden or cane handle, so the tool could be manipulated as a knife, or to a shaft for throwing as a projectile for hunting.[4]

Archaeological interest in the Middle Archaic of the lower Mississippi valley has increased dramatically in recent years, due to our realization that earthen mounds, stone beads, oversize bifaces, fired clay objects, and ground stone artifacts all date to this period. Such dramatic differences from the preceding Early Archaic period point to substantial economic, social, and ideological changes, none of which are well understood. The apparent complexity of chert bead manufacture raises the possibility that there were individuals who specialized in this task, which, if true, would be an indication of increasing social complexity.

Other Middle Archaic sites in Mississippi and Louisiana—Loosa Yokena (22WR691), Watson Brake (16OU175), and the Keenan Cache—have artifact assemblages remarkably like John Forrest's, particularly with respect to the beads, which have shaped an ongoing debate regarding craft specialization. Sam McGahey, former state archaeologist for Mississippi, has suggested that the nearly identical stone beadmaking debris found at the John Forrest and Loosa Yokena sites may represent "the activities of a single group of lapidarians who moved from one of the sites to the other."[5]

Analysis of the chipped chert beads from the Watson Brake mound site in Louisiana enabled archaeologist Jay Johnson at the University of Mississippi to define the sequential stages of stone bead production. Likewise, the Keenan Cache, a collection of 469 stone objects found in 1876 by a farmer in Jefferson Davis County, Mississippi, includes an array of bead preforms and tubular and zoomorphic beads comparable to those from Middle Archaic contexts. One unfinished bead in this cache retains the tip of a chert drill that broke in the incompletely drilled bore, clearly demonstrating the relationship between chert drills and chert beads.[6]

John Forrest, the site's landowner, had been picking up artifacts from the surface of his plowed field for many years when we met him in 2000. McGahey introduced Phil Carr and Alison Hadley (at the time, an undergraduate major in anthropology at the University of South Alabama) to Forrest, who generously loaned his collection for study. Forrest's surface collection includes 1,283 bifaces, 368 hafted bifaces, 422 cores, 99 chipped beads, and 1,169 pieces of debitage (waste flakes). Additionally, there are a variety of ground stone artifacts: 90 modified greenstone pebbles, 4 greenstone pebble beads, 21 abraders, 5 axe fragments, 1 plummet preform, 15 atlatl weight preforms, 3 hammerstones, 1 nutting stone, and 39 other objects of unknown function.[7]

That summer, Forrest hosted a joint field school by the University of South Alabama's Center for Archaeological Studies and the University of Southern Mississippi. Students dug shovel tests on a 5-meter grid at the south end of the site, where Forrest had observed concentrations of beads and bifaces. Soil from 534 shovel tests and 7 1 × 1-meter excavated units was screened through ⅛-inch mesh to retrieve even the tiniest chert drills. Artifacts came exclusively from an upper soil zone disturbed by plowing that had mixed together artifacts from different time periods. No features or intact midden were found that would allow us to assign dates to an artifact assemblage.

The ninety-nine artifacts in the bead production sequence recovered from the John Forrest site are particularly interesting (fig. 6.1). Chert gravel from the Citronelle Formation, the raw material selected for bead making, had been heat treated to improve workability, a process that turned this usually tan-colored stone pink to red. Local chert gravels had also been preferred for chipped stone bead making at the Loosa Yokena and Watson Brake sites. Once appropriately sized chert gravel was collected from nearby stream beds, the first step in making beads involved knapping these pebbles into pyramidal or cube shapes so that each face was roughly equal in size. Over half of the bead-related artifacts at John Forrest represent this first stage of the production process. The second step involved grinding the chipped edges to round them off and smooth the ends. Evidence for Stage 2 grinding can be seen on twenty-six beads, including one completely ground specimen. Drilling, the final stage of manufacture, is apparent in five artifacts. Just one complete chert bead was found during excavations at the John Forrest site.

Were Middle Archaic stone beads made by craft specialists as part of a lapidary industry? Anthropologists generally agree that making durable goods for one's self or one's dependents does not qualify as craft specialization, no matter the scale of production, expectations for consistency in form, requisite levels of specialized knowledge, or other factors. Making durable goods for others, whether for elites or nonelites, by either parttime or fulltime craftspeople, qualifies as craft specialization. It simply depends on who receives the fruits of the labor. From the spatial concentration and abundance of beadmaking debris at John Forrest, compared with the single finished bead, Hadley and Carr concluded that lapidary specialists produced chert beads here for others.

Chert beads were not part of what archaeologist Brian Hayden dubs a "practical technology," something intended "to solve practical problems of survival and basic comfort." Stone beads did not serve a practical purpose in the ways that the Sykes projectile points and other stone tools did. Beads were not designed primarily for reliability or maintainability. Reliable tools depend on high-quality materials and overdesign to ensure a tool will work when needed. Chert beads were overdesigned, although for other reasons. Less durable materials, such as tubular portions of animal bone, would have made perfectly serviceable tubular beads. If the beads had to be made of chert (for whatever reason), small chert pebbles of various shapes occur in abundance in nearby streams and could simply have been drilled through the center with less chance of failure than was likely with the thin-walled tubular beads. Some other factor besides simple utility clearly dictated this particular stone bead design.[8]

Perhaps Middle Archaic people valued these stone beads merely as objects of adornment, with no more complex function or meaning behind their design. Unfortunately, the contexts of the archaeological beads found thus far have been unhelpful in resolving their exact use. But we suspect that the inordinate amount of time and energy necessary to create these chert beads set them apart from common utilitarian ornaments. Anthropologists recognize a special category of products made by craft specialists, things designed to communicate social messages by the exaggerated time and energy costs involved in their creation. These costly

6.1. Several stages of stone bead production at the John Forrest site (22CB623): finished bead (*top row*); beads with incompletely drilled holes (*second to fourth rows*); Stage 2 preform with ground surfaces (*fifth row*). Each row offers multiple views of a single specimen. (Center for Archaeological Studies, University of South Alabama.)

"hypertrophic" items conveyed social messages or information, as prestige items or as objectifications of some meaning now obscure or entirely lost to us.[9]

New research into this fascinating category of artifact may yet reveal more about bead manufacture and meaning. Experimentation to replicate the stone beadmaking process could provide important insights, particularly into understanding the method of drilling used. And more extensive excavations of Middle Archaic sites could clarify the use contexts of stone beads. In any case, stone beads remind us once again of the complexities of fisher-forager-hunter societies that philosophers once relegated, through ignorance and an unfounded sense of superiority, to the realm of savagery.

CHAPTER 7

Lincoln County Mound

> . . . turns out to be five thousand years old, part of a pattern of mound construction during the Middle and Late Archaic periods that has defied the expectations of earlier archaeologists.

For about two decades now, the perilous condition of America's aging and deteriorating highway bridges has led to a lot of new bridge construction, which has, in turn, spurred archaeological fieldwork. Our modern transportation grid coincides fairly closely with much older networks of trails and river crossings. The long-term attractiveness of places with easy access to water, a prime consideration for settlement throughout human history, partially explains the overlap between old and new travel routes. So, replacements of modern highway bridges quite likely will impact archaeological remains of ancient settlements. The planned replacement of a failing bridge on State Highway 550, over the Homochitto River in southwestern Mississippi, led to just such an archaeological project.

In 2003 and 2006, teams from the Center for Archaeological Studies, led by Phil Carr, carried out testing and excavation at site 22LI504, a predominantly Archaic period site in Lincoln County, part of the Pine Hills region of south Mississippi, on a terrace overlooking the river (fig. 7.1). A local artifact collector's report of the site prompted the Mississippi Department of Transportation to request fieldwork in the area proposed for a new bridge approach. Of particular interest was a single conical mound measuring about two meters high and twenty-two meters in diameter.[1]

A test unit excavated into the mound recovered stemmed stone projectile points but no pottery, indicating that the mound and its contents date to the Archaic period. Radiocarbon dates confirmed that age assessment and further pinpointed the earthwork's origin to over five thousand years ago, at the cusp between Middle and Late Archaic periods. Late Archaic

7.1. Lincoln County Mound (22LI504), November 2003. (Center for Archaeological Studies, University of South Alabama.)

mounds have long been recognized at the Poverty Point site in Louisiana, although until recently that spectacular site was considered an anomaly. The gradual realization among southeastern archaeologists that mounds and entire mound complexes in fact date as early as the Middle Archaic in the lower Mississippi valley has been one of the most important discoveries in recent years. That finding has upended a century-long assumption that conical mounds date to the Woodland period.[2]

Worked stone artifacts, referred to by archaeologists as lithics, were recovered in abundance from excavated units at 22LI504. Small "knappable" (easily flaked) chert cobbles are abundant in the gravel bars of the Homochitto River adjacent to the site, a situation that resembles the environment at Watson Brake, the largest Middle Archaic mound group in Louisiana (fig. 7.2). As at Watson Brake, lithics from the Lincoln County mound include blade cores, chert drills, and various stages of chert bead manufacture (fig. 7.3). A great number of hafted bifaces—the projectile points and knives that were lashed at their stemmed or notched bases to spear shafts or handles—comprise much of the lithic assemblage (fig. 7.4). Since bifaces in use at a particular time by a single social group tended to look more or less similar, the variety of biface shapes found at 22LI504 suggests either interactions at the site between people with different stylistic traditions or reuse of the mound site as an important place on the landscape through time.[3]

7.2. Sarah Price inspecting a bed of chert gravel in the Homochitto River floodplain near site 22LI504, April 2006. (Center for Archaeological Studies, University of South Alabama.)

7.3. Carey Geiger sorting a fine-screened sample for stone flakes and other artifacts. (Center for Archaeological Studies, University of South Alabama.)

New York archaeologist William Ritchie coined the term *Archaic* in 1932 to describe the period of ancient North American history before the adoption of agriculture, mound building, and pottery making. The term has always carried negative connotations. By emphasizing the absence of various cultural achievements, Archaic culture seemed backward and

7.4. Tangipahoa points from site 22LI504. (Center for Archaeological Studies, University of South Alabama.)

impoverished in comparison to succeeding cultures. After nearly a century of additional archaeological research, we now know Ritchie was wrong about the Archaic period; in fact, he was wrong on all counts. During that period the Native peoples of eastern North America first domesticated local food plants, first built earthen mounds, and first made pottery, among many other impressive accomplishments. Considering the many new cultural practices evident at Archaic period archaeological sites such as 22LI504, the Lincoln County mound, perhaps that era is better labeled the Innovation period.[4]

CHAPTER 8

Silver Run

> . . . where a lack of local high-quality stone for tool manufacture led to long-distance foraging for stone and other subsistence needs, to careful husbanding of hard-to-replace tools, and to innovative recycling methods to create new tools from old during the Early Archaic period.

Archaeological sites are not pristine records of what happened in the past. In fact, most ancient archaeological sites have experienced cumulative damage from natural causes as well as from repeated reoccupation by human residents. Our investigation of the Silver Run site (1RU142) in Russell County, Alabama, showed how a complex interaction of human activities and natural processes can create an archaeological "palimpsest," a layered accumulation of residues left by sequential site occupants. Each layer is a compressed, partial, and imperfect record of a period of human occupation. That record is further degraded by natural processes that contribute to the gradual formation of an archaeological site, processes such as rodent burrowing or tree tips or freezing and thawing, all forces that can move artifacts around in the ground. Digging by site residents to create storage pits and other deep cultural features, and natural events such as tree tips during windstorms, can cause significant displacement of artifacts a meter or more in depth. Famed archaeologist Lewis Binford, who first applied the concept of palimpsest to archaeological sites, noted that "rates of deposition are much slower than the rapid sequencing of events which characterizes the daily lives of living peoples; even under the best of circumstances, the archaeological record represents a massive palimpsest" derived from many separate episodes of site occupation, with every successive occupation overprinting the previous ones.[1]

8.1. Excavation of Block 1 at the Silver Run site (1RU142) in 2004. (Center for Archaeological Studies, University of South Alabama.)

Archaeological testing at the Silver Run site by the Center for Archaeological Studies took place in 2004 because the Alabama Department of Transportation (ALDOT) intended to widen US Highway 431 in Russell County. Under federal law, ALDOT needed to know whether this site was eligible for the National Register of Historic Places. Could the site potentially yield historical information of local, regional, or national significance? Recovery of an Early Archaic projectile point during this initial archaeological survey, from over a meter deep in a shovel test, indicated the possibility of deeply buried Early Archaic occupation layers eight thousand to ten thousand years old. Even though the soil profile in test units looked like a single zone with a mixture of coarse to very fine sand-sized grains and no visibly distinct soil strata, the depth of that one Early Archaic discovery suggested the archaeological site could still have intact strata. In the jargon of cultural resource management, the Silver Run site appeared to have "integrity," with artifacts still in cultural layers associated with specific time periods.[2]

Because there were no observable soil strata, the site was excavated in ten-centimeter levels (fig. 8.1). However, Sarah Price and Phil Carr devised several additional excavation and laboratory procedures to tease out any patterns in the locations of artifacts that would reveal stratification no longer visible in the soil. Geoarchaeologist James Kocis analyzed the site's soils and determined that they formed as an upland terrace no later than the Pleistocene, the most recent Ice Age. On this stable land surface, artifact burial had occurred mainly in the biologically active A horizon, the uppermost soil zone that is most prone to movement of artifacts due to plant and animal activities, a process generally referred to as bioturbation.[3]

Another lab analysis looked at artifact size. If artifacts had moved vertically to any significant degree through the sandy soil profile, then one would expect to find larger artifacts concentrated in the upper levels and smaller ones in deeper levels (because small items are known to migrate downward more readily than large ones). When stone flakes were sorted by size and plotted by depth from the surface, the distribution of these artifacts did not show such a pattern. Despite the lack of stratification, the site appeared to retain sufficient integrity for further investigation. In subsequent excavations the field crew laboriously piece plotted individual artifacts, especially large artifacts, by surveying the precise horizontal and vertical position of each with an electronic total station.

Even with piece plotting artifacts and displaying the results in three-dimensional modeling, along with nine radiocarbon dates, cultural layers in the homogenous sandy soils at the Silver Run site were not readily definable. While the distribution of all artifacts revealed what appeared to be an extensive site, this overall impression resulted from many small, short occupations. Artifacts accumulated over a long span, a few at a time from numerous site visits. Various cultural and natural processes blurred the vertical distribution of artifacts, which made it very difficult to define individual occupation layers.

A sizable assemblage of worked stone was recovered from the Silver Run site consisting of a few stone tools and many debris flakes discarded during tool manufacture. The six Early Archaic stone tools are of particular interest from an organization of technology perspective, as are eleven tools resulting from radial breaks. Prominent archaeologist Robert Kelly has characterized "organization of technology" as "the spatial and temporal juxtaposition of the manufacture of different tools within a cultural system, their use, reuse, and discard, and their relation not only to tool function and raw material type and distribution, but also to behavioral variables which mediate the spatial and temporal relations among activity, manufacturing, and raw-material loci."[4]

Simply put, a person's choices about when and where to acquire raw materials, to manufacture a tool, to use and reuse that tool, and finally to discard it, all depend on the life circumstances of that individual. By working back from the clues evident in the tool itself, in the manufacturing debris, and where these are found, archaeologists gain insights into past human behaviors, especially the patterns of a people's movements across the landscape.

As the lithic landscape offered no nearby high-quality stone sources for the residents of the Silver Run site, we were particularly interested in the more distant sources they exploited for raw materials. Six projectile points from Silver Run are classified as the Early Archaic Big Sandy type (fig. 8.2). Three are Coastal Plain chert (from sources 90–190 kilometers away), and one each is clear quartz (0–20 kilometers), Auburn Formation gneiss (50–60 kilometers), and Tallahatta Sandstone (177–310 kilometers) (fig. 8.3). Measurements of these tools fall within standard ranges reported for Big Sandy points (including points classified as the Taylor type in Georgia) by other archaeologists working in the region. Tellingly,

8.2. Big Sandy hafted bifaces flaked from a variety of stone types: (*a*) Tallahatta sandstone, (*b, d–e*) Coastal Plain chert, (*c*) clear quartz, (*f*) Auburn gneiss. (Center for Archaeological Studies, University of South Alabama.)

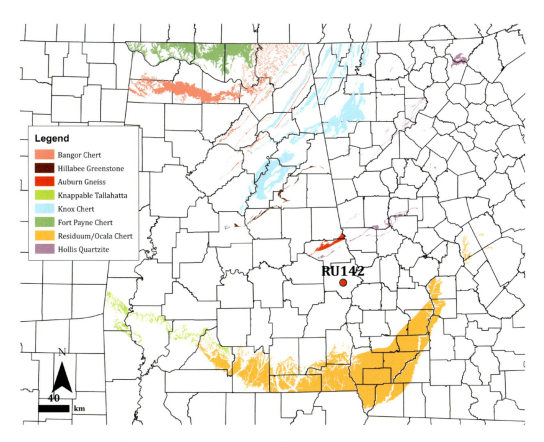

8.3. South central Alabama and Georgia with sources of lithic raw material types present at the Silver Run site. (Base map sources: Esri, DeLorme, USGS; graphic by Sarah Price, Center for Archaeological Studies, University of South Alabama.)

the Silver Run points fall on the short end of the length spectrum because of resharpening during their long use lives. These tools were evidently curated; that is, they were kept for a long time before eventual discard because high-quality raw material was hard to come by in this region. We make similar decisions in our own daily lives. Consider, for example, what items you "curate" in your luggage when you leave your house for an extended period of time, items you know you will need when you arrive at your destination. The diversity of raw materials coming from considerable distances from the site could be the result of travel from Silver Run to those locations by groups tasked with procuring these kinds of stone during forays to acquire plant and animal resources.[5]

One of the most interesting aspects of the Silver Run stone assemblage is the presence of eleven radially broken tools (fig. 8.4). Some archaeologists consider radial breaks as a distinctive form of flaking in which a

8.4. Examples of radially broken bifaces: (a–d, g–k) Coastal Plain chert, (e, f) quartz. (Center for Archaeological Studies, University of South Alabama.)

relatively thin artifact is struck at the center rather than at the margin. Others argue that radial break technology was a recycling technique used during the Archaic period to produce new tools in places lacking fresh raw materials. Archaeologist Kevin Bruce has shown through experiments how flakes produced from a radial break were used for specific tasks, such as scoring grooves in bone or antler. Only two of the Silver Run radially broken pieces exhibit use wear, one with wear damage attributable to drilling or boring into wood or soaked antler and the other with wear from cutting, sawing, or slicing hide, meat, or plant matter. Given the distance to raw materials, the presence of radially broken tools at the Silver Run site likely reflects a need to recycle bifaces into other tool types.[6]

No archaeological site is pristine. Despite the challenges of understanding artifacts found in an archaeological palimpsest, new methods give us the potential to draw additional insights from the Silver Run site artifacts. The diverse peoples who occupied the Silver Run site over time brought their stone tools from varying distances, employed radial break technology, and organized their technology to meet their daily and longer-term needs. Today, the Silver Run stone artifacts are permanently curated at the University of South Alabama for future study.

PART IV

WOODLAND PERIOD (1000 BC–AD 1150)

CHAPTER 9

Gulf Shores Canoe Canal

> . . . constructed around 1,400 years ago across Fort Morgan peninsula, one of just a handful of long canoe canals known from ancient Native North America.

In 1828, Capt. Daniel Burch reported to Gen. Thomas Jessup, quartermaster general of the US Army, on prospective routes for military roads to connect Mobile, Pensacola, and Fort Morgan, newly built at the mouth of Mobile Bay. America was then amid a great canal-building boom—this was the era of the Erie Canal—and since Burch had also been tasked with scouting locations suitable for canals, he appended this surprising observation: "You will notice on my sketch the vestiges of a Canal marked as existing between Bay John and the little Lagoon, near to Mobile point. This canal has never to my knowledge been spoken of before or noticed by any one and was shewn to me by one of the old residents of the Country who informed me that there was no account or tradition whatever respecting it among the oldest Inhabitants; so that it must refer itself for its history to some former period before the occupation of this Continent by the present race of white Inhabitants."[1]

Burch correctly inferred the mysterious canal's function and its precolonial origin without explicitly crediting Native Americans with its construction. Yet, succeeding generations of residents knew who built it. They referred to the unusual feature crossing Fort Morgan peninsula as the "Indian Ditch." Although little known outside the Mobile area, appreciation for this odd landscape feature was commonplace among south Alabama residents, such as Paul Boudousquie, an art instructor at Spring Hill College who led a field trip to the canal in 1899.[2]

However, the term *Indian Ditch*, it turns out, underestimates the engineering accomplishment of the ancient canal builders. Instead of a simple

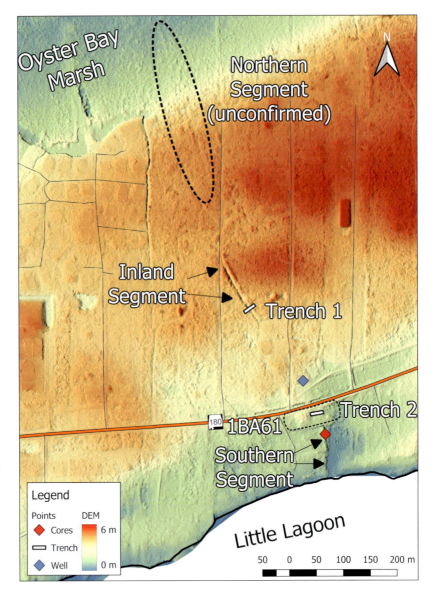

9.1. LiDAR digital elevation model of Fort Morgan peninsula between Oyster Bay and Little Lagoon, showing visible canal remnants (1BA709), small shell mound (1BA61), and archaeological test locations. (Graphic by Donald A. Beebe, Department of Earth Sciences, University of South Alabama.)

trench or ditch connecting two estuaries at sea level, the Gulf Shores canal took advantage of a naturally high water table to permit canoe traffic across a six-meter-high (nineteen-foot-high) peninsula during rainy seasons, most reliably in winter.[3]

The canal ran 1.39 kilometers (0.86 mile) between Oyster Bay (which Captain Burch in 1828 referred to as Bay John) and Little Lagoon, connecting the Mobile Bay watershed to a coastal route for canoe travel to Pensacola Bay and points east without the need to navigate in the Gulf's potentially turbulent waters (figs. 9.1 and 9.2). This extraordinary feature is only

9.2. Gulf Shores canoe canal, south end on Little Lagoon (*left*) and interior segment (*right*). (Center for Archaeological Studies, University of South Alabama.)

the seventh example of an ancient long-distance canoe canal documented in the country and the only one outside of Florida. But who built it, when, and for what purposes?[4]

Our study of this ancient canal began in 2017 at the prompting of Gulf Shores resident Harry King, who has worked for decades to raise public awareness and appreciation of this rare archaeological feature and to protect its remaining visible segments. With essential support from King and other local residents, as well as officials with the city of Gulf Shores, Greg Waselkov and Bonnie Gums organized a volunteer effort to hand excavate trenches across the two visible portions of the canal (site 1BA709) and to examine a small mound-like archaeological site (1BA61) near the canal's south end (figs. 9.3 and 9.4).

Geoarchaeologist Howard Cyr, a specialist in soils analysis, studied the canal's stratigraphy revealed in our trenches and in mechanically extracted soil cores. He learned that the canal bed in places had been just eighty centimeters (2.6 feet) deep. Hydrologist Alex Beebe, another team

9.3. Excavating a trench across the inland segment of the Gulf Shores canal, October 21, 2018; *left to right*: Harry King, Greg Waselkov, and Peter Waselkov. (Photograph by Lori Sawyer, Center for Archaeological Studies, University of South Alabama.)

member, compared modern fluctuating water table elevations over the course of a year in a monitoring well adjacent to the ancient canal. For a dugout canoe with a shallow draft of twenty to thirty centimeters, Beebe's calculations revealed the canal's navigability was limited to the year's coolest months, when the water table was highest. The canal's builders could have prolonged its seasonal utility by placing dams across the canal near

9.4. Cross-section trench across inland section of the Gulf Shores canal, October 21, 2018. (Center for Archaeological Studies, University of South Alabama.)

each end, thereby retaining water throughout much of the year. However, we have not yet uncovered evidence for the existence of dams.[5]

The creators of this canal very likely lived at a large village once located on nearby Plash Island, at the mouth of Oyster Bay and Bon Secour River, east of the Bon Secour Bay portion of Mobile Bay (fig. 9.5). Bon Secour is known today for its shrimp and oyster fisheries, and the

9.5. *"Industry of the Floridians in Depositing Their Crops in the Public Granary,"* from Theodor de Bry, *Der ander Theil, der newlich erfundenen Landschafft Americae* (1591, plate XXII). (Courtesy of Florida Memory, State Archives of Florida.)

year-round residents of the Plash Island site (1BA134) certainly consumed a lot of oysters. Although shrimp are essentially invisible in the archaeological record, we did recover abundant bony remains of croakers, sheepshead, seatrouts, mullets, catfishes, gars, and other fishes that were efficiently harvested in tidal traps, with nets, and by spearing. That village has been radiocarbon dated between AD 574 and 642, which corresponds to the Porter phase at the end of the Middle Woodland period, the same age as the Gulf Shores canoe canal.[6]

We know that the canal was contemporary with the Plash Island village because charcoal found beneath a canal berm has been radiocarbon dated to AD 580–650. Before construction, vegetation in the canal's path through the peninsula's pine and oak forest first had to be cleared by burning. Some of that charred wood was covered and preserved beneath the berms, which formed as dirt dug from the canal bed was piled on either side. Confirmation of the canal's age includes two more radiocarbon samples from the site of a small contemporary fishing camp, 1BA61, perched atop two small sand dunes straddling the canal's south end at Little Lagoon. The shellfish harvested at site 1BA61 were far more diverse than at oyster-rich Plash Island, with abundant hard clams, coquinas, periwinkles, and ribbed mussels, as well as blue crab claw parts. The canal surely simplified exploitation of Little Lagoon's high salinity fishery. And access to the interconnected streams, marshes, lakes, and bays behind the beaches of the northern Gulf offered sheltered canoeing as far east as

Choctawhatchee Bay. The Plash Island community's decision to expend immense effort to construct and maintain a long canoe canal must have involved many considerations—political, economic, even spiritual factors no doubt played a role—issues that we now only dimly perceive.[7]

What is clear is that this land was theirs. Centuries of modifications of the landscape across the continent by Native Americans—and many of their modifications are still visible today if we choose to see them—reflect their long occupation, deep knowledge, and intimacy with the land from which they were displaced.

CHAPTER 10

Bayou St. John

... where, on the south shore of Bear Point peninsula between AD 650 and 1050, Native Americans intensively harvested the local fishery and developed an ingenious and practical range of tools made from white-tailed deer bones, in a coastal zone largely devoid of flakeable stone.

Two private residential developments on Bear Point peninsula in the city of Orange Beach prompted the largest modern excavation of a Late Woodland village site on the Alabama coast between 2004 and 2006 (figs. 10.1 and 10.2). The center's field investigations were directed by Bonnie Gums, George Shorter, and Sarah Price, with Greg Waselkov and Phil Carr serving as coprincipal investigators and Price responsible for the project report. Staff were assisted by field school students and volunteers from the Southwest Chapter of the Alabama Archaeological Society, the Emerald Coast Chapter of the Florida Anthropological Society, and the Pensacola Archaeological Society, along with Caroline Girard, an exchange student from Université Laval, Québec, Canada.[1]

An earlier exploration of the Bayou St. John site (1BA21) evidently occurred in 1901, when pioneering archaeologist Clarence B. Moore dug into a small sand "mound with shell-fields adjoining" on or near this site. That mound, and most of the Bayou St. John site occupation, are attributable to the Weeden Island culture, a diverse group of societies that occupied most of the northern Gulf Coast and portions of interior Alabama and Georgia from the fifth to eleventh centuries AD.[2]

The Bayou St. John occupation spanned most of the late Weeden Island period, with calibrated radiocarbon dates ranging from AD 650 to 1041, a period known locally as the Tates Hammock phase. Well-made Weeden Island pottery was found in great abundance (fig. 10.3). The small

10.1. Deep feature excavation at the Bayou St. John site (1BA21), November 2004. (Center for Archaeological Studies, University of South Alabama.)

number of stone tools, by contrast, reflects a scarcity of flakeable stone on the Alabama coast, where wood, rivercane, and bone provided workable alternatives. Among the hundreds of bone tools, mostly made from deer leg bones, are many socketed spear points (fig. 10.4). Analysis of organic residue from the point sockets, by University of South Alabama chemist Alexandra Stenson and chemistry student Long Dinh, suggests that bitumen, originating as tar balls from natural oil seeps in the floor of the Gulf of Mexico and washed onto coastal beaches, served as an adhesive to attach the bone points to wooden spear shafts.[3]

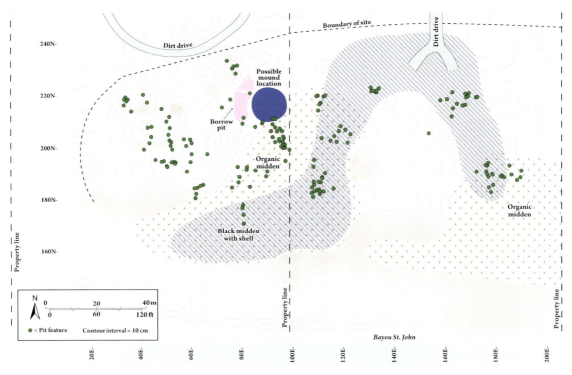

10.2. Map of the Bayou St. John site, based on excavations in 2004 and 2006. (Graphic by Sarah Mattics, Center for Archaeological Studies, University of South Alabama.)

10.3. Weeden Island pottery jar rim from the Bayou St. John site. (Center for Archaeological Studies, University of South Alabama.)

10.4. Socketed spear points made from the metapodial bones of white-tailed deer, Bayou St. John site. (Center for Archaeological Studies, University of South Alabama.)

A principal outcome of the Bayou St. John excavations is an enormous collection of animal remains left behind from fishing and shellfish collecting and food processing by the site's Late Woodland residents. Teams of zooarchaeologists from the University of Georgia, the University of Tennessee, the University of Alabama, and the University of South Alabama collaborated to identify a remarkable 278,517 elements from 73 species of vertebrates and invertebrates, by far the largest assemblage of food remains ever analyzed from an ancient Alabama coastal site (fig. 10.5).[4]

Fred Andrus at the University of Alabama supervised studies of the proportions of different oxygen isotopes found in layers of molluscan shells and carbonate structures of certain fish species. Because oxygen isotopes reflect changes in water temperature and salinity, Andrus's studies provided detailed information about shifts in fishing and shellfish collection strategies from season to season throughout the year. A composite picture assembled from various lines of evidence indicates a complex seasonal round of animal exploitation that took advantage of changes in species abundances and vulnerability to capture by humans. Due to their detailed knowledge of animal behaviors and habitats acquired from centuries of life along the coast, Late Woodland people knew at any given time which estuarine animals could be reliably harvested. The sheer abundance, diversity, and dependability of available coastal food resources meant that the occupants of the Bayou St. John site could live there throughout the

10.5. Fish bones in the water screen from Bayou St. John site midden. (Center for Archaeological Studies, University of South Alabama.)

year. Even without food surpluses, which later Native peoples derived from maize agriculture, the Weeden Island population of the northern Gulf Coast lived in permanent villages, such as the one at Bayou St. John.[5]

Great quantities of mullet and sea catfishes were acquired very efficiently with mass-capture technologies, such as by tidal weir or with small-gauge nets. No ancient tidal weirs have yet been found on the Alabama coast, although the discovery of river weirs in the Florida and Mississippi coastal plains argues for the use of this simple but effective technology throughout the region during Woodland and Mississippian times. Larger fish, such as jacks, sheepshead, and flounders, were taken in smaller numbers by spear or dip net—perhaps facilitated by jacklighting, luring fish toward the light of a fire kindled at night in a dugout canoe. Line fishing with hooks apparently played no role in subsistence, given the absence of bone fishhooks, which are common at contemporary riverside village sites farther inland. Considerable numbers of oysters and coquinas also contributed important amounts of meat to the Late Woodland diet, far more than white-tailed deer and other terrestrial mammals. The Bayou St. John animal remains provide our most detailed look at Late Woodland foodways from anywhere on the northcentral Gulf Coast.[6]

CHAPTER 11

Clarke County

> ... is well represented by numerous village sites in the floodplain of the Tombigbee River, where some are imperiled by highway construction and river navigation channel dredging.

Between AD 800 and 1150, during the Late Woodland period, a string of villages once lined the broad floodplain of the lower Tombigbee River, which presently forms the western boundary of Clarke County, Alabama. This once-populous Native American society is labeled, in archaeological jargon, the McLeod phase. Their most distinctive artifacts are several kinds of pottery, most with check-stamped or simple-stamped exterior surfaces (fig. 11.1). McLeod potters produced those effects with grooved wooden paddles, partly to seal clay seams, partly to create a textured surface, and partly, perhaps, for the pleasing pattern, judging from the care exercised in applying the stamped designs. McLeod stamped pottery types closely resemble ceramics made by other contemporary societies occupying much of southern Alabama, southern Georgia, and northern Florida during the Late Woodland period, all of whom shared a similar way of life referred to as the Weeden Island culture.[1]

These impressive McLeod village sites have attracted quite a bit of attention from archaeologists, beginning with excavations sponsored by the Alabama Museum of Natural History in the 1930s. Many McLeod sites have been documented during site surveys, including several led by Richard Fuller and Read Stowe with the University of South Alabama in the 1970s and 1980s and by Ian Brown and Fuller with the Alabama Museum of Natural History in 1997. In that same year, George Shorter with the Center for Archaeological Studies directed extensive excavations at four large village sites (1CK236, 1CK286, 1CK287, 1CK290) before the widening of Alabama Highway 177, near the city of Jackson. These sites

11.1. Wakulla check stamped, variety Bridge, potsherds from site 1CK56. (Center for Archaeological Studies, University of South Alabama.)

occupied the ends of small ridges extending from the upland hills into the floodplain. That study confirmed the minor presence of maize as early as AD 900, along with similarly small quantities of goosefoot, maygrass, and knotweed seeds. The McLeod people tended modest gardens and encouraged the growth of seedbearing weedy plants endemic to the Tombigbee floodplain—evidence of emergent agriculture that would become far more important for subsequent Mississippian populations in this region, beginning around AD 1250.[2]

An opportunity to investigate another McLeod village location, the Corps site (1CK56), arose through unusual circumstances. While Shorter's field crew were exploring the four sites near Jackson, the US Army Corps of Engineers created the St. Elmo Upland Dredge Material Disposal Area elsewhere in the Tombigbee River floodplain as a place to put sediments dredged from the river's navigation channel. Although this disposal area should have been surveyed in advance for archaeological sites, no survey was done. Over the next decade, 1CK56 would be severely damaged by dredge spoil disposal.

Although Corps of Engineers officials were initially unaware of archaeological site 1CK56, local Clarke County residents with an interest in archaeology did know about it and became increasingly concerned about the situation. Walter Davis (fig. 11.2), who has dedicated much of his life to preservation and public interpretation of the Clarke County historical record, took the initiative to do something about the disaster unfolding at 1CK56.

11.2. Walter Davis holding an iron rail used to support a cast iron evaporation pan at a Confederate salt works on Limestone Creek, Clarke County, 2007. (Courtesy of Ian Brown and Ashley Dumas.)

When Phil Carr with the Center for Archaeological Studies asked Davis in 2001 to guide him to some quarry sites and stone outcrops in the area, Davis also led Carr to 1CK56. By that point, the site had already suffered severe erosion from dredge spoil pumping. Even so, they could see an intact portion of site midden sitting atop a remnant of a ridge in the middle of the massive dredge spoil area, an archaeological island in a sea of sludge. Carr notified archaeologists with the Alabama Historical Commission and the Corps of Engineers and urged them to take action to protect what remained of 1CK56. Finally in 2007, after six more years of erosion to the site, Corps archaeologist Joe Giliberti successfully obtained his agency's permission and funding to mitigate the damage the site had sustained. Carr and Sarah Price developed an excavation strategy to retrieve as much information as possible from the remaining intact midden and cultural features.[3]

Nothing good would have come of the Corps site saga if not for Davis, who well exemplifies the essential contributions of avocational archaeologists to the preservation and study of our archaeological heritage. In the United States today, there are only about 7,600 professional archaeologists, individuals with formal training who are employed to conduct archaeological research. However, as the great proponent of public archaeology Hester Davis once said, an archaeologist is simply a person who sees artifacts as a means to learn about the past, whether that person is paid or unpaid, professional or nonprofessional. The smart professional will seek out preservation-minded nonprofessionals and involve them in every aspect of research because they frequently have a deep knowledge of their local archaeological landscape and the enthusiasm to share what they learn with others.[4]

There is, unfortunately, an archaeological underworld of looters, individuals with no preservation ethic who pillage archaeological sites for artifacts to possess them or to sell them for profit. Looters have done great damage to archaeological sites, such as the notorious incident at Slack Farm in Kentucky described by archaeologist Brian Fagan: "Ten pot hunters from Kentucky, Indiana and Illinois paid the new owner of the land $10,000 for the right to 'excavate' the site. They rented a tractor and began bulldozing their way through the village midden to reach graves. They pushed heaps of bones aside, and dug through dwellings and the potsherds, hearths and stone tools associated with them. Along the way, they left detritus of their own—empty pop-top beer and soda cans—scattered on the ground alongside Late Mississippian pottery fragments. Today, Slack Farm looks like a battlefield—a morass of crude shovel holes and gaping trenches. Broken human bones litter the ground, and fractured artifacts crunch under foot. . . . The ravagers of Slack Farm had no interest in science or prehistory. They were hunting for artifacts for their personal collections and for money." There have been equally horrifying episodes of looting in south Alabama, so readers will understand why we look forward to working side by side with the antithesis of looters—nonprofessional archaeologists who have much to contribute and who share our passion for the past.[5]

The excavations conducted at 1CK56 by faculty, staff, and students from the Center for Archaeological Studies would not have been possible without the participation of Davis and Maury Outlaw, another Clarke County resident. Working conditions at this site were extraordinarily difficult. Access roads became nearly impassable after every rain, and Davis's tractor pulled our vehicles out of the mud on several occasions. The duo cleared the site for initial mapping, and, without fail, the two of them arrived on site every morning ready to help with screening or any other task laid before them. Perhaps most importantly, by their enthusiasm about what we were finding and what it meant, they reminded us why we do archaeology.[6]

Although site 1CK56 had been partially destroyed by dredging activities, the remnant examined during excavations contained intact cultural midden and pit features. The pottery styles and radiocarbon dates from these deposits confirm a Late Woodland occupation, primarily from AD

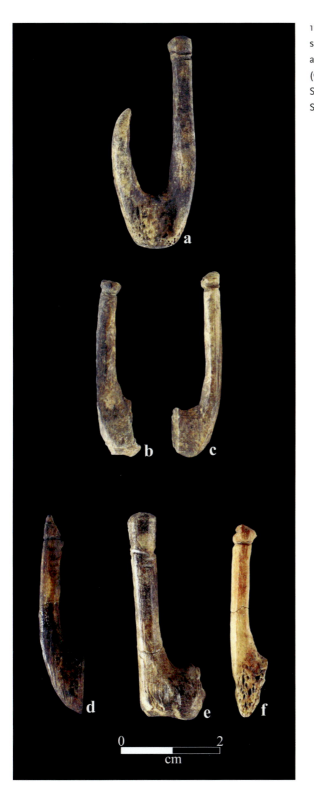

11.3. Bone fishhooks from site 1CK56: (*a*) complete and (*b–f*) fragmentary. (Center for Archaeological Studies, University of South Alabama.)

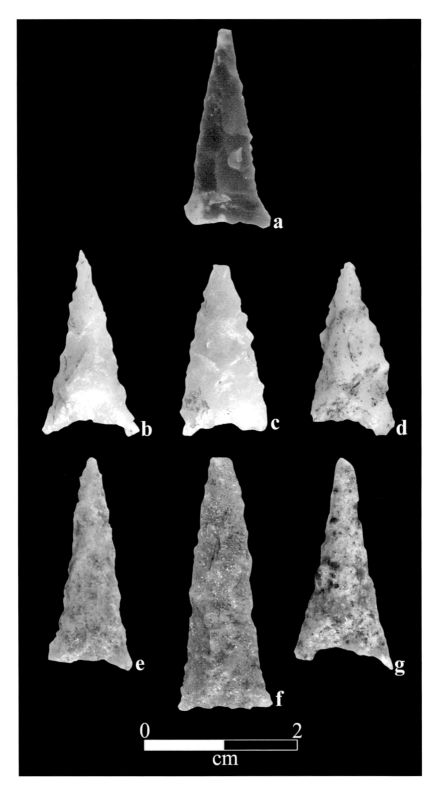

11.4. Hamilton points from site 1CK56: (*a*) chert, (*b–d*) quartz, (*e–g*) Tallahatta sandstone. (Center for Archaeological Studies, University of South Alabama.)

900–1100. The stone tool and bone tool technologies proved to be of particular interest.

Fishing by hook and line was preferred at 1CK56, rather than the mass-capture methods with nets or weirs preferred by Late Woodland coastal dwellers (see chapter 10). The vertebrate faunal assemblage supports this conclusion; fish bones came predominantly from large specimens of drum, gar, catfish, and bowfin (locally called grinnel). Excavation recovered thirty-two fishhooks carved from the leg bones of white-tailed deer (fig. 11.3). These were likely used on trotlines that can be left unattended, a particularly efficient fishing method that is still used today for all four kinds of fish.

Stone tools, like bone tools, can inform us in various ways about peoples' relationships with their environment. At 1CK56, most of the bifacially flaked stone tools with hafts functioned as arrowheads (fig. 11.4). Fourteen of them had broken from impact or at the haft, the kinds of damage that typically occur during use. Since we have no direct evidence of warfare at McLeod village sites, such as village palisades or arrows embedded in human skeletal remains, this breakage probably reflects hunting activities. Another nineteen bifaces were discarded undamaged, but almost all have extensively resharpened blade edges. This, along with an immense amount of flake debris ("reduction debitage"), indicates that retooling and restocking of arrowheads occurred here. These are all activities that point to long-term village occupation, either seasonal or year-round.

There are at least fourteen different raw materials in the worked stone ("lithic") assemblage. Except for two pieces of chert, all these lithic raw materials were likely acquired locally, within a five-kilometer walk from 1CK56. Quartz is the most abundant material and probably was procured from Pleistocene/Quaternary deposits along stream banks or from eroded slopes. All stages of tool production are present, from cobbles to early stages to finished tools to reworked, resharpened specimens. It would appear that many of the quartz bifaces arrived on site in finished form, which would account for the high rate of biface discard relative to the other raw materials.

Agate, the second most abundant material recovered from 1CK56, is available mainly in the uplands surrounding the site but also in some small creeks. Only six agate bifaces were recovered, which is odd when compared with the 2,497 pieces of flaked debris. Perhaps tools were produced on site, then used and discarded elsewhere.

Tallahatta Sandstone is the third most common material but significantly less common than quartz and agate, which is surprising because Tallahatta Sandstone is locally available, although more restricted

11.5. Tallahatta sandstone nodule 3, with seventy-one discarded flakes and two failed bifaces, from site 1CK56. (Center for Archaeological Studies, University of South Alabama.)

to upland ridge tops. Few Tallahatta Sandstone quarries or outcrops have been recorded in the vicinity of 1CK56.

One excavation layer with an exceptional quantity of Tallahatta Sandstone proved especially interesting. Different nodules of this material tend to have distinct color and texture, so Carr and Price were able to sort the 612 flakes and 5 bifaces into 9 nodules originally carried to 1CK56. Each nodule was represented by a pile of flakes, and, in some cases, one or more bifaces were discarded before completion (fig. 11.5). This location within the village was evidently a place where stone knapping occurred, and the resulting debris had been left where it dropped.

Salvage excavation of the remaining portion of 1CK56 allowed us to investigate significant research questions regarding site chronology and cultural lifeways. And the artifacts, permanently stored at the University of South Alabama, remain available for future analyses to address questions not yet imagined. All of this has been possible because of the interest, persistence, and participation of local (nonprofessional) archaeologist Walter Davis.

PART V

MISSISSIPPIAN PERIOD (AD 1150–1700)

CHAPTER 12

Bottle Creek Mounds

> . . . the largest Mississippian mound center on the northcentral Gulf Coast, in the heart of the Mobile-Tensaw delta, created around AD 1250 by Native people inspired by (or perhaps migrants from) the great Moundville chiefdom.

The intrepid people who first disembarked from dugout canoes with the intent to build a large ceremonial center at Bottle Creek, on a flood-prone island at the center of the Mobile-Tensaw delta, faced a formidable task. Today, most visitors to south Alabama miss out on the adventure of visiting this marvel of ancient construction, discouraged by any number of modern-day inconveniences: navigating a maze of waterways, parrying stinging insects, and keeping an eye out for biting reptiles. For those who seek out this hidden gem, however, the sight of Mound A, rising forty-five feet above the palmetto-strewn forest floor, is as awe-inspiring for modern visitors as it must have been for the Native inhabitants who reworked this watery landscape eight centuries ago.

With their evocative descriptor of the mound builders as "DaVincis of Dirt," geoarchaeologists Sarah Sherwood and T. R. Kidder remind us that those who built this place and others like it across the Southeast accomplished an engineering feat. Mounds that remain standing for hundreds of years, retaining their rectangular shapes despite floodwaters, hurricanes, and modern farming, are not simply piles of dirt but planned monumental edifices, built to plan by people who understood the structural properties of soils. We rightly marvel at the earthen structures of ancient Native America as brilliant examples of human ingenuity, skillful planning and creation, and massive effort.[1]

The first written account of ancient mounds on Bottle Creek appeared in the journal of Pierre Le Moyne d'Iberville, leader of the French expedition

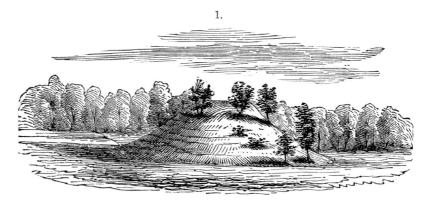

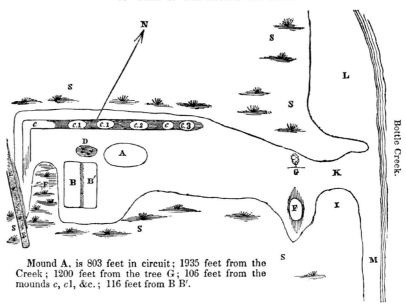

12.1. Artemas Bigelow's engravings of a mound and his plan view of the Bottle Creek archaeological site (1BA2). (From Bigelow, "Observations on Some Mounds," 188–89; Center for Archaeological Studies, University of South Alabama.)

that founded the colony of Louisiane. In his entry for March 4, 1702, Iberville noted how his brother, Jean-Baptiste Le Moyne de Bienville, had given a flintlock musket to a Mobilian Indian who had shown him "the place where their gods are." Having paddled to an island in the Mobile-Tensaw delta, "it took a search to locate them [the gods] on a little hill among the canes, near an old village that is destroyed, on one of these islands." From the mound-top temple, Bienville stole five statues—"a man, a woman, a child, a bear, and an owl"—which Iberville sent back to France, even though he considered them "not particularly interesting." Bienville's desecration gave the place its colonial name, Isle aux Statues, now called Mound Island.[2]

12.2. Modern topographic map of the Bottle Creek site, 2003. (Graphic by Sarah Mattics, Center for Archaeological Studies, University of South Alabama.)

In 1853 Artemas Bigelow, a young New England naturalist, published a crude map of the mound site (fig. 12.1), after having "botanized and geologized" for two years from his base at Hall's Landing, a few miles south of modern-day Stockton, on the eastern edge of the delta in northern Baldwin County. Bigelow rejected racist notions of non-Indigenous "Mound Builders" then current in mid-nineteenth-century American scientific circles and, instead, correctly attributed these earthworks "to some tribe of the present race of Indians." He also noticed a large ditch-like feature west of the mounds that had "the appearance of an ancient canal."[3]

Apart from small-scale excavations in 1932 by David DeJarnette with the Alabama Museum of Natural History, modern explorations of the extensive Mississippian Bottle Creek site (1BA2) have been limited to a brief period in the 1990s. Archaeologists Greg Waselkov, Diane Silvia, Richard Fuller, Craig Sheldon, Amy Carruth, and Edwin Jackson collaborated to draft a topographic map of the site in 1990 to improve on Bigelow's sketch (with additional mounds to the west and north added to the map in 1997 and 2007) (figs. 12.2 and 12.3). Ian Brown and Fuller, with the Gulf Coast Survey of the Alabama Museum of Natural History, carried out a thorough site survey of Mound Island (fig. 12.4) and accomplished excavations on several mounds between 1991 and 1994, with grant support from the Baldwin County Historic Development Commission, the Alabama Historical Commission, and the National Endowment for the Humanities.[4]

Brown, Fuller, and their team of researchers learned that major settlement and mound construction began at Bottle Creek around AD 1250, almost certainly by a group of immigrants from the Moundville chiefdom

12.3. Catherine Potter, Greg Waselkov, and Diane Silvia (*left to right*) mapping the Bottle Creek site in 1990. (Photograph by Steve Thomas, Center for Archaeological Studies, University of South Alabama.)

centered far to the north in the Black Warrior River valley of west-central Alabama. Brown suspects that initial Moundville colonization of the coastal region began around AD 1100, partly to control trade in salt, a vital commodity obtained by boiling water from saline springs in southern Clarke and Washington Counties. Bottle Creek proper, they determined, had been occupied primarily by elites, chiefly families in the site center and retainers on the smaller domiciliary mounds lining the western and northern edges of this important political and religious center. The rest of the

12.4. Ian Brown driving the boat to the Bottle Creek site, 1991. (Center for Archaeological Studies, University of South Alabama.)

Mississippian population lived primarily at small farmsteads scattered among their maize fields on the natural levees that line the delta's waterways. Fuller and Brown found some of those small sites during their 1991 survey. The abundance of carbonized maize kernels and cobs recovered from excavations documents the importance of farming to the inhabitants of Bottle Creek.

12.5. Mississippian anthropomorphic head effigy from a ceramic vessel, Bottle Creek site. (Center for Archaeological Studies, University of South Alabama.)

Part of the 1993–94 fieldwork included excavations at Mound L, carried out by Diane Silvia as part of her PhD research. From the hundreds of post features found there, she recognized the footprints of several structures occupied one after another over a period of several centuries. Most of those buildings corresponded to the Mississippian occupation between AD 1250 and 1550, but the last structure to stand atop the mound dated to the mid-eighteenth century. A sparse artifact assemblage of colonial-era Mobilian pottery and a handful of French items—a musket lock, a clasp knife blade, a military button, three handwrought nails, four glass beads—differs starkly from the abundance of pottery and trade goods found at an earlier eighteenth-century Mobilian house site, 1MB147, near

French Old Mobile. Brown suspects that the last occupants of Mound L at Bottle Creek were tending a temple, similar to or perhaps the very one violated by Bienville in 1702.[5]

Bottle Creek and other great Mississippian mound centers remained sacred to Native southeasterners well into the eighteenth century, and they continue to be important to Native Americans today (fig. 12.5). The isolation of the Bottle Creek site, on an island in the middle of one of our nation's largest swamps, has saved it from development, even as a park. The pristine nature of this forested site is due, in large part, to the foresight of the McMillan family who farmed Mound Island and protected the mounds from diggers for a century. In the 1990s, Scott Paper Company donated a large tract on Mound Island to the state of Alabama. The Bottle Creek archaeological site, a National Historic Landmark, is now a preserve administered by the Alabama Historical Commission and protected by enforcement officers with the Department of Conservation and Natural Resources.

Several state agencies cooperate to encourage educational visits to Mound Island and the Bottle Creek archaeological site. In 2002, Alabama State Lands Division established the Bartram Canoe Trails in the delta, including a 9.1-mile Mound Island Trail originating at Rice Creek Landing. Between 2003 and 2018, to help generate funds for financially strapped Historic Blakeley State Park, Greg Waselkov and Bonnie Gums guided several tours per year to Bottle Creek on the *Delta Explorer*, the park's fifty-passenger pontoon boat. Those tours, which are now led by park personnel, have raised money for the perpetually underfunded state park while introducing thousands of members of the public to one of the most impressive and remarkable ancient sites on the northern Gulf Coast.

CHAPTER 13

Dauphin Island Shell Mounds

. . . partially preserved within the bounds of Shell Mound Park and fiercely protected by birdwatchers as prime habitat for migratory birds, the big mound remnant is the largest ancient shell structure still standing on the Alabama coast, dating to around AD 1250.

Within the boundaries of Dauphin Island's Shell Mound Park (eleven acres administered by the Marine Resources Division of the Alabama Department of Conservation and Natural Resources) stands coastal Alabama's largest remaining ancient coastal shell midden, site 1MB72. In 1975 University of Alabama archaeologists, with a grant from the National Park Service, found evidence on the eastern edge of the site for occupations spanning the centuries between three thousand and one thousand years ago in the form of pottery from the Bayou La Batre-Tchefuncte, Porter Marksville, and Weeden Island Woodland cultures. However, far more impressive than those early deposits are the oyster shell mounds, created during the Mississippian period (between AD 1250 and 1700), that once dominated the landscape.[1]

When Pierre Le Moyne d'Iberville's colonizing expedition first arrived on the island in 1699, the French noticed "at the southwest end, a spot where more than sixty men or women had been slain." Based on those skeletal remains, the French named the place Isle Massacre. Soon afterward the newcomers learned, according to chroniclers Jean-François-Benjamin Dumont de Montigny and André-Joseph Pénigault, that Mobilian Indians periodically gathered the bones of their dead and "carried them into this spot" to form ossuaries. Colonists subsequently found a lone human skull on a small shell-midden-covered island north of the large shell mound, a discovery that reinforced their initial association of the island with burial rituals of Native peoples. They called that landmark Teste de mort (Tête de mort, in modern French), "death's head," invoking a common eighteenth-century French landscape metaphor recalling the inevitability of death. Eventually, however, Isle Dauphine, the island's official name honoring Louis XIV's great-grandson and heir to the French throne, superseded these macabre folk names and survives today in anglicized form[2] (fig. 13.1).

The first archaeologist to explore the shell mound site was Clarence B. Moore, a wealthy Philadelphian who spent winters from 1891 to 1918 touring waterways of the South with a crew of laborers aboard his small steamboat *Gopher*, stopping now and then to dig into the region's largest ancient sites. In January 1905, the *Gopher* pulled up to Dauphin Island's "considerable aboriginal deposit of shells, mainly of the oyster" to do "some digging." However, Moore found little to interest him besides broken pottery, including a few ceramic bird effigies.[3]

In 1922 this site was the scene of a remarkable discovery. A man digging foundation trenches for a neighbor's new house uncovered a large red stone smoking pipe carved in the shape of a crawfish (fig. 13.2). The material and style of the pipe indicate that it was made during the twelfth century AD in the central Mississippi River valley, at or near the great Mississippian city of Cahokia, one thousand miles northwest of Dauphin Island. Crawfish played a key role in Native southeastern origin legends as Earth Diver, who dove to the bottom of the primordial sea and returned with mud, creating the earth island on which humans would live.[4]

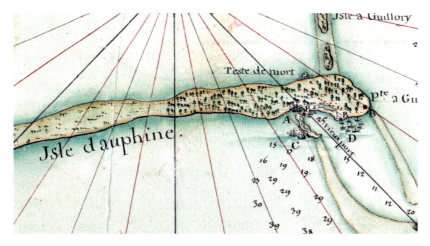

13.1. French colonial map of Dauphin Island. The northern portion of the large shell mound site (1MB72) is shown as a small island immediately to the right of the caption "Teste de mort" (death's head) (Le Moyne, Serigny, and Devin, "Carte de l'entrée"; source Bibliothèque nationale de France.)

13.2. Stone crawfish effigy pipe made of Missouri flint clay, an Earth Diver of southeastern Native American cosmology, found at site 1MB72 in 1922. (Courtesy of Steven L. Boles.)

A grant in 1990 to the University of South Alabama from the National Science Foundation's EPSCoR program enabled Greg Waselkov and Diane Silvia to excavate test units and draft a topographic map of the portion of the site located within the park (figs. 13.3 and 13.4). The site included several smaller shell mounds to the north, now damaged by shoreline erosion and Civil War–era placement of a Confederate artillery battery, similar to more extensive defensive works dug into the shell midden at Cedar Point on the mainland. Today the large mound stands about thirteen feet high at its tallest point and resembles a horseshoe with a hollowed-out center opening to the north. Shell middens in the shape of rings and horseshoes are known from elsewhere in the Southeast, particularly on the south Atlantic Coast from South Carolina to northeast Florida, where they signify circular and crescent-shaped village arrangements. But the unusual modern appearance of the large shell mound on Dauphin Island misleads us regarding the mound's original form.[5]

Nearly all large shell middens along the US coastline have been mined in recent centuries for construction material. For instance, eighteenth-century colonists routinely burned shells from ancient middens to produce tabby, a form of shell cement popularly used for sturdy wall construction (fig. 13.5). One such tabby house once stood on the shore north of the Dauphin Island shell mound, as shown in a photograph taken around 1900. Elsewhere in the area, Old Bay Shell Road (a toll road that

13.3. Amy Carruth and Warren Carruth excavating a test unit in the large shell mound on Dauphin Island, 1990. (Center for Archaeological Studies, University of South Alabama.)

ran from Choctaw Point to Brookley, south of downtown Mobile) and Old Shell Road (in west-central Mobile) were first paved in the 1850s with shells taken from ancient middens that once lined the city's waterfront and from as far away as the Andrews Place shell mound at Coden. An 1877 report to the Smithsonian Institution from the land commissioner

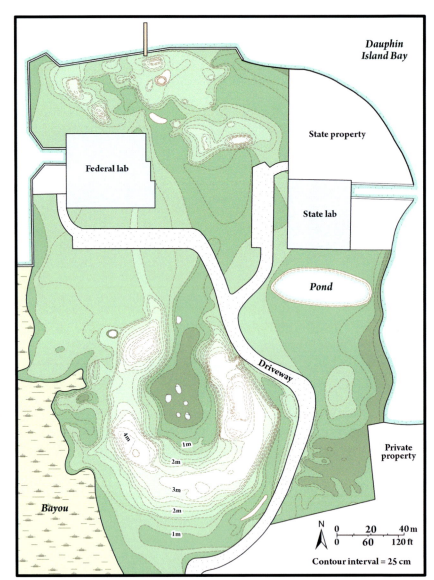

13.4. Topographic map of Dauphin Island Shell Mound Park, with elevations in meters, showing the southern large shell mound and northern smaller shell mounds. (Graphic by Sarah Mattics, Center for Archaeological Studies, University of South Alabama.)

of the Mobile & Ohio Railroad mentioned midden shells used to pave "the stockyards of the railroads, and the grounds around the cotton warehouses in Mobile."[6]

On Dauphin Island, longtime residents told historian Thomas Owen in 1900 that the center of the big mound had been mined in the 1820s and 1830s for midden shells burned in kilns to produce lime mortar used to construct nearby Forts Gaines and Morgan. Visitors to those masonry forts can still see, embedded in the lime mortar slathered between millions of

13.5. Colonial-era tabby wall on Little Dauphin Island Bay, north shore of Dauphin Island, near the Shell Mound, ca. 1900. (Doy Leale McCall Rare Book and Manuscript Library, University of South Alabama.)

bricks, bits of oyster shells and Native-made pottery from the Dauphin Island mound and other nearby middens.[7]

Despite its fame and cultural significance, this little-studied site remains poorly understood. In previous centuries, archaeologists thought all shell middens were formed in the same way, by the slow accretion of food remains discarded by visiting bands of shellfish gatherers. Repeated visits over many years led to substantial accumulations of shells, a normal result of shellfish gathering and processing that did occur at many coastal sites. However, recent research is revealing that many of the world's largest shell mounds were designed and constructed as impressive platforms, often supporting temples and chiefly houses, very much like their earthen counterparts, such as Mound A at the Bottle Creek site in the Mobile-Tensaw delta.[8]

One possible clue to the intentional layout of the Dauphin Island site is found on a pre–Civil War–era map of the island, drafted for the US Coast Survey in 1851. That detailed map shows a mysterious causeway crossing a marshy bayou that once separated the northern and southern shell mounds. Perhaps this walkway or road was built in the early nineteenth century simply to expedite removal of shell mined from the largest mound. However, soil cores recently analyzed by geoarchaeologist Howard Cyr support the notion that the causeway predates the colonial era. And studies of elaborate mound sites on the west coast of Florida have revealed previously unsuspected water courts, interior canals, and other elaborate features. Perhaps the marshy bayou at the heart of the Dauphin Island shell mounds served a similar purpose for the Mississippian residents.[9]

Now that we are beginning to look closely at the Dauphin Island shell mounds, the presence of Earth Diver at such a place seems most appropriate. Just as the great complex of mounds at Bottle Creek, in the Mobile-Tensaw delta, reflects a carefully engineered community plan built of earth, the contemporary Mississippian shell mounds on Dauphin Island likely represent a comparable townscape crafted from shells, at the edge of the southern sea.

CHAPTER 14

McInnis Site

> . . . on Bear Point peninsula in Orange Beach, was apparently a place of periodic feasting early in the Mississippian period, a large village later, and, around AD 1710, the home of a band of Towasa refugees from the Florida panhandle.

While clearing underbrush late in 2012 from his eight-acre Orange Beach property on Bear Point peninsula, overlooking Bayou St. John, part of Perdido Bay, John M. McInnis III discovered several heaps of oyster shells. Among the shells he spotted Native-made pottery, including two ceramic effigies, hand-modeled figures of strange-looking animals. McInnis intended to build his family's new home on this lot, but the finds seemed important. After seeking advice from the city's coastal resources manager, he decided to postpone house construction. McInnis contracted with Justin Stickler of Wiregrass Archaeological Consulting for a systematic shovel test survey and four test unit excavations to be supplemented with volunteer fieldwork by a variety of groups, including several troops of Boy Scouts. Once the Wiregrass team completed their fieldwork, the Center for Archaeological Studies' volunteer corps, supervised by Greg Waselkov and Bonnie Gums, devoted forty-six field days—many Saturdays between mid-March 2013 and early January 2015—to excavate another fifty units in seven areas of the site (fig. 14.1). At the conclusion of fieldwork, McInnis generously donated his own collection of ceramic effigies from the site to the University of South Alabama's Archaeology Museum, where the entire site assemblage is curated for future study and display.[1]

The McInnis site (1BA664), we now know, is the far western end of a very large and complex Mississippian village site with a long archaeological history. In the 1870s, George Sternberg, a US Army surgeon stationed

14.1. Lori Sawyer excavating at the McInnis site (1BA664), March 2014. (Center for Archaeological Studies, University of South Alabama.)

at the Pensacola Navy Yard, explored several ancient sites in the region, including an extensive shell midden on Bear Point peninsula. His account, although brief, is especially valuable because he visited at an ideal time to assess the size of this and other nearby archaeological sites that have subsequently become obscured by modern urban development.[2]

"The land has been cleared to some extent," Sternberg wrote in 1876, "for the purpose of cultivation," by local farmers, "as these 'shell-banks' are favorite locations for the raising of corn, watermelons, and fruit trees (orange, fig, and peach)." He saw oyster shells "scattered over the surface in irregular heaps, the contents of which vary from a few bushels to thousands of bushels" (fig. 14.2). Sternberg estimated the cleared portion of this site "at 60 acres" and consequently the largest ancient archaeological site on the Alabama coast. An even more immense shell midden, estimated at one hundred acres, covered much of Innerarity Point, directly east of Bear Point across Perdido Bay.[3]

"Present owners of the land" on Bear Point peninsula, Sternberg went on to state, "have occasionally picked up, while cultivating the 'shell banks,' clay images of the heads of birds and animals, and a single specimen of the 'human face divine.' . . . Some of them seem to have formed the handles of earthen vessels. One in the shape of a squirrel's head is evidently a rattlebox. It is hollow and contains fragments of something which rattle when it is shaken"[4] (fig. 14.3).

Sternberg's report attracted the attention of archaeologist William Henry Holmes at the Smithsonian Institution's Bureau of American Ethnology. In his 1903 landmark study of pottery made by Native peoples of eastern North America, the first comprehensive work on the topic, Holmes highlighted ceramics found on Bear Point peninsula by two other visitors. In 1889 the Smithsonian had received a donation of a group of pots from a sand mound at Bear Point (site 1BA1) from Francis H. Parsons of the US Coast and Geodetic Survey. Parsons had acquired the pots by digging in the mound while he was supposed to be mapping Perdido Bay. Holmes later corresponded with Clarence B. Moore, the wealthy Philadelphia archaeologist, who dug extensively in 1901 into the same burial mound despoiled by Parsons. Holmes commented on the numerous "heads of birds and other creatures" collected by both men and illustrated several, noting

14.2. Excavation Units 29–30, with shell midden in cross section, November 2014. (Center for Archaeological Studies, University of South Alabama.)

14.3. Ceramic zoomorphic effigy in shell midden, December 2014. (Center for Archaeological Studies, University of South Alabama.)

"these are not figurines in the true sense, but are merely heads broken from the rims of bowls"[5] (fig. 14.4).

We now know that site 1BA1, the sand burial mound at Bear Point essentially destroyed by Parsons's and Moore's depredations, dated to the mid-sixteenth to early seventeenth centuries. Sternberg's sixty-acre shell midden west of the mound was a complex site occupied throughout the Mississippian period (AD 1250–1700), judging from the pottery styles reported by all three early site investigators. A survey of private residential lots east of the McInnis property, carried out in 2022 by the center's volunteers and supervised by Greg Waselkov, has confirmed the enormous extent of this mainly Late Mississippian village site. The McInnis site, at the far west end of this site complex and the only portion studied in detail in modern times, offers valuable clues that help us interpret this important archaeological locale.

Archaeologist Richard Fuller analyzed pottery collected during the shovel-testing survey of the McInnis tract. In his report for Wiregrass, he concluded that the oyster shell middens at the west end of 1BA664 dated almost entirely to the Bottle Creek I period (AD 1250–1400). In fact, that

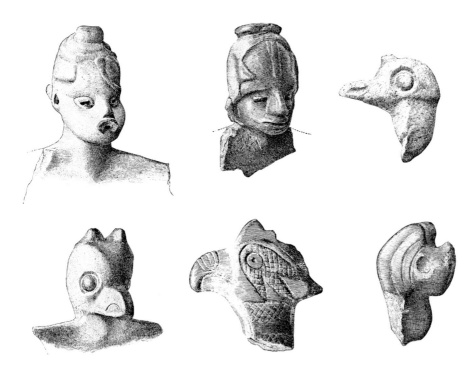

14.4. Drawing of ceramic effigies from the Bear Point shell middens, collected by Francis Parsons "about the year 1889." (From Holmes, "Aboriginal Pottery," plates LVIII–LIX; Center for Archaeological Studies, University of South Alabama.)

part of the McInnis site is the only shell midden yet excavated that dates exclusively—or nearly so—to Bottle Creek I. Sites occupied during a single period, while rare, are very helpful to archaeologists; this one clarifies the Mississippian ceramic chronology for the entire northern Gulf Coast. Very small amounts of later pottery types dating to Bottle Creek II (AD 1400–1550) and to post-Mississippian times (AD 1550–1650) did appear in the upper few inches of the McInnis site excavation.[6]

Shovel testing on the McInnis tract also revealed an even later Native occupation of the site, dating to around AD 1710 and located mainly west of the shell middens. Volunteers from the center excavated a block of units in the nonshell portion of 1BA664 and found a small pit with burned corn cobs, the sort of feature commonly encountered on colonial-era sites. Wet smoldering cobs produce a dense smoke that Native Americans used for two purposes: to preserve deerskins traded in vast numbers to colonists and to drive off mosquitoes, which were (and still are) a great annoyance in warm months of the year. Pottery types associated with the circa 1710 occupation resemble styles made by Muscogee Creeks and affiliated

MCINNIS SITE   101

14.5. Mississippian ceramic effigies and rim sherd from the McInnis site. (Courtesy of Jennifer Brown/Into Nature Films.)

14.6. Ceramic anthropomorphic effigy, probably dating to the seventeenth century, from the McInnis site. (Courtesy of John McInnis III.)

peoples living farther north. Greg Waselkov and Phil Carr have interpreted this early colonial-era occupation of the McInnis site as a small camp of Towasas, people who had once lived in central Alabama. In 1704–5, Towasas sought a new home near the French at Old Mobile after their refugee villages in the Florida panhandle were attacked by slave-raiding Creek warriors.[7]

Sternberg, Moore, and Holmes all remarked on the prevalence of ceramic effigies at the Bear Point shell midden (figs. 14.5, 14.6, and 14.7). During analysis by Waselkov and Erin Nelson, we, too, were struck by their number and diversity in the McInnis site collection. As Holmes noted, they once adorned the rims of shell-tempered bowls, although none remained attached to bowl rims. The McInnis site effigies had either broken off at a narrow part of the effigy's neck or become detached where the potter had originally pressed the base of the effigy into the outer rim of the bowl. In fact, the damage to these vessels is so severe and consistent that we think the bowls were broken deliberately at the end of their usefulness. All the pots that once displayed McInnis site effigies were well-made hemispherical bowls with smoothed burnished surfaces. Fuller identified the type as Mound Place Incised, variety Waltons Camp. Such bowls characteristically have a band of horizontal parallel incised lines running just below the rim on the vessel exterior. Where the incised band approaches the

14.7. Mississippian ceramic effigy bowl sherd (interior and exterior views) found in 1953 at the Dauphin Island shell mound (1MB72) by Wilson Duval of Pascagoula. (Center for Archaeological Studies, University of South Alabama.)

effigy, the band of lines either ends or abruptly curves beneath the effigy attachment.[8]

Archaeologists have recently made much progress in our understanding of Mississippian iconography, the decorative imagery found on many of their artifacts. For instance, we now know that the bands of incised lines encircling many Mississippian and later Native-made pots are cosmological markers that refer to one or another of the realms of the three-tiered cosmos—Beneath World, This World, Above World. In the case of the McInnis bowls, the open loops incised by potters beneath the rim effigies are thought to refer to the Above World, the realm of birds, bird spirits, and certain other legendary characters, all possessing great powers. Mississippian artists, including their potters, deployed these graphic symbols for several reasons. By incising these lines into clay, they expressed their worldview and conveyed respect for powers controlled by other-than-human persons who populated the other realms, the beings depicted in the ceramic effigies. The literature on Mississippian iconography is already quite extensive and far too complex to delve into here, but we can suggest several ways to interpret and understand the importance of the McInnis site effigies.[9]

Although the various forms of bowl rim effigies have characteristics that suggest they represent humans or seem to capture key identifying features of particular animal species, Mississippian art generally depicts mythological beings. Seemingly naturalistic effigies that resemble ducks, owls, woodpeckers, bears, and other familiar animals often combine features of different animals, thereby signaling that they, too, refer to beings not normally encountered in physical form in This World. Folklorist George Lankford and archaeologist David Dye have argued, regarding the anthropomorphic (humanlike) effigies, that one style with elaborate conical headwear represents Lightning-boy, one of the Twins highlighted in many Native myths told by descendants of Mississippian societies. In fact, there are reasons to think that all the humanlike effigies on bowl rims portray Lightning-boy.[10]

One intriguing distinction between anthropomorphic and animal effigies is consistently evident between their orientations on bowl rims. Among the McInnis site effigies, every anthropomorphic head once faced the interior of the intact bowl. In contrast, animal effigies invariably faced outward (a pattern, interestingly, not found everywhere in the Mississippian world). These divergent orientations are reinforced on "bird" effigy bowls by the placement of a stylized tail projecting from the rim opposite the outward-facing head. In effect, the entire bowl became an effigy. Similarly, some bowls from Mississippian sites in the Mississippi valley have upturned human feet jutting from the rim opposite the human head effigy. These patterns suggest that all bowls with rim effigies were thought of as corporeal with or without additional appendages.

These bowls were intended to hold something. Chemical analysis of content residues will someday provide us with specific information. But food of some sort was the most likely contents of open bowls because liquids would have been more effectively conveyed in beakers and bottles, ceramic vessels with narrow mouths that would have lessened spillage. Fuller suggested that the large number of effigy vessels found at the McInnis site may point to regular occurrences of ritual feasting at this location. If we think about these bowls as food containers, then placing food into an anthropomorphic effigy vessel with inward-facing head would have "fed" the bowl's body. The avian forms with outward-facing heads carried food on their backs. At the McInnis site the two effigy vessel forms—animal like and humanlike—therefore complemented each other in a thematic way.[11]

Perhaps they also played complementary roles in performative rituals. In 1700, Jesuit missionary Paul du Ru witnessed such a ritual enacted at a Taensa temple (in Louisiana) with wooden effigy bowls filled with cornmeal. The Taensa people had taken a *cabanne* or hut "of the newly dead chief to serve as a temple." According to du Ru, "they have surrounded it with screens made with canes, and we only see elders at the door of this temple moaning and howling, we only see cantors praying, we only see people carrying offerings, and that with order and an extraordinary modesty. Among other things there are six large wooden bowls, of which one handle represents the tail of a swan and the other the neck, filled with flour and carried gravely to the temple."[12] This rare observation of effigy vessels in use by Native people during a religious ritual, at the very beginning of French colonization on the Gulf Coast, suggests that Father du Ru witnessed one of the final performances of a five-hundred-yearlong tradition.

There is more than a little speculation in this, although archaeologists are making steady progress in the interpretation of Mississippian ritual behavior. Short-lived sites like the McInnis shell heaps also allow archaeologists to trace historic trends in effigy styles, tasks that Steve Wimberly, Fuller, and Diane Silvia began years ago. We now know that styles of anthropomorphic heads changed through time: the "topknot" form seen at the McInnis site during Bottle Creek I was replaced by a hollow "rattlebox" form with notched side and rear headwear crests during Bottle Creek II, found at the large shell midden east of the McInnis tract. Cherokee artist Teresa Horn suggested that carrying a bowl with a hollow head filled with clay pellets, causing it to rattle, brought the effigy vessel to life. That rattlebox style was followed by solid heads, some with zigzag "lightning" incising, attached to bowls made during the seventeenth century.[13]

The McInnis site's ceramic effigies are just one of the many fascinating aspects of Alabama coastal Mississippian culture. Unfortunately, these coastal sites are among the most threatened by development, storm surges, and rising sea level. They urgently need protection and study.

CHAPTER 15

Dugout Canoes

> . . . examples of which are occasionally found in the rivers of south Alabama, were skillfully crafted and durable watercraft that served across millennia as the principal mode of transport and travel in the Native South.

Before the nineteenth century, travel around the South relied on an intricate trail network crisscrossing the landscape, some trails for long-distance journeys, many more for local hikes between towns, fields, and hunting grounds. Complementing the land routes was an equally important "waterscape" of rivers and streams that, thanks to abundant rainfall, reached every corner of the region. Dugout canoes provided the principal means to move people and materials around the Southeast. In the coastal zone of the northern Gulf, travel by water was, until very recently, by far the predominant mode of transport. So discoveries here of very old dugout canoes are not surprising or particularly unusual.[1]

From the hundreds of ancient canoes found across the Southeast, we know that there were several distinct types: flatbottomed canoes for shallow waters; round-bottomed styles for deeper waters; and a multihulled catamaran style, with two canoes lashed together and straddled by a platform, perhaps for use in the open waters of the Gulf. Native Americans for at least ten thousand years made dugout canoes from logs of cypress and longleaf pine, both rot resistant woods, laboriously felled and shaped by burning and chopping with stone axes or adzes to form graceful watercraft (fig. 15.1). Early colonists observed the efficiency of these boats and copied the form for travel in coastal waters. They even employed well-worn portages (shown on several colonial-era maps), overland carrying places used for centuries to connect nearby waterways[2] (fig. 15.2).

Most of the ancient dugout canoes found in recent years come from

15.1. "The manner of makinge their boates," engraved by Theodor de Bry, after John White, of Native people of coastal North Carolina. (From Harriot, *A Briefe and True Report*, plate 12; Center for Archaeological Studies, University of South Alabama.)

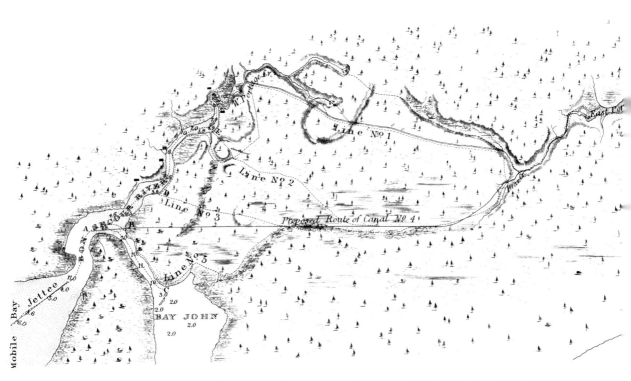

15.2. Detail of Lt. Henry G. Sill's 1833 "Survey for a Projected Canal," showing a five-hundred-foot-long portage (dotted line, *top middle*, above "Line No. 1") between the headwaters of Bon Secour River at left and East Portage Creek, a tributary of Perdido Bay. (Library of Congress, Geography and Map Division, 2018593269.)

southern lakes, where they were intentionally submerged, perhaps to preserve the wooden craft during periods of disuse. The fact that so many dugout canoes were never retrieved by their owners suggests, however, that permanent submersion may have been a form of burial or offering, an appropriate way to end a canoe's useful life. Other canoes were beached or tied up along riverbanks, only to be buried by the collapse of those riverbanks during intense storms. Modern-day floods sometimes shift sediments and uncover long-lost canoes, and in fact, many have reappeared after violent weather events. If ancient dugout canoes are buried beneath clay, in an anaerobic (oxygen-free) environment, the wood can emerge centuries later in good or even excellent condition.[3]

The first recorded discovery of a dugout canoe in southwest Alabama occurred in 1935 when laborers from a Works Progress Administration transient camp at Fort Morgan uncovered a cypress canoe near Ewing Bayou, ten miles east of the fort, while building State Highway 180 to Gulf Shores. After some years on display at the fort, the dugout canoe was given to the Alabama Department of Archives and History during World War II and now is an exhibit highlight at the Museum of Alabama in Montgomery. That canoe measures 4.92 meters long, 0.69 meters wide, and 0.3 meters tall. Because it lacks bow and stern platforms typically seen on Mississippian-era dugout canoes, this specimen may be of fairly recent age, although that has not been established by radiocarbon dating.[4]

In June 1973, Noel Read Stowe heard about a dugout canoe discovered on the bank of the Tombigbee River, southeast of Peavy's Landing in Clarke County, by Robert L. Grimes and J. J. Mason of Frankville in Washington County (fig. 15.3). Grimes and Mason had found the canoe a month earlier, lodged in some brush along a riverbank where it had floated after a flood. Now exposed to the elements, the canoe began deteriorating rapidly, which prompted the men to seek professional assistance from the University of South Alabama's Archaeological Research Laboratory. Grimes and Mason agreed to donate their find to the county if the university would take on the challenge of conserving the ancient artifact. Stowe and his students built a long stainless-steel conservation tank at their Brookley Field lab and submerged the canoe for three months in a 15 percent polyethylene glycol (PEG) solution, standard treatment at the time for stabilizing waterlogged wood. This canoe, referred to as Peavy's Landing No. 1, is now on display in the Washington County Courthouse Museum in Chatom.[5]

With a submersion tank now available, opportunities arose to conserve several other dugout canoes over the next two decades. In 1977, Richard Fuller and Stowe received a call from the father of two boys who had found a beautifully preserved canoe washing out of a sand bar in the

15.3. Dugout canoe found by J. J. Mason and Robert L. Grimes in May 1973 on the bank of the lower Tombigbee River near Peavy's Landing, Frankville, Alabama. The canoe is on display in the Washington County Courthouse Museum in Chatom. (Center for Archaeological Studies, University of South Alabama.)

lower Alabama River near Boatyard Lake. The boys had scooped out the remaining sand and paddled around in the ancient canoe for a while before informing their dad of their discovery. Fuller and Stowe treated this canoe with PEG too, and it was eventually purchased by the History Museum of Mobile, where it is prominently displayed.[6]

Several dugout canoes from other states were conserved in the Brookley conservation tank by Stowe and Fuller in succeeding years, under contract with the US Army Corps of Engineers (fig. 15.4). A second canoe turned up near Peavy's Landing on the lower Tombigbee River in the late 1980s. This canoe, Peavy's Landing No. 2, was not conserved, but the owners permitted Sam McGahey, chief archaeologist with the Mississippi Department of Archives and History, to view and record the canoe, observations he shared with Fuller.[7]

Finally, in 1991 a small dugout canoe discovered in the Chickasawhay River in southeastern Mississippi was donated to the University of South Alabama, where it remains available for study. The Chickasawhay specimen is made from longleaf pine and is the most recent, with steel axe marks visible on the canoe interior. Fuller compiled information on the Alabama River canoe and the two Tombigbee River canoes from Peavy's Landing and offered the following conclusions. All three are made of bald cypress wood and show evidence of charring and stone axe or adze cuts. Samples of wood submitted for radiocarbon dating from two of the canoes yielded these results. The calibrated date ranges (in parentheses) bracket the most likely ages of the canoes:

Alabama River Canoe, AD 1320 ± 55 years (cal AD 1279–1409)
Peavy's Landing No. 1, AD 1345 ± 60 years (cal AD 1284–1423)

Both radiocarbon-dated canoes fall comfortably within the Mississippian period, and all three are stylistically similar. All have short, flat, projecting platforms at either end, with a mooring hole present in the narrower bow platforms, a characteristic of most Mississippian dugout canoes found elsewhere in the Southeast. Dimensions of the southwest Alabama canoes are also similar to the majority of known Mississippian canoes.[8]

Alabama River Canoe (6.06 meters long; 0.46 meters maximum width; circa 0.3 meters maximum height)
Peavy's Landing No. 1 (6.03 meters long; 0.51 meters maximum width; circa 0.36–0.39 meters maximum height)
Peavy's Landing No. 2 (5.62 meters long; 0.44 meters maximum width; circa 0.37 meters maximum height)

Other ancient canoes will assuredly be discovered in the future by accident and by nonprofessionals who may or may not know that long-submerged wood will crack, warp, and decompose in short order if not

15.4. Salitpa canoe at the Archaeological Research Laboratory, University of South Alabama, Brookley Campus, June 1980. (Center for Archaeological Studies, University of South Alabama.)

conserved. These impressive artifacts give us a rare glimpse of the organic part of the archaeological record—the wooden tools and structures, river-cane mats and baskets, woven plant fiber textiles—that seldom survives to the present day but played an essential role in the lives of our predecessors in this region.

PART VI

FRENCH COLONIAL PERIOD (1699–1763)

CHAPTER 16

Old Mobile

> . . . capital of French colonial Louisiane from 1702 to 1711, a celebrated historic site, the place where modern Alabama began, yet also a place that remains nearly inaccessible for the public.

In 2002, and again in 2011, Mobilians celebrated their city's two tricentennials. Modern downtown Mobile sits atop the city's small colonial predecessor, the second colonial town by that name, established in 1711. The French had just abandoned their 1702 settlement at Twenty-Seven Mile Bluff, located that distance upstream from the mouth of the Mobile River. After relocating their capital, the French referred to the original townsite as Vieux Mobile, Old Mobile, as it has been known ever since.[1]

French Mobile and nearby Spanish Pensacola, founded in 1698 as Presidio Santa María de Galve, were the first successful European footholds established on the northern Gulf Coast. Those successes built on Spanish explorer Tristán de Luna's faltering effort at Pensacola in 1559–61, René-Robert Cavelier, sieur de La Salle's disastrous Texas colony near Matagorda Bay in 1685–88, and Pierre Le Moyne d'Iberville's short-lived Fort Maurepas on Biloxi Bay in 1699–1701. The presence of permanent colonizing outposts on the Gulf Coast profoundly impacted Native peoples throughout the South and altered the trajectory of southern history, which makes archaeological exploration of both historic sites imperative. Yet neither colonial townsite, neither Old Mobile nor the first Pensacola, revealed its secrets easily.

Despite being accurately pinpointed on eighteenth-century maps, unearthing evidence of the two colonial towns took both luck and persistence. After years of speculation as to its whereabouts, traces of Presidio Santa María de Galve turned up by chance in 1992 on the grounds of Naval Air Station Pensacola, during trenching for a utility line being monitored by US Army Corps of Engineers archaeologists. That revelation prompted negotiations with the US Navy, which eventually allowed full-scale excavations led by University of West Florida archaeologist Judith Bense from 1995 to 1998.[2]

Positive identification of Old Mobile's archaeological footprint took just as long. In 1897 Peter J. Hamilton, Mobile's pioneering historian, reportedly found distinctive French bricks and cannonballs at Twenty-Seven Mile Bluff. Other visitors retrieved souvenir colonial pottery there during the 1902 unveiling of a stone marker commemorating the two hundredth anniversary of the town's founding. In 1970 archaeologist Donald Harris took a busman's holiday from his excavation of Fort Condé, in downtown Mobile, to excavate for a few days near the 1902 commemorative marker but found little evidence of Fort Louis apart from some more cannonballs.[3]

Finally in 1989, James "Buddy" Parnell, an engineer working at Courtaulds Fibers, a rayon manufacturing plant that owned part of Twenty-Seven Mile Bluff, noticed several slight irregularities in the forest floor near the road to the river. When metal detecting turned up handwrought nails and other unusual artifacts, Parnell surmised that the low mounds he had spotted could be raised floors of French houses. Realizing he had found the long-sought townsite of Old Mobile, Parnell selflessly passed along word of his discovery to local historians Jay Higginbotham and John "Jack" Friend. They in turn contacted University of South Alabama archaeologist Greg Waselkov, who had previously excavated Fort Toulouse and other French colonial-era sites near Montgomery.[4]

Parnell had indeed found raised clay floors of French half-timber buildings, barely perceptible features preserved almost miraculously for three centuries atop a forested bluff (figs. 16.1 and 16.2). The old townsite had been largely spared the ravages of agricultural plowing and disturbance by industrial development. With grant assistance from the National Endowment for the Humanities and the National Science Foundation, the National Center for Preservation Technology, the Alabama State Legislature and Alabama Historical Commission, and many corporate and private donors, plus unwavering support from every level of university administration, Waselkov directed field projects at Old Mobile for twenty-nine years, until his retirement in 2017. During those years, students who enrolled in spring field methods courses dug side by side with professional staff from the Center for Archaeological Studies and dedicated volunteers to learn survey and excavation techniques at one of the premier archaeological sites in the country[5] (figs. 16.3 and 16.4).

Five years of intensive systematic shovel testing by a survey team led by Diane Silvia revealed the remains of over fifty French structures scattered

16.1. Drone photograph looking down at the footprint of Structure 1 at Old Mobile (1MB94), originally excavated in 1989 and re-excavated in June 2016. (Center for Archaeological Studies, University of South Alabama.)

16.2. Artist's impression of a poteaux-sur-sole building at Old Mobile. (Ink sketch by Philippe Oszuscik, colorized by Sarah Mattics, Center for Archaeological Studies, University of South Alabama.)

16.3. Iron bar shot excavated in 2000 at Structure 14, Old Mobile. (Center for Archaeological Studies, University of South Alabama.)

across some eighty acres along a half mile of river bluff. Old Mobile (site 1MB94) turned out to be the rarest sort of archaeological find, an entire colonial townsite without a modern city atop it. Quebec, Montreal, New Orleans, St. Louis, modern Mobile—each one sits astride its colonial forerunner, which only occasionally comes to light when utility work or new building construction offers archaeologists narrow, brief glimpses of deeply buried colonial deposits. At Old Mobile, the colonial townsite sits beneath an Alabama forest, unencumbered by layers of more recent history.[6]

Between 1989 and 2017, Waselkov, Silvia, and Bonnie Gums carried out excavations at places where ten structures once stood (fig. 16.5). This sample of the colonial town included five colonists' homes (Structures 1, 3–5, 14), three soldiers' barracks (Structures 30–32), a blacksmith's forge (Structure 2) (fig. 16.6), and a Native American house (site 1MB147) situated across a swamp from the French townsite. This archaeological cross section of a colonial community offers an unrivaled view of life in French Louisiane during the first decade of the eighteenth century. In 2004 and 2017, Joy Klotz and the Friends of Old Mobile sponsored two key field projects

118 CHAPTER 16

16.4. Berle Clay carries an electromagnetic earth conductivity meter during a geophysical survey at Old Mobile, December 2001. (Center for Archaeological Studies, University of South Alabama.)

that allowed us to correlate the colonial-era maps of Old Mobile with our archaeological finds and identify the owners of the private structures.[7]

Thanks to Higginbotham's excellent historical study, *Old Mobile*, published in 1977, we already had in hand a compelling narrative history of events experienced between 1702 and 1711 by the town's several hundred French-speaking colonists who hailed from France, Canada, and the Caribbean islands. For his book, Higginbotham necessarily relied solely on documentary historical sources, principally the official reports and letters that reflect the biases of their authors, the colony's literate elites, all of whom were white, male, and Eurocentric. Archaeology offers us ways to challenge biases of that sort that are inherent in the written historical record. The material evidence of daily existence experienced by Old Mobile's diverse residents often contrasts with official statements written to impress the French king and his ministers. Here, we can only hint at the knowledge gained from such a lengthy and productive research project and provide a few highlights.[8]

16.5. Historic sketch of Old Mobile's town layout ("Plan de la ville et du Fort Louis sur La Mobile" [1704]), overlaid with excavation maps of archaeological structures. (Graphic by Sarah Mattics, Center for Archaeological Studies, University of South Alabama.)

In many ways, the written and material records complement one another. Gaps or oversights in one are sometimes offset by evidence of the other sort. In fact, studying artifacts and documents in tandem often yields insights unachievable from either of them alone. For instance, our detailed archaeological survey of the townsite helped us understand the different purposes of the town's two historic maps, even though the intentions of the two anonymous mapmakers are not explained in period

16.6. Artists' impression of the blacksmith's shop, Structure 2, at Old Mobile. (Ink sketch by Patsy and Ed Gullett, Center for Archaeological Studies, University of South Alabama.)

documents. While the town plan drawn in 1702 (perhaps by military engineer Charles Levasseur) is best understood as a proposal for town development, a later town plan drafted in 1704–5 more realistically depicts the town revealed by archaeology. Once the French experienced firsthand the Gulf Coast's torrential winter and spring rains early in 1702, the settlers sensibly avoided building on low swampy land that had originally been platted for the north end of the settlement, in favor of drier terrain to the south. There, in fact, is where we found remains of numerous houses that correspond to private lots shown only on the latter town plan.[9]

Artifact finds largely confirm impressions from historic documents that great disparities in wealth existed between colonial households. Such social inequalities are dramatically evident when comparing objects such as dropped coins, which were found far more often at the Chauvin and Levasseur households (Structures 1 and 14) than at the soldiers' barracks (Structures 30–32), which housed the most impoverished of the colonists, members of the Troupes de la Marine, who lived just outside the hewn walls of Fort Louis[10] (fig. 16.7).

Far more challenging to the documentary record, however, were the many fragments of beautiful Chinese porcelain vessels—cups, saucers, plates—uncovered by excavations everywhere in Old Mobile, even at the barracks (fig. 16.8). In continental France during the first decade of the eighteenth century, only the social equals of the colony's wealthiest

OLD MOBILE   121

16.7. Artists' impression of barracks life, Structures 30–32, at Old Mobile. (Ink sketch by Patsy and Ed Gullett, Center for Archaeological Studies, University of South Alabama.)

residents could afford imported Chinese porcelain. In truth, more of these decorative cups and saucers, intended for serving tea and chocolate in elevated society, were found at the homes of the well-to-do Levasseur and the wealthy Chauvins. But some turned up at every Old Mobile structure, even at the blacksmith's shop. Why were such exotic, expensive status symbols ubiquitous at a rude outpost on the edge of the French empire?[11]

Proximity to Spanish ports—neighboring Pensacola, of course, but also not too distant Havana and Veracruz, across the Gulf—is certainly the principal reason. Few of the first wave of French colonists came to Louisiane to farm. Nearly all sought their fortunes in trade, legal or otherwise. Native hunters were eager to acquire firearms, cloth, and other merchandise in exchange for animal pelts and furs, which French colonists then endeavored to sell in Spanish colonial ports, exchanging them for silver coinage or imported luxury goods such as Chinese porcelain. Since both those forms of commercial transaction, trade in furs and intercolonial trade, were highly regulated by French and Spanish officials through monopolies, taxes, and embargoes, Old Mobile's artifacts amply document the ineffectiveness of official trade policies and regulations. Smuggling flourished in this new colony and remained prevalent for a century. Archaeological evidence from Old Mobile clearly points to the many surreptitious pathways to wealth available to enterprising colonists of every social level.[12]

The Old Mobile site has been listed on the National Register of Historic Places since Higginbotham nominated it in 1976. In 2001, the US Secretary of the Interior determined this preeminent historic site eligible for designation as a National Historic Landmark. However, landowner objections prevented actual listing as a National Historic Landmark, which is the highest level of recognition bestowed on historic sites by the National Park Service. Landowner objections have also stymied all efforts to make the site publicly accessible on a regular basis. The Archaeological Conservancy, a private nonprofit preservation organization, has acquired preservation easements on portions of the archaeological site, which affords the place some level of protection. But Old Mobile's educational and tourism potential, like that of nearby Mount Vernon Barracks/Searcy Hospital, remains unrealized, despite its immense historical importance.

16.8. Chinese porcelain cup rim sherd, Kangxi period (1662–1722), excavated from Structure 14 at Old Mobile. (Center for Archaeological Studies, University of South Alabama.)

CHAPTER 17

Port Dauphin

> . . . Mobile's deepwater port early in the eighteenth century, on the south shore of Dauphin Island, now sits beneath DeSoto Landing, a gated residential community.

During the first quarter of the eighteenth century, the French colony of Louisiane depended on a small harbor on Dauphin Island's Gulf side to serve as a port for supply ships arriving from Europe (fig. 17.1). In 1973–74, archaeologist Noel Read Stowe supervised excavation of a nearby palisaded fort (site 1MB61) that had protected the harbor and adjacent small village. University of South Alabama undergraduates and fifteen Girl Scouts (in the Deep South Girl Scout Council's "Archy" Program) participated in those digs. When subdivision development threatened the remains of the fort site, George Shorter conducted further excavations there in 1992–93, assisted by volunteers from the Alabama School of Mathematics and Science, and Shorter documented his findings in a master's thesis for Louisiana State University.[1]

In 1993 Stowe and Rebecca Lumpkin discovered a remnant of Port Dauphin village (1MB221) in DeSoto Landing subdivision. Despite damage to the village site from hurricane storm surges over the previous three centuries, remains of three household sites were found relatively intact under dune sand. Imminent destruction of the best-preserved house site by private home construction led to excavations there, directed by Shorter and Greg Waselkov in 1997. We were very appreciative of the property owner's willingness to delay construction of her home, especially as there were no legal requirements for archaeological investigations in advance of her planned construction. Her generosity permitted us to retrieve a vast amount of information from one of the most important colonial sites in Alabama.

17.1. Bird's-eye view of Port Dauphin village with fort at upper left, harbor in foreground. Watercolor by Sieur de Norlet, 1717. (Source Bibliothèque nationale de France.)

Fieldwork by university students and staff uncovered features of a large French colonial house (figs. 17.2 and 17.3), until we were interrupted on July 19 by Hurricane Danny, which inundated the island with an astounding 36.7 inches of rain, the equivalent of more than half a year's average precipitation. Excavation only resumed when the floodwaters receded after Labor Day, six weeks later. Despite that natural calamity, research at Port Dauphin village, which was partially supported by a grant from the Alabama Historical Commission, uncovered a barrel well and

17.2. University of South Alabama students excavating the Port Dauphin village midden (1MB221), 1997. (Center for Archaeological Studies, University of South Alabama.)

PORT DAUPHIN   125

17.3. Matthew Cooper preparing to piece plot artifacts in relation to wall trenches (lighter-colored sand) during excavations at Port Dauphin village, 1997. (Center for Archaeological Studies, University of South Alabama.)

foundations of a long post-in-ground building occupied from about 1715 to 1730. Among thousands of excavated artifacts were French ceramic plates and pitchers, English-made bottles and wine glasses, Native-made pottery, and food remains.[2]

The quantity and variety of artifacts associated with drinking suggest that this building served as a tavern as well as a private residence (figs. 17.4 and 17.5). Before 1733, taverns were not licensed in colonial Louisiane, and more than a few enterprising colonists operated wine shops out of their homes. We suspect that this was the case at Port Dauphin, where the

17.4. Artists' interpretation of house interior at Port Dauphin village. (Ink sketch by Patsy and Ed Gullett, Center for Archaeological Studies, University of South Alabama.)

17.5. English wine bottle discovered at Port Dauphin village, 1997. (Center for Archaeological Studies, University of South Alabama.)

nearby fort's garrison and the crews of ships intermittently anchored in the harbor undoubtedly furnished eager clientele. The most convincing evidence for a tavern on the premises is a rare signet (also known as a seal matrix) carved from semiprecious carnelian (fig. 17.6). The signet's owner used it to impress his personal emblem on wax seals attached to letters

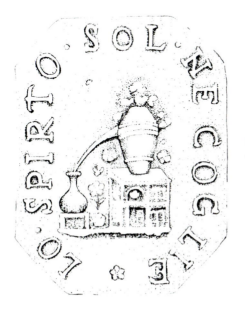

17.6. Drawing of signet or seal matrix impression from Port Dauphin village. (Ink drawing by Joann Okuzono, Center for Archaeological Studies, University of South Alabama.)

PORT DAUPHIN 127

17.7. View of a Cottage on the Island Massacre near the Mobile W. Florida. Octor. 1764, by Lord Adam Gordon. (British Library, King George III's Topographical Collection, Maps K.Top.122.94.2, CC BY-NC-SA.)

and legal documents. This small stone artifact, with a hole at one end for suspension, was certainly prized by its owner until damaged by fire and discarded or lost. The engraved end depicts an alembic, a distillation apparatus of the sort used in brandy making, encircled by a misspelled motto in Italian, "Lo spir[i]to sol ne coglie," which echoes the poet Petrarch's aphorism ("il più bel fiore ne coglie" [the best flower among others is chosen]). Italian language specialists who were consulted provided this English translation of the signet's text: "Among others, the spirit alone is chosen," with *spirito* doubling as a pun for distilled alcoholic drinks.[3]

The abundance of imported artifacts found at Port Dauphin came mostly from France, unsurprisingly, but also from England, Holland, and Mexico (colonial New Spain). Although the colonists on this isolated, sandy island depended on resupplies from their home country, they also proved resourceful (fig. 17.7). Merchant vessels from competing nations made surreptitious layovers at this little colonial outpost to carry on illicit trading, even in the midst of war. Indeed, smuggling via Port Dauphin became a mainstay of the Louisiane economy, which came to light during an official inquiry into the sinking of *La Bellone* off the island in 1725, with Gov. Jean Baptiste Le Moyne de Bienville's personal cargo of prohibited furs and other banned exports filling the ship's hold.[4]

Given the storm-ravaged state of the colonial village site, in a now thoroughly developed subdivision, these investigations may have provided our only archaeological glimpses of the port that served as French colonial Mobile's link to the Atlantic world during Louisiane's precarious early decades.

CHAPTER 18

Fort Condé

> . . . the site of a masonry fortress, which protected the town of Mobile throughout the eighteenth century, was defended by Mobile's resolute historic preservation community in the mid-1960s when threatened by interstate highway construction.

As happened in so many American cities during the 1950s and 1960s, plans to construct an interstate highway, I-10, through downtown Mobile threatened to divide neighborhoods and destroy a great swath of the city's architectural gems. In the proposed construction path also lay one of the region's most significant historic sites, archaeological remains of the colonial fort known successively as Fort Louis de la Mobile, Fort Condé, and finally Fort Charlotte (Fuerte Carlota, during the Spanish regime). Construction of I-10's Wallace Tunnel did indeed displace many residents and destroy a great portion of downtown Mobile's architectural and archaeological heritage (fig. 18.1). However, a truly heroic effort by members of the local historic preservation community, with key assistance from state and federal highway officials, saved more than anyone initially thought possible and set an important precedent for future preservation efforts in the region.[1]

Before the National Historic Preservation Act became law in October 1966 (thereby creating modern cultural resource management in the United States), preservationists had few tools to avert or mitigate loss of historically significant places during urban development. Fortunately for Mobile, Nancy N. Holmes and her husband Nicholas H. Holmes Jr., both members of the Mobile Historical Commission, recognized the preservation potential of an obscure section of the US legal code concerning federal highways. Enacted in 1958, Title 23, Section 305 permitted expenditure of highway funds "for archeological and paleontological salvage." By

18.1. Interstate-10 Wallace Tunnel construction, site of Fort Condé (1MB262), Condé-Charlotte House at right, January 1971. (Center for Archaeological Studies, University of South Alabama.)

the spring of 1966, the federal Bureau of Public Roads, the Alabama Highway Department, and the University of Alabama reached an agreement to conduct archaeology at the site of the colonial fort (1MB262)—the first highway salvage archaeology project in Alabama. David DeJarnette led the project, with Jerry Nielsen supervising initial survey work in the field. Donald Harris, at the time a graduate student at the University of Florida, directed excavations from September 1967 to the fall of 1970, when Noel Read Stowe took over that role until February 1972.

Before Harris moved to Nova Scotia to join the archaeology staff at Fortress of Louisbourg National Historic Site, he wrote a master's thesis and a subsequent final project report documenting many of Fort Condé's architectural elements, including masonry curtain walls, casemates. and barracks, as well as the dry moat. Three impressive stone-lined wells, which reached depths of ten to sixteen feet, proved technically challenging to excavate but yielded informative artifact assemblages, including well seats—massive wooden rings that supported each well's brickwork during construction of these critical fort features. A thick layer of debris deposited in 1780 near the bottom of each well relates to the Spanish siege of British Fort Charlotte, one of only two battles fought during the American Revolutionary War in what would become Alabama.[2]

Stowe monitored construction of the Wallace Tunnel, which uncovered (and then destroyed) remains of the King's Wharf, a long wooden causeway that once crossed a marsh between the fort's water gate and an anchorage in the Mobile River. At the anchorage, three cannons were found—one French, one Spanish, and a third either French or British in origin. The cannons and one of the well seats are now displayed in the History Museum of Mobile's exhibits at Colonial Fort Condé, a partial reconstruction of the masonry fort created in 1976, after completion of Wallace Tunnel, for Mobile's celebration of the nation's bicentennial. Most of the other excavated artifacts and all project documentation are curated at the University of Alabama Museums' facility in Moundville.[3]

As the first largescale investigation of a colonial-era site in Alabama, the pathbreaking Fort Condé excavations confirmed the benefits of salvage archaeology at a time when historically important sites were routinely bulldozed in the name of progress. Yet all did not go flawlessly. Scientific excavation was only permitted in limited areas of the site. Most of the fort's archaeological deposits were dug mechanically and hauled in dump trucks to Virginia Street, where local metal detectorists and bottle collectors combed through the spoil dirt. Tales still circulate through Mobile's preservation community about artifacts removed illegally from the construction site, including coins taken forcibly from students screening the excavated soil. Mobile's initial, imperfect attempt at urban archaeology taught some harsh practical lessons, such as the need for site security.

Since those pioneering days a half century ago, archaeological methods have improved greatly. Fortunately, peripheral remnants of the fort still exist in a few protected locations, particularly on the grounds of the Condé-Charlotte house (also known as the Kirkbride house, 1MB470) and other properties in Fort Condé Village (1MB132), a cluster of architecturally important buildings surrounded by the I-10 Water Street interchange. Work there by University of South Alabama field school students and staff from the Center for Archaeological Studies in 1992, 1998–2001, and 2010 identified small pockets of fort midden and structural remains that are preserved for future study (figs. 18.2 and 18.3). In 1978, north of the fort site, archaeologists from Auburn University at Montgomery retrieved some information from a fort-related barracks beneath the Mobile County Courthouse Annex. They also partially excavated a latrine belonging to the LeVert family, prominent members of mid-nineteenth-century Mobile society whose house once stood atop the fort site.[4]

Demolition of the former Mobile County Probate Courthouse (1MB387) to make way for Mardi Gras Park, at the north edge of the fort site, provided an opportunity for staff from the Center for Archaeological Studies to excavate a cross section of the fort moat in 2005 (fig. 18.4). That deep, waterlogged feature contained well-preserved plant and animal remains from the British colonial period, the sort of artifacts that were not collected systematically during the 1966–72 excavations. Most intriguing were large numbers of cow ribs used to make bone buttons, which, oddly

18.2. Condé-Charlotte House shovel testing (1MB470), January 2010. (Center for Archaeological Studies, University of South Alabama.)

enough, was a common pastime of troops stationed at colonial outposts throughout the British empire in the mid- to late eighteenth century.[5]

The fort's archaeological remains were just some of the historically significant aspects of Mobile's past put in jeopardy by construction of Interstate 10. Much of the city's architectural heritage that stood in the path of highway construction was demolished. Two exceptions—the Seaman's Bethel originally at 75 Church Street and the Marx House at the corner of Church and St. Emanuel Streets—were dismantled and rebuilt in 1968 on the campus of the University of South Alabama. In 1868 Isaac and Amelia Marx immigrated to Mobile, fleeing anti-Semitism in Germany, and built a fine Italianate side-hall-with-wing townhouse, a style of dwelling

18.3. Antomanchi House shovel testing, Fort Condé Village (1MB132), 2001. (Center for Archaeological Studies, University of South Alabama.)

18.4. Tara Potts excavating Fort Condé moat deposits, Mobile Probate Courthouse site (1MB387), 2005. (Center for Archaeological Studies, University of South Alabama.)

18.5. *Submarine Boat* H. L. Hunley, at Charleston, SC, December 1863, assembled in Mobile earlier that year; an 1867 etching of *H. L. Hunley* by J. G. Chapman, after a painting by C. W. Chapman. (Courtesy of Boston Athenæum, Prints and Photographs Department, A B54 Cha.c., no. 6.)

once common among the city's mercantile elite. The Seaman's Bethel, built in 1860, promoted nondenominational Protestant evangelism and temperance among mariners, until the US Navy's blockade of Mobile and other southern ports during the Civil War curtailed marine commerce. The building was commandeered by the Confederate military, specifically for assembly of the submarine *H. L. Hunley* during the spring of 1863 (fig. 18.5). The following year *H. L. Hunley* became the first submarine in history to sink an enemy vessel.[6]

PART VII

COLONIAL PLANTATIONS

CHAPTER 19

La Pointe-Krebs Plantation

> . . . now a park on the shore of Krebs Lake in Pascagoula, Mississippi, boasts the oldest standing residential structure on the northern Gulf Coast, as well as exceptional archaeological remains of a large colonial plantation.

The oldest standing structures in Alabama's narrow coastal zone—the Vincent-Doan house (now home of the Mobile Medical Museum) and a portion of the Jonathan Kirkbride house (aka Condé-Charlotte house), both in Mobile—are barely two centuries old. Every bit of the state's colonial-era built landscape fell into ruin long ago, an unsurprising fate in an environment routinely pummeled by tropical cyclones. One colonial survivor, however, still stands a few miles west of the Alabama state line, in Pascagoula, Mississippi, where the resilient mid-eighteenth-century La Pointe-Krebs house (fig. 19.1) has endured wars, hurricanes, termites, and decay—formidable hazards that leveled every one of its contemporaries.

That venerable building sits on land granted in 1715 to Joseph Simon *dit* La Pointe, a French Canadian who helped establish the first Mobile colonial settlement in 1702. His family in Québec had acquired "La Pointe" as a nickname (signified in French by the preceding *dit*, "called"), which Joseph later normalized to "de la Pointe." In 1704 he sailed to La Rochelle, France, on the supply ship *Pélican* and returned to the Louisiane colony in 1709 aboard the *Marguerite* with his wife, Marie Foucaud, and daughter, Élisabeth.[1]

Once settled on an embayment of the Pascagoula River, the family soon prospered. French military engineer Jean-François-Benjamin Dumont de Montigny visited in 1726 and sketched a view of their palisaded plantation, which comprised a two-story main house, storehouse, dairy,

19.1. La Pointe-Krebs house, southeast elevation. (Photograph by James Butters, April 1936, Library of Congress, Prints and Photographs Division, Historic American Buildings Survey, (HABS) MISS,30-PASCA,3—1.)

forge, sawmill, dovecote, garden, kitchen, and quarters for enslaved African and Native American laborers. At Simon's death in 1747, the property devolved to Hugo Ernestus Krebs, who had married Simon's daughter Marie Josephine Simon de la Pointe. The heart of the plantation remained in their family until 1914.[2]

Bernard Romans, a Dutch surveyor employed to chart the coastline of British colonial West Florida, experienced a slow-moving hurricane's impact on this portion of the northcentral Gulf Coast from August 30 to September 3, 1772. As Romans later recalled, "it destroyed the woods for about 30 miles from the sea coast in a terrible manner, . . . but the greatest fury of it was spent on the neighbourhood of the Pasca Oocolo river; the plantation of Mr. Krebs there was almost totally destroyed, of a fine crop of rice, and a large one of corn were scarcely left any remains, the houses were left uncovered, his smith's shop was almost all washed away, all his works and out houses blown down."[3]

When a team from the Historic American Buildings Survey (HABS) arrived in Pascagoula in 1936, as part of a nationwide Depression-era effort to record architecturally significant structures, only one colonial plantation building remained: the La Pointe-Krebs house. The oldest portion of the building consists of two rooms with walls of oyster shell tabby, a colonial form of concrete. A room subsequently added to the building's west end in the *charpente* style, a French-colonial half-timber technique, has walls infilled with *bousillage*, a mixture of clay, horsehair, and Spanish moss. Many of the house's roof beams and trusswork elements remain in place.

The HABS team's findings raised local interest in this unusual structure. In 1939 Jackson County acquired the house and four acres, all that remained of the once expansive plantation, and leased the property to the Jackson County Historical Society, which administers the park to this day. Efforts to restore the dilapidated house began immediately, with subsequent major preservation and stabilization efforts in 1979, 1992–96, and 2012–21. Research by staff from the Center for Archaeological Studies (principally led by Bonnie Gums, Greg Waselkov, and Diane Silvia) included excavations in 1994–95 inside the house and a shovel-testing survey of the surrounding grounds, major excavations in 2010 of plantation building sites and features, and later monitoring during restoration. Hurricane Katrina's storm surge severely damaged the building in 2005, which prompted a thorough restudy and most recent restoration of the old structure.[4]

The age of the La Pointe-Krebs house has long been disputed. Local proponents have claimed the house corresponds to one of the plantation workshops shown on Dumont's 1726 sketch, placing its construction near the onset of colonial settlement. However, excavations beneath the tabby floor uncovered foundation trenches of a prior French colonial post-in-ground house and artifact types dating to the mid- to late eighteenth century. Construction in the British colonial period seemed plausible, considering Romans's 1772 hurricane account.[5]

A thorough recent analysis of all evidence by architectural conservator George Fore has finally resolved the question. Fore identified ten stages of construction and alteration, beginning with the creation of the central tabby room in the 1750s, a conclusion supported by a dendrochronological study of wooden structural elements (fig. 19.2). Among the trusswork in the central room attic, three hewn timbers have outer growth rings dating to 1757, late in the French colonial period. According to Fore, successive construction episodes involved additions of the eastern tabby room in the 1770s, during the British colonial era, and the western *charpente*-and-*bousillage* room in the 1790s, around the middle of the Spanish colonial period. Three rafter timbers were felled in 1772, presumably to repair damage from that year's hurricane.[6]

Until recently, we knew of no other tabby construction by French colonists in La Louisiane. But reanalysis of the Bon Secour tabby structure (see chapter 20) now places its construction in the 1740s, and tabby

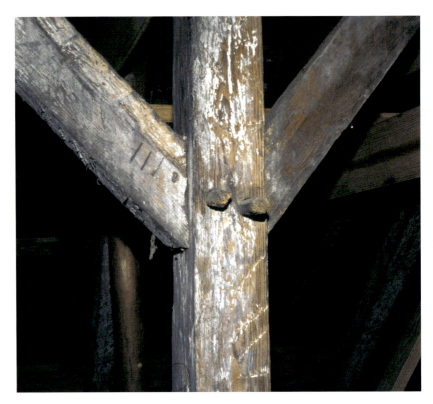

19.2. Kingpost (*aiguille*) with mortise-and-tenoned diagonal braces (*aisseliers*) supporting the roof above the tabby central room of the La Pointe-Krebs house, September 1994. Note the Roman numeral III on the left brace, a guide to assembly, and the bark still adhering to the bottom edge of that brace, indicating the presence of a terminal growth ring useful for dendrochronology. (Center for Archaeological Studies, University of South Alabama.)

footings for house gallery posts at Port Dauphin (see chapter 17) and the Augustin Rochon Plantation (see chapter 22) provide evidence that tabby played an architectural role throughout the French colonial regime. Despite its apparent rarity, French colonists knew how to make tabby and put it to use as needed.

Excavation of features in the lawn surrounding the La Pointe-Krebs house revealed a wonderfully preserved colonial plantation site (fig. 19.3). Here, we mention a few highlights. For instance, thousands of sherds of cooking and serving vessels—both traditional Native forms and copies of European wares—made by Pascagoula Indian potters at their villages a few miles upstream, attest to the deep entanglement of Indigenous peoples in the French colonial economy (fig. 19.4). Two sherds have tiny white glass beads pressed into the surface, a rare form of decoration[7] (fig. 19.5).

19.3. Greg Waselkov and Dennis Guy excavating a large pit (Feature 105), interpreted as a small storage cellar filled with refuse on abandonment; late French colonial to British colonial periods, La Pointe-Krebs Plantation site (22JA536). (Center for Archaeological Studies, University of South Alabama.)

19.4. Sherds of Doctor Lake Incised ceramic bowls, attributed to Pascagoula Indian potters, made for exchange with the colonists during the French colonial period; from the La Pointe-Krebs Plantation site. (Center for Archaeological Studies, University of South Alabama.)

19.5. Glass beads impressed into Doctor Lake Incised pottery, attributed to Pascagoula Indian potters; from the La Pointe-Krebs Plantation site. (Center for Archaeological Studies, University of South Alabama.)

19.6. Bowls of Canadian-style smoking pipes made of ceramic and stone from the La Pointe-Krebs Plantation site. (Center for Archaeological Studies, University of South Alabama.)

Judging from hundreds of seeds of the southern bayberry (known as wax myrtle) found discarded in refuse pits, the plantation economy involved exploitation of that local source of high-quality wax, which the colonists greatly valued for candle making as well as for export to islands in the French Caribbean. Wild resources also provided plantation residents with substantial amounts of meat from fish (mostly gars and several species of drum), turtles, alligators, waterfowl, bears, and white-tailed deer. Wild game equaled or surpassed dietary contributions from domesticated chickens, pigeons (from the dovecote), goats, cattle, and pigs throughout the entire colonial period.[8]

Finally, any number of artifact categories recovered from excavations reflect the French Catholic identity of the La Pointe-Krebs family, from imported European ceramics and glasswares to religious medallions, rosary beads, and crosses, and especially the distinctive Canadian-style smoking pipes (sometimes erroneously called Micmac pipes) favored by French colonists of Canadian descent[9] (fig. 19.6).

CHAPTER 20

Bon Secour River Sites

> . . . near its confluence with the Oyster Bay, the Bon Secour estuary has long attracted settlement, among them a Native American town circa AD 1400 and a 1740-era French colonial tabby house, known in recent times as the Mystery Fort.

Site 1BA53 is the most puzzling of several archaeological sites near the mouth of the Bon Secour River. In a 1902 address to the Iberville Historical Society, prominent Mobile historian Louis de Vendel Chaudron wondered what story lay behind Bon Secour's Old Fort or Indian Fort (fig. 20.1). Three decades later, Walter B. Jones, state geologist with the Alabama Museum of Natural History, described the ruin as "an old fort with a rectangular foundation of plaster & oyster shells . . . don't know [who] built it."[1]

David White, a precocious and energetic undergraduate enrolled in the anthropology program at Florida State University (FSU), would finally decipher the identity of this unusual ruin. He had grown up near Bon Secour, hearing stories of the "old fort," so settling the question of its origin seemed a good topic for a college term paper. In 1964–65, White ambitiously excavated some test units around the ruin. In a report of his findings, written for FSU professor Hale G. Smith, White correctly identified the sixteen-by-thirty-two-foot building's wall construction material as tabby, an early form of oyster shell concrete introduced into southeastern North America by European colonists. Judging from the domestic nature of the French, Spanish, and Native-made artifacts recovered from in and around the tabby structure, White rejected the fort identification. Instead, he thought the structure had likely served as a private residence for French colonists, and he dated the building's origin to the early eighteenth century. White's research effectively debunked speculations by Chaudron

20.1. Tabby wall remnants beneath a live oak at Bon Secour (site 1BA53). (Photograph by Paul Boudousquie in Villamil, "Round Bon Secours Bay"; Center for Archaeological Studies, University of South Alabama.)

and others attributing the building variously to the mythical Welsh prince Madoc, Mexican Aztecs, or the Spanish conquistador Hernando de Soto.[2]

Soon after White's study, the property owners decided to build their own home on the site and, not wishing to destroy the ruin, moved the tabby wall remains one-half mile downriver to a community park (fig. 20.2). Some thirty years later, in 1998, the same long-term site owners

20.2. Close-up view of a portion of the tabby wall, moved from site 1BA53 to a public park in Bon Secour, 1998. (Center for Archaeological Studies, University of South Alabama.)

BON SECOUR RIVER SITES 145

contacted the Center for Archaeological Studies for advice about returning the tabby walls to their original location. George Shorter and Greg Waselkov carried out limited test excavations in their yard, which established that the modern house had, in fact, been built on the original location of the tabby structure. Unfortunately, the combined impacts of house construction and tabby wall removal had effectively destroyed the archaeological site. However, recovery of additional artifacts pointed to a mid-eighteenth-century date for the tabby house, a few decades later than White had thought.

Apart from his college term paper, White wrote nothing further about Gulf Coast archaeology. During his youth in Pensacola, however, White clearly had a passion for the subject, and he became a charter member of the Society for Historical Archaeology at its founding in 1967. He pursued a PhD in cultural anthropology at Southern Methodist University, writing "Social Organization and the Sea: A Gulf Coast Shrimp Fishery," and maintained his interest into the 1990s. White started Applied Cultural Dynamics, a consulting firm in Santa Fe, New Mexico, that led to his

20.3. Colonial artifacts from David White's excavation at 1BA53. *Clockwise from top left*: San Agustín Blue on White majolica plate rim sherd, French musket side plate fragment of brass, French lead glazed coarse earthenware bowl rim sherd, and a French faience platter fragment. (Center for Archaeological Studies, University of South Alabama.)

20.4. Mississippian ceramic discoidals from site 1BA55. (Center for Archaeological Studies, University of South Alabama.)

involvement with ethnohistorical and ethnographic research projects for the National Park Service and to board positions with the Audubon Society. His last publication, *Zen Birding*, which appeared in 2010, was completed by his wife, Susan Guyette, after his death in July 2007.[3]

Soon after White's passing, his family in Pensacola decided to dispose of his archaeological collections, which were dispatched to a rummage sale. One of the bargain hunters at that sale, a member of the Pensacola Archaeological Society, happened to recognize the significance of the collections and fortuitously purchased them for donation to the Archaeology Institute at the University of West Florida. Elizabeth Benchley, the institute's director, contacted Waselkov about transferring the Alabama portion of White's collections, including the 1BA53 artifacts and notes, to the Center for Archaeological Studies at the University of South Alabama. With the benefit of another half century of research on colonial material culture, our reexamination of White's extensive artifact assemblage from 1BA53 revealed a likely date of construction in the 1740s, based on the presence of plain French faience, Spanish colonial San Agustín Blue on White majolica, and a French musket side plate of that era (fig. 20.3). White's precocious, well-recorded research, and the near-miraculous preservation of his collection and notes, have proven invaluable in resolving the longstanding enigma of the Mystery Fort.

In 2006, center archaeologists led by Sarah White (no relation to David) had an opportunity to explore another of the Bon Secour River sites recorded in 1933 by Walter B. Jones. Amid a building boom, owners of the property containing site 1BA55 requested an archaeological assessment in advance of possible condominium development. Test units revealed a complex shell midden site dating principally to the Late Mississippian period (AD 1400–1700), with less intensive occupations extending from Middle Woodland to colonial times. By far, the most surprising finds were twenty-four small discs made from ceramic and stone, dating to the Mississippian occupation (fig. 20.4). These are thought to have functioned as game pieces, although their true purpose remains uncertain.[4]

The Great Recession of 2007–9 stalled proposed development at 1BA55 and many similar waterfront construction projects initiated before the collapse of the 2005–6 housing bubble, thereby preserving, for a while longer, some of the most delightful parts of the Alabama coast. Despite that reprieve, a disproportionate number of the coastal region's archaeological sites occupy waterfront locations, where they remain vulnerable to development.[5]

CHAPTER 21

Rivière aux Chiens Plantation

> . . . at the mouth of Dog River, saw continuous occupation from the 1720s to 1848 by ethnic French and later American families, their enslaved labor forces of Native Americans and Africans, and, for a time, by a small village of Indigenous Chatos, refugees from Florida.

A decision in 1988 by Alabama's Department of Transportation to replace a picturesque but outmoded drawbridge, built in 1930 over Dog River near its mouth at Mobile Bay, launched a dozen years of exploration at one of the most informative and complex archaeological sites in the region. As the new two-span, eighty-foot-high concrete bridge gradually materialized above us, staff and students with the Center for Archaeological Studies meticulously uncovered the heart of a once-thriving plantation (site 1MB161), home to families of European colonists, enslaved Africans, and free and enslaved Native Americans from the early eighteenth to mid-nineteenth centuries[1] (fig. 21.1).

A few flaked stone tools and a handful of ceramic bowl sherds point to intermittent small-scale occupations of the river's south bank during the Bayou La Batre period (ca. 700–200 BC) and to occasional use of this low bluff during the Porter phase of the Middle Woodland period (ca. AD 300–650). Only with the establishment of French colonial Louisiane would this hitherto neglected spot on the western edge of Mobile Bay become a hub of economic activity, beginning with the arrival of Charles and Henriette Rochon about 1725.[2]

In 1701 Charles Rochon had crossed the continent, from Montreal to the Gulf Coast, with famed explorer Henri Tonti and lived for a time at the original French colonial settlement of Mobile on Twenty-Seven Mile Bluff. Around 1708, Charles moved to a Chato Indian village at Les

21.1. Archaeologists shovel skimming an excavation area (1MB161), September 1994. (Center for Archaeological Studies, University of South Alabama.)

Oignonets (Little Onions), where downtown Mobile now sits, to pursue a lucrative trade with Native hunters for furs and deerskins. Thus began a long and mutually beneficial relationship between the Rochon family and the Chato people, who had fled the Florida panhandle a few years earlier to escape slaving raids by English-allied Muscogee Creeks. When French officials moved their colonial capital from Twenty-Seven Mile Bluff to Les Oignonets in 1711, the Chatos, accompanied by the Rochons, relocated

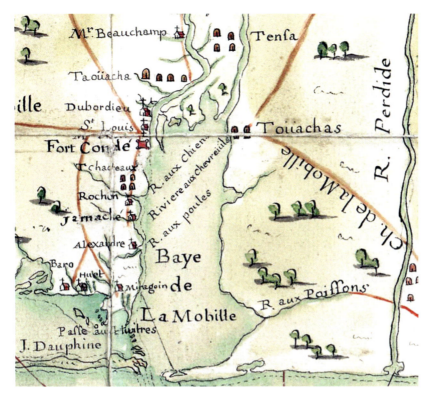

21.2. Detail of Baron de Crenay's "Carte de partie de la Louisianne, 1733," showing the Rochon plantation at Dog River, on the west side of Mobile Bay near "Chacteaux," a village of the Chatos south of Fort Condé. (Courtesy of Archives nationales d'outre-mer, Aix-en-Provence, France, Dépôt des Fortifications des Colonies, 04DFC Louisiane 1A.)

to the western shore of Mobile Bay, around the mouth of Dog River (fig. 21.2). There the Chatos and the Rochons remained, until the French ceded Louisiane to the British in 1763. Soon afterward the Chatos, Mobilians, Apalachees, and others known collectively as the *petites nations*—the various Native peoples who had found relative safety and economic benefit in proximity to the French for the previous half century—migrated west of the Mississippi River to Spanish colonial territory.[3]

Until our excavations at the Dog River bridge uncovered part of their village site, the Chato presence had been nearly invisible to archaeologists. The critical evidence of their archaeological presence appeared near a small bayou that once flowed eastward toward Mobile Bay. Highway engineers placed one of the bridge supports, referred to as Bent 16, in precisely the right location for our discovery of the Chatos. To the north lay remnants of the Rochons' plantation buildings and to the south lay the Chato village (fig. 21.3). After the Chatos' departure in 1764, Pierre Rochon (Charles's son) housed his enslaved workforce of Africans at their former village location, in small cabins raised on piers, buildings that replaced the older Native-built post-in-ground houses.[4]

The Chatos left behind stone arrowpoints and pieces of their own

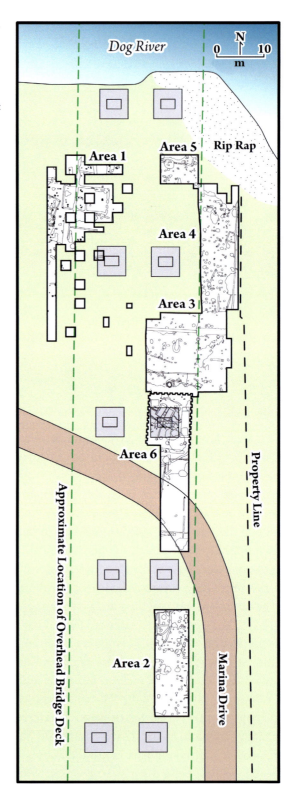

21.3. Extent of the 1994–95 excavations at the Dog River bridge site, showing postholes, pit features, and structural trenches, as well as Bent 16 in Area 6. (Center for Archaeological Studies, University of South Alabama.)

distinctive pottery, the key evidence we needed to recognize their presence here and elsewhere. Little ceramic cooking jars, tempered with sand, bore impressions of corncobs rolled onto the wet clay before firing. The presence of Africans living there in the late eighteenth century was likewise reflected in a characteristic form of pottery: small hemispherical unglazed shell-tempered bowls, many of them coated with a clay slip that fired a bright red hue (fig. 21.4). In the Gulf South, Native women potters first developed this style of bowl for trade to the colonists, but by the late eighteenth century, production had almost certainly shifted to African potters who created bowls for their own use. Archaeologists continue to debate the complex cultural interactions leading to the creation and use of these "colono" wares by the different peoples present in colonial America.[5]

Our extensive excavations and research at plantations owned by three close colonial kin—Pierre Rochon at Dog River; Pierre's brother Augustin and his first wife, Marie Jeanne Simon de La Pointe at modern-day Spanish Fort; and Marie Jeanne's birthplace at the La Pointe-Krebs family plantation in Pascagoula—documented the intimately intertwined lives of colonists, Natives, and Africans, free and unfree. At Dog River, after the death of his first wife Catherine Paux in 1751, Pierre Rochon (whose grandmother Catherine Exipakinoea was a Native Kaskaskia woman) had an openly acknowledged relationship with his mulatto slave Marianne.

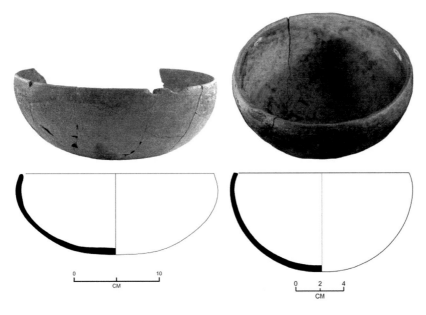

21.4. Shell-tempered ceramic bowls from Area 2 (*left*) and Area 6 (*right*). (Center for Archaeological Studies, University of South Alabama.)

He and Marianne had six children, all of whom Pierre held in bondage until a year before his death in 1771, at which time Marianne, too, was freed. The complex entanglements of colonial society on the Gulf Coast in the eighteenth century at times presented opportunities for freedom and economic advancement, as well as risks of violence and abuse. Dog River Plantation mapped Pierre Rochon's segregation and subjugation of his labor force onto the landscape. The narrow bayou that separated the planter from his enslaved workers represented a much deeper and broader social chasm that even his own offspring could only traverse on the occasion of the plantation owner's death.[6]

Our excavation at Bent 16, in the bayou, posed formidable logistical challenges but yielded great rewards. Archaeological deposits reaching two meters beneath the modern ground surface, and far below the water table, called for construction of a cofferdam (fig. 21.5). Sheet pilings inserted by a pile driver held the surrounding soil in place while an array of well points temporarily lowered the water table within the cofferdam. Artifacts and structural features, waterlogged since the eighteenth century, could then be unearthed from bayou soils and proved to be exceptionally well preserved.[7]

Among the many surprises emerging from the bayou were a wooden rice pestle and two wood-lined tanning vats for processing cowhides into leather. From a refuse pit near the vats, a nearly complete cow's skull appeared, the remains of a lowland Scottish medium-horned breed raised

21.5. George Shorter, Amy Carruth, and Catherine Potter mapping and excavating one of two British colonial tanning vats in the Bent 16 cofferdam, February 1995. (Center for Archaeological Studies, University of South Alabama.)

on the Rochon Plantation during the British colonial period, between 1763 and 1780 (fig. 21.6). Gulf Coast colonial plantations were highly diversified operations with maize, tobacco, indigo, cotton, rice, and sugarcane all serving as cash crops under the French, British, and Spanish regimes. But production of naval stores (pitch, tar, resin, and turpentine from pine trees), timber (particularly oak for barrel staves and ships' parts and pine for ships' masts), and livestock (preeminently, cattle) provided planters with reliable and often highly profitable incomes. Indeed, Pierre Rochon's colonial-era establishment at Dog River might be more accurately characterized as a cattle ranch with subsidiary agricultural endeavors rather than a typical crop-focused plantation.[8]

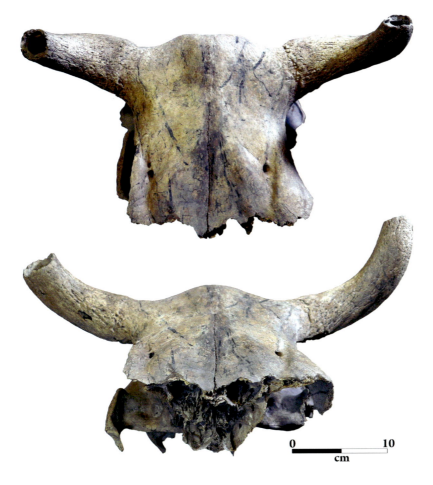

21.6. Cattle (*Bos taurus*) skull from a British colonial refuse pit in Area 6. The skull shows characteristics of medium-horned breeds from the Lowlands and Inner Hebrides of Scotland. (Center for Archaeological Studies, University of South Alabama.)

CHAPTER 22

Augustin Rochon Plantation

> ... burned on the first of October 1780 by raiding Choctaw warriors, allies of the British, testifies to the suffering endured by civilians caught up in the American Revolutionary War on the Gulf Coast.

In 1995 history enthusiast Shawn Holland spotted artifacts, pottery, and glass dating to the colonial era on undeveloped residential lots near her home in the city of Spanish Fort. Inspection of historic maps revealed that Holland's new site (1BA337) had been the British colonial-period plantation of wealthy colonists Augustin Rochon; his first wife, Marie Jeanne Simon de La Pointe; and his second wife, Louise Fievre. Augustin had grown up at another Rochon family plantation (see chapter 21), which center archaeologists excavated in the mid-1990s at the south end of the modern Dog River bridge. Owners of the Spanish Fort lots, Carlton Nell and William and Paula Barnhill, had a keen interest in history, and they kindly agreed to archaeological investigations. Greg Waselkov and Bonnie Gums directed site survey, testing, and eventually full-scale excavations by staff, field school students, and volunteers from 1996 to 1998. A grant from the Alabama Historical Commission and matching funds generously provided by the city of Spanish Fort supported our work.[1]

Artifacts and documentary evidence agree that the Rochon family occupation of this plantation spanned the entire brief existence of the British colony of West Florida, from 1764 to 1780 (fig. 22.1). A Spanish army commanded by Bernardo de Gálvez took Mobile from the British in March 1780, part of Spain's contribution to the American Revolution. Augustin died around the time of the siege of the city, but other family members signed oaths of loyalty to the new Spanish regime, just as Augustin had sworn allegiance to the British crown following French cession of the colony years before. This act of fealty should have allowed the Rochon family to remain on their plantations. By autumn, however, British forces in Pensacola persuaded their Native allies to attack plantations in Spanish-held territory. At dawn on October 1, Choctaw warriors raided the Rochon Plantation. They killed three members of the household (a young man named Trouillet "and one Negro and one Indian female, [enslaved] Servants") and captured the widow Rochon, her seven children, four other relatives, and two enslaved males. Before marching their stripped and bound prisoners to Pensacola, where they were ransomed by the British commander, the Choctaws looted and torched the plantation's buildings. The Rochon homesite would remain virtually unoccupied for more than eighty years, until the American Civil War.[2]

Although the Rochons' occupation of their plantation site coincided neatly with British colonial rule in this region of the Gulf Coast, none of the occupants were British. Augustin's father, Charles, a voyageur from Montreal, had been among the first French-speaking colonists to arrive on the Gulf Coast in 1701. And Augustin's mother, Henriette Colon, was the daughter of a Frenchman and a Kaskaskia Indian woman from the Illinois country. Madame Rochon, Augustin's widow taken by the Choctaws

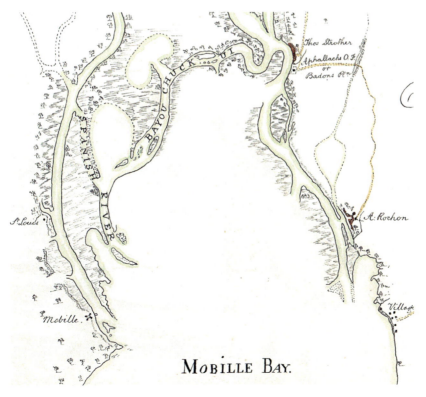

22.1. Detail, "A Plan of Part of the Rivers Tombecbe, Alabama, Perdido, & Scambia in the Province of West Florida, 1771" by David Taitt, showing Augustin Rochon's plantation on the bluff in the modern-day city of Spanish Fort. (Library of Congress, Geography and Map Division, 73691550.)

AUGUSTIN ROCHON PLANTATION   157

22.2. Burned structural features from the 1780 destruction of the Augustin Rochon plantation (1BA337), excavated in April 1998. (Center for Archaeological Studies, University of South Alabama.)

in 1780, was Louise Fievre, whose mother, Marie Anne Grise, had been deported to the Louisiane colony from France for tobacco smuggling. The workforce at their three plantations (including two upriver) consisted of thirty men and women, some of African and some of Native descent, who tended hundreds of cattle in the surrounding woods, raised crops, and processed pitch and tar for naval stores.[3]

22.3. Smoking pipes from the Augustin Rochon Plantation: (*a, b*) ceramic Canadian-style and (*c*) argillite stone calumet-style. (Center for Archaeological Studies, University of South Alabama.)

Archaeology revealed the burned remains of a Creole-style house, home for the ethnic French plantation owners (fig. 22.2). This substantial building, which measured sixteen by thirty feet, had post-in-ground walls covered with *bousillage* (clay daub, baked by the fire that destroyed the home's wooden elements). A gallery ran the length of the east side, with support posts resting on sandstone and shell tabby slabs. Adjacent fenced enclosures, built in the French colonial palisade style, probably safeguarded vegetable and herb gardens and chickens kept near the main house. Nearby stood six smaller post-in-ground outbuildings, a kitchen and quarters for the plantations' enslaved workers, all burned. The artifact assemblages from the seven buildings differ, as one would expect given the differences in ethnicity and social status of the occupants. Fine tablewares and other furnishings in the Rochon house were mostly imported from England, France, and New Spain (as Mexico was known at the time). In contrast, simple unglazed pottery bowls were abundant in quarters for the enslaved people. Among the most unusual finds are several distinctive Canadian-style smoking pipes (sometimes erroneously called Micmac pipes) (fig. 22.3). By their use, a French-speaking family living under British rule quietly but proudly asserted their ethnic identity.[4]

CHAPTER 23

Lisloy Plantation

> . . . on the grounds of Bellingrath Gardens and Home, briefly served as the residence of a retired French military officer, his family, and enslaved African labor force during the early days of British colonial rule.

Walter and Bessie Bellingrath's estate, Bellingrath Gardens and Home, is one of Alabama's premier sightseeing attractions, with two hundred thousand annual visitors touring their 1935 home and sixty-five-acre showplace of camelias and azaleas. However, an earlier occupation of the bluff in the fork of Fowl River, south of Mobile and west of Mobile Bay, attracted our archaeological interest in 2000–2001. Somewhere in this vicinity, Henri Montault de Monberaut, a prominent French military officer, once owned a plantation called Lisloy (a corruption of the French *l'isle aux oies*, Goose Island).[1]

Montault, who arrived in Louisiane from France in 1739 at age twenty-one, was a lieutenant in the colonial Troupes de la Marine. From 1756 to 1759, Captain Montault commanded a small garrison at Fort Toulouse (in modern-day Wetumpka, Alabama), an important French outpost among the Indigenous Alabama villages on the edge of the Muscogee Creek Nation. The colonial governor considered Montault "quite intelligent" and valued his ability to maintain French influence with Native American leaders. But he also thought him "brutal, muddleheaded, and dangerous." Montault probably began construction of Lisloy at the time of his recall to Mobile in 1759. By 1762 the plantation was providing much of his income when he retired from French military service due to ill health.[2]

Early in 1763, Montault received confirmation of a formal grant of this land on Fowl River. By then a widower, the wealthy Montault and his household (consisting of his children, a steward, and a cook) alternated between three residences—his house in Mobile, a plantation on the Mobile River, and Lisloy down the bay. Twenty-six enslaved Africans generated wealth for him by operating a tar works and tending five hundred cattle, fifty horses, and numerous sheep and pigs.[3]

With the departure of most French colonial troops and officials from Mobile at the end of 1763, the newly arrived governor of British West Florida, George Johnstone, recognized a need to negotiate new treaties with the Muscogee Creek and Choctaw Nations that controlled most of the interior Southeast. Johnstone recruited recently retired Montault and his seventeen-year-old son, Louis Augustín, who had grown up among the Alabamas, to serve as translators and negotiators with Native leaders on behalf of the incoming British colonial regime. The Montaults proved adept as diplomats by helping Johnstone conclude a treaty with the Creeks. But the obstreperous elder Montault soon quarreled with his British employers. By mid-1765, he had sold all his Mobile properties, including Lisloy, and moved to Spanish colonial New Orleans. Montault returned to France in August 1769.[4]

Considering Lisloy's brief existence, for perhaps fewer than six years, we were uncertain what we would find on the well-tilled grounds of Bellingrath Gardens. One crucial clue to the locations of Montault's plantation structures proved to be a sketch—outlines of two buildings surrounded by a palisade fence—found on an anonymous 1775 British map of the Mobile area. There, at the fork of Fowl River, was an inscription: "Chevalier Mombereaut's Plantn. deserted."[5]

Our archaeological search began in the spring of 2000 with a site survey by field school students, staff, and volunteers directed by Greg Waselkov and Bonnie Gums. Hundreds of shovel tests eventually revealed two clusters of colonial bricks, tabby, ceramics, and other artifacts in a maintenance area south of the Great Lawn at Bellingrath Gardens (fig. 23.1). Discovery of Lisloy Plantation (site 1MB313) led to test unit excavations in the spring of 2001, supported by grants from the Bellingrath-Morse Foundation and the Alabama Historical Commission (fig. 23.2). Those findings enabled us to prepare an archaeological stewardship plan to assist the Bellingrath-Morse Foundation in protecting this and other archaeological sites on their property.[6]

The two clusters of colonial artifacts correspond to the two buildings described as "deserted" on the 1775 map. Montault's family residence is presumably the densest cluster of structural debris, with imported French roof tiles and tabby gallery supports, while the other probably represents housing for the plantation's enslaved workers. One evocative artifact, a small fragment of carved red stone pipe bowl, part of a calumet pipe traditionally used in southeastern Indian diplomacy, recalls Montault's brief but critical role in Gulf Coast colonial history (fig. 23.3).

23.1. Students shovel testing the Great Lawn in front of the Bellingrath Home, January 2000. (Center for Archaeological Studies, University of South Alabama.)

23.2. Students preparing a test unit at site 1MB313 for drawing and photographs, May 2001. (Center for Archaeological Studies, University of South Alabama.)

23.3. Artifacts from Lisloy plantation (1MB313). *Clockwise from top*: rim fragment of a calumet smoking pipe made of catlinite, with carved X motif; brass button from French colonial military uniform coat; fired lead musket ball. (Center for Archaeological Studies, University of South Alabama.)

CHAPTER 24

The Village

> ... an ethnic French settlement of plantations and smaller households on the Eastern Shore of Mobile Bay that witnessed skirmishes and a major battle between Spanish and British forces during the American Revolutionary War.

A small community of ethnic French households and plantations once lined a milelong stretch of Mobile Bay's northeastern shoreline, south of Yancey Branch in modern-day Daphne. The Village, as it was commonly known, coalesced in the 1750s. David Taitt's map of 1771 shows a cluster of six buildings on the bay bluff south of Village Point. A horse path led southeastward to Pensacola, which made the Village a natural departure point for westward-bound boat traffic across the bay to Mobile. In 1775 an anonymous mapmaker depicted ten fenced enclosures and several land grants at the Village, including "Miller's Plantation deserted" (fig. 24.1). British traveler Edward Mease, who toured British West Florida in this era, briefly described the Village as "a few stragling Houses. The Inhabitants are French & they raise great Quantities of Poultry of all Kinds, with some Corn Potatoes, &ca and have Herds of Cattle, but they look poor like the Country"—presumably referring to the cattle and not necessarily the inhabitants.[1]

Apart from a brief period of chaos in 1780–81 (discussed later), residents of the Village focused on agricultural pursuits. Dominique D'Olive settled on the old Miller grant in 1781, acquired legal title in 1787, and operated a sawmill on Yancey Branch. In 1813–14, Redstick Creek warriors raided the Village, taking 130 head of cattle and three enslaved workers with French names—Hector, Isidore, and Michel—accomplished hewers, sawyers, and brickmakers from the D'Olive Plantation at the north end of the Village. Local legend insists that Gen. Andrew Jackson addressed his

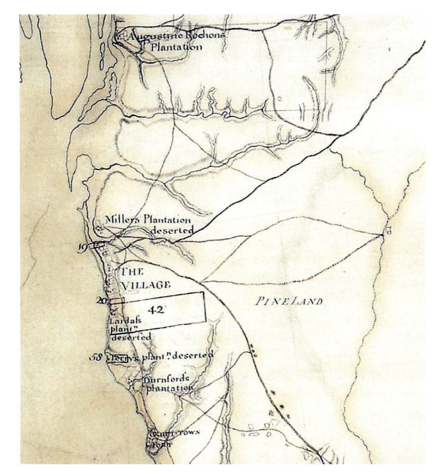

24.1. Detail, "Survey of the Bay and River Mobile, 1775," showing the Village on Mobile Bay, in modern-day Daphne. (Courtesy of Colonial Office, National Archives, Kew, UK, CO 700/Florida 51.)

troops from the low limb of a huge live oak tree, the Jackson Oak on the D'Olive property, before marching against Pensacola in 1814, despite documentation of his army's more northerly line of march.[2]

The Village maintained its distinct identity through the 1820s. Afterward, maps show only the D'Olive Plantation, which remained in the family's possession until the 1960s, when Campark trailer court and campground purchased the property. The city of Daphne in turn acquired the land in 1999 for a park, Village Point Preserve.

Some ancient sites are known in this area, including an earthen mound explored by Clarence B. Moore in 1905. University of South Alabama archaeologists have investigated eighteenth- and nineteenth-century sites associated with the Village and D'Olive Plantation, beginning with site surveys and testing in 1973–75, 1978–79, 1983, and 1997 directed by Noel Read Stowe. Before construction of a boardwalk in 2000, Bonnie Gums surveyed a small area around a live oak, one of several candidates

THE VILLAGE   165

for Jackson Oak designation, and a year later carried out extensive testing of site 1BA190, the D'Olive mansion site in the city's preserve.[3]

Center surveys led by Gums documented eight archaeological sites associated with the Village (1BA538–1BA545) in 2002–3 with grant support from the Alabama Historical Commission and located two more (1BA608, 1BA609) on the Paradiso tract in December 2007. Over the next two years Gums, Greg Waselkov, and center staff excavated the Paradiso sites, with help from thirty-one volunteers and fifteen University of South Alabama field school students.[4]

Forty-five trench features found at 1BA608 delineated two palisaded plantation compounds (figs. 24.2 and 24.3). A maze of forty crisscrossing trenches in the center of the site comprised Complex 1, the remains of repeated rebuilding over several decades. This is thought to be the location of the plantation owner's principal residence. Complex 2 consisted of palisade fences and two walls of a subsidiary plantation building only partially explored. These post-in-ground structural remains and associated palisade fences are typical of French Creole architecture found at mid- to late eighteenth-century colonial sites throughout the Mobile area.[5]

Here, as elsewhere in the Village, buildings sat near the edge of a twenty-five-foot-high bluff, two hundred yards east of the bay. Colonial settlers may have chosen this location because Native Americans—Pensacolas, Mobilians, and Towasas—had already cleared the forest here for their

24.2. University of South Alabama field school students troweling Block 2 (1BA608), revealing soil stains of fence foundation trenches and pit features, February 2009. (Center for Archaeological Studies, University of South Alabama.)

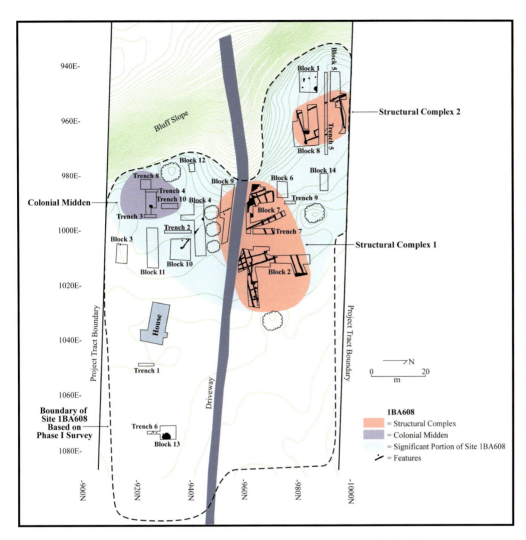

24.3. Excavation overview of site 1BA608, Paradiso Tract, 2008–9. (Graphic by Sarah Mattics, Center for Archaeological Studies, University of South Alabama.)

own houses and gardens between 1650 and 1750. A road graded through the bluff in the mid-twentieth century destroyed all but a small remnant of dark earth midden from that earlier occupation. Artifacts point to establishment of the Village in the 1750s and subsequent changes in the ethnic French community under British, Spanish, and American rule (figs. 24.4 and 24.5).

Our research at the Village raised the prospect of finding some trace of a Revolutionary War battle fought there on January 7, 1781. Although

THE VILLAGE   167

24.4. Tin-glazed earthenware sherds from 1BA608; French faience and English delft (*lower right*). (Center for Archaeological Studies, University of South Alabama.)

24.5. Spanish coins from 1BA608, Paradiso Tract. *Top*: cut one *real* "piece of eight" dating to 1772–88, on an image of a complete peso (eight *reales*) coin for scale; *bottom*: one-half *real* "cob," minted in Mexico City, 1700–1746. Two views of each coin. (Graphic by Sarah Mattics, Center for Archaeological Studies, University of South Alabama.)

we have not yet located that battlefield, we offer these thoughts about the kinds of battle evidence that are someday bound to appear.[6]

Few modern-day residents of the northern Gulf Coast know that the region played an important, if underappreciated, role in the American Revolution, thanks to the efforts of Spain, one of the few allies of the newly formed United States. In March 1780, Bernardo de Gálvez, governor of Spanish colonial Luisiana, took British Mobile by siege and a year later completed his conquest of British West Florida with the capture of Pensacola. Between those signal events were several small skirmishes and one significant battle at the Village.[7]

In the summer of 1780, José de Ezpeleta, Gálvez's commander in Mobile, decided that defense of the town required a military presence on the Eastern Shore of Mobile Bay, specifically at the Village (La Aldea, to the Spaniards). From that strategic spot, his troops could monitor the British in Pensacola, deprive them of the cattle they had been rounding up from plantations in the area, and encourage desertions from that demoralized and isolated British garrison. Ezpeleta established an outpost there on July 28 with a contingent of twenty-five men, soon increased to forty. When British-allied Choctaw warriors fired on the Spaniards on the night of October 5, without inflicting any casualties, Ezpeleta boosted the detachment to eighty men. That reinforcement failed to deter the Choctaws, who returned on the thirteenth and killed a soldier at the post's corral.[8]

At midday on November 2, two hundred Choctaws, accompanied by trader John Pitchlynn and six Royal Forester mounted militia, killed three Spanish soldiers working on the beach, prompting the garrison, now reinforced to 120 men, to take positions in the trenches of their redoubt. Artillerists at the outpost dispersed the raiders by firing two 4-pounder cannons in the direction of the Pensacola road. During this brief engagement, the Choctaws shot fire arrows into the fort, which set alight the officers' quarters and burned some huts (*casillas*) containing the officers' baggage.[9]

By January 7, 1781, the Spanish force at the Village totaled 190 men from Príncipe, España, Navarra, and Havana regiments of the line, supported by members of the New Orleans Colored Militia and the Royal Artillery Corps with their two small cannons. The advancing British force numbered about two hundred soldiers drawn from the Sixtieth Infantry Regiment (who had two brass 3-pounder field artillery pieces), West Florida Royal Forester militia, Maryland and Pennsylvania Loyalists, and a portion of the Third Waldeck Regiment of German mercenaries, as well as four hundred to five hundred allied Choctaw warriors.[10]

Under cover of fog, the attackers approached at dawn in three columns. The Choctaws moved between the fort and the bay shoreline, where an armed provisions vessel (*la bercha*, one of two barges or lighters in the Spanish fleet, either *La Mobileña* or *La Panzacoleña*) lay at anchor. The British left column slipped through the Spanish militia camp located behind an outlying earthwork (*Lengua de sierpe*) protecting the fort's entrance, while the Waldeckers on the right approached the north flank of the rectangular fort. Once they reached the outer trenches, which protected the three landward sides of the fort, but not the bluff side toward the bay at the fort's rear, the British and German troops unexpectedly found a palisade on or inside the parapet. At that moment the defenders opened fire. The Spaniards inside the parapet fought from the cover of a barracks building and a hut (*casilla*) until their artillerists dried some fuses that had become soaked in the night's rain and fired one of their cannons, ending the attack. The British force lost seventeen killed, presumably buried nearby. Spanish losses were similar: fourteen dead and twenty-three wounded.[11]

Spanish and British accounts of the 1781 battle at the Village agree in many particulars. The Spanish defensive work was a rectangular earthen redoubt situated on a bluff some distance from the bay, with trenches and parapets on the three land faces, an outer work defending the entrance on the east side (toward the road to Pensacola), and a four-sided interior palisade enclosing one substantial building and a few simpler huts. Considering the prevalence of dwellings, outbuildings, and palisade fences at the Village, the Spaniards likely enclosed existing plantation structures with their redoubt. These structural features, plus the distinctive weaponry and uniforms of the various units represented in this battle, should someday permit a firm identification of the battle's location based on archaeological evidence.

We can dispense with the persistent notion that the battle at the Village occurred at the Spanish Fort, site of the 1865 Civil War siege that took place 3.5 miles north of the Village. British and Spanish descriptions of the earthwork at the Village in no way resemble the elaborate water battery, called the Spanish Fort (see chapter 34), with its imposing bayside parapet. Furthermore, our excavations immediately adjacent to the Spanish Fort revealed the presence of the Augustin Rochon Plantation, destroyed in a Choctaw raid on October 1, 1780, four days before the first Choctaw raid on the Village. These were separate events in different locations.[12]

CHAPTER 25

Water Street, Mobile

> . . . where a colonial rice field, with footprints of the people who tended the rice plants, emerged from a buried marsh during excavations beneath the Water Street exit ramp from I-10, south of downtown Mobile.

Considering seafood's prominent role in Gulf Coast cuisine and culture, modern residents might be surprised to learn about the longstanding importance of crop agriculture in the region, reaching back more than one thousand years. From at least AD 900 onward, Indigenous women tilled riverbank maize fields to feed their families. Maize and other crops supported the chiefly society that ruled the coast from the great mound center at Bottle Creek. At the dawn of the eighteenth century, Mobilian and Tomé townspeople farming in the Mobile-Tensaw delta traded their agricultural surpluses to the first French colonists, who soon added maize to their repertoire of crops, as well as animals domesticated in other parts of the world. Settlers during the colonial era and first half century of American rule depended on (and compelled) the labor of enslaved Africans to raise cattle and tend plantation crops including tobacco, indigo, cotton, rice, and maize. Even today, truck farming contributes significantly to local commerce, especially in Baldwin County.[1]

Archaeologists routinely add to our knowledge of earlier foodways, particularly through studies of discarded animal bones, carbonized plant parts, and even food residues preserved in and on pottery. Direct evidence of agricultural fields, however, rarely turns up. One such exceptional find occurred in 2014, during excavations by University of South Alabama archaeologists at site 1MB510 near downtown Mobile, beneath the Water Street exit ramp from I-10 (fig. 25.1). For many years that grassy space beneath the interstate ramps has filled every spring with parked recreational vehicles belonging to hundreds of Mobile's Mardi Gras celebrants visiting from out of town. The Alabama Department of Transportation (ALDOT) has long planned to revamp the interchanges south of the Wallace Tunnel, where I-10 dives beneath the Mobile River. In fact, the Center for Archaeological Studies' first project for ALDOT, in 1992, investigated the area immediately west of the Water Street site for proposed revisions to the Virginia Street interchange.[2]

The environment of the Water Street site has changed substantially over the last two centuries (fig. 25.2). To the east is Water Street, which today generally follows the original right bank of the Mobile River as it existed in the eighteenth century. To the west was a low bluff (delimited roughly by Royal Street) occupied by the colonial town. A low, marshy stretch of ground, at least one hundred yards wide, lay between the bluff and the natural levee at the river's bank. By the 1790s, during the Spanish colonial regime, Mobile's residents understood the unhealthy consequences of living next to this mosquito-infested marsh and the economic advantages to be had from filling in that marsh for riverfront development. Abundant proof of nineteenth-century marsh reclamation has appeared in excavations by New South Associates at the site of Mobile's Convention Center and by the Center for Archaeological Studies at the Exploreum, the History Museum of Mobile, RSA Tower, the site of the 1865 ordnance explosion, and other locations.[3]

25.1. Aerial photograph of I-10 construction, circa 1970, with archaeological site 1MB510 located south of the Water Street ramp. (Center for Archaeological Studies, University of South Alabama.)

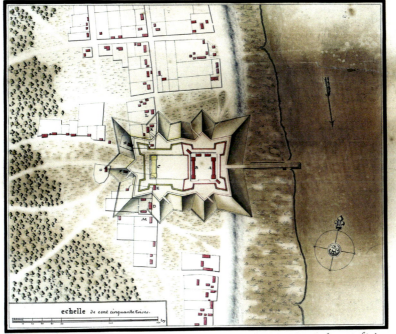

25.2. "Plan du Fort Condé de la Mobille" (1743), showing marshes east (*right*) of the fort and the Mobile River bluff (in blue). Archaeological site 1BM510 is at the middle lower map edge. (Library of Congress, Geography and Map Division, 2009581264.)

Excavations at the Water Street site, however, told a different story (fig. 25.3). This location, at the extreme south end of the colonial town, saw little land reclamation and consequently still suffers from flooding, as we experienced during our fieldwork with each summer afternoon's thunderstorm. Our large excavation—in the middle of a former city block originally bordered by Eslava, St. Emanuel, Madison, and South Royal Streets—encompassed the backyards of two private residences occupied by African Americans and property of the Star Ice Company, based on Sanborn Fire Insurance Company maps drafted between 1885 and 1955. Digging beneath the backyard privies of those residences revealed a foot-thick layer of water-sorted yellow and gray sand, devoid of artifacts. Geoarchaeologist Howard Cyr, a specialist in interpreting soils, identified this sand as flood-deposited sediment. Its thickness and homogeneity indicated a single major flood, almost certainly the storm surge of a powerful hurricane.[4]

Careful removal of the storm-deposited sand exposed the uneven surface of the riverside marsh. At the western edge of our excavation a small colonial-era house (Feature 52, on our site map) and nearby barrel well

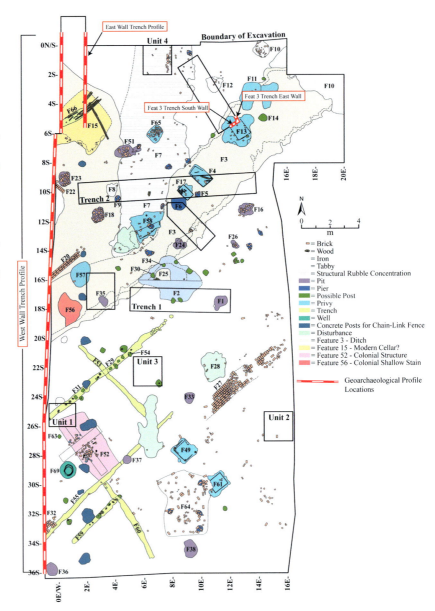

25.3. Plan view of excavated area at site 1MB510, showing an extensive ditch (Feature 3) and associated colonial structure (Feature 52), well (Feature 69), and palisade fencing (in olive green) to the south. Intrusive privy pits (in aqua) date to the late nineteenth century. (Graphic by Sarah Mattics, Center for Archaeological Studies, University of South Alabama.)

(Feature 69), enclosed by palisade-type fencing, once stood on a high spot in the marshy terrain (fig. 25.4). Barrel wells are not uncommon at colonial sites in the Mobile area. At coastal sites where estuary waters are brackish and undrinkable, colonists learned how to tap into just the right part of the natural water table to obtain drinking water. Two wooden barrels (with ends removed) stacked in a shallow pit dug into sandy soil would hit that sweet spot and fill with potable water, since a thin layer of fresh groundwater floats above salty groundwater.

North of the colonial house, in a low part of the marsh, an erosional gulley had been intentionally deepened and widened into a broad ditch (Feature 3), judging from hoe marks on the edges and the feature's artificially flat bottom surface. Wooden planks and an associated earthen berm that crossed a northern branch of the ditch were apparently part of a check dam to control water level. The need for such a device only became evident as excavators reached the deeply black organic-rich layer at the bottom of the ditch. In that "wet meadow soil," typical of a tidal marsh environment, were hundreds of small depressions filled with yellow sand (figs. 25.5 and 25.6). Close inspection revealed some to be prints left by bare human feet, other starshaped depressions were plant root casts, and the smallest were snail and insect burrows. All were preserved and made visually distinct from the black marsh soil, when the storm event filled them with the same yellow hurricane-deposited sand that capped the entire ditch.

The unusual landscape features found at the Water Street site are best explained as elements of a wetland agricultural field specifically designed for rice farming. The broad shallow ditch probably began in the mid-eighteenth century as part of an extensive network of ditches and check dams designed to control water levels in portions of the marsh. Rapid accumulation of "wet meadow soil" in the ditch and the presence of footprints, root impressions, and hoe marks all point to rice planting as a likely activity there, an endeavor that ended abruptly with massive sand

25.4. Colonial-era barrel well (Feature 69), dating to the British colonial period, 1763–80. (Center for Archaeological Studies, University of South Alabama.)

25.5. Greg Waselkov (*left*) and Howard Cyr (*right*) uncovering dark marsh soil with human footprints and plant casts. Human footprint cross-sectioned at right. (Center for Archaeological Studies, University of South Alabama.)

25.6. Human footprints and plant casts visible in black marsh soil, preserved when filled with storm-deposited yellowish sand. (Center for Archaeological Studies, University of South Alabama.)

deposition during a great hurricane. Considerable numbers of pearlware ceramics in the buried marsh soil help date the hurricane to either 1819 or 1821, when we know large storms devastated Mobile.[5]

Nearly half a century ago, historian Peter Wood, in his book *Black Majority: Negroes in Colonial South Carolina from 1670 through the Stono Rebellion*, first pointed to similarities in rice cultivation in west Africa and the colonial American South and suggested how importation to the South of enslaved Africans, knowledgeable in rice cultivation, shaped southern plantation agriculture in ways previously unacknowledged (fig. 25.7). Historians have debated Wood's hypothesis and generally conclude that southern agriculture developed by incorporating domesticates and farming expertise from everyone involved—Native Americans, Europeans, and Africans—just as southern cuisines evolved from diverse cultural roots. Yet, there is much we do not know about this complex process of creolization because historical documents were largely written by literate whites, not by the Indigenous and African contributors to this process. Archaeology can help us fill in the missing pieces of our shared past by examining

25.7. "Planting the Rice," from *Harper's New Monthly Magazine* (Richards, "Rice Lands of the South"). (Center for Archaeological Studies, University of South Alabama.)

physical evidence unfiltered by social biases. We should also recognize how the normally destructive force of powerful hurricanes has, ironically, in this case preserved pieces of the historic landscape, which we can study through archaeology.[6]

The remarkable discovery at the Water Street site of a colonial rice field's archaeological "footprint," including even literally the footprints of the last people to tend the rice plants growing in that field, people who were certainly enslaved Africans, is a powerful reminder that archaeology can expand our view of the Gulf Coast region's complex colonial history.

PART VIII

LATE COLONIAL/ EARLY FEDERAL PERIOD (1764–1859)

CHAPTER 26

The Southeast in 1773

> ... seen in a map of the Native South, reconstructed from British colonial military maps, provides a more balanced historical context than typically seen in American history textbooks.

Between 2005 and 2014, staff at the Alabama Department of Archives and History in Montgomery developed a comprehensive new exhibit for the state's history museum. The *Museum of Alabama* offers visitors state-of-the-art displays that trace the development of Alabama across three centuries through the voices of its diverse inhabitants. Archaeological artifacts figure prominently in the exhibit, particularly in those displays relating to eighteenth- and early nineteenth-century interactions between Native peoples of the region, Europeans colonists and their descendants who intermittently (and repeatedly) appropriated Native lands, and the peoples of Africa brought here against their will, in perpetual servitude, to work for others on the land that would become Alabama. This exhibit challenges visitors to confront some hard truths about Alabama's history and offers fresh perspectives on aspects of life in earlier times that are generally misunderstood.

The entire United States consists of the homelands of hundreds of Native American societies, a fact too often forgotten by many Americans, so this Alabama exhibit opens appropriately with a map of the Indigenous nations that once populated the mid-eighteenth-century South. Maps of colonial-era America, whether drafted in colonial times or in our own era, typically show towns and roads in the colonized coastal regions but leave out those details in regions owned and occupied by Native peoples. Such maps implicitly convey the erroneous message that Native America was a trackless wilderness, devoid of roads or permanent towns. In fact, there

26.1. Detail of the Stuart-Gage map of the Southeast, showing "Creek Country" in 1773. (Courtesy of William L. Clements Library, University of Michigan, Thomas Gage Papers, Maps 6-E-12.)

26.2. Sheet 5 of the Stuart-Purcell map of the Southeast in 1775, showing Creek and Cherokee towns and the boundary with colonial Georgia, South Carolina, and North Carolina. (Courtesy of Newberry Library, Chicago, Edward E. Ayer Collection, Ayer MS map 228.)

were many Native towns, some of them larger in population, established far earlier, occupied longer than most colonial settlements, and linked together by efficient transportation and communication networks of overland trails and navigable waterways. To overcome this inaccurate historical legacy of a trackless Native America, we need a fresh perspective.[1]

To provide museum visitors with a more balanced picture of human settlement in the pre-Revolutionary Southeast, Steve Murray, director of the Department of Archives and History, asked Kathryn Braund, historian at Auburn University, and Greg Waselkov and Sarah Mattics at the University of South Alabama's Center for Archaeological Studies to create a better map. We turned to two manuscript maps of southeastern North America drafted by British colonial surveyors and military engineers that document the locations of 185 Native towns occupied around the year 1773[2] (figs. 26.1 and 26.2).

These remarkable historical documents resulted from a determined effort by John Stuart, superintendent of Indian affairs for the southern district of British colonies in North America, to comprehend the physical and cultural geography of the entire Southeast. From 1769 to 1775, Stuart commissioned coastline navigation charts, surveys of newly negotiated boundaries between the southern colonies and Native nations, hydrographic surveys of major interior rivers, and maps of Native towns, paths, and hunting grounds. Stuart additionally drew on maps compiled by French military officers in earlier decades. French and British cartographers frequently took information on rivers and trails from maps drawn by American Indians and included that Indigenous knowledge into their own maps, usually without crediting their sources. Whether acknowledged or not, a lot of the geographical data compiled by Stuart's mapping team came from Native Americans willing to share their own deep familiarity with the region, information distilled from hundreds of generations of accumulated firsthand experience. In the years leading up to the Revolutionary War, Stuart was able to present Gen. Thomas Gage, commander-in-chief of British forces in North America, with several large, detailed, and reasonably complete maps of the Native Southeast.[3]

For the *Museum of Alabama* exhibit, we primarily relied on the 1773 Stuart-Gage map, which exists only in manuscript form in the Clements Library at the University of Michigan. Additional details are taken from the revised 1775 Stuart-Purcell map, which survives in manuscript copies at the British National Archives in London and the Newberry Library in Chicago. Neither map is perfect, but together, they give us enough landmarks to correct mistakes in river course and determine reasonably precise locations of nearly two hundred Native American towns, which were

26.3. "The land is ours," based on the Stuart-Gage map of 1773, with modern state borders. (Courtesy of Alabama Archives and History Foundation, Montgomery, Alabama.)

homes to about fifty-five thousand Native people. A British colonial official's monumental mapping project gives us, centuries later, a uniquely detailed picture of the Cherokee, Muscogee Creek, Choctaw, and Chickasaw cultural landscapes in the years immediately before formation of the United States (figs. 26.3 and 26.4). This map at the Museum of Alabama, countless archaeological investigations across the South, and modern-day Native peoples with origins in the Southeast remind the rest of us that this land was theirs.

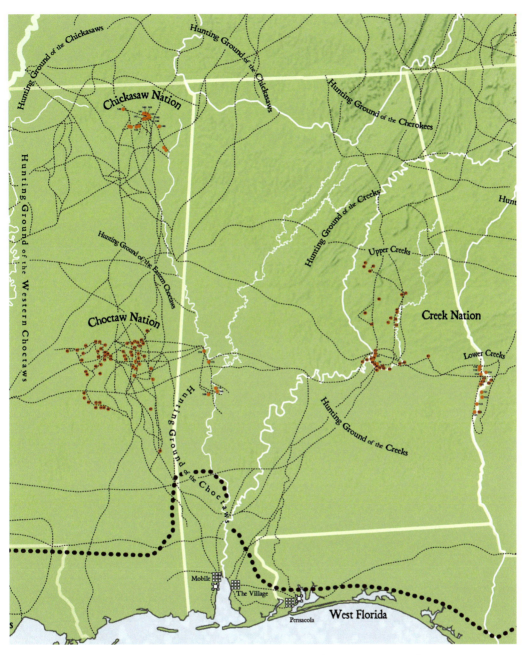

26.4. Detail of the original version of "The land is ours," based on the Stuart-Gage map of 1773, showing Creek, Choctaw, and Chickasaw towns, trails, and hunting grounds. (Graphic by Sarah Mattics, Center for Archaeological Studies, University of South Alabama.)

CHAPTER 27

Exploreum Science Center and History Museum of Mobile

. . . where archaeologists found domestic features from the Espejo family residence dating to the Spanish colonial era (1780–1813), a walkway and midden from Montuse's Tavern and Wharf (1805–35), cotton warehouse foundations from the 1820s to 1850s, and 11.5 feet of rubble and artifacts dumped into the Mobile River marsh, an early effort at land reclamation on Mobile's waterfront.

In the late 1990s, downtown Mobile underwent a rejuvenation. Historic buildings were restored, and new construction brought life back to the riverfront of Alabama's oldest city. Unfortunately, Mobile's archaeology rarely figures in urban renewal plans. Portions of the city's underground history still persist in places, hidden (and preserved) for centuries until threatened by major construction. In Mobile's city center, new construction typically involves driving concrete pilings deep into subsoil and the complete removal of surface soils that are replaced with structurally stable sand. This "removal of surface soils" effectively eradicates the archaeological record unless steps are taken in advance of construction. Archaeology ended prematurely after initial testing at the Mobile Convention Center, and no scientific excavation at all occurred before construction of the Riverview Plaza complex, the downtown Hampton Inn, and other irreplaceable portions of Mobile's historical heart.

If not for one vigilant employee of the Federal Highway Administration, largescale excavations would not have happened at the site of the new Exploreum Science Center either. During a review of a grant funded by the Intermodal Surface Transportation Efficiency Act, Faye Demassimo

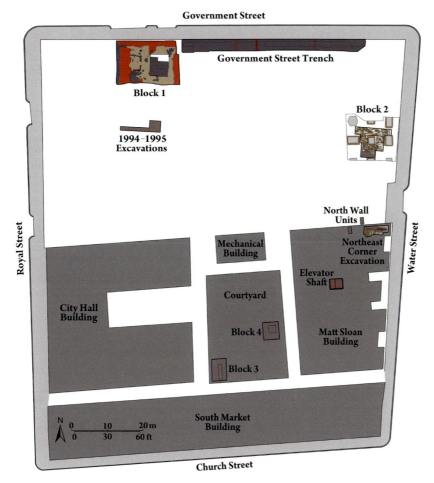

27.1. Site 1MB189, with archaeological excavation blocks in the Exploreum Science Center area on the north, and in the History Museum of Mobile Courtyard on the south, 1996–98. (Center for Archaeological Studies, University of South Alabama.)

noticed that the site's archaeology had been overlooked during project planning. Exploreum's project director Marian Pfeifer immediately asked the Center for Archaeological Studies to develop and implement a research plan.

Through July and August 1996, Bonnie Gums and George Shorter supervised center staff and student assistants working in two excavation blocks (fig. 27.1). Construction in the 1950s of a Mobile City Police building with a deep basement had already seriously impacted archaeological deposits in much of the planned footprint of the Exploreum. However, testing by a private archaeology firm in 1994–95 did reveal intact deposits at several locations outside the basement. We decided to focus on two of those spots.[1]

Block 1, adjacent to Government Street, contained Spanish colonial features associated with Antonio Espejo's household dating as early as the

1780s. Block 2, abutting Water Street, proved to be near Montuse's Tavern and Wharf, dating roughly from 1805 to 1835—in other words, from late in the Spanish colonial period through the first decades of American rule. By 1837, all earlier structures had been torn down and replaced by a long row of brick commercial buildings known as Hitchcock's Row, which in turn were demolished in 1955 for the police building.

In addition to those two large excavation blocks, we sampled deposits inside the Matt Sloan Building. Built in 1916 as a fire station, this structure was scheduled for renovation to house the Exploreum's children's gallery and administrative offices. Previous digging by the project's architects to inspect the building's foundations had left a large hole in the floor, which we expanded to document the site's deepest stratigraphy. Our excavation in the Matt Sloan Building reached 11.5 feet below the modern street level, well into marsh soils that once bordered the Mobile River. There we found a brass military button stamped "CUBA," from Mobile's post-1790 Spanish colonial garrison, specifically the Regimiento Infantería de Cuba, Fijo de la Habana, the Fixed Cuba Regiment who supported local Creole troops.[2]

Late eighteenth-century wall trenches found in Block 1 related to an Espejo family residence. The decayed remains of widely spaced upright posts in these trenches indicated a timber-frame post-in-ground building with clay daubed walls and a door in the middle of the east wall. Just beyond the northeast and southeast corners of the building footprint, excavators found small smudge pits filled with carbonized corncobs. Smoldering wet corncobs would have emitted copious smoke to drive away mosquitoes, an important consideration when living next to the Mobile River marshes. Artifacts found in the vicinity of this structure comprise a fine assemblage of late eighteenth-century Spanish colonial household items. Rare sherds of Catalonian and Triana majolica plates, ceramic tableware imported directly from Spain, strongly suggest that members of the wealthy Espejo family occupied this modest-looking house. Quarters for the household's enslaved people probably lay twenty-five feet to the east, near a midden of unglazed ceramic bowl fragments. Unfortunately, construction of Hitchcock's Row destroyed evidence of Spanish colonial structures in that location.[3]

In 1804, Espejo obtained permission from Spanish authorities to fill in the mosquito-infested riverfront marsh bordering his grant, land labeled as "low and miry" on an 1815 map of the town. Shortly afterward, Espejo died from mosquito-borne yellow fever. One year later his business partner, Sylvain Montuse, married Espejo's widow, Catalina. The couple ran a tavern and commercial wharf on the river's edge, and after Montuse's death in 1819, Catalina and her son-in-law Richard Tankersley continued to operate those businesses for some years. We know from Montuse's estate inventory that their household included five enslaved females—three adults (Rose, Nanny, and Amy) and two children, Milito and Rosetta.[4]

Reclaiming riverfront marsh land remained a concern of Espejo's successors. Excavation in Block 2 revealed an extensive layer of sawn timbers laid side by side in the marsh (fig. 27.2). Each timber had one end sharpened with an axe and signs of rot at the other. We interpreted these reused timbers as fraising—massive, pointed stakes set in the ground around nearby Fort Charlotte (previously known to the French as Fort Condé and to the Spanish as Fuerte Carlota). The US government decommissioned the obsolete fort in 1820 and soon thereafter sold its millions of bricks and other structural components to the local populace. Atop that layer of recycled fort timbers, the Espejos laid out a two-foot-wide walkway, a thick layer of marsh clam shells edged with wooden boards. The shells came from an ancient midden, judging from associated Native-made pottery. Some years later a pile of debris from the tavern accumulated on the path, pieces of 49 glass bottles, mostly English "beer-style quarts" with a few French wine bottles, along with 218 bottle corks, all dating to the 1820s and 1830s. In the 1830s, a small wooden structure had a floor made from three unfinished British millstones, a grindstone, and a layer of coral sand, materials that arrived in Mobile as ballast in the hold of a European ship.[5]

Once Exploreum construction got underway, city officials decided to move the History Museum of Mobile from an old house on Government Street (now the Mardi Gras Museum) into historic structures occupying the rest of the city block—the City Hall and Southern Market complex (a National Historic Landmark) dating to 1855–57. To accommodate interpretive exhibits about the city's long history, the museum board decided to build a new gallery in a central courtyard space, which led to excavations by staff from the Center for Archaeological Studies in that courtyard from late 1997 to mid-1998.[6]

Excavation Blocks 3 and 4 exposed key architectural features of enormous cotton warehouses in use from the late 1820s until their demolition in the 1850s (fig. 27.3). These warehouses were massive commercial structures designed to store the most valuable export commodity of the antebellum era, cotton. Given the unstable soils of Mobile's waterfront, builders of these imposing structures had to devise ways to support the immense weight of thousands of bales of cotton, each bale weighing four hundred to five hundred pounds. One approach to this problem, seen in Block 3, involved the use of spread footings, massive cypress planks resting side

27.2. Greg Waselkov vacuuming water from the wooden platform associated with Montuse's Tavern in Block 2, 1996. (Center for Archaeological Studies, University of South Alabama.)

by side on the boggy ground. Pine boards laid on top, perpendicular to the spread footing planks, supported short brick walls spanned by floor joists. Huge masonry piers, seen in Block 4, likewise broadly distributed the weight borne by roof support columns[7] (figs. 27.4 and 27.5).

Moving the Exploreum Science Center and the History Museum of

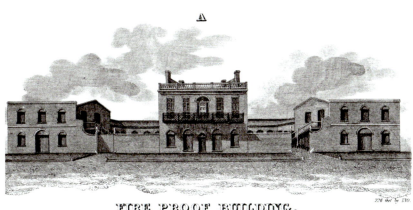

27.3. Engraving of a brick cotton warehouse at the corner of Royal and Conti Streets from James M. Goodwin and C. Haire's 1824 *Plan and View of the City of Mobile*. (Library of Congress, Geography and Map Division, 2012593360.)

27.4. Block 4 cotton warehouse pier. Excavation crew (*clockwise from left*): Bonnie Gums, Matthew Cooper, Dawn Smith, and Ashley Dumas, 1997. (Center for Archaeological Studies, University of South Alabama.)

Mobile to the city block bounded by Government, Water, Church, and Royal Streets in the 1990s helped revitalize downtown Mobile. Archaeology contributed to that process, while adding significantly to our understanding of the city's development before the Civil War. Archaeology is sometimes blamed for delaying construction projects, but that has not been our experience. The center completed this fieldwork on schedule, as always. There are, however, lessons still to be learned. Although development continues in the downtown area, archaeology is rarely considered in advance

27.5. Fort Condé fraising log being removed during Block 3 excavation by Eric Perkins, George Shorter, and Sarah Mattics, March 1998. (Center for Archaeological Studies, University of South Alabama.)

of construction, despite the cultural and educational benefits that accrue. And, while the History Museum of Mobile effectively incorporates archaeology into its interpretive exhibits, no mention of the remarkable history revealed by scientific excavation on the Exploreum site appears anywhere inside the city's premier science center.

CHAPTER 28

Historic Blakeley Park

> . . . wherein are found ancient shell middens, colonial-era sites of an Apalachee mission village and the Badon Plantation, the early nineteenth-century townsite of Blakeley, and well-preserved Confederate and Union earthworks from the 1865 siege, all protected within a two-thousand-acre nature preserve.

An underappreciated natural and cultural treasure sits six miles north of Interstate 10, on the east edge of the Mobile-Tensaw delta. Historic Blakeley State Park encompasses two thousand acres of ecologically diverse bottomland swamp and upland forest, as well as nearly the entire extent of a major Civil War battlefield, the historic townsite of early nineteenth-century Blakeley, a British colonial-era plantation site, an Apalachee Indian village and mission site, and ancient shell middens. Archaeologists affiliated with the University of South Alabama have long partnered with park staff to study and interpret this historic place.

Before the park's creation by the state of Alabama in 1981, Noel Read Stowe and Dan Jenkins directed a survey and test excavations funded by grants from the Historic Blakeley Foundation and the Alabama Historical Commission. Their fieldwork revealed the extents of two important archaeological sites: a large, ancient shell midden (1BA229) and the town of Blakeley (1BA221). For a brief period from 1819 to 1825, Blakeley rivaled Mobile in population and economic activity. Its two thousand residents supported a newspaper, a hotel, waterfront cotton warehouses, and a booming business district. However, the combined effects of a raging yellow fever epidemic and river channel dredging, which improved oceangoing ship access to Mobile, convinced most of Blakeley's residents to relocate, leaving the place a veritable ghost town. Stowe's early work at Blakeley located the remains of twenty substantial frame and brick structures

28.1. Archaeologist Richard Fuller and field school students excavating the pottery kiln at Historic Blakeley State Park, February 1977. (Center for Archaeological Studies, University of South Alabama.)

from the early nineteenth-century town, as well as a two-chambered pottery kiln built in the late nineteenth-century from bricks salvaged from abandoned buildings[1] (fig. 28.1).

In 2003, park director Jo Ann Flirt invited university archaeologists to return to Historic Blakeley State Park. Greg Waselkov and Bonnie Gums brought students enrolled in field methods courses and volunteers back for a closer look at the riverfront business district. An intensive shovel-testing survey across that elevated area, centered on the modern picnic pavilion, uncovered evidence of two major occupations that preceded Blakeley: a French colonial-era Apalachee Indian village and an ethnic French plantation from the British colonial period (fig. 28.2).

When Christian Apalachees from San Luis Mission (modern-day Tallahassee) fled Spanish Florida in the wake of slave raids in 1704, some of those refugees established towns near the French colonial settlement of Mobile, on the west side of the Mobile-Tensaw delta. Beginning in 1733, one group shifted their settlement east of the delta, to the low bluff immediately south of Baptizing Creek, a place that would later become Blakeley. A priest maintained a mission there for the Apalachees until 1763, the year the French crown ceded the eastern portion of colonial Louisiane to the British. That political transition prompted the Apalachees to migrate once again in search of a place where they could maintain their Catholic faith, finally resettling in the Red River valley west of the Mississippi River, an area controlled by Spain. Their descendants, the Apalachee Indians of the Talimali Band, live there today, in Libuse, Rapides Parish, Louisiana.

28.2. Volunteer Traci Cunningham and her find, an Early Woodland projectile point/knife from a shovel test at Historic Blakeley State Park, January 2003. (Center for Archaeological Studies, University of South Alabama.)

As colonial governments changed periodically on the Gulf Coast during the eighteenth century, some colonists left with departing officials. But many resilient families weathered the shifting political winds, learned new languages, and adapted to unfamiliar legal regimes. Most found ways to keep their property intact and maintain their livelihoods. The Badons, one such family, were ethnic French colonists who tended a farm in the vicinity of Eight Mile Creek, north of Mobile. In 1764 Joseph Badon swore an oath of allegiance to the new ruler of colonial British West Florida and promptly married Catherine Montelimar. Her parents had claimed the recently abandoned Apalachee town and mission site, which became her dowry. There the Badons established a plantation—essentially a cattle ranch—and raised a family. When Spanish general Bernardo de Gálvez besieged and took Mobile from the British in the spring of 1780, Badon swore another oath of allegiance, this time to the Spanish crown. In succeeding months, while the British garrison in Pensacola held out against the Spanish military onslaught, Badon apparently struggled with conflicting loyalties. When officials in Mobile observed two British spies coming and going from his plantation and then discovered he had harbored a Spanish deserter, Badon was arrested and sentenced to six years hard labor. He died imprisoned in Havana's El Morro castle a few years later.[2]

Our survey and test excavations recovered artifacts from the Apalachees and the Badon Plantation, although we found few intact features from either. Construction of Blakeley town, as well as digging by bottle collectors and metal detectorists during the years before creation of Historic

28.3. Archaeological field school students cleaning a portion of the brick floor of the courthouse at Historic Blakeley State Park, January 2011. (Center for Archaeological Studies, University of South Alabama.)

Blakeley State Park, did a lot of damage to the site's shallow colonial layers. One providential exception was a short length of foundation trench from a French-style house, probably attributable to the Badon era. The most abundant colonial artifact category is Native-made pottery, some in distinctive forms made by Apalachee potters and others attributable by decoration to Choctaws, who moved into the Mobile area after the Apalachees' departure. The origin of a third category of colonial pottery—simple unglazed bowls decorated with a red clay slip—remains uncertain. But we suspect that Africans made some proportion of those bowls for their own use as they worked and lived in bondage on the Badon Plantation.[3]

Since 2003, staff members with the Center for Archaeological Studies have continued to cooperate closely with park personnel as they developed visitor facilities, including various ground-disturbing activities ranging from interpretive sign placement to restroom construction and campground expansion. University of South Alabama students helped clear part of the Union siege trenches of downed trees felled by Hurricane Ivan in 2004. And in 2010, field methods course students sampled a two-thousand-year-old Middle Woodland shell midden first investigated in 1905.[4]

In 2011, center staff and volunteers joined students in a major effort to uncover, document, and preserve the ruins of one of Baldwin County's earliest courthouses, discovered during the 1977 survey. An 1820 legislative act defining the modern boundaries of Baldwin County, Alabama, also established Blakeley as the county seat, with its obligatory courthouse. The brick features excavated in 2011 relate to the second courthouse, constructed in 1833, with the county's jail on the ground level and a courtroom on the second floor. Portions of the building's masonry foundation walls and piers, as well as herringbone-patterned brick floors of the two jail cells (fig. 28.3), remain in place and are now safeguarded by an interpretive shelter.[5]

When the Civil War overtook Blakeley in the spring of 1865 (fig. 28.4), little remained of the old town apart from that well-built courthouse and jail. The park today preserves a remarkably intact siege landscape from that terrible conflict. Miles of Confederate defensive trenches, interspersed with redoubts, still stand opposite Union parallel and zigzag trenches (fig. 28.5). Although these battlefield features afforded the major impetus for creation of Historic Blakeley State Park four decades ago, the park is so much more, with a rich diversity of natural and cultural resources unsurpassed in an increasingly urbanized part of the state.[6]

28.4. Attack of federal forces against the Confederate stronghold at Blakeley on April 9, 1865, from *Harper's Weekly*, "The Fight Before Mobile—Storming of Fort Blakeley." (Courtesy of Digital Collections, University of Michigan Library.)

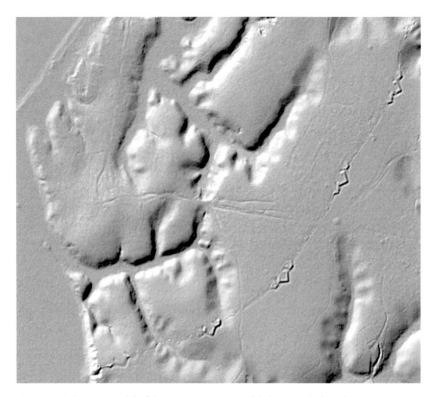

28.5. LiDAR elevation model of the terrain in Historic Blakeley State Park, with tree cover digitally removed, showing redoubts 4 to 9 of the Confederate defensive line east and south of the old town, which occupied the peninsulas at upper left. (US Geological Survey National Map, 3D Elevation Program, based on 2018 data.)

CHAPTER 29

Fort Mims

> . . . where a battle's outcome in 1813 changed the course of American history and contributed to the political decision in the 1830s to expel Native Americans from the eastern United States, the ethnic cleansing known as Indian Removal.

At noon on the thirtieth of August 1813, as Zachariah McGirth and two of his enslaved African laborers gathered "corn & pumpkins" from McGirth's farm on the Alabama River, they heard "heavy firing in the direction of the Fort." Over the previous month, such runs upriver for provision had sustained their families and hundreds of other civilians taking refuge behind a crude stockade called Fort Mims. This settler fort had been hastily erected by Mississippi Territorial militiamen around the plantation home of Samuel Mims. The population of this remote frontier, anticipating attacks by Redstick Creeks, had spent the last four weeks huddled inside Fort Mims and a score of similar fortified houses strung along the Creek Nation's southwestern boundary with the United States. All afternoon the three men "listened at the firing with great anxiety & pain." Running their raft into a nearby canebrake, they lay still until "all firing ceased." When "immense volumes of smoke" rose over the fort, they knew "all was lost."[1]

Decades of land encroachments on the Muscogee people (known to English-speakers as Creeks) and US political pressure to cede their land and assimilate to American ways had contributed to the rise of the militaristic anti-American Redstick movement. However, the scale of the Redstick victory at Fort Mims—a garrisoned fort overrun, at the cost of nearly three hundred dead—triggered a three-pronged American military invasion of the Creek Nation that burned sixty towns and killed thousands. Andrew Jackson's decisive American victory at Horseshoe Bend just seven months later, and a subsequent treaty ceding twenty-one million acres of Creek land to the United States, immediately opened to American settlement much of the territory that would become Alabama. The American public's perception of the Fort Mims battle as an unprovoked attack and a massacre of white civilians (both inaccurate oversimplifications) influenced the federal government's abandonment of the assimilation program. A longer-term repercussion was the eventual decision to carry out a mass expulsion of Native peoples from the eastern states, resulting in the numerous Trails of Tears known as Indian Removal. The fire that engulfed Fort Mims had lasting consequences for not only the Muscogee people but for all Americans.[2]

Within a generation of the event, the compelling tragedy of Fort Mims attracted the scholarly attention of Albert James Pickett, a wealthy Alabama planter who published the first comprehensive history of his state in 1851. Pickett based his narrative of the Creek War of 1813–14 on interviews with participants, and his notes and correspondence remain important primary sources on that conflict. Thanks largely to Pickett's influence, the story of Fort Mims endures as a key part of Alabama's foundational mythology.[3]

Throughout the nineteenth and early twentieth centuries, the historic site of Fort Mims attracted visitors who could purchase battle memorabilia from the tenant farmer or pick them up themselves from adjacent fields (fig. 29.1). (Two of the oldest residents of Tensaw recalled for us their memories as boys in the 1930s, picking up lead balls from the battle site for use as fishing sinkers.) In 1953 some Tensaw residents, most of them descendants of battle survivors, obtained use of a bulldozer and scraped the perimeter of the fort site, uncovering what they thought were charred remains of the fort's stockade. On that basis, the site's owners, the Till family, donated a five-acre parcel to the state in 1955, with the understanding that the land would be developed as a public park within ten years. Nine years passed with no progress toward a park, and the property was about to revert to the Till family, when engineers at the Department of Conservation (DOC) finally fenced the site, set up two picnic tables, and undertook archaeological excavations.

The DOC excavations in 1964 and 1968 retrieved many important artifacts, particularly from two deep wells inside the fort, and confirmed the state's right to the property. However, the DOC's engineers lacked any archaeological expertise and essentially approached archaeology as an artifact mining operation, stripping off arbitrary four-inch levels of soil without recording (or even recognizing) subsurface features.[4]

In 1971 control of the park transferred from the DOC to the newly created Alabama Historical Commission (AHC), which soon contracted with

29.1. Sheet brass arrow points and lead rifle balls from the Fort Mims site (1BA218). (Center for Archaeological Studies, University of South Alabama.)

Read Stowe at the University of South Alabama for artifact conservation. Grants from the National Park Service enabled Stowe to begin new excavations in 1973 with students from his field methods course, volunteers, and a local Girl Scout troop. Additional fieldwork occurred in 1975 and 1981. Stowe identified a southern portion of the stockade (which did not correspond to the area bulldozed in 1953) and established the locations of the Mims house, kitchen, and other plantation structures within the fort[5] (fig. 29.2).

After five seasons of extensive excavation, AHC staff recognized the need for a comprehensive analysis and report on the archaeology at Fort Mims. In 2000 the state contracted with the University of South Alabama's Center for Archaeological Studies for Greg Waselkov and Bonnie Gums to direct that study. We soon realized the scale of damage the site had sustained from the bulldozing and DOC excavations and recommended that additional targeted fieldwork be undertaken to resolve several important outstanding questions. Paramount among them was a need to ascertain the true appearance and shape of the fort.[6]

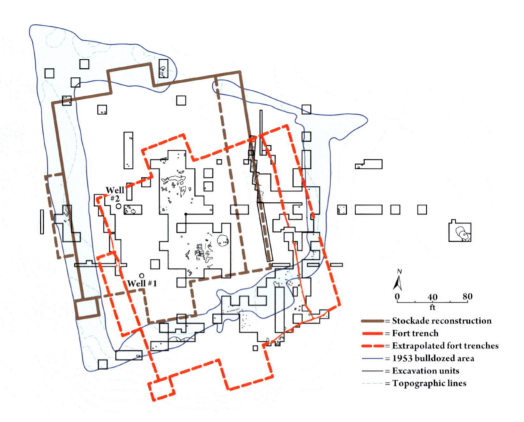

29.2. Composite map of the Fort Mims site excavations, with the 1953 bulldozed search area shaded light blue, the 1975–2013 excavations outlined in black, the actual fort stockade outline in solid red and interpolations in dashed red, and the reconstructed palisade in brown. (Graphic by Sarah Mattics, Center for Archaeological Studies, University of South Alabama.)

To help address that question, a team led by Jay Johnson from the University of Mississippi carried out a geophysical survey of the park in 2003 using ground penetrating radar, electrical resistance, electromagnetic conductivity, and magnetometry. Although those high-tech methods identified many promising-looking geophysical anomalies, test excavations quickly determined their modern origins as gravel walkways, a flagpole base, erosional gullies, and forgotten utility lines. Unfortunately, the fainter geophysical signals from historic features had been effectively obscured by the 1953 bulldozing and subsequent park development.[7]

Therefore, in October 2004 Waselkov organized a volunteer dig to locate the western stockade wall of Fort Mims. One of our units west of the well-established location of the Mims house revealed a narrow, north-south-bearing feature filled with dark brown soil, charcoal, fired clay, melted bottle glass, burned creamware pottery fragments, and lead

29.3. Amy Barker and other field school students, center staff, and volunteers tracking down the western palisade of Fort Mims, February 2006. (Center for Archaeological Studies, University of South Alabama.)

shot—the same evocative artifacts found to the east, inside the burned fort. To the west we recovered virtually nothing. The feature, which turned out to be the western stockade footing trench, was very shallow, reduced by a century of agricultural plowing to a depth of just seven inches. At the bottom we uncovered a row of charcoal-rimmed semicircles, stains in the soil from decayed split pine poles, placed upright side by side in the trench early in August 1813, then scorched by the fires that consumed Fort Mims at the end of the battle.[8]

Waselkov and Gums directed further small-scale excavations with field methods students and volunteers from 2005 to 2013, a few days every year, to trace more of the stockade line (fig. 29.3). In the end, our excavations confirmed that a historic fort sketch (fig. 29.4), drawn by Lt. Benjamin Salvage of the Mississippi Territorial Volunteers in September 1813, several weeks after the battle, accurately depicted Fort Mims but in no way resembled the larger trapezoid outline created by the 1953 bulldozing. One notable discovery, just inside the east gate of the fort, was a large, shallow, rectangular pit full of very dark brown soil (fig. 29.5). Among the few artifacts in this highly organic muck was a broken chamber pot, confirming our suspicions that we had found a latrine—a "sink," to use military jargon of the early nineteenth century—the only one known within the fort.[9]

Now that the appearance of Fort Mims and its method of construction have been clarified, this settler fort can be compared with dozens of other

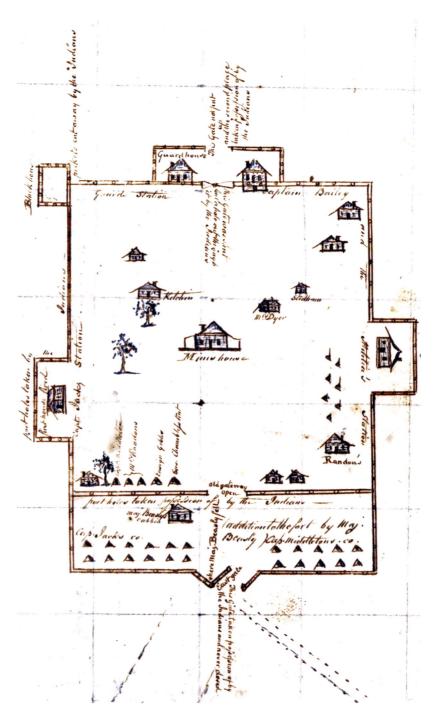

29.4. Detail of sketch of Fort Mims (with north to the right) drawn in September 1813, after the fort's destruction, by Lt. Benjamin Salvage, Quartermaster for the Mississippi Territorial Volunteers. (Courtesy of Alabama Department of Archives and History, Pickett Family Papers, LPR185.)

29.5. Field school students and center staff excavating Feature 3, a large privy pit inside the east palisade of Fort Mims, March 2007. (Center for Archaeological Studies, University of South Alabama.)

such forts hurriedly thrown up in times of trouble by American settlers. These amateur fort builders generally had little or no military training, but they drew upon a wealth of folk knowledge based on two centuries of prior frontier conflicts in eastern North America. Archaeologists have sought out and explored similar frontier stockades from earlier conflicts, such as Revolutionary War Boonesborough in Kentucky and other less famous settler forts in Virginia, West Virginia, and Pennsylvania. These comparisons generally confirm the many deficiencies of Fort Mims noted by critics soon after its fall, including a weakly constructed stockade and the lack of a second blockhouse.[10]

During our ten years of involvement with the park, we worked closely with members of the Fort Mims Restoration Association (FMRA), then led by Davis Smith (fig. 29.6), a relative of the Till family who had donated the fort site to the state many years before. To enhance public interpretation of the historic site, Smith and the FMRA, in conjunction with the AHC, undertook an ambitious reconstruction of the west, north, and east stockade walls, built at 1:1 scale. To limit the potentially detrimental impact of stockade reconstruction on the site's remaining subsurface archaeological features, the reconstructed walls were offset from the actual fort footprint several meters to the west and north, where they still effectively mirror the original fort outline.

Every year in August, when the FMRA and the AHC host their annual commemoration of the battle, those rebuilt walls offer visitors the opportunity to appreciate the cramped quarters endured by over four hundred refugees confined to that walled acre. The stockade also helps convey some sense of the horror of the attack on that overcrowded space and the panic felt by those trapped within. A visit to Fort Mims Park is unsettling on many levels. In this place of memory, where the slain yet rest in two mass graves, visitors can reflect on the causes of a conflict spawned by social, cultural, and racial issues still resonant today.

One unanticipated outcome of the University of South Alabama's archaeology at Fort Mims was Waselkov's decision to write a book on the historical context of the battle, a review long overdue since Albert James Pickett's 1851 magnum opus. Waselkov's research brought to the fore the Creek métis. This dispersed community at the far southern limits of the Creek Nation were a diverse mix of ethnicities—mainly offspring of marriages between European colonists and Muscogees but also some of African-Muscogee descent. They had moved near the US boundary line in search of greater political and economic autonomy than the leadership of the Creek Nation permitted. In close proximity to white and Black residents of the Tensaw district of Mississippi Territory, the Creek métis could maintain their Indigenous identity, independence, language, and customs, while enjoying ready access to the Mobile and Pensacola markets.

29.6. Davis Smith, with his dog Bubba, March 2008. As president of the Fort Mims Restoration Association, Davis oversaw reconstruction of the palisade at Fort Mims Park. (Center for Archaeological Studies, University of South Alabama.)

Our archaeology confirmed the presence of Creek métis inside Fort Mims, as refugees alongside their Black and white neighbors, by the abundance of traditional Creek pottery found mostly in the northeast quadrant of the fort. Descendants of those Creek métis who survived the battle at Fort Mims are today counted among the tribal rolls of the Muscogee Nation in Oklahoma and the Poarch Band of Creek Indians in Alabama. The documentary history and archaeology of Fort Mims, when viewed afresh, expose the social complexity of early Alabama and compel us to set aside the tired historical trope of an American frontier divided neatly between settlers and Native people.[11]

Many Muscogee Creeks trace their ancestry back to Zachariah McGirth and his Muscogee wife, Levitia (Vicey) Cornells. As he hid in a canebrake near the raging battle, Zachariah (whose broad axe was found in one of the Fort Mims wells) felt sure that his wife and six children had all perished. Their son did die that day, but the victorious Redstick Creeks took Vicey and their five girls north to the town of Oce Vpofv/Hickory Ground, where they subsisted on sweet potatoes until retaken the following spring by Capt. Uriah Blue's company of Choctaw and Chickasaw warriors. Zachariah also survived the war, recklessly riding as a courier several times across the Creek Nation to deliver correspondence coordinating the American invasion. When the McGirths reunited at a dock in Mobile, Zachariah barely recognized his war-weary wife and daughters. For the McGirths, this story that began with suffering at Fort Mims ended with redemption from captivity and a chance for a renewed life together, but of course, that sentimental tale is merely a brief snippet of their life stories set in the broad panorama of American history.[12]

CHAPTER 30

Ekvncakv/Holy Ground

> . . . discovered and preserved in 2010, where excavation of log cabin remains contributed to a better understanding of the Redstick movement, an effort to revitalize Muscogee society that contributed to the war of 1813–14.

During the spring and summer of 1813, the Redstick prophetic movement swept through the Muscogee Creek Nation inspired by the nativist teachings of the Shawnee prophet Tenskwatawa and his brother Tecumseh. As war became increasingly likely between the Redstick faction of the Creeks and the United States, several prophet's towns arose in defensible places made stronger by invocations of spiritual protection. Tohopeka, the best known of these new towns, occupied the great Horseshoe Bend of the Tallapoosa River and served as a stronghold for Creeks living in nearby towns. Other new sacred towns fulfilled similar functions for Muscogees living elsewhere in the Upper Creek country. According to George Stiggins, a Natchez Creek writing many years later, the Redsticks hoped to "repel any invading army" at those strongholds, rather than having "a war at the door of every town, and the repeling of the foe to be left to be done alone by the warriors of each town and village."[1]

Another such prophet's town was Ekvncakv (written in modern Muscogee orthography; formerly Ikanachaka), usually translated as Holy Ground, located south of the Alabama River in what is now Lowndes County. A force of Americans and allied Choctaws attacked and destroyed Holy Ground on December 23, 1813, midway through the Creek War.[2]

Heles Haco (also known as Josiah Francis), the Alabama prophet, had gathered his followers at Holy Ground from Koasati, Alabama, and Muscogee towns clustered near the confluence of the Coosa and Tallapoosa Rivers (north of modern-day Montgomery). One prominent resident was

William Weatherford, Opunvkv Fvccetv or Truth Teller, a leader of the successful Redstick assault on Fort Mims on August 30, 1813. Dubbed "Red Eagle" by later romantic poets, Weatherford is known to every credulous Alabama grade schooler for his legendary leap from a bluff on horseback into the Alabama River at the end of the battle. Skepticism has long dogged that fabled but improbable exploit. According to his acquaintance Thomas Woodward, Weatherford had, instead, ridden his horse down a ravine into the river to escape encirclement by American troops. Nevertheless, engravings of Weatherford's leap have appeared in Alabama history textbooks for generations, firmly tying Holy Ground to the banks of the river in the public's imagination.[3]

Searches for the site of Holy Ground during the twentieth century repeatedly failed to uncover any archaeological evidence of that Redstick Creek town on the bluffs bordering the Alabama River. In 2010, Greg Waselkov teamed with Craig T. Sheldon Jr., recently retired from Auburn University–Montgomery, to find Holy Ground. Supported by a grant from the National Park Service's American Battlefield Protection Program, center staff and volunteers sought the battle site in a ninety-two-acre tract extending well south of the Alabama River. Shovel testing and metal detecting did eventually uncover Creek pottery and other early nineteenth-century artifacts in a ten-acre area, recorded as site 1LO210, about one-quarter mile south of the river. Ekvncakv had been rediscovered.[4]

Our satisfaction at having relocated a major Creek town site was tempered by the realization that the entire site area had been platted for private home development. We immediately contacted The Archaeological Conservancy (TAC), a marvelous private nonprofit organization that saves sites by buying them. The TAC staff straight away recognized Holy Ground's national historical significance, and their regional director, Jessica Crawford, opened negotiations with the landowner. The TAC's purchase of a large portion of the archaeological site saved it from development.[5]

Over the following eight years, in partnership with TAC, we carried out a series of targeted, small-scale archaeological investigations designed to understand more about this historically and culturally important place, while respecting the need to preserve the site in its pristine condition. For we soon learned that this Redstick Creek prophet's town had never been subjected to plow agriculture. Plowing has disrupted and churned the upper zone of most archaeological sites in the eastern United States, so the absence of a plowzone here is surprising and noteworthy. This allowed the fragile, shallow remains of log cabins to survive.

Log cabins are notorious for leaving behind little to no archaeological trace. Because traditional Creek structures of the eighteenth century were supported by upright posts set deep in the ground in a rectangular arrangement, houses of that sort can be identified from soil stains left by the decayed lower portions of the support posts, which will be partially preserved even beneath a site's plowzone. When National Park Service archaeologists excavated the plowed site of Tohopeka in the 1960s and 1970s, the absence of rectangular house post patterns suggested to them that the town's residents lived in log cabins. But absence of evidence is a poor substitute for evidence, which makes the Holy Ground cabin remains so important and informative. By the time we concluded fieldwork late in 2018, five complete or partial log cabin footprints had been uncovered, photographed, and mapped. At project's end we backfilled our excavations, leaving the site as we found it.[6]

Despite the log cabin's northern European origins, Native peoples of the Southeast found much to like about that architectural form. Holy Ground cabins were small, averaging 10.5 feet wide and 15 feet long. American participants in the battle at Holy Ground estimated they destroyed 150 to 200 houses in the 10-acre town, a figure we suspected the victors had inflated until we saw how closely packed together the cabins stood, separated from one another by only a few feet. Later Seminole towns were similarly crowded, probably for defensive purposes (fig. 30.1).[7]

To meet their own needs with this foreign housing form, the Creeks modified several cabin features, as the archaeological remnants at Holy Ground revealed. When the Americans and their Choctaw allies burned

30.1. Detail of *Burning of the Town Pilak-Li-Ka-Ha by Gen. Eustis*, a lithograph from the Seminole War published by T. F. Gray and James, 1837. (Library of Congress, Prints and Photographs Division, LC-USZC4–2727.)

Holy Ground, that conflagration baked the clay used to daub each cabin's walls and stick-and-mud chimneys and to build the hearths. That burning preserved impressions in the clay of wooden structural elements and other missing house construction details. From impressions in fired daub, we know the cabin walls consisted of round logs that had been split lengthwise, notched at the ends, and stacked with the flat split surfaces facing inward. Once the inner surfaces were covered with a thin layer of clay, these well-insulated cabins would have had smooth interior walls, much like earlier traditional Creek houses. At one end of each cabin the residents of Ekvncakv built a raised wooden bench for sleeping, opposite a wide, open hearth.[8]

Holy Ground chimney bases at first glance seemed much like those found in settler cabins of the era. Closer inspection, though, revealed how Holy Ground chimneys each sat atop a rectangular raised clay hearth formed in a shallow, semicircular pit. Cabin occupants deposited ashes from their household hearths in those pits at the base of chimneys (fig. 30.2). Specially burned hickory ash was an essential ingredient in the preparation of *sofke*, predecessor to grits and hominy, but normal hearth ashes from cooking fires were carefully disposed outside each cabin chimney. This probably signaled respect for the origin of a family's hearth fire, rekindled each year during the *poskita* or Green Corn ceremony with embers from the town's sacred square ground fire. That practice, and the

30.2. Excavation of the Structure 3 hearth at Holy Ground (1LO210), by Lori Sawyer, Traci Cunningham, and Craig Sheldon (*left to right*). The rectangular, orange clay hearth in the center of the photograph is partially encircled by a shallow ash pit. (Center for Archaeological Studies, University of South Alabama.)

presence of a raised clay hearth, a domestic feature with a history dating back thousands of years in the Southeast, reflects a thorough integration of classic Muscogee architectural design elements with the recently introduced log cabin house form.[9]

30.3. Ocmulgee Fields Incised carinated bowl rim sherds with remnants of red filming, from Structure 3. (Center for Archaeological Studies, University of South Alabama.)

30.4. African-style earthenware smoking pipe bowl (two views) from Structure 3. (Center for Archaeological Studies, University of South Alabama.)

Artifacts found within each cabin's footprint similarly reveal how the Redstick Creeks selectively adopted some elements of American material culture and rejected others (figs. 30.3 and 30.4). Native-made pots are very abundant, although supplemented at each cabin by a few British-made tablewares. The latter could have been taken from Fort Mims or from settler farms destroyed during raids launched from Holy Ground in the early days of the war with the Americans. Far less common are glass beads and silver adornments, once so popular but now proscribed by the prophet's injunctions against imported goods, indulgences that the Quaker traveler William Bartram had labeled "foreign superfluities." Archaeology at Ekvncakv/Holy Ground has opened a window on the everyday lives of Redstick Creeks who sought to redress more than a century of political, economic, and cultural harm inflicted on their society by colonizing Europeans and Americans.[10]

CHAPTER 31

Old St. Stephens

> ... Alabama's territorial capital and a boomtown in the early nineteenth century, now a ghost town preserved in a historical park that integrates archaeological research and interpretation into public education activities.

Peter Hamilton, Mobile's preeminent historian at the turn of the twentieth century, encouraged broad appreciation of this region's past by organizing anniversary commemorations at key historic sites. The man knew how to throw a party. Hundreds attended his bicentennial event at French colonial Old Mobile, held on January 23, 1902, at Twenty-Seven Mile Bluff on the Mobile River, the city's original location. Hamilton and his colleagues in the Iberville Historical Society mobilized an enthusiastic public celebration of that legendary place and left behind an impressive stone monument, which stands on the site to this day—a memorial with the rare distinction among historical markers of actually celebrating the correct location.[1]

Three years earlier, Hamilton had staged an equally popular commemoration at the remote Washington County site of Old St. Stephens. By 1899 this once-booming frontier capital of Alabama Territory had become a forested ghost town, with telltale piles of limestone and brick rubble marking where homes and businesses once stood. On May 6, a contingent of celebrants took the Mobile & Birmingham Railroad line from Mobile to Jackson, in Clarke County, and caught a ride on the steamboat *Minnie Lee* for a nine-mile voyage up the Tombigbee River. On arrival at the St. Stephens bluff, a two-gun salute from the USS *Winona*, a US Coast Guard revenue cutter, welcomed a crowd numbering in the hundreds, locals as well as dignitaries assembled to celebrate the anniversary of the transfer of this region from Spanish to American rule in 1799.[2]

Among the centennial orations delivered that day, one still resonates. Mary Welsh offered reminiscences on her first ten years of childhood in "the dear old town," since her birth there in 1823: "The localities, events and people of the St. Stephens of more than sixty-five years ago are as present to my memory now as they ever were to my physical sight." Since Hamilton could find no map of the town from that era, Welsh, now nearly blind, sketched one from memory with help from a longtime friend. The two women plotted locations of many of the town's government and commercial edifices, long since gone, as Welsh recalled how they had been constructed of limestone "quarried from the hills near by in blocks smooth and white as marble; the foundations were laid and the cellars walled up of the same durable material." Over a century later, Welsh's map has proven of inestimable value to modern archaeologists.[3]

St. Stephens had its origin in the Spanish colonial period. In 1789 Juan Vincente Folch, governor of Spanish West Florida, ordered construction of Fuerte San Esteban de Tombecbé, just downstream from a treacherous stretch of rapids on the lower Tombigbee River later known as McGrew's Shoals. Folch's original earthen fort was strengthened in 1792, then rebuilt in 1795 at a slightly different location on the river bluff. When a 1799 American-Spanish survey of the disputed international boundary between Mississippi Territory and colonial West Florida revealed that Fuerte San Esteban in fact fell on the US side of the line, the Spanish garrison turned over their fort to an American trader and departed.[4]

Official American occupation of the site began in 1803. The Choctaw Trading House, a federally operated store for Indian trade, was established in the abandoned fort to help maintain peaceful relations between the United States and the Choctaw Nation, which lay immediately north of St. Stephens. George Strother Gaines, initially an assistant factor at the trading house, became federal agent to the Choctaws in 1805. Toward the end of his long life, Gaines wrote a narrative of the town's rapid rise and lengthy decline, which he witnessed firsthand[5] (fig. 31.1).

Washington County surveyors platted lots for the town of St. Stephens in 1807, but few settled there until the land rush known as Alabama Fever. A federal land office opened at St. Stephens in 1815 to sell parcels of the twenty-one million acres ceded by the Creek Nation at the end of the Redstick War. Within a few years, the population of St. Stephens reached three thousand residents, rivaling Mobile.[6]

Thomas Eastin began publishing a newspaper, the *Halcyon and Tombeckbe Public Advertiser*, in 1815 with an old printing press and type he found at the Mount Vernon Cantonment, equipment used in 1811–12 to print the *Mobile Centinel* at Fort Stoddert. Articles and advertisements

31.1. High Street in Old St. Stephens (1WN1), 1999. (Center for Archaeological Studies, University of South Alabama.)

in the *Halcyon* document the political, economic, and social development of this southwestern corner of early nineteenth-century Alabama. Particularly revealing are the numerous advertisements requesting assistance with the recapture of enslaved Black laborers who fled into the Mobile-Tensaw delta from nearby plantations. One such "runaway[,] . . . a Negro Man by the name of Isaac," was described in the April 3, 1820, issue of the *Halcyon* as "stout made, about six feet high, dark complexion and an impudent look when spoken to." For more than a year Isaac had been "lurking near Blakely" until shot and wounded and "since that time has been concealed on Tensaw river." His goal, the advertiser surmised, was to reach Pensacola "or some other place in the Spanish government for refuge."[7]

On March 3, 1817, the US Congress created Alabama Territory from the eastern half of Mississippi Territory, and in December of that year, the new territorial legislature met at the Douglas Hotel in St. Stephens. A state constitution drafted in Huntsville in August 1819 led to Congress granting statehood to Alabama on December 14, 1819, at which time Cahawba became the first state capital. That brief two-year interval as territorial capital coincided with the heyday of St. Stephens, which witnessed the launch of the first steamboat in the state, the *Alabama*, in February 1818 at the head of navigation on the Tombigbee River. The town continued to thrive economically for a few more years, but by 1830, most residents had moved to new St. Stephens, a few miles inland. By the outbreak of the Civil War, Old St. Stephens had been abandoned almost entirely.[8]

The ghost town lay undisturbed for nearly a century, until Lone Star Cement Company began quarrying chalky and shelly limestone from the north part of the site in the 1920s. Rock was shipped by barge to the company's plant at New Orleans for manufacture into Portland cement until the St. Stephens quarry closed in 1981. The several enormous pits opened for materials mining incidentally exposed the most complete cross section of marine deposits of Oligocene age (thirty-four to twenty-three million years) accessible to paleontologists in North America. But that boon to fossil hunters came at a heavy archaeological price—destruction of the Spanish fort ruins and about one-quarter of Old St. Stephens.[9]

A century after Mary Welsh's return to the place of her birth, Jim Long, director of the St. Stephens Historical Commission, contacted the Center for Archaeological Studies for advice. Long needed to know how to preserve and interpret some house cellars and collapsed chimneys that his workers had uncovered during preparations for an event scheduled for May 9, 1999, to celebrate the two hundredth anniversary of Fuerte San Esteban's transfer to US dominion. St. Stephens Historical Park, created a decade earlier to protect the old townsite, had been acquiring land gradually through purchase and donation, by then totaling two hundred acres, as well as contracting for some preliminary archaeological surveys. Washington County residents flocked to the park's seventy-acre quarry lake, which provides the only safe place for recreational swimming in the county, but Long hoped also to develop the park's educational and heritage tourism potential.[10]

During our initial visit to the old townsite, we were astounded by the scale of the exceptionally well-preserved archaeological remains. There were structural ruins visible everywhere we looked. (We also encountered the first of many large rattlesnakes we would meet in the park over the next twenty years.) Here was a worldclass archaeological site, 1WN1, clearly of great historical significance and essentially undisturbed since the town's abandonment more than 150 years earlier. George Shorter quickly took the lead on research at Old St. Stephens for the center and worked closely with Long and other park personnel until fieldwork ended in 2019.

Several initial archaeology projects, from 2000 to 2004, were funded jointly by grants from the St. Stephens Historical Commission and the Alabama Historical Commission. Our initial goal was to survey systematically the entire area within the park's boundaries, a lengthy process during which Shorter found and documented remains of fifty-two buildings on the sixty-five acres of the intact townsite. Fifteen of those building ruins had quantities of limestone blocks and bricks visible on the ground surface. Because those surface ruins had the potential to tell us about the layout and appearance of the buildings, and they also seemed especially vulnerable to damage by illicit metal detectorists and bottle hunters, their detailed mapping became our next priority.[11]

Once Shorter's team had maps in hand detailing the site's many building ruins, another problem rose to the fore: erosion of two substantial stone ruins on the Tombigbee River bank. Read and Rebecca Stowe had test excavated that location in 1995–96, but every year afterward the river carried away another half meter of riverbank. Shorter directed excavations in 2001 and 2003 to retrieve what remained (fig. 31.2). The buildings are thought to have originally been part of the Spanish church and rectory that Gaines reused as warehouses for the Choctaw Trading House. Artifacts were sparse, as one might expect at both a rectory and a warehouse, but among them were fragments of two small red-filmed ceramic bowls decorated with the combed incising characteristic of Choctaw pottery, as well as twenty-one small glass beads in styles routinely traded to the Choctaws during the early nineteenth century.[12]

The most ambitious excavation accomplished at Old St. Stephens targeted town lots 137 and 151, the Globe Hotel property at the intersection of High and Spring Streets (figs. 31.3 and 31.4). In 1820 Col. Benjamin Smoot owned the hotel, which soon became the property of Reuben Chamberlain, whose family resided there and ran a dry goods store out of the lower floor. Elsewhere in the hotel lots stood a stable, kitchen, well, and quarters for enslaved workers. For this long-term project, Shorter partnered with the Alabama Museum of Natural History to bring a Museum Expedition to Old St. Stephens in 2002, 2003, and 2009. Museum Expedition, a program devised by science educator John Hall, offered middle and high school students and members of the general public a chance to participate

31.2. Structure 51 on the bank of the Tombigbee River, September 2003. The flat surface of limestone blocks in the foreground is a hearth, surrounded by limestone rubble from a fallen chimney. (Center for Archaeological Studies, University of South Alabama.)

in scientific field research somewhere in the state of Alabama, every year from 1979 to 2018. The experience was intended to be an adventure for the young participants, who lived in a tent camp in remote settings and worked side by side with professionals in paleontology, archaeology, and ecology. Museum Expedition summer camps at the Globe Hotel excavations at Old St. Stephens were immensely popular with participants and greatly enhanced public interpretation at the park.[13]

31.3. Excavation of the Globe Hotel in 2001 revealed the front gallery's brick floor, laid in a herringbone pattern, just outside a wall made of limestone. (Center for Archaeological Studies, University of South Alabama.)

Public engagement remained a major goal of the center's partnership with St. Stephens Historical Park for twenty years. Shorter also developed a management plan for park personnel to care for the park's archaeological resources. He and Sarah Mattics created a website as well as educational outreach programs for the park. Programs included a trail through the old town with interpretive signage; exhibits for the St. Stephens Historical Commission's museum in new St. Stephens; talks to the community; and special events in the park, such as volunteer digs (at the Douglas Hotel site in 2017–19) and the annual Founders Day every October. We hope that the next generation will continue to value and preserve this extraordinary archaeological site, in the spirit of Mary Welsh, who looked forward with confidence and faith that "the massive ruins will doubtless remain through all future years, testifying to the wealth, enterprise and public spirit of the founders of Old St. Stephens."[14]

31.4. George Shorter reconstructing a "ghost" version of the Globe Hotel at 137 High Street in 2009. The original Globe Hotel stood from 1818 until its destruction by fire in 1847. (Center for Archaeological Studies, University of South Alabama.)

PART IX

CIVIL WAR ERA (1860–1868)

CHAPTER 32

Africatown Visitor Center

> . . . will soon arise at the place where 110 Africans, stolen from their homeland and transported to Mobile on *Clotilda*, the last slaving ship to enter the United States, created a new community after emancipation.

Discovery and confirmation in 2018–19 of the wreck of *Clotilda*, America's last slaving ship, ranks among south Alabama's most community-inspiring archaeological finds. The story that begins with *Clotilda* has now gained national recognition. A wager in 1860 between two wealthy slaveowners dispatched that ship to steal the freedom of 110 Africans and carry them as contraband from Ouidah in the kingdom of Dahomey (modern Benin) into slavery at Mobile. *Clotilda* arrived on the eve of the Civil War, fifty-two years after a ban on slave imports into the United States. Upon emancipation after five years in slavery, the survivors built a cluster of cabins north of the city on a plot of poor land (the location of their original disembarkation from *Clotilda*) that became known as Africatown. The fierce determination of those Africans and their descendants to create a community and to tell and hold onto their own history during the subsequent 160 years has inspired our nation and propelled continuing archaeological research on Africatown and the ship *Clotilda*.[1]

Public interest in Africatown's compelling history has grown steadily for over a century. In 1914, Mobile writer and artist Emma Langdon Roche first published a version of the *Clotilda* epic based on her conversations over many years with the few *Clotilda* Africans still living in her day: "Five women, Abaché (Clara Turner), Monabee (Kitty Cooper), Shamber, Kanko, and Zooma; and three men, Poleete, Kazoola (Cudjoe Lewis), and Olouala (Orsey Kan)" (fig. 32.1). Roche used their Yoruba names in her narrative,

32.1. Abaché and Kossula in Africatown, ca. 1912, photographed by Emma Langdon Roche (*Historic Sketches of the South*, opposite page 79). (Center for Archaeological Studies, University of South Alabama.)

"at their request, . . . because in some way these names might drift back to their native home, where some might remember them."[2]

By the mid-1920s, Roche's sympathetic account attracted the attention of Franz Boas, the preeminent anthropologist of his day, at Columbia University. Boas saw ethnographic potential in the Africatown residents' story, so he sent one of his most promising graduate students, a young Black woman from Notasulga, Alabama, named Zora Neale Hurston, to Mobile to conduct additional interviews. Hurston's initial fieldwork at Africatown went poorly. Kossula or Cudjo (as his names are usually spelled today) was initially reluctant to talk with her, and she had difficulty understanding his heavily accented English (fig. 32.2).

32.2. Kossula (Cudjo Lewis) at his home in Africatown, circa 1928. (Courtesy of Erik Overbey Collection, Doy Leale McCall Rare Book and Manuscript Library, University of South Alabama, N-3446.)

Perhaps because she collected little new information, Hurston's resultant 1927 article, published in the *Journal of Negro History*, was largely plagiarized from Roche's book. Boas detected the plagiarism, confronted a regretful Hurston—who would soon become an accomplished novelist, playwright, folklorist, anthropologist, and an important contributor to the Harlem Renaissance—and sent her back to Mobile. Over the course of several months in 1928, Kossula warmed to Hurston, who successfully conducted many hours of interviews. She devoted much of the next three years to crafting an innovative manuscript that captured, to the best of her ability, Kossula's own dialect, in contrast to the florid reworked quotes found in Roche's account. At the time, no publisher would accept this experiment in "literary anthropology"; *Barracoon* at last appeared in print to much acclaim in 2018.[3]

Historical research by Natalie Robertson and Sylviane Diouf (published in 2008 and 2009) unearthed a great deal more information on Kossula's life in Africa, as well as the history of Africatown, which sparked archaeological interest in that community and a renewed search for the long-lost *Clotilda*. While the discovery and ongoing study of the *Clotilda* wreck (site 1BA704) is a fascinating saga, well told by others, involvement by staff with the University of South Alabama's Center for Archaeological Studies has focused on the Africatown site (1MB592).[4]

Modern industrial and highway developments since 1960 have severely

32.3. Buried utilities and other features revealed by ground-penetrating radar (GPR) survey at the Africatown Visitor Center site. (Center for Archaeological Studies, University of South Alabama.)

impacted Africatown, leveling historic structures and physically dispersing community members. With the current rise in interest in *Clotilda* and Africatown, community leaders have constructed a Heritage House that will help refocus the community and provide descendants of *Clotilda* survivors with a place to commemorate their families' stories. Plans also call for a Visitor Center to inform and accommodate tourists. This new building will occupy a prominent landform known as Graveyard Alley, adjacent to historic Old Plateau Cemetery.

In 2010 Neil Norman, from the College of William and Mary, carried out the first substantial archaeological fieldwork at Africatown at the Peter Lee house site, Lewis Quarter, and in Old Plateau Cemetery. Earlier preservationists had already located and mapped 1,699 graves, including those of *Clotilda* survivors Innie (Annie) Keeby and Lottie Dennison. Norman documented interments from the 1870s and suggested that earlier graves would have been marked with wooden crosses that have not survived.[5]

Because a place named Graveyard Alley clearly needed to be investigated before construction of the Visitor Center, Justin Dunnavant (assistant professor of anthropology at the University of California, Los Angeles) and Phil Carr codirected investigations there in 2019 for the Center for Archaeological Studies (fig. 32.3). To determine whether Old Plateau Cemetery, which is listed on the Alabama Historic Cemetery Register, extended into the proposed location of the Africatown Visitor Center, Dunnavant devised a four-pronged approach: a ground-penetrating radar (GPR) survey, limited archaeological excavation, historical records research, and oral histories. Each segment of the study was conducted independently to provide multiple lines of evidence that together would permit strong conclusions about the presence or absence of graves or any other significant archaeological deposits in the project tract.[6]

Concerns for the possibility of human burials at Graveyard Alley were heightened by a rumor that Africatown community elders recalled marked graves there during their youth. Folklorist and historian Kern Jackson, who had conducted oral history interviews previously in the community, explored this rumor with elders who documented memories of graves outside the current boundaries of Old Plateau Cemetery but not in the proposed location of the Visitor Center. Interviewees instead recalled houses once standing at that location, and one elder remembered delivering newspapers to those houses over fifty years ago.[7]

Standard archaeological techniques included a walkover, called a pedestrian survey, to look for artifacts and clues ("lumps and bumps") in

32.4. Shovel testing the Africatown Visitor Center site. (Center for Archaeological Studies, University of South Alabama.)

the terrain, digging 101 shovel tests systematically across the project tract, and excavation of two units. Shovel testing recovered seventy-nine artifacts: glass, ceramics, and nails, as well as modern debris (plastic, rubber, clothing), most dating to the mid- to late twentieth century (fig. 32.4). The few nineteenth-century artifacts included transfer-printed whiteware. All of these finds point to residential occupation of the tract. Unit excavations revealed that the site had suffered modern disturbances from demolition of the residential structures, land leveling, and construction.

Historical records researchers located deeds pertaining to the project area from 1868 to 2017. The tract was originally part of a ten-acre parcel containing a residential dwelling purchased by L. McKay in 1868, before the earliest interments identified in the Old Plateau Cemetery. Historic maps and records consistently document the area of the proposed Visitor Center as residential.

The success of GPR for revealing human graves is well documented, although early cemeteries can be difficult to delineate because burial accoutrements are minimal, caskets decompose, and soil formation processes mute the differences between graves and undisturbed soil. Howard Cyr of GeoArch Solutions conducted the GPR survey of the Visitor Center tract and found two kinds of linear radar reflections likely associated with buried utilities and possible house foundations.

Each line of evidence, gathered independently by different research teams, concluded that graves are not located at the proposed Visitor Center site. This area had been occupied by private residences, with primary occupation in the mid-twentieth century. Furthermore, judging from results of the shovel testing, unit excavations, and GPR survey, the house locations indicated by the oral history interviews and historical records research were shown to have been severely impacted by modern disturbances to the landscape.

Doing archaeology in a public space so thoroughly rooted in the injustice of slavery and the continuing impacts of racialized inequality in America has challenged us all to consider how we can advocate and act for justice and equality. Dunnavant joined six other African American archaeologists in a forum-style article in a 2021 issue of the professional journal *American Antiquity*. "'The Future of Archaeology Is Antiracist': Archaeology in the Time of Black Lives Matter" offers several recommendations for the discipline. Dunnavant and his coauthors urge archaeologists to identify and break down barriers to racial equity in archaeology, build an antiracist foundation for a new kind of archaeology, expand one's own understanding, and share a commitment to mentorship. They wrote, "We believe that the foundation of a house of antiracist archaeology is built in collaboration with accomplices.... This complicity comes in the form of placing one's privilege, body, career, and future on the line, all for the advancement and equitable treatment of those who have been historically oppressed."[8]

There remains a great untapped potential for significant archaeological research in the Africatown community. With the high-level of attention brought by the play *An Ocean in My Bones* and by Margaret Brown and Kern Jackson's recent award-winning documentary film, *Descendant*, which highlights the ongoing efforts of descendants of *Clotilda*'s survivors to reclaim their history, well-deserved attention continues to shine on Africatown and the story of its people. The University of South Alabama's Center for Archaeological Studies stands ready to support the people of the Africatown community in the investigation of their past. We will strive toward an antiracist archaeology and becoming accomplices in these efforts.[9]

CHAPTER 33

Camp Withers

> . . . a Confederate cavalry camp and a base for beach patrols during the Civil War, before the fall of Fort Morgan, provides a rare glimpse of everyday life experienced by common soldiers during periods of relative inactivity between battles.

Before the Battle of Mobile Bay on August 5, 1864, when Adm. David Farragut's Union fleet famously ran past Confederate-held Forts Morgan and Gaines at the mouth of Mobile Bay, federal naval vessels stationed off Alabama's coast blockaded the strategically vital port of Mobile (fig. 33.1). To retain Confederate control of the coast in this region, from August 1863 until the fall of Fort Morgan one year later, two companies of the Sixth and Seventh Alabama Cavalry Regiments patrolled the beaches of Baldwin County from their base at Camp Withers, located in modern-day Gulf Shores.[1]

33.1. Sketch of USS *Pocahontas* capturing blockade runner *Antona* near Mobile, by Alfred R. Waud and William Waud, 1863. (Library of Congress, Prints and Photographs Division, J. P. Morgan Collection of Civil War Drawing, DRWG/US-Waud, no. 458, 2004660864.)

Camp Withers played a strictly defensive role in the Civil War. No battles occurred there. Historians and archaeologists have largely ignored minor posts of this sort, although the day-to-day activities of troops at Camp Withers were the normal experiences of soldiers on both sides during the war.

One day after Christmas in 1863, Pvt. C. P. Watt of the Sixth Alabama Cavalry wrote to his young children from Camp Withers to explain his absence during the holiday: "The Yankees have boats in the Gulf, and we have boats in the Bay. On a narrow place between the two we have two forts, with large guns mounted on them so that the Yankees cannot pass into the Bay without being shot at. So they keep their boats in the gulf watching our boats. . . . We cavalry are stationed all along the shore below the fort way down to the Saltworks to keep them from landing and attacking the fort or breaking up the Saltworks. . . . We ride along [the shore] all times of the night & the day." In mid-January Watt wrote to his wife, Fannie: "We have been doing finely however, notwithstanding the cold and inclement weather. . . . We sit around the fire and parch corn when we cannot get Potatoes or Ground peas. About the only inconvenience is not getting any mail."[2]

Cavalrymen rode the shoreline continually, from outpost to outpost. The Baldwin County coastal zone was divided into three patrol areas: between Fort Morgan and Lagoon Post (twelve miles east of the fort, on Little Lagoon), on to Camp Withers (ten miles farther east), and thence to Camp Andrew at the Bon Secour salt works and Camp Powell near Perdido River (an additional twenty miles). Failure to complete a patrol between Camp Withers and Lagoon Post on the night of April 7, 1864, led to a private's court martial and sentence "to stand upon the head of a barrel" for two hours a day for five days.[3]

Watching smugglers evade Union gunboats provided some entertainment for the coastal cavalry pickets. In July, a closely pursued blockade runner "had to throw overboard part of her cargo in order to increase her speed." One box floated ashore and was found to contain stationery, ink, and pencils valued at $5,000. Pvt. C. T. Pope, Company B, Seventh Alabama Cavalry, wrote to his wife from Camp Withers about the incident on a sheet of that smuggled stationery.[4]

Camp Withers lost its purpose after the fall of Fort Morgan. Proceeding to the rail head at Pollard, the regiments' horses were loaded into boxcars and the men rode on top to join Gen. Nathan B. Forrest in Mississippi. In March 1865, as Union forces converged on the Confederate stronghold at Spanish Fort, several divisions of the Thirteenth US Army Corps marched past abandoned Camp Withers, burning the camp's buildings on their departure (fig. 33.2).

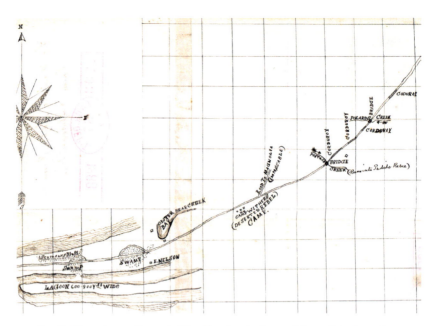

33.2. Detail of Capt. Arnout Cannon's "Map Showing the Route of the 1st Brigade, 2nd Division, 13th Army Corps, from Pilot town to Spanish Fort, Ala., March 18 to March 31, 1865," with "Camp Withers (Deserted Rebel Camp)." (National Archives, RG 77, Papers Related to Campaign of Mobile, Box 7, File A2203, Entry 87.)

In October 1995, proposed construction of an apartment complex prompted shovel testing, metal detector survey, and test excavation of site 1BA330, with Warren Carruth and George Shorter leading field efforts by Center for Archaeological Studies staff, assisted by Ray Keene and Jody Badillo. A one-hundred-foot diameter artifact scatter turned out to be the burned remains of a rectangular wooden plank building containing Civil War–era artifacts. Local historian John O'Donnell-Rosales relayed information he had heard from three relic hunters who thought they had found Camp Withers in the 1960s. Although they wished to remain anonymous, the trio told O'Donnell-Rosales that they had metal detected minié balls, horse bits, brass military buttons, and cut nails at the intersection of State Highways 59 and 180, where a shopping center now stands. Site 1BA330, with similar finds, lay a few hundred yards to the west, evidently an outlying part of the Confederate cavalry camp.[5]

The artifact assemblage from 1BA330 includes few domestic items: sherds of a large stoneware storage crock, a stoneware beer bottle, and four whiteware table vessels. The more abundant glass came from apothecary bottles, wine and bitters bottles, and lamp globes. Apart from hundreds of nails and brick fragments (but no window glass), most of the remaining

33.3. Minié balls melted together inside a now-vanished wooden box (site 1BA330). (Center for Archaeological Studies, University of South Alabama.)

artifacts are military: two "dropped" minié balls (one .69 caliber and one Sharps .54 caliber), iron gun parts, buckles, a broken Confederate-style brass spur, a six-pound laundry iron, a harmonica reed, two ceramic smoking pipes, and burned peach pits and pecan shells. Perhaps most interesting are four prewar brass military buttons—two US General Service and two of a type worn by US Infantry officers—and a 5.5-pound slab of melted lead, the remains of a burned wooden box of minié balls (fig. 33.3).

The scarcity of Confederate military artifacts remains puzzling twenty-five years later. Federal forces may have briefly occupied the building on their march north to Spanish Fort, but we suspect the eclectic nature of provisioning for state troops better explains the presence of prewar buttons.

CHAPTER 34

Spanish Fort

> . . . an earthwork water battery built by the Spanish military next to an abandoned British plantation sometime after 1780 was altered by Confederate engineers and underwent a siege in 1865, as revealed by archaeological excavation.

One of the final major battles of the Civil War, the siege of Spanish Fort, occurred between March 27 and April 8, 1865, on high bluffs overlooking the northeast corner of Mobile Bay, now part of the modern city of Spanish Fort. This extensive battlefield remained essentially undisturbed until the 1950s when the Fuller family began developing Spanish Fort Estates. That era also brought advances in metal detector technology and a boom in hobbyist metal detecting, which led to Spanish Fort (and all other Civil War–related sites around the country) being stripped of metal artifacts. Housing developments continue to whittle away at the battlefield, although the Fullers and other private landowners, as well as the city, have set aside significant areas for preservation. The Center for Archaeological Studies has had several opportunities to investigate portions of the Confederate defenses and Union siege works in the city of Spanish Fort.[1]

The name Spanish Fort implies the existence of a pre–Civil War structure dating to Mobile's Spanish colonial period (1780–1813). In his 1894 reminiscence of the Civil War siege, Maj. Gen. Dabney Maury, commander of the Confederacy's Department of the Gulf, wrote: "Spanish Fort was an old earth work on the east bank of Apalachia river [now, Blakeley River], which had been erected and occupied by the Spaniards more than a hundred years ago." We have no reason to doubt Maury's statement, but to date, we lack unambiguous documentary evidence for a colonial fort in that spot. In the ambiguous evidence category is Maxfield Ludlow's depiction of an "Old British [not Spanish] Fort" on his 1817 map of the Gulf Coast, north of D'Olive Creek in roughly the correct location.[2]

Confederate commanders in the Mobile area ordered construction of defensive works at "the old Spanish Fort" on August 12, 1864, following Union success in the Battle of Mobile Bay on August 5. A manuscript map drafted that summer for Confederate chief engineer Victor von Sheliha shows the state of the colonial earthwork before modification by his work force, with five cannon embrasures on the river side and two bastions on the land side (fig. 34.1). Between mid-August and the end of October, according to Sheliha, the 2,100-man garrison and an enslaved workforce brought downriver from the salt works in Clarke County raised the height of the old fort's parapets, built gun platforms, constructed two bombproof magazines (for munitions and the commissary), added a postern (a concealed rear entrance on the landward side), and mounted artillery in the old fort. To further protect the rear (landward) side of this water battery, newly built Fort McDermott and two other redoubts were connected by 1.25 miles of breastwork trenches, rifle pits, and abatis (sharpened stakes).[3]

In 1997, University of South Alabama field archaeology students directed by Greg Waselkov and Bonnie Gums carried out preliminary mapping, shovel tests, and test unit excavations at the fort site, 1BA336. Over

34.1. Detail of "Map of Spanish Fort and Vicinity, Drawn under the Direction of Lieut. Col. V. Sheliha." (Courtesy of Jeremy Francis Gilmer Papers, #276. Southern Historical Collection, Wilson Library, University of North Carolina at Chapel Hill.).

34.2. Ashley Dumas troweling a stepped excavation trench though the Spanish Fort parapet (1BA336), January 1998. (Center for Archaeological Studies, University of South Alabama.)

the course of three days in January 1998, center archaeologists Waselkov, Gums, George Shorter, and Ashley Dumas directed a larger excavation across the Spanish Fort parapet, assisted by volunteers from the Twenty-First Alabama Infantry Civil War Reenactors group led by Donnie Barrett and by members of the Spanish Fort Historical Society led by Shawn Holland. A grant from the Alabama Historical Commission and matching funds from the city of Spanish Fort supported this public archaeology event, made possible by landowners William and Paula Barnhill.[4]

The parapet today stands 3.5 meters above the fort interior, reduced from its wartime height by erosion. Our twenty-one-meter-long trench cut through the eastern parapet, from the exterior moat edge to the fort interior (fig. 34.2). The soil profile exposed in the trench walls consisted of many thin, multicolored layers of soil, which revealed how the parapet had been constructed in stages (fig. 34.3). Evidently the original builders used horse-drawn slips to spread soils brought from different locations—yellow sand from the 1.4-meter-deep moat, along with brown silty topsoil and orange clays from elsewhere.

We then widened our trench to intersect the eastern entryway to Spanish Fort, a low section of the parapet that looked like a gateway or sally port. However, excavations revealed a postern (as Sheliha had reported), an earth-covered, plank-lined tunnel connecting the fort interior to the moat. Intense burning had consumed the supporting pine posts and roof boards, causing the collapse of the tunnel and overlying dirt. Once these dramatic features were photographed and recorded, we backfilled the trench and restored the parapet to its prior appearance to help preserve this rare composite colonial/Civil War battlefield structure. Remains of magazines, gun platforms, and other features may still exist in the fort interior, although unfortunately the entire western half of the Spanish Fort was demolished in the 1960s for construction of a private home (fig. 34.4).

34.3. Profiles through the Spanish Fort parapet, showing construction layers stacked above the dark-brown British colonial-era plowzone, January 1998. (Center for Archaeological Studies, University of South Alabama.)

34.4. Old Spanish Fort, from a postcard dating ca. 1920, showing two of five cannon embrasures in the western portion of the earthwork that was destroyed in the 1960s by house construction. (Courtesy of Alabama Department of Archives and History, Q70068.)

We had hoped to find physical evidence of the original Spanish construction activities beneath the Confederate rebuilding layers. Despite screening all excavated parapet dirt and moat fill through one-quarter-inch mesh to retrieve small artifacts, we found none attributable to the Spanish colonial period. In fact, apart from a few Civil War–era minié balls and percussion caps and some flaked stone tools dating to a Late Archaic (ca. 3000–1000 BC) occupation of the bluff, most artifacts relate to Augustin Rochon's nearby British colonial plantation (1764–80). Fragments of creamware ceramic vessels and shell tabby cement came from a plowed layer of brown silty loam at the base of the fort parapet profile, a buried portion of the Rochons' agricultural field that predates fort construction (fig. 34.5).

As a consequence, we know the earthwork does not date to the British colonial period since it was constructed after destruction of the Rochon Plantation in 1780, which marks the beginning of Spanish colonial rule in this location. Despite the absence of Spanish colonial artifacts, we can conclude with considerable confidence that the lower portion of the parapet revealed in our excavation was built during the Spanish colonial period. The shape of the "old Spanish Fort" drawn on the 1864 Confederate engineer's preconstruction plan is essentially identical to the partial fort outline that exists today. Our excavations confirmed Sheliha's statement that the Confederates altered a Spanish colonial earthwork by raising the parapet height and adding a postern tunnel.[5]

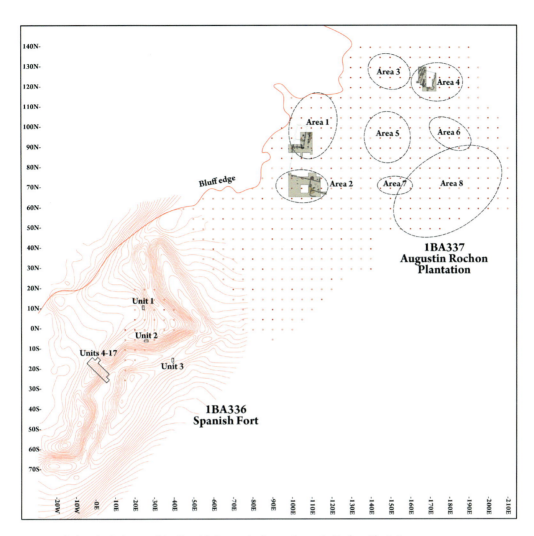

34.5. Archaeological map of the Spanish Fort and adjacent Augustin Rochon Plantation site, with shovel tests (positive tests darkened) and excavation Units 4–17 placed across the collapsed fort postern. (Graphic by Sarah Mattics, Center for Archaeological Studies, University of South Alabama.)

In 2006, center archaeologist George Shorter, with assistance from Donnie Barrett, mapped features of Carr's Front, part of the north siege line preserved by Spanish Fort Estates Trail, a city-owned park located between Watch Tower Drive and Cora Slocomb Drive. This included the Union Army's first parallel trenches, a large portion of the second parallel, approach trenches, the Eighth Iowa sap trench, redoubts, batteries, magazines, shelters, and rifle pits. At least one Confederate rifle pit was identified on the west side of the park.[6]

One year later, Shorter returned to map three lunette earthworks—Batteries 8, 9, and 11—and associated trenches at the center of the Union siege line, on property being developed as Garrison Ridge Subdivision. On March 27, 1865, Brig. Gen. William P. Benton's Third Division of the Thirteenth Army Corps occupied this location, eight hundred to one thousand meters east of the Confederate defensive line. Construction and strengthening of these features continued throughout the siege. We recommended preservation of these exceptionally well-preserved battlefield features, archaeological site 1BA594. However, the site owners and developers did not consider avoidance of any earthworks to be economically feasible and elected to proceed with mitigation of their development by full-scale archaeological excavation. Shorter's field crew documented the siege works and recovered a variety of associated artifacts, but the loss of these intact features of a major Civil War battlefield was a great disappointment.[7]

CHAPTER 35

1865 Ordnance Explosion

> ... which leveled a large part of Mobile's waterfront district, with great loss of life, destroyed all but the foundations of antebellum cotton warehouses preserved in the waterlogged soils found at the northern industrial end of the Civil War–era city.

In the 1920s Peter Joseph Hamilton, Mobile's preeminent colonial historian, jotted down his childhood memories of a traumatic event known simply as the Great Explosion. On Thursday, May 25, 1865, at half past two in the afternoon, a vast stockpile of Confederate munitions blew up, killing hundreds and destroying much of the city's port district (fig. 35.1). As a six-year-old, Peter recalled, he "was on top of the fence at the foot of the garden with my Mammy," when the ground shook violently, three

35.1. *Explosion of the U.S. Magazine at Mobile, 1865*, lithograph drawing by J. F. Young. (Courtesy of Wisconsin Historical Society, WHS-70628, Lithograph PH 5–1254.)

times in quick succession. "As we looked fearfully toward the city, over it swept a black cloud, dividing in two in the wind." A poetic insurance adjuster, Charles Fondé, described the fearsome cloud as "a writhing giant—gaunt and grim—poised in mid air, from whose wondrous loins sprang bursting shells, flying timbers, bales of cotton, barrels of rosin, bars and sheets of iron, bricks, stones, wagons, horses, men, women and children, commingled and mangled into one immense mass."[1]

Since the city's surrender to federal forces on April 12, fatigue parties of Union troops had been dismantling defensive fortifications and seizing all manner of weaponry abandoned by departing Confederate forces. The US Army Ordnance Department had commandeered four warehouses on the north end of town near the river to serve as magazines for small arms and artillery munitions—gunpowder, minié ball cartridges, carbine and pistol ammunition, canister and solid shot, percussion shells and fuses, as well as "torpedoes" (naval and land mines).[2]

The explosion occurred while a work detail of men drawn from the Fifty-First US Colored Troops, Twenty-Third Wisconsin Volunteers, and Twenty-Ninth Illinois Volunteers unloaded artillery shells from wagons for storage in Pomeroy and Marshall's Warehouse at Lipscomb and Water Streets. A military court of inquiry, held in June, found evidence for "gross and culpable carelessness on the part of the fatigue party in handling the fixed ammunition," although the immediate cause of the explosion could not be determined, "as there are no survivors of the accident."[3]

"The explosion was distinctly heard at this place," wrote Capt. William McMicken to his wife, Rowena, from an encampment of the Tenth Minnesota Infantry Volunteers near Meridian, Mississippi, 140 miles from Mobile. "Many were killed and maimed at the distance of a mile from where the powder was confined. Carriages were smashed to pieces at the same distance, and the sash and glass of the intire city broken. The number killed will never be known, as many were blown to fragments, and nearly all so mutalated that they could not be recognized. Up to yesterday morning, 300 bodies had been removed from the ruins, and they were still finding more"[4] (fig. 35.2).

Up to that point, Mobile, the last major port of the Confederacy to fall to Union forces, "had, under a kind Providence," according to one resident, "been mercifully spared the destruction that had befallen other Southern cities." Mobile's fortunes changed in an instant, as the blast devastated thirty-four blocks of the city's industrial infrastructure, everything north of St. Anthony and east of Conception Street (fig. 35.3). An appeal to the federal government for indemnity, compiled in August 1865 by Fondé for the Mobile Insurance Company, documented personal losses of $728,892.

35.2. "Awful calamity at Mobile, Ala.—Scene among the ruins after the explosion of the Ordnance Depot and Magazine, May 25," from *Frank Leslie's Illustrated Newspaper*, June 17, 1865, 200–201. (Center for Archaeological Studies, University of South Alabama.)

35.3. "Explosion in Mobile, Ala., 1865," spliced photographic panorama. (Courtesy of Doy Leale McCall Rare Book and Manuscript Library, University of South Alabama, Carlisle Barracks C-4184.)

The company's clients requested compensation for eleven thousand cotton bales and partial or total destruction of thirty-nine warehouses, eight cotton presses, three wharves, three machine shops and foundries, a blacksmith shop, stables, a marble works, an icehouse, at least thirty-four masonry store buildings, four residences, the Battle House Hotel, and the Mobile & Ohio Railroad freight and passenger depots. The steamboats *Kate Dale* and *Col. Cowles*, docked at Mobile River wharves, were also lost to fire. No compensation was ever awarded to affected business owners.[5]

An opportunity for archaeology in Mobile's antebellum warehouse district arose in 1999 during planning for improved highway access to the Alabama State Docks. Engineers with the Alabama Department of Transportation proposed building an elevated roadway over Dekle Street and the adjacent CSX and Amtrack rail line, a route that would require construction in the block bounded by Beauregard (formerly Hunt), Magnolia, Lipscomb, and Delchamps (formerly Water) Streets. Pomeroy and Marshall's

35.4. Weighing cotton, Magnolia Cotton Warehouse, 1894. (Courtesy of Doy Leale McCall Rare Book and Manuscript Library, University of South Alabama, Windsor Negative Sleeve 11 #30, C-196.)

35.5. Block 2 excavation at Dekle Street site (1MB34), looking east. Wall A, on salvaged wooden grillage in the middle, and associated piers to left are all parts of the ca. 1852 Ketchum Warehouse. Wall B, in distance at far right, is part of the postwar Magnolia Warehouse. (Center for Archaeological Studies, University of South Alabama.)

Warehouse, epicenter of the 1865 magazine explosion, stood immediately east of the location that the Center for Archaeological Studies excavated.[6]

This area had been a low-lying marshland during Mobile's colonial period. However, land reclamation efforts during the early nineteenth century, involving routine disposal of refuse and building demolition debris, eventually raised ground surfaces and permitted new construction

35.6. Block 2 excavation at Dekle Street site, looking northeast. Wall B, on rough sawn pine plank grillage in foreground, is associated with an open shed of the circa 1885 Magnolia Warehouse. Wall A, from the circa 1852 Ketchum Warehouse, is in background. (Center for Archaeological Studies, University of South Alabama.)

throughout the city's burgeoning waterfront commercial district. By 1852, Ketchum's Warehouse stood in the project area.

From January to May 1999, George Shorter and Bonnie Gums with the Center for Archaeological Studies directed archaeological testing and excavations in this location. Their work revealed structural remains of two cotton warehouses, the earlier Ketchum Warehouse destroyed by the 1865 explosion and the Magnolia Warehouse built in its place after the war and (fig. 35.4). A five-meter-long section of masonry wall and four associated brick piers from the Ketchum Warehouse had been built on timbers designed to spread and support the weight of the massive structure on unconsolidated marshland (fig. 35.5). These "floating" wooden support beams, called grillage, which remained well preserved in the waterlogged soils, had mortises, tenons, and wooden pegs, reflecting the eighteenth- and early nineteenth-century origins of these salvaged and recycled timbers. A short segment of masonry wall from the postwar Magnolia Warehouse also rested upon grillage, in this case pine planks rough sawn to length specifically for this purpose, not salvaged wood (fig. 35.6).

Munitions from the 1865 explosion turned up in several locations.

A 12-pound spherical cannonball, three iron canister shot, iron shrapnel, four minié balls, and other assorted lead shot were found in and around a wooden walkway in the warehouse's cotton yard, and a single lead canister shot was discovered embedded in the top of the Ketchum Warehouse wall. Unauthorized metal detection probably took away additional evidence of the explosion before our arrival on the site.

To our surprise, we found no trace of the rubble created by the 1865 explosion, no sign of the millions of brickbats and other materials from the buildings destroyed by the blast. Instead of simply leveling the debris field and rebuilding on it, evidently the site had been thoroughly cleared before rebuilding. Why did the survivors of this disaster choose to sweep the lot clean and where did the debris end up? Those questions remain unanswered, although we suspect additional land reclamation of Mobile River marshland to the east occurred in the aftermath of the Great Explosion.

PART X

LATE NINETEENTH CENTURY

CHAPTER 36

Spring Hill College

. . . where construction of a new library at this Jesuit school provided an opportunity to recover the material remains of campus life experienced by students, staff, and faculty during the nineteenth and early twentieth centuries.

In 2002, administrators at the University of South Alabama called on staff at the Center for Archaeological Studies to check campus locations before development of a proposed research park, a campus shuttle route, and an expansion of the Department of Psychology's primate research center. Those surveys turned up five small sites south of Three Mile Creek (1MB175, 1MB176, 1MB350, 1MB358, 1MB360). All had been plowed in recent times, leaving scatters of pottery and stone artifacts accumulated during multiple occupations dating to the Early Woodland Bayou La Batre phase (ca. 700–100 BC) and Late Woodland Tates Hammock and Coden phases (ca. AD 650–1150). Several of these sites were also occupied during the late nineteenth and early twentieth centuries by tenant households living in wooden frame structures built on piers of stone and brick.[1]

In 2007, we took a different approach to campus archaeology and hosted a summer camp, directed by Phil Carr and Deborah Lawrence, designed specifically for disadvantaged youths who excavated a mockup of an archaeological site created behind the center's facility. In addition to piece plotting stratified faux-archaeological deposits, participants engaged with center staff and students in laboratory processing of artifacts, and, at session's end, they gave oral reports of their findings. Archaeology became more than a treasure hunt for these youths immersed in the full process of archaeological research. Such intense and time-consuming experiences have the desired impact, but the cost has precluded a repeat of this educational opportunity.

Archaeology on our own campus has proven worthwhile in a variety of ways, but those projects were not designed to delve into the origins and evolution of our relatively young university, established in 1963. At universities with deeper historical roots, campus excavations have uncovered important evidence of student life during earlier eras. Perhaps unsurprisingly, archaeological field school digs at Harvard University (founded as Harvard College in 1631) have led to many revelations about student life in the seventeenth and eighteenth centuries. Students comprise one of those all-too-common social categories (along with women, the impoverished, the illiterate, the enslaved, the racially or ethnically marginalized) who have been poorly served by a historical record written largely by and about adult males of privileged social classes. Of course, college students—likewise, until quite recently, mostly males from elite backgrounds—have typically belonged to that privileged category too. But the written historical record is also remarkably silent about the everyday lives of children and adolescents, no matter their upbringing, including young persons lodged in residential institutions, such as workhouses for the poor, orphanages, juvenile detention centers, and boarding schools.[2]

An opportunity arose in May 2002 to learn about student life in nineteenth-century Mobile when Father Gregory Lucy, president of Spring Hill College, requested an archaeological survey of a site proposed for a new library. Later that year, staff and students with the Center for Archaeological Studies conducted a major excavation in the heart of the Spring Hill College campus, directed by Bonnie Gums, at a location referred to as site 1MB356.[3]

The community of Spring Hill first formed around 1800, late in the Spanish colonial period, on the first high ground encountered on the road leading west from low-lying Mobile (now, the city's downtown), six miles away. That elevated location appealed to the town's wealthiest residents as a healthier summer home during yellow fever season, much preferable to swamp-encircled Mobile. In 1830, those same prominent families, many of French descent, supported Bishop Michael Portier's establishment of St. Joseph's College at Spring Hill. Portier recruited seminary priests from France to instruct Catholic young men at his diocesan school, the first permanent Roman Catholic college in the South and the second institution of higher learning in Alabama. (Classes began at the University of Alabama a few months before those at St. Joseph's College, in 1831.) When financial difficulties forced a reorganization of the college in 1847, Portier asked priests of the Society of Jesus from Lyons, France, to take charge of the school, renamed Spring Hill College.[4]

During those early years, three Jesuit professors and five lay teachers

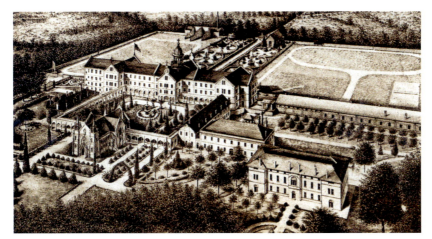

36.1. *Bird's-eye View Drawing of Spring Hill College, ca. 1915*, by art professor Paul Boudousquie, view to the south-southeast. (Spring Hill College Archives and Special Collections, Burke Memorial Library, Mobile, Alabama.)

provided instruction, mainly held in French, for a classical education emphasizing grammar, mathematics, history, geography, other languages (English, Latin, Greek, German, Spanish), and catechism, as well as philosophy, music, art, and sports. Such rigorous training produced more than a few exceptional graduates, including internationally renowned chess champion Paul Morphy. For many years boys as young as nine years old were admitted, until elementary and high school grades were discontinued in 1935. Faculty ties to Jesuit missions in Mexico and South America have always brought Hispanic students to the college. Women were first admitted in 1952, and, with the enrollment of eight Black students two years later, Spring Hill College became the first white college in the South to desegregate[5] (fig. 36.1).

Center excavations occurred in the original area of the Spring Hill College campus, which has undergone considerable rebuilding since 1830. The main school building (now the Administration Building), chapel, and library burned in 1869, and another fire in 1909 destroyed the chapel and damaged the main building. The site of our excavations, where Burke Memorial Library now stands, lay north of Moore Hall (originally the infirmary, dating to 1866) and the Administration Building and east of St. Joseph's Chapel, completed in 1910. Historic maps indicate that a kitchen, storehouse, and stables once stood in the area of Excavation Blocks 1 and 2, from circa 1830 to 1870 (fig. 36.2). Excavation Block 4 encompassed the site of a large wooden building described in documents as a laborer's residence, in use from 1830 to about 1870. And Excavation Block 3 corresponded to the location of a substantial, two-story brick structure that served mainly as a classroom building from circa 1870 to 1910. A large privy pit (Feature 13) found in Block 4 dated to the same period as the brick structure in Block 3[6] (fig. 36.3).

SPRING HILL COLLEGE   255

36.2. Block 1 excavations, view to the east from the second story of Moore Hall, July 2002. (Center for Archaeological Studies, University of South Alabama.)

36.3. Archaeologists Bryan Tate and Harriet Richardson Seacat recording the upper half of a large earthenware storage jar from Biot, France, used as a planter outside the entrance to Moore Hall and found during sewer line construction monitoring. (Center for Archaeological Studies, University of South Alabama.)

Feature 13, the privy pit, contained an amazing trove of artifacts, nearly ten thousand objects representing every aspect of life at Spring Hill College around the turn of the twentieth century. How these artifacts came to be discarded together around 1910 remains unclear. The fire of 1909 and subsequent construction of beautiful St. Joseph's Chapel, immediately to the west, may have prompted removal of the old classroom building and discard of obsolete furnishings into the privy pit. Certainly, the end of the privy's use and demolition of the classroom building coincided closely with the chapel's dedication (figs. 36.4 and 36.5).

Because students, Jesuit professors, lay instructors, and staff worked (and, in most cases, lived) in close proximity, these artifacts cannot be attributed to one group or another but instead represent the activities of the

36.4. Ceramic and glass inkwells from Feature 13 privy pit, Block 4. (Center for Archaeological Studies, University of South Alabama.)

36.5. Ironstone ceramic tablewares, in the plain white patterns often preferred by institutions, from various features dating ca. 1870–1910, Block 4. (Center for Archaeological Studies, University of South Alabama.)

entire college community. As one would expect, classroom-related artifacts are especially abundant, including pens and ink wells, hundreds of slate and wooden pencils, and many fragments of blackboard slate.

Among the most intriguing finds are 109 pieces of broken terracotta ceramic figurines, mostly human figures, all males (fig. 36.6). The larger busts clearly depict specific individuals, with clothing, hair, and facial features expertly sculpted in fine detail. Other figures, which stood on flat bases, seem to portray Asian men in dress of the period, accompanied by miniature hand-modeled loaves of bread, dinner plates and a pitcher, a bird, a pineapple, and a rifle. Nothing about these figures points to a religious or symbolic purpose; they bear no indications of Jesuit or Catholic iconography, even though religious medals and porcelain figurines are also present in the artifact assemblage (fig. 36.7). Rather, these well-wrought, but unglazed, low-fired sculptures seem simply to be art projects, perhaps attributable to students of Paul Boudousquie, the college's Paris-trained lay professor of art from 1872 until his death in 1925.

There is abundant evidence from the Spring Hill College excavations of the Jesuit faculty's continuing ties to France and French culture, in the many bottle seals from the major Bordeaux export wineries of Château Léoville, St. Julien Médoc, and Châteaux Lafite; French mineral water bottles; faience platters and ointment jars; a silver brooch made by a Paris

36.6. Terracotta figures from Feature 13 privy pit, Block 4. (Center for Archaeological Studies, University of South Alabama.)

36.7. French religious medals dedicated to St. Benedict, St. Gonzaga, the Guardian Angel, and the Virgin Mary (Miraculous medals), Blocks 3 and 4. (Center for Archaeological Studies, University of South Alabama.)

jeweler; a button from a Paris manufacturer; a suspender clasp made by the French company Chez Guyot; a brass signet for sealing wax; and numerous French religious medals. These artifacts document resilient economic connections and sentimental attachments to France, at least on the part of the Jesuit faculty. Considering Mobile's French colonial origins, though, these objects also reflect continuity in cultural tradition. To many modern-day Americans, annual Mardi Gras celebrations may seem the last lingering vestige of French influence on the Gulf Coast, but Spring Hill College and the archaeological remnants of its history reflect deeper and more meaningful ties to France.[7]

CHAPTER 37

Eastern Shore Potteries

> . . . examples of a once thriving industry on Mobile Bay, were intensively researched in the late 1990s, before most kiln sites were lost to urban development.

One day in mid-June 1995, a phone call from local historian and preservationist John H. "Jack" Friend alerted archaeologists at the Center for Archaeological Studies to the imminent destruction of a nineteenth-century pottery kiln (site 1BA276) in Montrose, on the Eastern Shore of Mobile Bay. Janie and Jim Shores (Janie was the first woman justice to serve on the Alabama Supreme Court) were about to build their new home atop a long-abandoned kiln. Jack asked the Shores, who were excited to learn about the old kiln on their property, if they would permit archaeological research. They readily agreed, but construction was already scheduled to begin the following Monday, leaving just one weekend for fieldwork.

During those two days of frenetic digging, a dozen volunteers uncovered the complete footprint of a rectangular kiln built from handmade bricks and oriented west to east to catch the prevailing onshore breeze during firing (fig. 37.1). Beneath the collapsed roof vaults were a pair of long rectangular chambers where newly turned stoneware pots had once been stacked for firing. At the west end, a recessed firebox inside the mouth of each chamber held the wood that fueled the kiln. A chimney once stood, probably at the east end, although no trace survived. Inside the kiln, thick deposits of emerald-green soda glass coated the remaining lower courses of bricks, residue from salt thrown into the kiln to glaze stoneware vessels over the course of dozens of firings.

Historical research unraveled the site's history. Augustin and Francis LaCoste, father and son immigrants from France, ran a stoneware pottery

37.1. Archaeologists Ray Keene, Amy Carruth, and Warren Carruth excavate a two-chambered salt glaze pottery kiln (1BA276) believed to have been used by the LaCoste and McAdam families from 1875 to 1895, Montrose, 1995. (Center for Archaeological Studies, University of South Alabama.)

in Baldwin County by 1830. Francis purchased the location of our kiln excavation in 1852 and operated the LaCoste Pottery in this general vicinity until his death twenty years later, when John and Peter McAdam, brothers recently immigrated from Glasgow, Scotland, acquired the business. Artifacts found in and around the excavated kiln date it to the McAdam era, 1875 to 1895.[1]

The fascinating results of this initial kiln excavation prompted us to seek out as many pottery production sites as possible. An upswing in the pace of private home construction on the Eastern Shore was rapidly obliterating remnants of what had once been a major industry on the north-central Gulf Coast. While center archaeologists carried out additional volunteer excavations at threatened pottery kiln sites, Greg Waselkov and Bonnie Gums obtained a grant from the Alabama Historical Commission in 1997 to survey all extant potteries. We collected information and artifacts at fifteen kiln sites, including Bluff (1BA524) (fig. 37.2), Cedar Brook (1BA326), James Beasley (1BA412, 1BA413), Steadman's Landing (1BA414), Fly Creek (1BA226, 1BA406), Gabel (1BA526), Howard (1BA404), Wingender (1BA418), Daphne (1BA370), and Captain O'Neal (1BA405, 1BA407, 1BA408). Gums reported the results of that research in her 2001 book, *Made of Alabama Clay: Historic Potteries of Mobile Bay*.

Pottery making has ancient roots along the Gulf Coast, with the oldest fiber-tempered pots dating to 1000 BC or earlier. As far as we know, all pottery made in Alabama before the nineteenth century was earthenware, which can be fired in the open at relatively low temperatures, between

37.2. Interior of one side of a nearly intact two-chambered salt glaze stoneware kiln (1BA524) built into the bluff at Montrose, in use during the 1880s and 1890s. (Center for Archaeological Studies, University of South Alabama.)

500° and 800°C (900° to 1500°F), which can be achieved with a wood fire on the ground surface. In contrast, clays found along the bayside bluffs (figs. 37.3 and 37.4) from Daphne to Fairhope proved to be particularly suitable for making a much harder kind of pottery, stoneware, which is fired to around 1300°C (2400°F), a temperature that requires a kiln. With an abundance of high-quality stoneware clay at hand, coupled with seemingly limitless supplies of firewood, dependable onshore breezes for kiln firings, and low-cost water transport of finished products to the nearby Mobile market, the Eastern Shore attracted potters familiar with stoneware production.[2]

In his classic study, *Alabama Folk Pottery*, folklorist Joey Brackner considers the Eastern Shore of Mobile Bay "the earliest and one of the most productive areas of historic pottery manufacture in Alabama." First to arrive were three families of French potters—the Mareschals, LaCostes, and Lefevres—who established potteries in the 1820s and 1830s producing salt-glazed stonewares. Recent archaeological excavations of stoneware production sites in France have documented the origin of the two-chambered kiln form seen at the LaCoste-McAdam site and three other Eastern Shore potteries, as well as a kiln at the town of Blakeley in northern Baldwin County (excavated in 1977 by University of South Alabama archaeologist Noel Read Stowe). An unusual variety of kiln furniture, including tall columnar stilts and eared shelves used to stack vessels in the kilns, also derives from traditional French methods of stoneware manufacture. The success of those pioneers in stoneware production attracted other immigrants from different parts of western Europe, including Scotland

37.3. Red Bluff, Ecor Rouge, a source of potting clay on the Eastern Shore of Mobile Bay in Montrose, 2003. (Center for Archaeological Studies, University of South Alabama.)

(McAdam), Ireland (Deady), and Germany (Wingender), as well as northern states (Howard, Miller).[3]

Between 1995 and 2002, center archaeologists, along with some enthusiastic volunteers and descendants of potting families, documented sixteen pottery production sites, including one at Fly Creek in Fairhope and three on Fish River south of the Eastern Shore potteries (fig. 37.5). Many of these kiln sites are now gone, although a few are preserved on private property. Fortunately, the pottery-making tradition that flourished here during the nineteenth century continues along several different paths. Descendants of Abraham Miller, who worked at the LaCoste pottery in the late 1860s, still operate Miller's Pottery near Brent, Alabama, carrying on a folk tradition with very deep roots in the South.

37.4. Unidentified worker at the Daphne Pottery Company clay pit in 1929. (Courtesy of University of Alabama Museums, photograph 5A-972A, Tuscaloosa.)

After the heyday of commercial stoneware potteries during the nineteenth century, those enterprises gradually lost ground to industrial bottle production and other competing technologies, as well as changing social norms. Demand for ceramic jugs, for instance, plummeted with Prohibition in 1919, never to recover. Artisans at the Daphne Pottery Company carried on the longest, until the 1950s, experimenting with new forms such as flowerpots, turpentine cups, puzzle jugs, flue thimbles, cemetery fence posts—anything ceramic the public might purchase (fig. 37.6).

37.5. Donnie Barrett and Kate Waselkov excavate a waster dump of salt glazed kiln furniture at the Montrose bluff kiln site (1BA524), 1995. (Center for Archaeological Studies, University of South Alabama.)

37.6. Potter, possibly Ed Grace, at the Daphne Pottery Company, October 15, 1929. (Courtesy of University of Alabama Museums, photograph 5A-973, Tuscaloosa.)

Charcoal braziers, a form unique to the Eastern Shore potteries, proved popular as portable heaters, smudge pots in orchards, and especially as cookers to prepare meals for picnics and on fishing boats, both commercial and private vessels.[4]

As folk and industrial pottery production faded, the superb clays of the Eastern Shore have continued to attract ceramic artists. In 1939 Edith Harwell, a ceramicist in the Arts and Crafts Movement, established Pinewood Pottery in Fairhope, where her kiln still stands today behind the Eastern Shore Arts Center. Tom Jones (a student of Harwell's), John Rezner, Lowell Webb, and Maria Spies are a few of today's studio-trained descendants of the region's early twentieth-century potteries.[5]

CHAPTER 38

Mount Vernon

. . . once the terminus of the Old Federal Road at Fort Stoddert, then the site of Mount Vernon Arsenal/Barracks, which held Apache prisoners of war, and finally Searcy Hospital, a state mental facility originally for Black patients, desegregated in 1969 and shuttered in 2012, now deteriorating and neglected, a worldclass historic site falling into ruin.

Centennials and bicentennials—anniversaries marking the passage of a century or two since certain momentous events—afford us opportunities to reflect on key moments in American history, ponder their consequences and current relevance, and perhaps reconsider their significance. The state of Alabama recently celebrated two bicentennials; one commemorated the establishment of Alabama Territory in 1817 and the other Alabama's statehood in 1819. The wave of immigration that spurred a rapid transition to statehood during those two years occurred, to a surprising degree, thanks to the prior existence of the region's first military and postal road, now known as the Old Federal Road, blazed between Milledgeville, Georgia, and Fort Stoddert, Mississippi Territory, in 1811.[1]

In 1805 Pres. Thomas Jefferson's administration negotiated treaties with leaders of all of the most populous southeastern Indigenous nations, including the Muscogee Creek Nation. Most ordinary Creeks, however, generally opposed concessions to the ever-acquisitive Americans and specifically disliked the treaty clause permitting construction of a military and postal road through their country. After several false starts at roadbuilding and some strongarm American diplomacy, the Creeks eventually permitted axe-wielding soldiers from the US Third Infantry Regiment to cut a road across their nation. As the Creeks had feared, conflicts with American travelers along the road increased tensions in the nation, which contributed to the rise of an anti-American political and religious faction, the Redsticks, and finally to outbreak of war with the Americans in 1813.

In anticipation of the Old Federal Road's bicentennial in 2011, Greg Waselkov obtained a grant for the Center for Archaeological Studies from the Alabama Department of Transportation to trace the road's original path through the state's modern landscape. He and Raven Christopher surveyed the entire route in 2010, with crucial assistance from local historical society members intimately familiar with their own counties. Two additional grants in 2009 and 2011 from the American Battlefield Protection program of the National Park Service enabled us to locate Redstick War–related sites near the Old Federal Road. Included among them was Samuel Moniac's homesite, where the Pintlala Historical Society sponsored a Public Archaeology Day event for local school children in 2010. All this road-related research culminated in a 2019 publication (with historian Kathryn H. Braund), an illustrated guide to the Old Federal Road for adventurous souls who wish to explore remnants of early Alabama on the ground.[2]

President Jefferson had promoted the road to Congress as the best way to bind newly acquired New Orleans and the Louisiana Purchase to the rest of the country. However, the road's actual southern terminus was not New Orleans but Fort Stoddert, a US military post on the Mobile River thirty miles north of Mobile (since that city remained part of Spanish West Florida). Established in 1799 on the southern boundary of Mississippi Territory, Fort Stoddert also served as an official port of entry along the US-Spanish border. Publication there of the *Mobile Centinel* in 1811 introduced journalism to Alabama, but the fort lost its strategic importance and was abandoned by 1815, not long after transfer of Mobile from Spanish to American hands at the end of the Redstick War.[3]

The fort site is privately owned today and has never been investigated by professional archaeologists, although students enrolled in a University of South Alabama field methods class led by Noel Read Stowe in 1976 gathered a small collection of artifacts eroding from a riverside ravine once used as a trash dump by the fort's garrison. Richard Fuller studied that collection in the 1990s and recognized many pieces of ceramic bowls decorated with fine parallel incised lines as a distinctive Choctaw pottery type called Chickachae Combed. Fort Stoddert, situated on the west bank of the Mobile River, had been constructed at the southeastern limits of the Choctaw homeland. The Mobile-Washington County (MOWA) Choctaws who live in the area today descend from some of the women who made the combed bowls purchased, used, and discarded by soldiers at Fort Stoddert.[4]

38.1. US Arsenal at Mount Vernon, Alabama, an inset of John La Tourette's 1838 *Map of the State of Alabama*. (Courtesy of David Rumsey Map Collection, David Rumsey Map Center, Stanford Libraries.)

The fort was considered an unhealthy place, with high mortality every summer mainly due to yellow fever, rightly attributed at the time to the proximity of the swampy Mobile-Tensaw delta. In 1811 the US Army built Mount Vernon Cantonment on a high hill four miles west of Fort Stoddert, where most of the garrison relocated during the hottest and sickliest months. After a decade of abandonment, that hill became the site of Mount Vernon Arsenal, which served as a federal depot for military small arms and munitions from the mid-1830s onward (fig. 38.1).

38.2. First Apache village at Mount Vernon Barracks. Photograph by G. B. Johnson, 1891. (Courtesy of Alabama Department of Archives and History, Silas Orlando Trippe Photograph Collection, SPP46.)

Mount Vernon Barracks, as the arsenal was known after 1873, gained nationwide notoriety with the arrival in 1887–88 of nearly four hundred Apaches (Chiricahua, Chokonen, and Chihene Southern Apaches, and some intermarried Mescalero Western Apaches). Here Geronimo and his small band, consisting of family and followers, were incarcerated alongside other Southern Apache bands who had fought with US troops against Geronimo—all treated, with astounding injustice, as Apache prisoners of war[5] (fig. 38.2).

Many of their relatives had died of malaria and tuberculosis the previous year while imprisoned in St. Augustine, Florida, so officials, and the Apaches themselves, hoped the move to Mount Vernon would improve their health. But the new internment camp added dysentery from contaminated drinking water to their troubles. Deep despair of ever returning to the mountains of Arizona claimed many more lives. Years later, Eugene Chihuahua, a small boy during the Apache's exile in Alabama, recalled how his people had not "known what misery was till they dumped us in those swamps" at Mount Vernon Barracks. "There was no place to climb to pray.... If we wanted to see the sky we had to climb a tall pine."[6]

The Apaches were put to work on arrival, building sixty-two small log cabins outside the west wall of the military compound, a location prone to swarms of mosquitoes, lack of breeze, and contaminated water supply.

38.3. Young girls at the second Apache village, Mount Vernon Barracks, circa 1894. (Courtesy of William Wallace Wotherspoon Collection, United States Army Heritage and Education Center, Carlisle, Pennsylvania.)

MOUNT VERNON 269

After an inquiry by Walter Reed, the post surgeon, into the prisoners' living conditions, in 1892 the Apaches were permitted to construct larger frame houses on a ridge about a mile away, overlooking Mount Vernon Barracks (fig. 38.3). In 1894, the federal government moved the fewer than three hundred surviving Southern Apaches at Mount Vernon to their next place of exile, Fort Sill, Oklahoma.[7]

With the Apaches' departure, the US Army had no further use for Mount Vernon Barracks and transferred control of the property to the state of Alabama in 1895. Seven years later the state opened the Mount Vernon Insane Hospital for segregated care of Black mental patients under the direction of James Searcy (for whom it was renamed in 1919). The hospital was desegregated in 1969.[8]

Soon after the hospital opened, physician George Searcy, the superintendent's son, reported an epidemic of pellagra among his mental patients. He and other public health workers across the South had noted a correlation between poor diet and pellagra, a disease manifesting severe skin lesions, extreme weakness, intractable diarrhea, and dementia. Dementia was often characterized by early twentieth-century physicians as "acute mania" on death certificates. Research in the 1920s and 1930s identified pellagra as a nutritional disorder caused by deficiencies of vitamin B_3 (niacin) and the amino acid tryptophan. Most prone to pellagra were those in the South with diets consisting largely of corn (maize); they were the poor and the institutionalized, particularly those in orphanages, prisons, and mental hospitals where meal expenditures amounted to a few cents a day. Many centuries earlier, Native Americans discovered that soaking maize in alkaline water (made with wood ash), the same method used to produce hominy and grits in recent times, enhanced health. We now know this process releases niacin and tryptophan in maize that is otherwise undigested. The 1906 pellagra epidemic is thought to have been caused by a change in commercial maize processing that removed the germ from maize kernels, the source of most of the protein and niacin in corn. Searcy's efforts to publicize and treat pellagra played an important role in controlling and eventually preventing this devastating disease.[9]

Changing attitudes on the treatment of mental health patients led to closure in 2012 of Searcy Hospital. Alabama's Department of Mental Health successfully negotiated for outright ownership of the property with the US Department of Defense, which had retained title since 1895. Yet, since 2012, almost nothing has been done to maintain the historic structures there, apart from basic security of the premises. Many of the original arsenal buildings and much of the milelong brick perimeter wall built in 1836 still stand today, although steadily deteriorating due to abandonment and neglect. Historic preservation groups at the local, state, and national level have repeatedly lobbied the state to provide basic site maintenance or find partners for adaptive reuse of the property, to no avail.[10]

To assist in the overall effort to raise public awareness of this nationally significant historic site, Greg Waselkov and Bonnie Gums brought the University of South Alabama's archaeological field methods classes to the Searcy Hospital grounds in 2013 and 2015, with permission from the Department of Mental Health (fig. 38.4). Along with volunteers at the Center for Archaeological Studies, we carried out a shovel test survey of the arsenal site. The first Apache village site turns out to have been destroyed by hospital construction in the 1960s, but the second Apache village site was found in 2015, essentially undisturbed. A team of advanced students also mapped and recorded 167 graves in the mental hospital cemetery, a fraction of the thousand or more graves visible in the woods, the final resting places of patients who died there between 1905 and 2012. Markers of cast iron, concrete, or wood bear punched, incised, or painted patient numbers that have become difficult to read due to weathering (fig. 38.5). Many are deteriorated and broken; other markers seem to be missing altogether. Those unnamed patients who suffered so much in life deserve better.

Each layer of this neglected site—Mount Vernon Cantonment, Mount Vernon Arsenal, Mount Vernon Barracks, Searcy Hospital—tells a remarkable chapter of Alabama and US history. Twice, in 1995 and 2018,

38.4. Searcy Hospital survey. *Left*: recently collapsed portion of the outer wall of Mount Vernon Barracks (1MB509), February 2013; *right*: Sarah Wraight mapping the Searcy Hospital cemetery. (Center for Archaeological Studies, University of South Alabama.)

38.5. Grave markers in the Searcy Hospital cemetery. *Left to right*: from oldest to most recent) cast iron, patient number #547; concrete, patient number #8005; wood, patient number #9623. (Center for Archaeological Studies, University of South Alabama.)

the Alabama Historical Commission listed this site as a Place in Peril, and in 2019, it made the National Trust for Historic Preservation's nationwide roster of Most Endangered Historic Places. One wonders whether any other state in this country would place so little value on such a historical treasure.

CHAPTER 39

Lucrecia Perryman's Well

> ... discovered during athletic ballfield renovation, is an extraordinary early twentieth-century time capsule of discarded artifacts that tell the story of a remarkable African American woman's career as a midwife.

Serendipity—an unexpected happening with fortuitous results—often aptly defines the process of archaeological discovery. Rarely can we anticipate precisely what we will find. When the city of Mobile in 1993 began renovations to Crawford Park, one of the oldest parks in the city, a review of historic maps had suggested only that Civil War earthworks, leveled soon after the war, once occupied the tract. No one foresaw the trove of artifacts and information revealed by scientific excavation of a long-forgotten well on the former residential property of an African American couple, Marshall and Lucrecia Perryman.

Park renovation called for regrading the ground surface for modern recreational facilities—a football field, basketball court, Little League baseball field—and a new parking lot and stormwater retention pond. Although initial grading uncovered nothing of archaeological significance, that earthmoving attracted the attention of "bottle diggers," who routinely monitor construction sites in the downtown area for historic privies and other bottle-rich targets. In this instance, their efforts were thwarted by the presence of a subcontractor on the project, landscape architect George Shorter, then a graduate student in anthropology at Louisiana State University (LSU).

One day in August 1994, during a morning inspection of new grading, Shorter noticed four dark surface stains, archaeological features with brickbats, broken glass and ceramics, iron debris, and other historic artifacts. These were just the sort of thing that would attract illicit digging.

Three of the features proved to be shallow and were quickly sampled, but the fourth, a backfilled well (labeled Feature 1), would require careful excavation. The construction contractor agreed to shift work to other parts of the project area while Shorter began excavating the well. Laurie Wilkie, a PhD candidate in anthropology at LSU, soon joined him (fig. 39.1).

39.1. Laurie Wilkie screening soil from well excavation at the Perryman site (1MB99), in Crawford Park, Mobile, September 1994. (Center for Archaeological Studies, University of South Alabama.)

Between August 28 and September 18, with several interruptions caused by heavy rains typical of Mobile weather in late summer, they excavated and screened the contents of the well in 10-centimeter layers to a depth of 1.3 meters. A pump became essential to cope with the downpours and to lower the groundwater table while digging the last 60 centimeters. At that point, with conditions unsafe for further excavation, the feature was filled with sand, and park construction resumed.

Research in Mobile's probate records on the well's location documented how Marshall Perryman purchased three lots between 1869 and 1883. Several households of his extended family resided there until his children sold the future park property in 1923. Wilkie and Shorter gradually pieced together Marshall and Lucrecia's family history, with invaluable help from their descendants, Katheryn and Marshall Butler, Harriet Goode, and Wiley Butler Jr., some of whom still lived on Marshall's 1883 parcel.[1]

In 1830 Marshall was born into slavery in Jamaica, probably to parents enslaved by North Carolina Loyalists who fled there after the American Revolution and then returned to North Carolina just before Britain abolished slavery in 1835. Lucrecia (fig. 39.2) was born in North Carolina in 1836, almost certainly into slavery as well. Her first three children—Carolyn, Sarah, and Frank—were born between 1855 and 1862 in North Carolina, Missouri, and New Orleans (respectively), a pattern that suggests movement by owners of the enslaved people.[2]

With emancipation, our confidence in the documentation of Marshall and Lucrecia Perryman's lives becomes more robust. The couple married in 1866, somewhere in Alabama, and by 1869, they were living in Mobile, where Marshall purchased his first parcel of land. According to the 1870 federal census, Marshall worked "in grocery," Lucrecia was a laundress, and their older children had attended school and were literate. Marshall worked as a store porter until his death from consumption (tuberculosis) in 1884. During those years, Lucrecia raised her eleven children, took in laundry, and worked their small farm on a nearby tract. Beginning in 1889, Mobile city directories for the first time listed her as nurse/midwife, an apprentice for the first two years, then a professional until at least 1907. She died in 1917 at the age of eighty-one from complications of heart disease.[3]

The well's abundant contents date between 1890 and 1910. Filling the well with household refuse may have been prompted by the arrival of city water and indoor plumbing at the Perryman household around 1910. That commonplace event, abandonment of an old-fashioned water well, incidentally created an extraordinary time capsule corresponding to Lucrecia's career as a midwife. Lucrecia's well provided Wilkie with an ideal sample

39.2. Lucrecia Perryman, 1905 or earlier, from glass plate negative by Mobile photographer William E. Wilson. (Courtesy of Historic Mobile Preservation Society, 1-W-P-132.)

of material culture and a unique opportunity to consider the life of an African American midwife practicing in the Deep South before state legislatures in the 1920s required licensure of doctors of obstetrics and gynecology. The resulting precipitate decline in midwifery only began to reverse in the 1960s.[4]

Included in the well were pieces of 166 different ceramic objects, mostly vessels for food preparation, storage, and serving, but also other kinds of containers and porcelain dolls, figurines, and vases (fig. 39.3). The glass assemblage represents 448 items: lamps, decorative tableware, food containers, soda bottles, beer and liquor bottles, and (the largest category) medicine bottles. Wilkie offers some fascinating interpretations of Lucrecia's glass and ceramic inventory. The diversity and quality of Lucrecia

Perryman's dining wares indicate her middleclass aspirations and economic success. Wilkie believes the prominence of teacups, saucers, and teapots reflects Lucrecia's use of "social teas" to convey a sense of Black womanhood and motherhood denied African America women during enslavement. By her decision to stay and work in her home during her married life, raising her own children, and sharing a social life with other Black mothers, Lucrecia exercised an option previously forbidden and now enjoyed by a great many Black women in the immediate aftermath of emancipation.

Lucrecia Perryman's occupation is, not surprisingly, evident in the high proportion (30 percent) of medicine-related items in the well assemblage—122 medicine bottles and 19 food medicine and extract bottles. Most numerous are patent medicine bottles, mostly from Mobile pharmacies, the contents probably administered for their ostensible benefits for stomach, lung, and kidney ailments. Others, however, suggest a range of homemade pharmaceuticals in the ethnomedical toolkits of African American midwives, such as various extracts (especially peppermint) added to medicinal teas. The prevalent use of sassafras tea to induce labor and black haw root

39.3. Pair of cherub vases, bisque porcelain, from Feature 1 well. (Center for Archaeological Studies, University of South Alabama.)

tea to prevent miscarriage by midwives suggests an additional medical significance for the many tea service vessels found in Lucrecia's well.

Wilkie has published extensively on the archaeology of midwifery and motherhood, inspired to a considerable degree by her study of Lucrecia Perryman's material culture. If not for serendipity, a timely intervention by George Shorter, and Wilkie's fortuitous interest in midwifery, the Perryman site could have easily been lost to "bottle diggers," and our society as a whole would never have learned about one of Mobile's most extraordinary historical figures.[5]

PART XI

MODERN TIMES (1900–PRESENT)

CHAPTER 40

Bayou La Batre

... where filmed oral histories of a resilient community of fisherfolk document their adaptation to environmental and social changes as they struggle to maintain traditional livelihoods.

Intensive harvesting of seafood—fish, shellfish, crustaceans—has a long history on the northern coast of the Gulf of Mexico. Centuries of water-focused lifeways are plainly evident from the massive shell mounds at Dauphin Island and other ancient sites on Alabama's coast. In a few fortunate places, estuarine and marine resources still support commercial fisheries.

The people of Bayou La Batre, a small coastal community near the Mississippi line that writer Winston Groom made famous by his novel (and the movie) *Forrest Gump*, have practiced traditional fishing methods for generations (fig. 40.1). Longtime resident Stephanie Nelson Bosarge characterized the sea-based rhythm of their lives as "shrimp, fish, crab, and oyster, that's your four seasons." Resettlement of refugee fishing families from Vietnam, Cambodia, and Laos in Bayou La Batre during the 1970s and 1980s added new ethnic and cultural dimensions to the community. Now neighbors of diverse backgrounds but converging values struggle together to retain a complex fishing industry.[1]

By boatbuilding, netmaking, trawling for fish and shrimp, running crab traps, tonging for oysters, processing the catches, and distributing to retailers, the industrious and resilient people of Bayou La Batre continue to make their livings from the water. Their dynamic adaptations continue, despite unrelenting challenges, including devastating hurricanes like the unnamed storm of 1906 and Katrina in 2005, which periodically threaten to obliterate the low-lying town. In recent years, their problems increasingly have underlying human causes. International market pressures,

40.1. Bayou La Batre docks, August 2008. (Center for Archaeological Studies, University of South Alabama.)

government regulations, competition with recreational fishing, technological changes, pollution of coastal waters, overfishing, rising sea level, and coastal erosion pose new and ever more formidable complications to a fishing way of life.[2]

In 2007, Harriet Richardson Seacat, staff ethnographer at the Center for Archaeological Studies, suggested that we record oral histories of residents still engaged in traditional fishing activities at Bayou La Batre. In the wake of Katrina and decades of declining shrimp harvests, long-term prospects for a viable fishery on the Alabama coast seemed to be diminishing. As anthropologists, we also shared with the Bayou La Batre fisherfolk an interest in fishing technologies, the material aspects of fishing that have traditions dating back thousands of years. That winter, Richardson Seacat, along with archaeologists Greg Waselkov, Mike Stieber, and Ashley Dumas, secured a federal grant from the Mississippi-Alabama Sea Grant Consortium to film interviews about a possibly dying way of life.

Fifteen residents of the bayou gave permission for their interviews to be filmed and made available to the public. All, in fact, were eager to record their work skills and their thoughts on the history and future of Bayou La Batre's fisheries-based economy. Lynn Rabren, a professional videographer, filmed the interviews, most conducted by Stieber in August and September 2008 (fig. 40.2). Nine interviews can be viewed at the National Oceanic and Atmospheric Administration (NOAA) website, Voices

Oral History Archives, under the collection name "Preserving Oral Histories of Waterfront-Related Pursuits in Bayou La Batre."[3]

Participants included Avery Bates (former commercial oysterman and crabber, vice president of Organized Seafood Association of Alabama), Joe Bennett (captain of the *Miss Carlie Page*, a large Gulf shrimp boat), David Bosarge (wooden boatbuilder and oyster tongs handlemaker), Brett Dungan (commercial boatbuilder, general manager of Master Marine), James Lawrence Johnson (commercial oysterman and fisherman), Minh Van Le (branch director of Boat People SOS and owner of two shrimp boats), Rodney Lyons (former shrimper and oysterman, seafood dealer, owner of Murdock's Market & Rod Noker's Bar), Jim Marshall (commercial crabber and co-owner of a crab boat), Souksavanh Phasadvona (commercial crabber, co-owner of a crab boat, electrician at Master Marine), George Henry Sprinkle (commercial fisherman, shrimp net shop owner), B. G. Thompson (commercial fisherman, fishery statistician with NOAA, family-owned BLB Seafood processing plant), Dillard Wilkerson (former commercial fisherman, shrimper, net mender, boat owner), and Milton Zirlott (former commercial shrimper and owner of several shrimp boats). Midge Zirlott and Bonnie Sprinkle joined interviews with their commercial fisherman husbands (figs. 40.3 and 40.4).

Despite the severe impact of the BP Deepwater Horizon oil spill in 2010 on their livelihoods, the fisherfolk of Bayou La Batre continue to

40.2. Avery Bates interviewed by Harriet Richardson Seacat and videographer Lynn Rabren, Bayou La Batre, April 2008. (Center for Archaeological Studies, University of South Alabama.)

40.3. Dillard Wilkerson weaving a shrimp net at his shop in Bayou La Batre, August 2008. (Center for Archaeological Studies, University of South Alabama.)

40.4. Souksavanh Phasadvona and Jim Marshall hauling a trap onto their crab boat, off Bayou La Batre, September 2008. (Center for Archaeological Studies, University of South Alabama.)

find ways to maintain most of their fisheries. Oysters, essentially gone a few years ago, have made a comeback via intensive oyster farming in Portersville Bay. Interviews with Bates, Dungan, Lyons, Thompson, and the others provide practical advice for maintaining a healthy marine habitat, encouraging good stewardship of waterways, and ongoing efforts at habitat restoration. Most importantly, their recorded interviews invite all of us to appreciate the joys of working on the water and to share their fascination with simply being on the water, a perspective gained over generations (fig. 40.5).

40.5. Charcoal brazier used on coastal and bay fishing boats for cooking and in the winter for heat, manufactured in earthenware at the Daphne Pottery, early twentieth century. (Center for Archaeological Studies, University of South Alabama.)

CHAPTER 41

I-10 Mobile River Bridge

> . . . a colossal construction project that has posed an immense challenge for the Center for Archaeological Studies yet also presents an opportunity for a collaborative reevaluation of Mobile's history.

This book's publication occurs amid the largest single project in the Center for Archaeological Studies' thirty-year history. Ever-increasing frequencies of traffic jams on the Interstate 10 Bayway over Mobile Bay have finally led to serious preparations for expansion of the Bayway and construction of a massive new highway bridge spanning the Mobile River. After several stops and starts, intensive fieldwork is now completed at fifteen archaeological sites in the path of that expanding roadway. At least two more years of intensive artifact analysis and additional archival and oral historical research will be accompanied by public presentations, exhibits, and other community outreach activities, such as a monthly booth at Mobile's Artwalk. Our incorporation of oral history, expertly led by Kern Jackson (African American Studies program director and assistant professor, University of South Alabama), complements the archaeology. Together their synergy adds a whole new level of public engagement with the project. In its overall scope, number of participants, and timeframe, the I-10 Mobile River Bridge archaeological project is a massive undertaking with the potential for truly consequential impacts on the Mobile community.

Like many large cultural resource projects, the I-10 Mobile River Bridge archaeological project has already had a long history. Beginning in 2006 with initial consideration of potential bridge routes, preliminary phases consisted of traditional shovel tests paired with hydraulic coring and heavy equipment, such as Gradall excavators used to remove fill and disturbed deposits to reach deeply buried, but intact, archaeological strata. Urban archaeology is often challenging in the extreme, with meters of demolition rubble and fill dirt covering older landscape surfaces. Yet the effort can reward us with otherwise unobtainable knowledge about the history of our largest cities and their predecessor settlements from the premodern past.

Archaeology for the current project, led by Phil Carr in partnership with Sarah Price and Justin Stickler of Wiregrass Archaeological Consulting, includes further exploration of the Water Street site, 1MB510 (see chapter 25), and examination of other eighteenth-, nineteenth-, and early twentieth-century sites along Water and Conception Streets in downtown Mobile, as well as two Native American sites in Baldwin County occupied between five hundred and three thousand years ago at the eastern terminus of the I-10 Bayway (fig. 41.1). William Turner, formerly chief archaeologist for the Alabama Department of Transportation, masterfully shepherded this project from the start and has come out of retirement to see it finished.

41.1. I-10 Mobile River Bridge project. (Base map sources: Esri, DigitalGlobe, GeoEye, USGS; Center for Archaeological Studies, University of South Alabama.)

The recent nature of many of the I-10 Mobile River Bridge project sites, some of them occupied into the 1960s when properties were acquired through eminent domain for highway construction, has led us to ponder how the study of the recent past can add value to the community. In fact, this has become a major driver of the project. Today, all of us, as citizens of the United States, grapple almost daily with unresolved aspects of our collective past. Recent events, such as the January 6, 2021, Capitol riot, and more distant ones, such as ongoing legacies of racialized slavery and the subjugation, dispossession, and forced removal of Native Americans, continue to have relevance in our everyday lives. The American Historical Association has developed the "Teaching History with Integrity" initiative to help history educators cope when confronted with intensifying controversies that arise around the teaching of American history. As part of a society faced with such challenges, we decided to bring archaeologists, historians, oral historians, public outreach professionals, and members of the Mobile community together in a collaborative way. We hope the I-10 Mobile River Bridge archaeological project can overcome the limits of our individual perspectives and offer new explanations and a fuller understanding of Mobile's past.[1]

An article in the March 1968 issue of *National Geographic* magazine, titled "Mobile: Alabama's City in Motion," featured the I-10 Bayway then under construction. Today's commuters, who deal daily with the near-perpetual traffic jams on the Bayway, can appreciate the irony of that title and the hubris that demolished a thriving Mobile neighborhood for what turned out to be only a temporary solution to Mobile's transportation dilemma. Our research is an opportunity to reevaluate the long-term social consequences of engineering decisions reached in the 1960s. We hope to write an innovative history of the region, enlighten and engage the public with our findings, and honor the people of Mobile and southwest Alabama. The I-10 Mobile River Bridge archaeological project, and the others discussed in this volume, demonstrate the value of archaeology done by and for a community.[2]

Epilogue

Gregory A. Waselkov

South Alabama has been my home for more than thirty-five years. My wife, Lin, and I raised our three children here, and this is the place where I have done most of my teaching and research as an archaeologist. I must tell you, the archaeology here is wonderful. I have never been bored. During my time on the teaching faculty at the University of South Alabama from 1988 to 2017, and ever since as a retiree and volunteer, each year has delivered startling discoveries and opportunities. I have been able to delve into some of the most challenging and fascinating sites on the northcentral Gulf Coast, several of which rank among the most important of their kind in the country.

This region holds more than its share of worldclass archaeological treasures. One turned out to be a 1,400-year-old dugout canoe canal in Gulf Shores, an ancient, engineered marvel, nearly a mile in length, traversing the Fort Morgan peninsula. The French colonial townsite of Old Mobile is another, the first formal European town established on the US Gulf Coast—our region's counterpart to Virginia's Jamestown. And even though I've always been strictly a terrestrial archaeologist—a landlubber—I, too, was thrilled to follow reports by underwater archaeologists studying another spectacular site, the wreck of the infamous slaver's ship *Clotilda*, which continues to attract worldwide media attention. Rare high-profile sites such as these deservedly claim headlines, but, honestly, every archaeological site has a potential to disclose new secrets about the human past. Each one can yield intellectual and emotional rewards through close study.

In this collection of essays, my colleague Philip Carr and I have tried to paint a balanced portrait of archaeology in south Alabama, including some places probably unfamiliar to you that deserve to be better known. Even so, we had to be selective. From the northcentral Gulf Coast's deep roster of outstanding archaeological sites, all of them once important to our predecessors on this landscape, we chose to highlight a few dozen in our essays. To give you a glimpse at our dilemma, here are some other worthy subjects that we left on the cutting room floor:

- Greenwood Island (site 22JA516) in Pascagoula, Mississippi, a few miles west of the Alabama border, was inhabited as early as 1200 BC, from Late Archaic to Middle Woodland, Late Woodland, and

E.1. Carey Geiger (*left*) on Greenwood Island and at the Paradiso site (1BA608) (*right*), 2008. (Center for Archaeological Studies, University of South Alabama.)

E.2. Multiple views of a projectile point and a copper ear spool from Greenwood Island (22JA516). (Center for Archaeological Studies, University of South Alabama.)

Mississippian times. Camp Jefferson Davis also occupied this coastal location during the US war with Mexico, 1846–48. Bonnie Gums supervised a volunteer crew during test excavations here in 1997, at the urging of Carey Geiger, a dedicated avocational archaeologist who observed encroachment on the site by industrial development[1] (figs. E.1 and E.2).

- An outlier of Oce Vpofv/Hickory Ground (site 1EE639), consisting of two house remains on the far eastern edge of the Muscogee Creek town (located on the east bank of the Coosa River in Wetumpka, Alabama), was excavated by center archaeologists in 2008 for the Alabama

E.3. Structure 1 posthole pattern and interior storage pits at Oce Vpofv/Hickory Ground Outlier (1EE639), 2008 excavation. (Center for Archaeological Studies, University of South Alabama.)

E.4. Ocmulgee Incised carinated bowl from Structure 2 at Oce Vpofv/Hickory Ground Outlier. (Center for Archaeological Studies, University of South Alabama.)

Department of Transportation, before widening US Highway 231. A field team led by Tara Potts uncovered post-in-ground remains of traditional-style Creek houses dating to circa 1770[2] (figs. E.3 and E.4).

- The Little Market Well (site 1MB193) at Springhill and Dauphin Streets in downtown Mobile, built in 1847 to serve one of the city's fresh meat and vegetable markets, had been demolished in 1926, paved over, and forgotten until uncovered and reported in 1995 to the Mobile Historic Development Commission by Timmy Connell, project supervisor for a construction project to repave Dauphin Street. Greg Waselkov led a team that recorded the discovery before paving continued[3] (fig. E.5).

- Construction of the Retirement Systems of Alabama (RSA) Tower, adjacent to the Battle House Hotel and now the tallest building in downtown Mobile, triggered excavations in 2002 (at site 1MB475) sponsored by RSA and the Alabama Historical Commission (fig. E.6). This "big dig" in Mobile's original business district revealed five major periods of construction and demolition from the 1820s to 1960s, including abundant artifacts from a crockery store operated by Irish immigrant Thomas Henry, a wholesale drug business, the National Commercial Bank, and a livery, most dating to the 1850s to 1890s. Inspired by this challenging project, the "stratigraphy wall" exhibit at the University of South Alabama's Archaeology Museum instructs inquisitive visitors in two basic elements of modern archaeological practice: careful excavation and the law of superposition.[4]

- Fort Albert Sidney Johnston (1MB369) was constructed in 1864–65 under the direction of Col. Victor von Sheliha as the eastern terminus of the center line of Confederate defensive works around the city of Mobile. The fort never came under fire and was dismantled at war's end, but it represents the pinnacle of Confederate military defensive engineering. Planned expansion of the Alabama State Dock facility at

E.5. Little Market Well (1MB193) at Springhill and Dauphin Streets, Mobile, September 1995. (Center for Archaeological Studies, University of South Alabama.)

E.6. Mechanical excavator clearing demolition rubble at the RSA Tower site (1MB475) in downtown Mobile, 2002. (Center for Archaeological Studies, University of South Alabama.)

Choctaw Point led to survey and testing in 2014–15 and 2017–18 directed by Bonnie Gums, who located subterranean features associated with the fort's magazine[5] (figs. E.7 and E.8).

- The Mobile Main Library dig, test unit excavations at Bienville Square, major excavations at De Tonti Square, an oyster growth experiment on Dauphin Island, the search for the oldest pottery on the northern Gulf Coast—the list of fascinating research projects accomplished or still underway is nearly endless.

E.7. Craig Sheldon metal detecting the site of Fort Albert Sidney Johnston (1MB369), 2014. (Center for Archaeological Studies, University of South Alabama.)

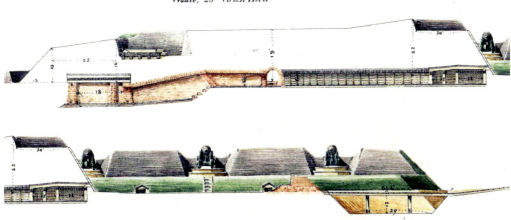

E.8. Confederate engineer's ink and watercolor drawing of a magazine cross section, Fort Albert Sidney Johnston, 1865. (Courtesy of National Archives, Cartographic Division, War Department, RG77, Office of the Chief of Engineers, Fortifications, File Drawer 121, Sheet 18–2.)

Part of our motivation in publishing this overview of south Alabama's archaeology is the hope that other archaeologists and historians, professionals and graduate students, will take an interest in this region's rich (and underexploited) research potential. While my colleagues at the Center for Archaeological Studies and I have published articles and books on a few of our projects, we have exhausted the research potential of none. Excavation notes, photographs, and artifact collections from our nearly 1,300 projects are permanently curated at the University of South Alabama's Archaeology Museum, where they can be studied by future students of the past.

In several ways, the collections curated on campus will only become more valuable with time, valuable not in a monetary sense, of course, but in their value for teaching and learning. Many years ago, during my graduate student days at the University of North Carolina, my advisor, Joffre Coe, would frequently remind my young impatient self that "archaeologists have all the time in the world." Coe alluded to the several million years of human history that archaeologists claim as their disciplinary domain. But this elder statesman of archaeology had also grown keenly aware that the study of the past is endless.

In another sense, time is running out for specific archaeological sites (and for specific archaeologists, come to think of it). Every year I have watched sites disappear in the face of development or storm damage or some other disaster (fig. E.9). Throughout my career, from my first exhilarating day on a field crew for the Cleveland Museum of Natural History in 1968 until today, I have always felt a real urgency to retrieve as much information from the site I am working on now because that site will very likely not be available for a second look. Only rarely have I seen sites preserved securely for the future, although the infrequent successes—Blakeley, Bottle Creek, Old St. Stephens, Ekvncakv/Holy Ground, and partial preservation of the Old Mobile site and the Gulf Shores canal—are immensely important victories. But the more prevalent losses are deeply troubling. Those that have suffered intentional damage or thoughtless neglect—including the USS *Tecumseh* and most other Civil War sites in the area, the Indian Meeting House site at the Hampton Inn location in downtown Mobile, and especially Mount Vernon Barracks/Searcy Hospital—those losses are heartbreaking. We could and should take much better care of our foremost historic places.

    I hope that these essays have conveyed to readers the benefits gained from proper archaeological study of artifacts and sites. Archaeology's popularity continues to grow. The international press—whether via radio, television, online, or print—offers stories virtually daily about stunning finds of buried or submerged treasure, discoveries of ancient statuary and mosaics, or newly found clues to longstanding questions about the origins of the human species. Articles, blogs, and videos describing novel technological applications of DNA analysis, geophysical survey, satellite imaging, or human bone chemistry garner innumerable social media likes. For a populace weary of incessant political wrangling and dire updates on pandemics, floods, megastorms, fires, wars, and refugee crises, archaeology offers a welcome respite, a source of relatively harmless diversion about people long dead. We can vicariously share in the thrills of discovery through our news feeds. However, we hope readers will agree that archaeology can do more than distract and entertain. There are social benefits to be gained and lessons learned from our predecessors on this earth.

    What perhaps is not always clear in media reports, particularly those about treasure, is the critical role of context in all worthwhile archaeological research. Every one of the most important finds discussed in these essays depended on someone, usually a professionally trained archaeologist, carefully recording where each artifact was found in the ground, its relationship to other artifacts, and its place in the historical record. Documenting archaeological finds is essential; irresponsible individuals who dig up artifacts solely for their own enjoyment or profit, and do not share what they have learned, have destroyed part of the historical record. The

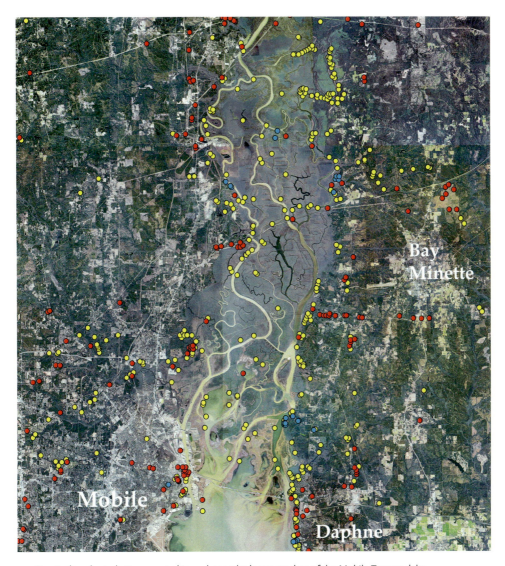

E.9. Archaeological sites reported in and near the lower reaches of the Mobile-Tensaw delta and upper end of Mobile Bay, as of 2012. Sites in blue have some degree of legal protection, yellow sites are considered threatened, and red sites have been destroyed. (Base map source: USGS; graphic by Sarah Mattics, Center for Archaeological Studies, University of South Alabama.)

artifacts excavated scientifically from Lucrecia Perryman's well provide a lovely example of the crucial importance of context. If that well had been dug for its bottles, without awareness or concern for the story that the well's contents could tell us about a prominent African American midwife in Mobile at the turn of the twentieth century, we would all have lost a key part of our shared history.

Yet, there are productive and responsible ways for the public to engage personally in archaeology. The University of South Alabama's professional archaeologists have been assisted in every instance by nonprofessionals. Members of the community are frequently the first to notice newly exposed or threatened archaeological sites, recognize their likely importance, and bring those previously unrecorded sites to the attention of professionals. If Buddy Parnell had not alerted others to his discovery of colonial house platforms at Old Mobile, if Harry King had not insisted that archaeologists look closely at the "Indian Ditch" in Gulf Shores, or if Jack Friend had not told Judge Janie Shores about the significance of the stoneware pottery kiln about to be destroyed by construction of her dream home, we might have (and very likely would have) lost those sites and all the information they could provide us about the region's past.

Two other groups of nonprofessionals—students and volunteers—have figured prominently in our essays. A small but dedicated number of volunteers have participated in field and lab work from the inception of the archaeology program at the university. Their enthusiasm, skill, and intelligence have contributed to the success of nearly every major project accomplished by the center's faculty and staff. In more than a few instances (most notably at the McInnis site, Ekvncakv/Holy Ground, and the Gulf Shores canoe canal), their contributions were essential.

Students, of course, are the foremost reason an archaeology program exists at the University of South Alabama. Undergraduate student demand for archaeology, ethnography, and human origins courses led to the creation of an anthropology major in the 1980s, and interest in anthropology remains strong today. The courses in archaeological field methods always attract students from diverse backgrounds. Nearly every class includes one or two "nontraditional" students who have experienced life in the real world and now want to find out whether archaeology is their true passion. The dirt and sweat of field archaeology do not always mesh with every student's sometimes romantic preconceptions. But most know immediately whether archaeology is for them. I think that students have generally enjoyed opportunities to participate in genuine field research projects, and the most motivated among them have remained passionate about the past.

Since 1970, there have been just four fulltime archaeology faculty affiliated with the center at the University of South Alabama. Throughout that time, external funding in the form of grants and contracts has supported fulltime professional staff, first at the Archaeological Research Laboratory and more recently at the Center for Archaeological Studies. Those several hundred dedicated staff members have accomplished most of the research, while also mentoring students and supervising volunteers. Modern archaeology is always a team effort. Successful archaeology at the University of South Alabama has depended on sincere engagement by all parties: knowledgeable, committed, and welcoming faculty and staff; motivated and intellectually curious students; passionate and energetic volunteers; supportive university administrators; and a public eager to learn about this region's deep history.

The University of South Alabama's long and productive commitment to regional archaeology has led directly to the discovery of hundreds of archaeological sites in south Alabama, contributed to a robust education program that now features the Archaeology Museum on the main campus, and fostered an abundance of community goodwill nurtured by constant outreach activities and public engagement. The artifacts from this region's archaeological sites, and the all-important photographs, data, and field records generated during surveys and excavations, are now safely curated at the University's Archaeology Museum, where future archaeologists can restudy them, ask new research questions unthought of today, and continue to write new chapters on the northern Gulf Coast's extraordinary past.

Philip J. Carr

Those of us who immerse ourselves in the study of humanity's past can testify that life was just as dynamic in previous eras as it is today. For those who lived through it, no time was static or uneventful. The future, however, remains a mystery, although one whose general trends are perceptible in broad terms through informed conjecture. Asking an archaeologist to speculate about "what comes next?" may solicit unexpected answers. The eminent archaeologist Robert Kelly offers one bold answer to this question in his book *The Fifth Beginning: What Six Million Years of Human History Can Tell Us about Our Future*. Echoing an inscription found in the tomb of Tutankhamun—"I have seen yesterday; I know tomorrow"—Kelly skillfully applies the strengths of archaeology to document four previous beginnings: the emergence of technology, culture, agriculture, and the state. These were momentous times when our ancestors set a new unalterable course, without knowing precisely where that course would lead and always with unanticipated consequences. Kelly predicts a fifth new beginning, a remarkable human future that we have the potential to not only witness but influence. Archaeologists commonly answer questions about the relevance of their discipline with vague allusions to the present and future, but here one archaeologist delivers. We encourage you to read his book, evaluate its premises, and work toward the future you want.[6]

We also encourage you to continue to explore the human past in the many ways available to you, from the online anthropological magazine *Sapiens* to local museums, from classrooms to professionally led field experiences and publicly accessible archaeological sites. The wonders of the past are within your reach in more ways than ever before, ways that both inspire and instruct. We hope to meet you on your next archaeological journey!

Notes

Foreword

1. Richebourg G. McWilliams, ed. and trans., *Iberville's Gulf Journals* (Tuscaloosa: University of Alabama Press, 1981), 168–69.

2. Paul Conrad, *The Apache Diaspora: Four Centuries of Displacement and Survival* (Philadelphia: University of Pennsylvania Press, 2021), 261

Chapter 2

1. Glenn E. Plumb, "A Brief History of the Mobile-Tensaw River Bottomlands National Natural Landmark," in Waselkov, Andrus, and Plumb, *State of Knowledge*, 5–6.

2. Gregory A. Waselkov, C. Fred Andrus, and Glenn E. Plumb, eds., *A State of Knowledge of the Natural, Cultural, and Economic Resources of the Greater Mobile-Tensaw River Area*. Natural Resource Report NPS/NRSS/BRD/ NRR—2016/1243. Fort Collins, CO: Biological Resources Division, National Park Service, 2016.

3. Edward O. Wilson, "Foreword," in Waselkov, Andrus, and Plumb, *State of Knowledge*, xx.

4. David W. Morgan, "Archeology—Arrival to AD 1550," in Waselkov, Andrus, and Plumb, *State of Knowledge*, 131–39.

5. Gregory A. Waselkov, "Archeology and History," in Waselkov, Andrus, and Plumb, *State of Knowledge*, 141–49.

6. Ben Raines, "Modern Cultures of the Mobile-Tensaw Delta," in Waselkov, Andrus, and Plumb, *State of Knowledge*, 151–54; David B. Schneider et al., "National Historic Landmarks," in Waselkov, Andrus, and Plumb, *State of Knowledge*, 155–66. For additional readings on the delta and its people, see Watt Key, *Among the Swamp People: Life in Alabama's Mobile-Tensaw River Delta* (Tuscaloosa: University of Alabama Press, 2015); Ben Raines, *Saving America's Amazon: The Threat to Our Nation's Most Diverse River System* (Montgomery, AL: New South Books, 2020); John S. Sledge, *The Gulf of Mexico: A Maritime History* (Columbia: University of South Carolina Press, 2019), and *The Mobile River* (Columbia: University of South Carolina Press, 2015); Robert Leslie Smith, *Gone to the Swamp: Raw Materials for the Good Life in the Mobile-Tensaw Delta* (Tuscaloosa: University of Alabama Press, 2008).

Chapter 3

1. Tara Potts and Cameron Gill, *Coastal Survey, Site Assessment, and Testing in Mobile and Baldwin Counties, Alabama* (Mobile: Center for Archaeological Studies, University of South Alabama, 2011).

2. Brian Ostahowski and Alison Hanlon, *Archaeological Investigations in Support of the MC252 (Deepwater Horizon) Oil Spill Response in the State of Alabama* (New Orleans: HDR Environmental, Operations and Construction, 2014); John H. Blitz and Lauren E. Downs, eds., *Graveline: A Late Woodland Platform Mound on the Mississippi Gulf Coast*, Archaeological Report No. 34 (Jackson: Mississippi Department of Archives and History, 2015); Bonnie L. Gums and Gregory A. Waselkov, *Archaeology at La Pointe-Krebs Plantation in Old Spanish Fort Park (22JA526), Pascagoula, Jackson County, Mississippi*, Archaeological Report no. 35 (Jackson: Mississippi Department of Archives and History, 2015); H. Edwin Jackson, ed., *Archaeological Investigations of Coastal Shell Middens in the Grand Bay Estuary, Mississippi*, Archaeological Report no. 37 (Jackson: Mississippi Department of Archives and History, 2015); Edmond A. Boudreaux III, *Archaeological Investigations at Jackson Landing: An Early Late Woodland Mound and Earthwork Site in Coastal Mississippi*, Archaeological Report 36 (Jackson: Mississippi Department of Archives and History, 2015).

3. Vernon J. Knight Jr., "Professionalization of Archaeology in the Alabama Museum of Natural History: 1929–1950," *Alabama Review* 75, no. 1 (2022): 24, 29.

4. John H. Blitz and C. Baxter Mann, eds., *Fisherfolk, Farmers, and Frenchmen: Archaeological Explorations on the Mississippi Gulf Coast*, Archaeological Report No. 30 (Jackson: Mississippi Department of Archives and History, 2000); John H. Blitz and Grace E. Riehm, eds., "Andrews Place (1MB1): A Late Woodland-Mississippian Shell Midden on the Alabama Gulf Coast," *Journal of Alabama Archaeology* 61, nos. 1–2 (2015): 1–117; Vernon J. Knight Jr., *Archaeological Investigations on Dauphin Island, Mobile County, Alabama* (Tuscaloosa: Department of Anthropology, University of Alabama, 1976); E. Bruce Trickey, "A Chronological Framework for the Mobile Bay Region," *American Antiquity* 23, no. 4 (1958): 388–96.

5. Potts and Gill, *Coastal Survey*.

6. David G. Anderson et al., "Sea-Level Rise and Archaeological Site Destruction: An Example from the Southeastern United States Using DINAA (Digital Index of North American Archaeology)," *Plos One* 12, no. 11 (2017): e0188142; Dylan S. Davis, Katherine E. Seeber, and Matthew C. Sanger, "Addressing the Problem of Disappearing Cultural Landscapes in Archaeological Research Using Multi-Scalar Survey," *Journal of Island and Coastal Archaeology* 16, nos. 2–4 (2021): 524–40; R. Barry Lewis, "Sea-Level Rise and Subsidence Effects on Gulf Coast Archaeological Site Distributions," *American Antiquity* 65, no. 3 (2000): 525–41.

Chapter 4

1. Gregory A. Waselkov et al., "History and Hydrology: Engineering Canoe Canals in the Estuaries of the Gulf of Mexico," *Journal of Field Archaeology* 47, no. 7 (2022): 486–500; James P. Delgado et al., *Clotilda: The History and Archaeology of the Last Slave Ship* (Tuscaloosa: University of Alabama Press, 2023).

2. Vernon J. Knight Jr., "Professionalization of Archaeology in the Alabama Museum of Natural History: 1929–1950," *Alabama Review* 75, no. 1 (2022): 14–49.

3. Richard S. Fuller, Diane E. Silvia, and Noel R. Stowe, *The Forks Project: An Investigation of Late Prehistoric–Early Historic Transition in the Alabama-Tombigbee*

Confluence Basin (Mobile: Archaeological Research Laboratory, University of South Alabama, 1984); Noel R. Stowe, ed., *A Cultural Resources Assessment of the Mobile-Tensaw Bottomlands: Phase II* (Mobile: Archaeological Research Laboratory, University of South Alabama, 1981), and *A Preliminary Cultural Resource Literature Search of the Mobile-Tensaw Bottomlands* (Mobile: Archaeological Research Laboratory, University of South Alabama, 1978); Stephen Lau and Oscar W. Brock Jr., *An Archaeological Survey and Test Excavations at Ideal Basic Industries, Inc., Theodore Park Plant Site, Mobile County, Alabama* (Mobile: Archaeological Research Laboratory, University of South Alabama, 1978).

4. Noel R. Stowe et al., *A Preliminary Report on the Pine Log Creek Site (1BA462)* (Mobile: Archaeological Research Laboratory, University of South Alabama, 1982); Amy Snow and Jennie Trimble, *Archaeological Excavation of the Ginhouse Island Site, 1WN86* (Mobile: Archaeological Research Laboratory, University of South Alabama, 1983); Richard S. Fuller, "Indian Pottery and Cultural Chronology of the Mobile-Tensaw Basin and Alabama Coast," *Journal of Alabama Archaeology* 44, no. 1 (1998): 1–51. Other major surveys include Judith A. Bense, *Archeological Investigations at the Dead Lake Site (1MB95), Creola, Alabama* (Pensacola, FL: Heritage Company, 1980); H. Blaine Ensor, Eugene M. Wilson, and M. Cassandra Hill, *Historic Resources Assessment: Tennessee-Tombigbee Waterway Wildlife Mitigation Project, Mobile and Tensaw River Deltas, Alabama* (Tuscaloosa, AL: Panamerican Consultants, 1993); David W. Morgan, *The Tensaw Bluffs Project: An Archaeological Survey of the Eastern Upland Margin of the Mobile-Tensaw Delta, Alabama* (Tuscaloosa: Alabama Museum of Natural History, University of Alabama, 1997), and "Mississippian Heritage: Late Woodland Subsistence and Settlement Patterns in the Mobile-Tensaw Delta, Alabama," PhD diss., Department of Anthropology, Tulane University, New Orleans, 2003; Richard S. Fuller and Ian W. Brown, *The Mound Island Project: An Archaeological Survey in the Mobile-Tensaw Delta*, Bulletin 19 (Tuscaloosa: Alabama Museum of Natural History, 1998); Ian W. Brown, *An Archaeological Survey in Clarke County, Alabama*, Bulletin 26 (Tuscaloosa: Alabama Museum of Natural History, 2009).

5. Nicholas H. Holmes Jr. and E. Bruce Trickey, "Late Holocene Sea-Level Oscillations in Mobile Bay," *American Antiquity* 39, no. 1 (1974): 122–24; E. Bruce Trickey, Nicholas H. Holmes Jr., and Janet R. Clute, "Archaeological and Historical Investigations at Pinto Battery or Battery Gladden, Site 1MB17, Mobile Bay, Alabama," *Journal of Alabama Archaeology* 32, no. 1 (1986): 39–62.

6. Jack B. Irion, *Underwater Archaeological Investigations, Mobile Bay Ship Channel, Mobile Harbor, Alabama* (Austin, TX: Espey, Huston and Associates, 1986); Tim S. Mistovich and Vernon James Knight Jr., *Cultural Resources Survey of Mobile Harbor, Alabama* (Moundville, AL: OSM Archaeological Consultants, 1983).

7. David Smithweck, *The USS Tecumseh in Mobile Bay* (Charleston, SC: History Press, 2021); W. Wilson West Jr., *USS Tecumseh Shipwreck Management Plan* (Washington, DC: Naval Historical Center, 1997).

8. Angus Konstam, *Confederate Submarines and Torpedo Vessels, 1861–65* (Oxford, UK: Osprey, 2004); William W. Schroeder and N. Read Stowe, *Archaeological Survey of a Portion of Mobile Bay*, Technical Report 74–001 (Dauphin Island, AL: Dauphin Island Sea Lab, 1974); David Smithweck, *In Search of the CSS Huntsville and CSS Tuscaloosa: Confederate Ironclads* (Mobile, AL: printed by author, 2016). David Smithweck (personal communication, July 12, 2023) has found evidence in files of

the US Army Corps of Engineers that the wreck of the *Pioneer II* was destroyed by channel dredging late in 1864.

9. Alabama State Archaeological Site File, maintained by the University of Alabama's Office of Archaeological Research, Moundville Archaeological Park, Moundville.

10. Herbert Aptheker, "Maroons within the Present Limits of the United States," *Journal of Negro History* 24, no. 2 (1939): 167–84; Sylviane A. Diouf, *Slavery's Exiles: The Story of the American Maroons* (New York: New York University Press, 2014), and "Borderland Maroons," in *Fugitive Slaves and Spaces of Freedom in North America*, ed. Damian Alan Pargas, 168–96 (Gainesville: University Press of Florida, 2018); Nathaniel Millett, *The Maroons of Prospect Bluff and Their Quest for Freedom in the Atlantic World* (Gainesville: University Press of Florida, 2013); Holly K. Norton and Christopher T. Espenshade, "The Challenge of Locating Maroon Refuge Sites at Maroon Ridge, St. Croix," *Journal of Caribbean Archaeology* 7 (2007): 1–17.

11. *New-York Spectator*, "Mobile, June 21st," July 17, 1827, 2; *Torch Light and Public Advertiser* (Hagers-Town, MD), "Mobile Register," July 12, 1827, 2; Jack D. L. Holmes, ed., *Documentos inéditos para la historia de la Luisiana, 1792–1810* (Madrid, Spain: Ediciones José Porrúa Turanzas, 1963), 370; B. F. Riley, "Hal's Lake," *Watson's Magazine* 4, no. 3 (May 1906): 391–93.

12. Daniel O. Sayers, *A Desolate Place for a Defiant People: The Archaeology of Maroons, Indigenous Americans, and Enslaved Laborers in the Great Dismal Swamp* (Gainesville: University Press of Florida, 2014). See J. Brent Morris, *Dismal Freedom: A History of the Maroons of the Great Dismal Swamp* (Chapel Hill: University of North Carolina Press, 2022); Marcus P. Nevius, *City of Refuge: Slavery and Petit Marronage in the Great Dismal Swamp, 1765–1856* (Athens: University of Georgia Press, 2020).

Chapter 5

1. Patrick W. Andrus, "How to Apply the National Register Criteria for Evaluation," National Register Bulletin 15 (1997): 2.

2. Roger C. Smith, "Introduction," in *Submerged History: Underwater Archaeology in Florida*, ed. Roger C. Smith (Sarasota, FL: Pineapple Press, 2018), v.

3. John G. Franzen, Terrance J. Martin, and Eric C. Drake, "*Sucreries* and *Zïïzbaakdokaanan*: Racialization, Indigenous Creolization, and the Archaeology of Maple-Sugar Camps in Northern Michigan," *Historical Archaeology* 52, no. 2 (2018): 164–96; James R. Wettstaed, "Cutting It Back and Burning It Back: Archaeological Investigations of Charcoal Production in the Missouri Ozarks," *Journal of the Society for Industrial Archaeology* 29, no. 2 (2003): 29–46; John G. Franzen, *The Archaeology of the Logging Industry* (Gainesville: University Press of Florida, 2020).

4. Jan F. Simek et al., "The Red Bird River Shelter (15CY52) Revisited: The Archaeology of the Cherokee Syllabary and of Sequoyah in Kentucky," *American Antiquity* 84, no. 2 (2019): 302–16; Kevin C. Ryan et al., *Wildland Fire in Ecosystems: Effects of Fire on Cultural Resources and Archaeology*, General Technical Report RMRS-GTR-42-vol. 3 (Fort Collins, CO: US Department of Agriculture, 2012); Grant Snitker et al., "A Collaborative Agenda for Archaeology and Fire Science," *Nature Ecology and Evolution* 6, no. 7 (2022): 835–39; Michael J. Dockry, Sophia A. Gutterman, and Mae A. Davenport, "Building Bridges: Perspectives on Partnership and Collaboration

from the U.S. Forest Service Tribal Relations Program," *Journal of Forestry* 116, no. 2 (2018): 123–32; Steven M. Meredith, "Culture History of the Middle Cahaba River Drainage in Alabama before AD 1800," *Journal of Alabama Archaeology* 63, nos. 1–2 (2017): 13–93; Harry O. Holstein, "An Investigation of Parallel Lineal Stone Walls along Alabama Mountain Slopes: Historic Agricultural Terraces or Native American Sacred Stone Monuments?," *Journal of Alabama Archaeology* 65, nos. 1–2 (2019): 87–108.

Chapter 6

1. Samuel O. McGahey, "Prehistoric Stone Bead Manufacture: The Loosa Yokena Site, Warren County, Mississippi," *Mississippi Archaeology* 40, no. 1 (2005): 3–29; Charles Rau, "The Stock-in-Trade of an Aboriginal Lapidary," *Smithsonian Institution, Annual Report for 1877*, 1–4 (Washington, DC: Smithsonian Institution, 1878).

2. Karl Widerquist and Grant S. McCall, *Prehistoric Myths in Modern Political Philosophy* (Edinburgh, Scotland: Edinburgh University Press, 2018), 29 (for the Hobbes quote and the "noble savage" phrase); David Graeber and David Wengrow, *The Dawn of Everything: A New History of Humanity* (New York: Farrar, Straus and Giroux, 2021).

3. Jessica F. Crawford, "Archaic Effigy Beads: A New Look at Some Old Beads," master's thesis, Department of Anthropology, University of Mississippi, Oxford, 2003.

4. Samuel O. McGahey, *Mississippi Projectile Point Guide*, rev. ed., Archaeological Report no. 31 (Jackson: Mississippi Department of Archives and History, 2004).

5. McGahey, "Prehistoric Stone Bead Manufacture," 16 (quote); Jay K. Johnson, "Beads, Microdrills, Bifaces, and Blades from Watson Brake," *Southeastern Archaeology* 19, no. 1 (2000): 95–104; Rau, "Stock-in-Trade of an Aboriginal Lapidary"; R. B. Fulton, "Prehistoric Jasper Ornaments in Mississippi," *Publications of the Mississippi Historical Society* 1 (1898): 91–95; John M. Connaway, "The Keenan Bead Cache," *Louisiana Archaeology* 8 (1981): 57–71.

6. Johnson, "Beads, Microdrills, Bifaces, and Blades."

7. Philip J. Carr and Alison M. Hadley, "Bifaces, Adzes, and Chert Beads: The Lithic Assemblage from the John Forrest Site (22CB623)," paper presented at the 58th Annual Meeting of the Southeastern Archaeological Conference, Chattanooga, TN, November 2001; Alison M. Hadley, "Beads, Bifaces, and Blade Cores from the Middle Archaic," senior honors thesis, Department of Sociology, Anthropology, and Social Work, University of South Alabama, Mobile, 2003; Alison M. Hadley and Philip J. Carr, "The Organization of Lithic Technology and Role of Lithic Specialists during the Archaic," paper presented at the 67th Annual Meeting of the Southeastern Archaeological Conference, Lexington, KY, 2010); Alison M. Hadley and Philip J. Carr, "Archaic Chert Beads and Craft Specialization: Application of an Organization of Technology Model," in *Exploring Southeastern Archaeology*, ed. Patricia K. Galloway and Evan Peacock, 71–98 (Jackson: University Press of Mississippi, 2015).

8. Brian Hayden, "Practical and Prestige Technologies: The Evolution of Material Systems," *Journal of Archaeological Method and Theory* 5, no. 1 (1998): 2.

9. John E. Clark and William J. Parry, "Craft Specialization and Cultural Complexity," *Research in Economic Anthropology* 12 (1990): 289–346.

Chapter 7

1. Kevin L. Bruce, Bruce J. Gray, and Cliff Jenkins, *Cultural Resources Survey of Proposed Bridge Replacement on Mississippi Highway 550 at the Homochitto River (MDOT Project No. 85-0171-00-009-10/102486201000) Lincoln County, Mississippi* (Jackson: Report to the Mississippi Department of Archives and History, 2000); Kevin L. Bruce, *Supplement to Cultural Resources Survey of Proposed Bridge Replacement on Mississippi Highway 550 at the Homochitto River, Lincoln County, Mississippi* (Jackson: Report to the Mississippi Department of Archives and History, 2002); Philip J. Carr, *Phase II Investigations at 22LI504, Lincoln County, Mississippi* (Mobile: Center for Archaeological Studies, University of South Alabama, 2004); Philip J. Carr and Evan Peacock, eds., *Archaeology at Site 22LI504* (Mobile: Center for Archaeological Studies, University of South Alabama, 2006).

2. Michael Russo, "Southeastern Archaic Mounds," in *Archaeology of the Mid-Holocene Southeast*, ed. Kenneth E. Sassaman and David G. Anderson, 259–87 (Gainesville: University Press of Florida, 1996); David G. Anderson, "Archaic Mounds and the Archaeology of Southeastern Tribal Societies," in *Signs of Power: The Rise of Cultural Complexity in the Southeast*, ed. Jon L. Gibson and Philip J. Carr, 270–99 (Tuscaloosa: University of Alabama Press, 2004); Joe W. Saunders et al., "Watson Brake: A Middle Archaic Mound Complex in Northeast Louisiana," *American Antiquity* 70, no. 4 (2005): 631–68.

3. J. W. Cambron and D. C. Hulse, *Handbook of Alabama Archaeology: Part One, Point Types* (Huntsville: Alabama Archaeological Society, 1964); Philip J. Carr and Andrew P. Bradbury, "Contemporary Lithic Analysis and Southeastern Archaeology," *Southeastern Archaeology* 19, no. 2 (2000): 120–35; Donald E. Crabtree, *An Introduction to Flintworking*. Occasional Papers 28 (Moscow: Idaho Museum of Natural History, 1972); M. L. Inizian, H. Roche, and J. Tixier, *Technology of Knapped Stone* (Meudon, France: CREP, 1992); Noel D. Justice, *Stone Age Spear and Arrow Points of the Midcontinental and Eastern United States: A Modern Survey and Reference* (Bloomington: Indiana University Press, 1987); Robert L. Kelly, "The Three Sides of a Biface," *American Antiquity* 53, no. 4 (1988): 717–34.

4. William A. Ritchie, "The Lamoka Lake Site," *Researches and Transactions of the New York State Archeological Association* 7, no. 4 (1932): 79–134.

Chapter 8

1. Lewis Binford, "Behavioral Archaeology and the 'Pompeii Premise,'" *Journal of Anthropological Research* 37, no. 3 (Fall 1981): 197.

2. Sarah E. Price, ed., *Phase III Archaeological Testing at the Silver Run Site, Archaeological Site 1RU142, Russell County, Alabama, Associated with Adding Lanes to US 431* (Mobile: Center for Archaeological Studies, University of South Alabama, 2008).

3. James J. Kocis, "Geoarchaeology of Site 1RU142," in Price, *Phase III Archaeological Testing*.

4. Robert L. Kelly, "The Three Sides of a Biface," *American Antiquity* 53, no. 4 (1988): 717.

5. Noel D. Justice, *Stone Age Spear and Arrow Points of the Midcontinental and Eastern United States: A Modern Survey and Reference* (Bloomington: Indiana University Press, 1987); John S. Whatley, "An Overview of Georgia Projectile Points and Selected Cutting Tools," *Early Georgia* 30, no. 1 (2002): 7–133; Zeljko Rezek et al., "Aggregates, Formational Emergence, and the Focus on Practice in Stone

Artifact Archaeology," *Journal of Archaeological Method and Theory* 27, no. 4 (2020): 887–928.

6. Donald E. Crabtree, *An Introduction to Flintworking*, Occasional Papers 28 (Moscow: Idaho Museum of Natural History, 1972); Kevin L. Bruce, "All Rocks Are Not Alike," *Southeastern Archaeology* 20, no. 1 (2001): 78–92.

Chapter 9

1. Clarence Edwin Carter, ed., "Daniel E. Burch to the Quartermaster General, Pensacola, March 10th, 1828," in *The Territorial Papers of the United States*, vol. 23, *The Territory of Florida, 1824–1828* (Washington, DC: National Archives, 1958), 1042.

2. Luciano Villamil, "Round Bon Secours Bay," *Spring Hill Review* 1, no. 1 (1899): 71–73.

3. Walter B. Jones, "Alabama," in "Archaeological Field Work in North America during 1934: Part 1," ed. Carl E. Guthe, *American Antiquity* 1, no. 1 (1935): 47–48; Gregory A. Waselkov et al., "History and Hydrology: Engineering Canoe Canals in the Estuaries of the Gulf of Mexico," *Journal of Field Archaeology* 47, no. 7 (2022): 486–500; Gregory A. Waselkov, "Gulf Shores' Ancient Canoe Canal," *Mobile Bay* 39, no. 7 (2023): 72–75.

4. On Florida canals and similar features, see Andrew E. Douglass, "Ancient Canals on the South-West Coast of Florida," *American Antiquarian and Oriental Journal* 7 (1885): 277–85; George M. Luer, "Calusa Canals in Southwestern Florida: Routes of Tribute and Exchange," *Florida Anthropologist* 42, no. 2 (1989): 89–130, and "The Naples Canal," *Florida Anthropologist* 51, no. 1 (1998): 15–24; George M. Luer and Ryan J. Wheeler, "How the Pine Island Canal Worked: Topography, Hydraulics, and Engineering," *Florida Anthropologist* 50, no. 2 (1997): 115–31; Victor D. Thompson et al., "Ancient Engineering of Fish Capture and Storage in Southwest Florida," *Proceedings of the National Academy of Sciences* 117, no. 15 (2020): 8374–81; Ryan J. Wheeler, "Aboriginal Canoe Canals of Cape Sable," *Florida Anthropologist* 51, no. 1 (1998): 15–24, "The Ortona Canals: Aboriginal Canal Hydraulics and Engineering," *Florida Anthropologist* 48, no. 4 (1995): 265–81, and "Walker's Canal: An Aboriginal Canal in the Florida Panhandle," *Southeastern Archaeology* 17, no. 2 (1998): 174–81.

5. Waselkov et al., "History and Hydrology."

6. Sarah E. Price, ed., *Phase III Archaeology at Plash Island, Archaeological Site 1BA134, in Baldwin County, Alabama* (Mobile: Center for Archaeological Studies, University of South Alabama, 2008); Elizabeth J. Reitz et al., "Woodland-Period Fisheries on the North-Central Coast of the Gulf of Mexico," *Southeastern Archaeology* 40, no. 2 (2021): 135–55.

7. Carla S. Hadden et al., "Temporality of Fishery Taskscapes on the North-Central Gulf of Mexico Coast (USA) during the Middle/Late Woodland Period (AD 325–1040)," *Journal of Anthropological Archaeology* 67 (September 2022): 101436.

Chapter 10

1. Sarah E. Price, ed., *Archaeology at Orange Beach: Phase III Data Recovery at 1BA21, the Bayou St. John Site, Orange Beach, Baldwin County, Alabama* (Mobile: Center for Archaeological Studies, University of South Alabama, 2009).

2. Clarence B. Moore, "Certain Aboriginal Remains of the Northwest Florida Coast, Part I," *Journal of the Academy of Natural Sciences of Philadelphia*, 2nd ser., 11, no. 4 (1901): 432; Craig T. Sheldon Jr., ed., *The Southern and Central Alabama*

Expeditions of Clarence Bloomfield Moore (Tuscaloosa: University of Alabama Press, 2001), 80. On Weeden Island culture, see Gordon R. Willey, "The Weeden Island Culture: A Preliminary Definition," *American Antiquity* 10, no. 3 (1945): 225–54, and *Archeology of the Florida Gulf Coast*, Smithsonian Miscellaneous Collections, vol. 113 (Washington, DC: Smithsonian Institution, 1949); Jerald Milanich et al., *Archaeology of Northern Florida AD 200–900: The McKeithen Weeden Island Culture*, rev. ed. (New York: Academic Press, 1997); Terry L. Lolley, "Weeden Island Occupation in the Borderland: An Example from South Alabama," *Southeastern Archaeology* 22, no. 1 (2003): 63–76; Thomas J. Pluckhahn, *Kolomoki: Settlement, Ceremony, and Status in the Deep South, A.D. 350–750* (Tuscaloosa: University of Alabama Press, 2003).

3. Carla S. Hadden and Alexander Cherkinsky, "Spatiotemporal Variability in ΔR in the Northern Gulf of Mexico, USA," *Radiocarbon* 59, spec. iss. 2 (2017): 343–53; Carla S. Hadden et al., "Radiocarbon in Marsh Periwinkle (*Littorina irrorata*) Conchiolin: Applications for Archaeology," *Radiocarbon* 61, no. 5 (2019): 1489–1500; Gregory A. Waselkov et al., "A Woodland-Period Bone Tool Industry on the Northern Gulf of Mexico Coastal Plain," in *Bones at a Crossroads: Integrating Worked Bone Research with Archaeometry and Social Zooarchaeology*, ed. Markus Wild et al, 259–88 (Leiden, Netherlands: Sidestone Press, 2021).

4. Kelly L. Orr, "Coastal Weeden Island Subsistence Adaptations: Zooarchaeological Evidence from Bayou St. John (1BA21), Alabama," PhD diss., Department of Anthropology, University of Georgia, Athens, 2007; Elizabeth J. Reitz et al., *Final Project Report: Woodland Seasonality on the Northern Coast of the Gulf of Mexico*, Report on Awards BCS-1026166, BCS-1026168, and BCS-1026169 (Washington, DC: National Science Foundation, 2013).

5. Elizabeth J. Reitz et al., "Woodland-Period Fisheries on the North-Central Coast of the Gulf of Mexico," *Southeastern Archaeology* 40, no. 2 (2021): 135–55; Carla S. Hadden et al., "Temporality of Fishery Taskscapes on the North-Central Gulf of Mexico Coast (USA) during the Middle/Late Woodland Period (AD 325–1040)," *Journal of Anthropological Archaeology* 67 (September 2022): 101436.

6. On southeastern fish weirs, see John M. Connaway, *Fishweirs: A World Perspective with Emphasis on the Fishweirs of Mississippi*, Archaeological Report No. 33 (Jackson: Mississippi Department of Archives and History, 2007); R. Christopher Goodwin, Gregg Brooks, and Martha R. Williams, *Archeological Evaluation of "Feature A," the Wakulla River Fishweir Site (8WA843)* (Frederick, MD: R. Christopher Goodwin and Associates, 2008).

Chapter 11

1. Steve B. Wimberly, *Indian Pottery from Clarke County and Mobile County, Southern Alabama*, Museum Paper 19 (Tuscaloosa: Alabama Museum of Natural History, University of Alabama, 1960).

2. Richard S. Fuller, Diane E. Silvia, and Noel R. Stowe, *The Forks Project: An Investigation of Late Prehistoric–Early Historic Transition in the Alabama-Tombigbee Confluence Basin* (Mobile: Archaeological Research Laboratory, University of South Alabama, 1984); Ian W. Brown, *An Archaeological Survey in Clarke County, Alabama*, Bulletin 26 (Tuscaloosa: Alabama Museum of Natural History, 2009); George W. Shorter Jr., ed., *The Late Woodland Period on the Lower Tombigbee River*, Archaeological Monograph 6 (Mobile: Center for Archaeological Studies, University of South

Alabama, 1999). Also see Ned J. Jenkins and Richard A. Krause, *The Tombigbee Watershed in Southeastern Prehistory* (Tuscaloosa: University of Alabama Press, 1986); David W. Morgan, "Mississippian Heritage: Late Woodland Subsistence and Settlement Patterns in the Mobile-Tensaw Delta, Alabama," PhD diss., Department of Anthropology, Tulane University, New Orleans, 2003.

3. Philip J. Carr, *Lithic Use in the Forks: An Archaeological Survey in Choctaw and Clarke Counties* (Mobile: Center for Archaeological Studies, University of South Alabama, 2003).

4. Hester Davis, "The Future of Archaeology: Dreamtime, Crystal Balls, and Reality," *American Journal of Archaeology* 93, no. 3 (1989): 451–58.

5. Brian Fagan, "Black Day at Slack Farm," *Archaeology* 41, no. 4 (1988), 15.

6. Sarah E. Price, ed., *Archaeology on the Tombigbee River: Phase III Data Recovery at 1CK56, the Corps Site, Clarke County, Alabama* (Mobile: Center for Archaeological Studies, University of South Alabama, 2009).

Chapter 12

1. Sarah C. Sherwood and Tristram R. Kidder, "The DaVincis of Dirt: Geoarchaeological Perspectives on Native American Mound Building in the Mississippi River Basin," *Journal of Anthropological Archaeology* 30, no. 1 (2011): 69–87.

2. Richebourg G. McWilliams, ed. And trans., *Iberville's Gulf Journals* (Tuscaloosa: University of Alabama Press, 1981), 168–69.

3. Artemas Bigelow, "Observations on Some Mounds on the Tensaw River," *American Journal of Science and Arts* 15, no. 44 (Article 21, 1853): 186–92; James W. Grimes and Sue Keller, "The Herbarium of Wesleyan University, Middletown, Connecticut," *Brittonia* 34 (1982): 368, 370; Frank W. Nicolson, ed., *Alumni Record of Wesleyan University, Middletown, Conn.*, 4th ed. (New Haven, CT: Tuttle, Morehouse, and Taylor, 1911), 18. On the possible canal, see Christopher B. Rodning, "Water Travel and Mississippian Settlement at Bottle Creek," in Brown, *Bottle Creek*, 194–204.

4. Gregory A. Waselkov, "A Contour Map of the Bottle Creek Site," *Journal of Alabama Archaeology* 39, no. 1 (1993): 30–35; Richard S. Fuller and Ian W. Brown, *The Mound Island Project: An Archaeological Survey in the Mobile-Tensaw Delta* (Tuscaloosa: Alabama Museum of Natural History, 1998); Ian W. Brown and Richard S. Fuller, eds., "Bottle Creek Research: Working Papers on the Bottle Creek Site (1BA2), Baldwin County, Alabama," *Journal of Alabama Archaeology* 39, nos. 1–2 (1993): 1–169; Ian W. Brown and Richard S. Fuller, *Master Plan for Managing the Bottle Creek Site National Historic Landmark* (Tuscaloosa: Gulf Coast Survey, Alabama Museum of Natural History, University of Alabama, 1999); Ian W. Brown, ed., *Bottle Creek: A Pensacola Culture Site in South Alabama* (Tuscaloosa: University of Alabama Press, 2003); Ian W. Brown, *Bottle Creek Reflections: The Personal Side of Archaeology in the Mobile-Tensaw Delta* (Tuscaloosa, AL: Borgo Publishing, 2012).

5. Diane Silvia, "Indian and French Interaction in Colonial Louisiana during the Early Eighteenth Century," PhD diss., Department of Anthropology, Tulane University, New Orleans, 2000.

Chapter 13

1. Vernon J. Knight Jr., *Archaeological Investigations on Dauphin Island, Mobile County, Alabama* (Tuscaloosa: Department of Anthropology, University of Alabama, 1976).

2. Richebourg G. McWilliams, ed. and trans., *Iberville's Gulf Journals* (Tuscaloosa: University of Alabama Press, 1981), 38; Jean-François-Benjamin Dumont de Montigny, *The Memoir of Lieutenant Dumont, 1715–1747: A Sojourner in the French Atlantic*, trans. Gordon M. Sayre, ed. Gordon M. Sayre and Carla Zecher (Chapel Hill: University of North Carolina Press, 2012), 108, 117; B. F. French, *Historical Collections of Louisiana*, vol. 5, *Historical Memoirs from 1687 to 1770* (New York: Lamport, Blakeman and Law, 1853), 2–3; Richebourg G. McWilliams, ed. and trans., *Fleur de Lys and Calumet: Being the Pénicault Narrative of French Adventure in Louisiana* (Tuscaloosa: University of Alabama Press, 1988), 11; Joseph Le Moyne, Sieur de Serigny, and Valentin Devin, "Carte de l'entrée de la Baye de la Mobile et de L'Isle, 1719," Département des cartes et plans, Ge SH 18, portefeuille 138, division 10, p 12 D, Bibliothèque Nationale de France, Paris.

3. Clarence B. Moore, "Certain Aboriginal Remains on Mobile Bay and on Mississippi Sound," *Journal of the Academy of Natural Sciences of Philadelphia*, 2nd ser., 13, no. 2 (1905), 295–96; Craig T. Sheldon Jr., ed., *The Southern and Central Alabama Expeditions of Clarence Bloomfield Moore* (Tuscaloosa: University of Alabama Press, 2001), 42–45.

4. Steven L. Boles, "Earth-Diver and Earth Mother: Ancestral Flint Clay Figures from Cahokia," *Illinois Archaeology* 29 (2017): 127–46.

5. Paul Brueske, *The Last Siege: The Mobile Campaign, Alabama 1865* (Havertown, PA: Casemate, 2018), 41.

6. Jason A. Gardner and Clare E. Farrow, "Introduction to the Andrews Place Site (1MB1)," in "Andrews Place (1MB1): A Late Woodland-Mississippian Shell Midden on the Alabama Gulf Coast," ed. John H. Blitz and Grace E. Riehm, *Journal of Alabama Archaeology* 61, no. 1 (2015): 5–6; A. S. Gaines and K. M. Cunningham, "Shell-Heaps on Mobile River," in *Annual Report of the Board of Regents of the Smithsonian Institution for the Year 1877*, 290–91 (Washington, DC: Smithsonian Institution, 1878); W. D. Gates, "Pottery of the Mound Builders," *American Archaeologist* 2, no. 5 (1898): 114.

7. Thomas M. Owen, "Prehistoric Works," in *Report of the Alabama History Commission*, vol. 1, ed. Thomas M. Owen (Montgomery, AL: Brown Printing, 1901), 366, and "Mounds and Prehistoric Works in Alabama," in *Handbook of the Alabama Anthropological Society, 1910*, ed. Thomas M. Owen (Montgomery, AL: Brown Printing, 1910), 36, 51, and "Some Notes on the Shell Banks of the Alabama Coast," *Arrow Points* 4, no. 1 (1922): 5–6.

8. Gregory A. Waselkov, "Shellfish Gathering and Shell Midden Archaeology," *Advances in Archaeological Method and Theory* 10 (1987): 115–17.

9. Alexander D. Bache, "Entrance to Mobile Bay, 1851," in *Maps and Charts of the United States Coast Survey, A. D. Bache, Superintendent, to July 1854* (Washington, DC: US Coast Survey, 1854); Victor D. Thompson et al., "Ancient Engineering of Fish Capture and Storage in Southwest Florida," *Proceedings of the National Academy of Sciences* 117, no. 15 (2020): 8374–81.

Chapter 14

1. Sarah E. Price and Justin Stickler, *The McInnis Site, Orange Beach, Alabama*, with photographs by Lyle Ratliff (Orange Beach, AL: published by author, 2015).

2. G. M. Sternberg, "Indian Burial Mounds and Shellheaps near Pensacola, Florida," *Proceedings of the American Association for the Advancement of Science* 24 (1876): 282–92.

3. Sternberg, "Indian Burial Mounds and Shellheaps," 283–84.

4. Sternberg, "Indian Burial Mounds and Shellheaps,"286.

5. William H. Holmes, "Archaeological Collections from Alabama," *American Anthropologist* 2, no. 4 (1889): 350, and "Aboriginal Pottery of the Eastern United States," *Twentieth Annual Report, Bureau of American Ethnology 1898–1899* (Washington, DC: Smithsonian Institution, 1903), 107 (quotes); Clarence B. Moore, "Certain Aboriginal Remains of the Northwest Florida Coast, Part I," *Journal of the Academy of Natural Sciences of Philadelphia*, 2nd ser., 11, no. 4 (1901): 423–32; Craig T. Sheldon Jr., ed., *The Southern and Central Alabama Expeditions of Clarence Bloomfield Moore* (Tuscaloosa: University of Alabama Press, 2001), 35–37.

6. Richard S. Fuller, "An Analysis of Indian Pottery Recovered during Shovel Testing at the McInnis Site (1BA664), Orange Beach, Alabama," manuscript on file at the Center for Archaeological Studies, University of South Alabama, Mobile, 2015.

7. Gregory A. Waselkov and Philip J. Carr, "Avoidance Strategies of a Displaced Post-Mississippian Society on the Northern Gulf Coast, circa 1710," in *Contact, Colonialism, and Native Communities in the Southeastern United States*, ed. Edmond A. Boudreaux III, Maureen Meyers, and Jay K. Johnson, 126–39 (Gainesville: University Press of Florida, 2020); Gregory A. Waselkov and Bonnie L. Gums, *Plantation Archaeology at Rivière aux Chiens, ca. 1725–1848*, Archaeological Monograph 7 (Mobile: Center for Archaeological Studies, University of South Alabama, 2000), 31–32; Ives Goddard et al., "Small Tribes of the Western Southeast," in *Handbook of North American Indians*, vol. 14, *Southeast*, ed. Raymond D. Fogelson (Washington, DC: Smithsonian Institution Press, 2004), 186–87.

8. Fuller, "Analysis of Indian Pottery"; Ian W. Brown and Richard S. Fuller, *Sorting Manual of Pensacola Culture Pottery* (Tuscaloosa: Gulf Coast Survey, Alabama Museum of Natural History, 1992).

9. Several important references that relate specifically to rim effigies include Madelaine C. Azar, "Making Heads or Tails: An Iconographic Analysis of Late Mississippian Rim-Effigy Bowls in the Central Mississippi River Valley," master's thesis, Department of Anthropology, University of North Carolina, Chapel Hill, 2020; Madelaine C. Azar and Vincas P. Steponaitis, "Modeling the Cosmos: Rim-Effigy Bowl Iconography in the Central Mississippi Valley," in *Archaeologies of Cosmoscapes in the Americas*, ed. J. Grant Stauffer, Bretton T. Giles, and Shawn P. Lambert, 25–45 (Oxford, UK: Oxbow Books, 2022); David H. Dye, "Ceramic Wares and Water Spirits: Identifying Religious Sodalities in the Lower Mississippi Valley," in *Ceramics in Ancient America: Multidisciplinary Approaches*, ed. Yumi Park Huntington, Dean E. Arnold, and Johanna Minich, 29–61 (Gainesville: University Press of Florida, 2018); Alice Eileen Muntz, "Interpreting Ritual in Ceramics of Late Mississippian Southern Illinois," master's thesis, Department of Anthropology, Southern Illinois University, Carbondale, 2018; Vincas P. Steponaitis, *Ceramics, Chronology, and Community Patterns: An Archaeological Study of Moundville* (New York: Academic Press, 1983).

10. George E. Lankford and David H. Dye, "Conehead Effigies: A Distinctive Art Form of the Mississippi Valley," *Arkansas Archeologist* 53 (2014): 37–50.

11. Fuller, "Analysis of Indian Pottery."

12. Paul Du Ru, "Journal d'un voyage fait avec Mr. d'Iberville de la rade de Bilocchis dans le haut du Mississippi," February 1 to May 8, 1700, Vault Ayer MS. 262, f. 64, Edward Ayer Collection, Newberry Library, Chicago; Ruth L. Butler, ed. And

trans, *Journal of Paul du Ru (February 1 to May 8, 1700) Missionary Priest to Louisiana* (Chicago: Caxton Club, 1934), 42.

13. Steve B. Wimberly, "Indian Pottery Human Effigy Heads from the Mobile Bay Region of Alabama," *Journal of Alabama Archaeology* 14, no. 1 (1968): 30–37; Richard S. Fuller and Diane E. Silvia, "Ceramic Rim Effigies in Southwest Alabama," *Journal of Alabama Archaeology* 30, no. 1 (1984): 1–48; Richard S. Fuller, *An Alternative Rim Effigy Typology for the Pensacola Mississippian Variant* (Tuscaloosa: Gulf Coast Survey, Museum of Natural History, University of Alabama, 1993); Mark Howell, "Sonic-Iconic Examination of Adorno Rattles from the Mississippian-era Lake George Site," *Music in Art* 36, nos. 1–2 (2011): 231–44.

Chapter 15

1. Helen Hornbeck Tanner, "The Land and Water Communication Systems of the Southeastern Indians," in *Powhatan's Mantle: Indians in the Colonial Southeast*, rev. ed., ed. Gregory A. Waselkov, Peter H. Wood, and Tom Hatley, 27–42 (Lincoln: University of Nebraska Press, 2006).

2. Brandon Charles Ackermann, "Archaeological Computer Modeling of Florida's Pre-Columbian Dugout Canoes: Integrating Ground-Penetrating Radar and Geographic Information Science," master's thesis, Department of Anthropology, University of Denver, Denver, CO, 2019; Frank Hamilton Cushing, "Exploration of Ancient Key Dwellers' Remains on the Gulf Coast of Florida," *Proceedings of the American Philosophical Society* 35, no. 153 (1896): 329–448; Mark Joseph Hartmann, "The Development of Watercraft in the Prehistoric Southeastern United States," PhD diss., Department of Anthropology, Texas A&M University, College Station, 1996; Richard P. Kandare, "A Contextual Study of Mississippian Dugout Canoes: A Research Design for the Moundville Phase," master's thesis, Department of Anthropology, University of Arkansas, Fayetteville, 1983; Lee Ann Newsom and Barbara A. Purdy, "Florida Canoes: A Maritime Heritage from the Past," *Florida Anthropologist* 43, no. 3 (1990): 164–80; Peter H. Wood, "Missing the Boat: Ancient Dugout Canoes in the Mississippi-Missouri Watershed," *Early American Studies* 16, no. 2 (2018): 197–254.

3. Julie Duggins, "Canoe Caching at Transit Points: Inferring Florida's Ancient Navigation Routes Using Archaeology and Ethnohistory," in *Iconography and Wetsite Archaeology of Florida's Watery Realms*, ed. Ryan J. Wheeler and Joanna Ostapkowicz, 82–110 (Gainesville: University Press of Florida, 2019); David Sutton Phelps, *Ancient Pots and Dugout Canoes: Indian Life as Revealed by Archaeology at Lake Phelps* (Creswell, NC: Pettigrew State Park, 1989).

4. Noel R. Stowe, "A Preliminary Report on Four Dugout Canoes from the Gulf Coast," *Journal of Alabama Archaeology* 20, no. 2 (1974): 194–203.

5. Stowe, "Preliminary Report on Four Dugout Canoes."

6. Richard S. Fuller, "Mississippian Canoes in the Deep South: Examples from Mississippi and Alabama," paper presented at the 49th Annual Meeting of the Southeastern Archaeological Conference, Little Rock, AR, 1992.

7. Fuller, "Mississippian Canoes in the Deep South."

8. Fuller, "Mississippian Canoes in the Deep South."

Chapter 16

1. Jay Higginbotham, *Old Mobile: Fort Louis de la Louisiane, 1702–1711* (Mobile, AL: Museum of the City of Mobile, 1977); Peter J. Hamilton, *Colonial Mobile: An*

Historical Study, 2nd ed. (Boston: Houghton Mifflin, 1910), and *Mobile of the Five Flags* (Mobile, AL: Gill Printing, 1913).

2. Judith A. Bense, ed., *Presidio Santa María de Galve: A Struggle for Survival in Colonial Spanish Pensacola* (Gainesville: University Press of Florida, 2003), and *Presidios of Spanish West Florida* (Gainesville: University Press of Florida, 2022).

3. Hamilton, *Colonial Mobile*, 52–53; Louis de Vendel Chaudron, "How We Found the Site of Fort Louis de la Mobile," manuscript, Iberville Historical Society Collections, Mobile History Museum, Mobile, AL, 1902; Donald A. Harris, "An Archaeological Survey of Fort Louis de la Mobile," report on file, Mobile Historic Development Commission, Mobile, AL, 1970. A cannon probably once deployed at Old Mobile is illustrated by David Smithweck, *Historic Cannons of Mobile, Alabama: An Illustrated Guide* (Mobile, AL: printed by author, 2014).

4. Gregory A. Waselkov, *Archaeology at the French Colonial Site of Old Mobile (Phase I: 1989–1991)* (Mobile: University of South Alabama, 1991), xiii, 7–8.

5. Some of the results of this long-term project include Ann S. Cordell, *Continuity and Change in Apalachee Pottery Manufacture* (Mobile: Center for Archaeological Studies, University of South Alabama, 2001); James Austin Gazaway, "A Comparison and Analysis of the Specie (Coins) Recovered from French Colonial Sites around Old Mobile and Spanish Colonial Sites around Pensacola," master's thesis, Department of Anthropology, University of West Florida, Pensacola, 2023; Kristen J. Gremillion, "Archaeobotany at Old Mobile," *Historical Archaeology* 36, no. 1 (2002): 117–28; James N. Gundersen, Gregory A. Waselkov, and Lillian J. K. Pollock, "Pipestone Argillite Artifacts from Old Mobile and Environs," *Historical Archaeology* 36, no. 1 (2002): 105–16; Marvin T. Smith, "Eighteenth-Century Glass Beads in the French Colonial Trade," *Historical Archaeology* 36, no. 1 (2002): 55–61; and a graphic novel by Barbara Filion, Gregory Waselkov, and Brandon Mitchell, *Jean-Paul's Daring Adventure: Stories from Old Mobile* (Mobile: Archaeology Museum, University of South Alabama, 2014). For a broader archaeological context, see Gregory A. Waselkov, *The Archaeology of French Colonial North America, English-French Edition* (Uniontown, PA: Society for Historical Archaeology, 1997); Marcel Moussette and Gregory A. Waselkov, *Archéologie de l'Amérique Coloniale Française* (Montréal, Canada: Lévesque Éditeur, 2013).

6. Gregory A. Waselkov, "French Colonial Archaeology at Old Mobile: An Introduction," *Historical Archaeology* 36, no. 1 (2002): 3–12; Gilles-Antoine Langlois, *Des villes pour la Louisiane française: Théorie et pratique de l'urbanistique coloniale au 18e siècle* (Paris: L'Harmattan, 2003).

7. Waselkov, "French Colonial Archaeology at Old Mobile"; Bonnie L. Gums, "Earthfast (*Pieux en Terre*) Structures at Old Mobile," *Historical Archaeology* 36, no. 1 (2002): 13–25; Diane E. Silvia, "Indian and French Interaction in Colonial Louisiana during the Early Eighteenth Century," PhD diss., Department of Anthropology, Tulane University, New Orleans, 2000, and "Native American and French Cultural Dynamics on the Gulf Coast," *Historical Archaeology* 36, no. 1 (2002): 26–35.

8. Higginbotham, *Old Mobile*.

9. Gregory A. Waselkov, *Old Mobile Archaeology* (Tuscaloosa: University of Alabama Press, 2005), 5–9; cf. Langlois, *Des villes pour la Louisiane française*.

10. Waselkov, *Old Mobile Archaeology*, 49.

11. Linda R. Shulsky, "Chinese Porcelain in Old Mobile," *Antiques* 150, no. 1 (July 1996): 80–89, and "Chinese Porcelain at Old Mobile," *Historical Archaeology*

36, no. 1 (2002): 97–104; Scott S. Williams and Roberto Junco, eds., *The Archaeology of Manila Galleons in the American Continent: The Wrecks of Baja California, San Agustín, and Santo Cristo de Burgos (Oregon)* (Cham, Switzerland: Springer, 2021).

12. Gregory A. Waselkov, "Old Mobile: Archaeological Treasures in Louisiana's First Capital." *64 Parishes* (Fall 2022): 44–52; Shannon Lee Dawdy, *Building the Devil's Empire: French Colonia New Orleans* (Chicago: University of Chicago Press, 2008); Marcel Giraud, *A History of French Louisiana*, vol. 1, *The Reign of Louis XIV, 1698–1715*, trans. Joseph C. Lambert (Baton Rouge: Louisiana State University Press, 1974); Nancy M. Miller Surrey, *The Commerce of Louisiana during the French Régime, 1699–1763*, with an introduction by Gregory A. Waselkov (Tuscaloosa: University of Alabama Press, 2006).

Chapter 17

1. Noel R. Stowe, *Archaeological Excavations at Port Dauphin* (Mobile: Archaeological Research Laboratory, University of South Alabama, 1977); George W. Shorter Jr., "The Archaeological Site of Port Dauphin (1MB61): Its Role in the French Colony on Mobile Bay," master's thesis, Department of Geography and Anthropology, Louisiana State University, Baton Rouge, 1995. For Fort Port Dauphin's history, see Marcel Giraud, *A History of French Louisiana*, vol. 1, *The Reign of Louis XIV, 1698–1715*, trans. Joseph C. Lambert (Baton Rouge: Louisiana State University Press, 1974), *A History of French Louisiana*, vol. 2, *Years of Transition, 1715–1717*, trans. Joseph C. Lambert (Baton Rouge: Louisiana State University Press, 1993), *Histoire de la Louisiane française*, vol. 3, *L'époque de John Law, 1717–1720* (Paris: Presses de Universitaires de France, 1966), and *Histoire de la Louisiane française*, vol. 4, *La Louisiane après le système de Law, 1721–1723* (Paris: Presses de Universitaires de France, 1971).

2. George W. Shorter Jr., "Status and Trade at Port Dauphin," *Historical Archaeology* 36, no. 1 (2002): 135–42.

3. Gregory A. Waselkov, *Old Mobile Archaeology* (Tuscaloosa: University of Alabama Press, 2005), 28–30. Joan DeJean provided the translation and literary reference for the signet's inscription. On taverns, see Nancy M. Miller Surrey, *The Commerce of Louisiana during the French Régime, 1699–1763*, with an introduction by Gregory A. Waselkov (Tuscaloosa: University of Alabama Press, 2006), 273–77.

4. For a recent study of French women who landed at Port Dauphin as exiles to the Louisiane colony, see Joan DeJean, *Mutinous Women: How French Convicts Became Founding Mothers of the Gulf Coast* (New York: Basic Books, 2022).

Chapter 18

1. On the history of Fort Condé/Charlotte, including the 1780 siege, see René Chartrand, *The Forts of New France: The Great Lakes, the Plains, and the Gulf Coast, 1600–1763* (Oxford, UK: Osprey Publishing, 2010); William S. Coker, ed., *The Military Presence on the Gulf Coast* (Pensacola, FL: Gulf Coast History and Humanities Conference, 1977); William S. Coker and Hazel P. Coker, *The Siege of Mobile, 1780, in Maps* (Pensacola, FL: Perdido Bay Press, 1982); Francisco de Borja Medina Rojas, *José de Ezpeleta, gobernador de La Mobila, 1780–1781* (Seville, Spain: Escuela de Estudios Hispano-Americanos de Sevilla, 1980).

2. Donald A. Harris, "Fort Condé: A Problem in Salvage Archaeology," master's thesis, Department of Anthropology, University of Florida, Gainesville, 1969, and

"A French Colonial Well: Its Construction, Excavation and Contents," in *Conference on Historic Site Archaeology Papers 5*, ed. Stanley South, 51–80 (Columbia: University of South Carolina, 1970); Donald A. Harris and Jerry J. Nielsen, *Archaeological Salvage Investigations at the Site of French Fort Condé, Mobile, Alabama* (Tuscaloosa: Department of Anthropology, University of Alabama, 1972).

3. David Smithweck, *Historic Cannons of Mobile, Alabama: An Illustrated Guide* (Mobile, AL: printed by author, 2014).

4. Nicholas H. Holmes, "Restoration of Mobile's First Court House Jail, Later Known as the Kirkbride House," manuscript on file, Condé-Charlotte House Museum, Mobile, AL, 1947; Diane E. Silvia and Gregory A. Waselkov, *Roads to the Past: Phase II Archaeological Research and Testing Prior to Interstate-10 Revisions in Mobile, Alabama (Virginia Street Interchange to West Tunnel Interchange)* (Mobile: Center for Archaeological Studies, University of South Alabama, 1993); George W. Shorter Jr., et al., *Phase I and II Archaeological Investigations in Fort Condé Village (1MB132), Mobile, Alabama* (Mobile: Center for Archaeological Studies, University of South Alabama, 2001); Bonnie L. Gums and Gregory A. Waselkov, *Limited Test Excavations at Condé-Charlotte Museum House (1MB470), Mobile, Mobile County, Alabama* (Mobile: Center for Archaeological Studies, University of South Alabama, 2010); Craig T. Sheldon and John W. Cottier, *Origins of Mobile: Archaeological Investigations at the Courthouse Site, Mobile, Alabama*, Archaeological Monograph 5 (Auburn, AL: Department of Sociology and Anthropology, Auburn University, 1983).

5. Bonnie L. Gums, *Archaeological Investigations on Site 1MB387, the Mobile Country Probate Courthouse Block, Mobile, Alabama* (Mobile: Center for Archaeological Studies, University of South Alabama, 2006); Walter E. Klippel and Bonnie E. Price. "Bone Disc Manufacturing Debris from Newfoundland to Antigua during the Historic Period," in *Bones as Tools: Current Methods and Interpretations in Worked Bone Studies*, ed. Christian Gates St-Pierre and Renee B. Walker, 133–42, International Series 1622 (Oxford, UK: BAR, 2007).

6. For a cartographic history of changes to the built environment of downtown Mobile, see Bonnie L. Gums, Gregory A. Waselkov, and Sarah B. Mattics, *Planning for the Past: An Archaeological Resource Management Plan for the City of Mobile, Alabama*, Archaeological Monograph 5 (Mobile: Center for Archaeological Studies, University of South Alabama, 1999).

Chapter 19

1. Ellen Foster, France Miller, and Gladys Rutan Daw, comps. And eds., *The Krebs Family History* (Pascagoula, MS: printed by author, 1991); Bonnie L. Gums and Gregory A. Waselkov, *Archaeology at La Pointe-Krebs Plantation in Old Spanish Fort Park (22JA526), Pascagoula, Jackson County, Mississippi* Archaeological Report no. 35 (Jackson: Mississippi Department of Archives and History, 2015), 10.

2. Jean-François-Benjamin Dumont de Montigny, *The Memoir of Lieutenant Dumont, 1715–1747: A Sojourner in the French Atlantic*, trans. Gordon M. Sayre, ed. Gordon M. Sayre and Carla Zecher (Chapel Hill: University of North Carolina Press, 2012), 119–20.

3. Bernard Romans, *A Concise Natural History of East and West Florida*, ed. Kathryn E. Holland Braund (Tuscaloosa: University of Alabama Press, 1999), 90.

4. Gums and Waselkov, *Archaeology at La Pointe-Krebs Plantation*, 11–17; Thomas J. Padgett, *Archaeological Testing at the Old Spanish Fort, Pascagoula* (Hattiesburg:

Department of Sociology and Anthropology, University of Southern Mississippi, 1979); Gregory A. Waselkov and Diane E. Silvia, *Archaeology at the Krebs House (Old Spanish Fort), Pascagoula, Mississippi*, Archaeological Monograph 1 (Mobile: Center for Archaeological Studies, University of South Alabama, 1995); Bonnie L. Gums, *Archaeology Survey of Old Spanish Fort Park, Pascagoula, Mississippi* (Mobile: Center for Archaeological Studies, University of South Alabama, 1996); Bonnie L. Gums and Gregory A. Waselkov, *House and Excavation Photos from the La Pointe-Krebs House Site (22JA526), Pascagoula, Mississippi* (Mobile: Center for Archaeological Studies, University of South Alabama, 2010); Cameron Gill and Bonnie L. Gums, *Limited Archaeological Survey for Historic-Period Native American Sites in Jackson County, Mississippi* (Mobile: Center for Archaeological Studies, University of South Alabama, 2012); Bonnie L. Gums, *Summary of Examination of Museum Collections of La Pointe-Krebs House, Pascagoula, Jackson County, Mississippi* (Mobile: Center for Archaeological Studies, University of South Alabama, 2013); Bonnie L. Gums, *Results of Fieldwork for Archaeological Monitoring of Sand and Backfill Removal at La Pointe-Krebs House (22JA526), City of Pascagoula, Jackson County, Mississippi* (Mobile: Center for Archaeological Studies, University of South Alabama, 2015); Bonnie L. Gums, *Results of Fieldwork for Second Archaeological Monitoring of Restoration Activities at La Pointe-Krebs House (22JA526), City of Pascagoula, Jackson County, Mississippi* (Mobile: Center for Archaeological Studies, University of South Alabama, 2015); Bonnie L. Gums, *Results of Fieldwork for Third Archaeological Monitoring of Restoration Activities at La Pointe-Krebs House (22JA526), City of Pascagoula, Jackson County, Mississippi* (Mobile: Center for Archaeological Studies, University of South Alabama, 2016).

5. Waselkov and Silvia, *Archaeology at the Krebs House*, 30–38.

6. George T. Fore, *The La Pointe-Krebs House, Pascagoula, Mississippi: Architectural Development and Interpretation* (Pascagoula, MS: La Pointe-Krebs Foundation, 2017); Grant L. Harley et al., "Precision Dating and Cultural History of the La Pointe-Krebs House (22JA526), Pascagoula, Mississippi, USA," *Journal of Archaeological Science: Reports* 20 (August 2018): 87–96.

7. Gregory A. Waselkov, David W. Morgan, and Billie Coleman, "Ceramics and Glass Beads as Symbolic Mixed Media in Colonial Native North America," *Beads: Journal of the Society of Bead Researchers* 27 (2015): 3–15.

8. Elizabeth J. Reitz and Gregory A. Waselkov, "Vertebrate Use at Early Colonies on the Southeastern Coasts of Eastern North America," *International Journal of Historical Archaeology* 19, no. 1 (2015): 21–45.

9. Gregory A. Waselkov, "Smoking Pipes as Signifiers of French Creole Identity," in *Tu Sais Mon Vieux Jean-Pierre: Essays on the Archaeology and History of New France and Canadian Culture in Honour of Jean-Pierre Chrestien*, ed. John Willis, 137–59, Mercury Series, Archaeology Paper 178 (Ottawa, Canada: Canadian Museum of History and University of Ottawa Press, 2017); Marie-Hélène Daviau and Roland Tremblay, "Le calumet canadien comme symbole d'un mode de vie fondateur," In *Feu, lueurs et fureurs: Archéologie du Québec*, ed. Christian Gates St.-Pierre and Yves Monette, 146–47 (Montréal, Canada: Pointe-à-Callière and Les Éditions de l'Homme, 2022).

Chapter 20

1. Louis de Vendel Chaudron, "Old Fort and Indian Canal at Bon Secours, from an Essay Read before the Iberville Historical Society," *Lorgnette* 1, no. 1 (1902): 1;

Luciano Villamil, "Round Bon Secours Bay," *Spring Hill Review* 1, no. 1 (1899): 71–73; Walter B. Jones, "Archaeological Survey of Baldwin County," manuscript on file, Center for Archaeological Studies, University of South Alabama, Mobile, 1933; Kay Nuzum, "Bon Secour," *Baldwin County Historical Society Quarterly* 1 (1973): 10–14.

2. David M. White, "The 'Mystery Fort' Site in Bon Secour, Alabama: Excavations, 1964–65," manuscript on file, Center for Archaeological Studies, University of South Alabama, Mobile, 1965; Thomas Spalding, "On the Mode of Constructing Tabby Buildings, and the Propriety of Improving Our Plantations in a Permanent Manner," *Southern Agriculturalist* 3, no. 12 (December 1830): 617–24.

3. David M. White and Susan M. Guyette, *Zen Birding* (Ropley, UK: O-Books, 2009).

4. Sarah E. White, *Phase II Investigations at 1BA55: Midden, Mounds, and Chungke Stones on the Bon Secour River* (Mobile: Center for Archaeological Studies, University of South Alabama, 2006).

5. Charley Wakeford and Meme Wakeford, *Food, Fun, and Fable: Recipes and Tales of the River Country* (Bon Secour, AL: printed by author, 1965).

Chapter 21

1. Preliminary fieldwork at the Dog River bridge site included Gregory C. Spies and Michael T. Rushing, *Archaeological Investigations at the Bay Oaks Site on Dog River, Mobile County, Alabama* (Mobile, AL: Northern Gulf Coast Archaeological Research Consortium, 1983); Noel R. Stowe and Diane E. Silvia, *Report of the Preliminary Archaeological Testing of the Alabama Highway Department's Proposed New Dog River Bridge* (Mobile: Archaeological Research Laboratory, University of South Alabama, 1988); Julie Barnes Smith, *Archaeological Investigations of Site 1MB161, Dog River, Mobile County, Alabama*, Report of Investigations 73 (Moundville: University of Alabama Museums, Office of Archaeological Services, 1995).

2. Gregory A. Waselkov and Bonnie L. Gums, *Plantation Archaeology at Rivière aux Chiens, ca. 1725–1848*, Archaeological Monograph 7 (Mobile: Center for Archaeological Studies, University of South Alabama, 2000), 124, 133–36.

3. Waselkov and Gums, *Plantation Archaeology at Rivière aux Chiens*, 1–110.

4. The first archaeological indication of the Chatos near Dog River was reported by Noel R. Stowe, "Pot Sherds and a Brass Kettle: Continuity and Change at 1MB82," *Journal of Alabama Archaeology* 21, no. 1 (1975): 68–78. Historical documentation on the Chatos is summarized in Waselkov and Gums, *Plantation Archaeology at Rivière aux Chiens*, 30–31; George E. Lankford, "Chacato, Pensacola, Tohomé, Naniaba, and Mobila," in *Handbook of North American Indians*, vol. 14, *Southeast*, ed. Raymond D. Fogelson, 664–68 (Washington, DC: Smithsonian Institution Press, 2004); Ives Goddard et al., "Small Tribes of the Western Southeast," in *Handbook of North American Indians*, vol. 14, *Southeast*, ed. Raymond D. Fogelson, 174–90 (Washington, DC: Smithsonian Institution Press, 2004). For a broad view of the *petites nations*, see Elizabeth N. Ellis, *The Great Power of Small Nations: Indigenous Diplomacy in the Gulf South* (Philadelphia: University of Pennsylvania Press, 2022).

5. Waselkov and Gums, *Plantation Archaeology at Rivière aux Chiens*, 124–130; Ann S. Cordell, *Continuity and Change in Apalachee Pottery Manufacture* (Mobile: Center for Archaeological Studies, University of South Alabama, 2001). On Native-made ceramics of the colonial era, see Richard S. Fuller, "A Ceramic Lingua Franca? The Origins, Attributes, and Dimensions of a Historic Period Indian Pottery Tradition

on the Northern Gulf Coastal Plain," manuscript on file, Alabama Museum of Natural History, University of Alabama, Tuscaloosa, 1991, and "Indian Pottery and Cultural Chronology of the Mobile-Tensaw Basin and Alabama Coast," *Journal of Alabama Archaeology* 44, no. 1 (1998): 1–51.

6. Waselkov and Gums, *Plantation Archaeology at Rivière aux Chiens*, 98–105. In recent decades there has been some excellent historical research on interactions between European colonists and Native and African peoples, free and enslaved, in colonial Louisiane, including Robin F. A. Fabel, *The Economy of British West Florida, 1763–1783* (Tuscaloosa: University of Alabama Press, 1988); Daniel H. Usner Jr., *Indians, Settlers, and Slaves in a Frontier Exchange Economy: The Lower Mississippi Valley before 1783* (Chapel Hill: University of North Carolina Press, 1992); Ira Berlin, *Many Thousands Gone: The First Two Centuries of Slavery in North America* (Cambridge, MA: Harvard University Press, 1998); Brett Rushforth, *Bonds of Alliance: Indigenous and Atlantic Slaveries in New France* (Chapel Hill: University of North Carolina Press, 2012); Kathleen DuVal, *Independence Lost: Lives on the Edge of the American Revolution* (New York: Random House, 2015).

7. Waselkov and Gums, *Plantation Archaeology at Rivière aux Chiens*, 116–18.

8. Waselkov and Gums, *Plantation Archaeology at Rivière aux Chiens*, 169–78; Elizabeth J. Reitz and Gregory A. Waselkov, "Vertebrate Use at Early Colonies on the Southeastern Coasts of Eastern North America," *International Journal of Historical Archaeology* 19, no. 1 (2015): 21–45.

Chapter 22

1. Bonnie L. Gums, *Material Culture of an 18th-Century Gulf Coast Plantation: The Augustin Rochon Plantation, ca. 1750s–1780, Baldwin County, Alabama* (Mobile: Center for Archaeological Studies, University of South Alabama, 2000); Gregory A. Waselkov and Bonnie L. Gums, *Plantation Archaeology at Rivière aux Chiens, ca. 1725–1848*, Archaeological Monograph 7 (Mobile: Center for Archaeological Studies, University of South Alabama, 2000), 80.

2. Gregory A. Waselkov and Mike Bunn, "A Tale of Two Forts," *Alabama Heritage* 145 (Summer 2022): 32–45; Francisco de Borja Medina Roja, *José de Ezpeleta, gobernador de La Mobila, 1780–1781* (Seville, Spain: Escuela de Estudios Hispano-Americanos de Sevilla, 1980).

3. Jacqueline Oliver Vidrine, *Love's Legacy: The Mobile Marriages Recorded in French, Transcribed and Annotated Abstracts in English, 1724–1786* (Lafayette: Center for Louisiana Studies, University of Southwestern Louisiana, 1985); Robin F. A. Fabel, *The Economy of British West Florida, 1763–1783* (Tuscaloosa: University of Alabama Press, 1988); Joan DeJean, *Mutinous Women: How French Convicts Became Founding Mothers of the Gulf Coast* (New York: Basic Books, 2022), 235.

4. Gums, *Material Culture of an 18th-Century Gulf Coast Plantation*; Gregory A. Waselkov, "Smoking Pipes as Signifiers of French Creole Identity," in *Tu Sais Mon Vieux Jean-Pierre: Essays on the Archaeology and History of New France and Canadian Culture in Honour of Jean-Pierre Chrestien*, ed. John Willis, 137–59, Mercury Series, Archaeology Paper 178 (Ottawa, Canada: Canadian Museum of History and University of Ottawa Press, 2017); Marie-Hélène Daviau and Roland Tremblay, "Le calumet canadien comme symbole d'un mode de vie fondateur," in *Feu, lueurs et fureurs: Archéologie du Québec*, ed. Christian Gates St.-Pierre and Yves Monette, 146–47 (Montréal, Canada: Pointe-à-Callière and Les Éditions de l'Homme, 2022).

Chapter 23

1. Howard Barney, *Mister Bell: A Life Story of Walter D. Bellingrath, Founder of Bellingrath Gardens* (Mobile, AL: Bellingrath-Morse Foundation, 1979).

2. Carl A. Brasseaux, *France's Forgotten Legion: Service Records of French Military and Administrative Personnel Stationed in the Mississippi Valley and Gulf Coast Region, 1699–1769* (Baton Rouge: Louisiana State University Press, 2000); Milo B. Howard Jr. and Robert R. Rea, "Introduction," in *The Memoire Justificatif of the Chevalier Montault de Monberaut: Indian Diplomacy in British West Florida 1763–1765*, trans. Milo B. Howard Jr. and Robert R. Rea (Tuscaloosa: University of Alabama Press, 1965), 17.

3. Howard and Rea, "Introduction," 21.

4. Howard and Rea, "Introduction," 49–51; Peter J. Hamilton, *Colonial Mobile*, ed. Charles G. Summersell (Tuscaloosa: University of Alabama Press, 1976), 237. On the social turmoil accompanying French withdrawal from their Louisiane colony, see Daniel H. Usner Jr., "'A Prospect of the Grand Sublime': An Atlantic World Borderland Seen and Unseen by William Bartram," in *The Attention of a Traveller: Essays on William Bartram's Travels and Legacy*, ed. Kathryn H. Braund, 19–36 (Tuscaloosa: University of Alabama Press, 2022).

5. "Survey of the Bay and River Mobile, 1775," CO 700/Florida 51, 1775, Colonial Office, National Archives, Kew, UK.

6. Bonnie L. Gums, *Archaeology at Lisloy Plantation, Site 1MB312, Bellingrath Gardens and Home, Mobile County, Alabama* (Mobile: Center for Archaeological Studies, University of South Alabama, 2001).

Chapter 24

1. David Taitt, "A Plan of Part of the Rivers Tombecbe, Alabama, Perdido, & Scambia in the Province of West Florida, 1771," Geography and Map Division. Library of Congress, Washington, DC; "Survey of the Bay and River Mobile, 1775," CO 700/Florida 51, 1775, Colonial Office, National Archives, Kew, UK; Dunbar Rowland, ed., *Peter Chester: Third Governor of the Province of British West Florida under British Domination 1770–1781*, vol. 5 (Jackson: Mississippi Historical Society, 1925), 60 (Mease quote); Bonnie L. Gums, "Eighteenth-Century Plantations in the Northern Gulf Coast Region," *Gulf Coast Historical Review* 14 (1998): 120–42.

2. Walter Lowrie, *American State Papers, Public Lands*, vol. 3 (Washington, DC: Duff Green, 1984), 11; "Plan no. 1815, Luis Dolive, Mobile, 1808," Pintado Papers, Special Collections, Louisiana State University Libraries, Baton Rouge; Richard S. Lackey, comp. *Frontier Claims in the Lower South* (New Orleans, LA: Polyanthos, 1977), 41–42; William L. D'Olive, comp. "The D'Olive Family History and Data, 1999," manuscript on file, Mobile Public Library, Local History and Genealogy Division, Mobile, AL; Prescott A. Parker, *Story of the Tensaw: Blakely; Spanish Fort; Jacksons Oak; Fort Mims* (Montrose, AL: P. A. Parker, 1922).

3. Clarence B. Moore, "Certain Aboriginal Remains on Mobile Bay and on Mississippi Sound," *Journal of the Academy of Natural Sciences of Philadelphia*, 2nd ser., 13, no. 2 (1905): 287–89; Bonnie L. Gums, *Archaeological Survey of the D'Olive Plantation (1BA190) and The Village in Daphne, Baldwin County, Alabama* (Mobile: Center for Archaeological Studies, University of South Alabama, 2003).

4. Bonnie Gums et al., *Phase III Archaeological Data Recovery at Sites 1BA608 and 1BA609 for the Proposed Paradiso Subdivision, Daphne, Baldwin County, Alabama* (Mobile: Center for Archaeological Studies, University of South Alabama, 2009).

5. Greg Waselkov and Mike Bunn, "A Tale of Two Forts," *Alabama Heritage* 145 (Summer 2022): 38–39. Remains of similar palisade fenced compounds have been found at other excavated French colonial sites, such as reported by Craig T. Sheldon, Ned J. Jenkins, and Gregory A. Waselkov, "French Habitations at the Alabama Post, ca. 1720–1763," *Archéologiques, Collection Hors Série* 2 (2008): 112–26.

6. Waselkov and Bunn, "Tale of Two Forts."

7. Francisco de Borja Medina Rojas, *José de Ezpeleta, gobernador de La Mobila, 1780–1781* (Seville, Spain: Escuela de Estudios Hispano-Americanos de Sevilla, 1980).

8. Medina Rojas, *José de Ezpeleta*, 295–96, 368; K. G. Davies, ed., *Documents of the American Revolution, 1770–1783*, vol. 18, *Transcripts, 1780* (Dublin: Irish University Press, 1978), 219–20.

9. Medina Rojas, *José de Ezpeleta*, 378–80.

10. Jack D. L. Holmes, "Alabama's Forgotten Settlers: Notes on the Spanish Mobile District, 1780–1813." *Alabama Historical Quarterly* 33 (Summer 1971): 87–97, "Alabama's Bloodiest Day of the American Revolution: Counterattack at the Village, January 7, 1781," *Alabama Review* 29, no. 3 (1976): 207–19, and "German Troops in Alabama during the American Revolution: The Battle of January 7, 1781." *Alabama Historical Quarterly* 38 (Spring 1976): 5–9; Bruce E. Burgoyne, *The 3rd English-Waldeck Regiment in the American Revolution* (Bowie, MD: Heritage Books, 1999); Bruce E. Burgoyne, ed. and trans., *Eighteenth-Century America: A Hessian Report on the People, the Land, the War as Noted in the Diary of Chaplain Philipp Waldeck (1776–1780)* (Bowie, MD: Heritage Books, 1995); Edwin W. Besch, Shawn Holland, and Dave W. Morgan, "A Bayonet and a Musket Barrel from the 3d Waldeck Regiment at the Museum of Mobile, and Action at 'The Village' on 7 January 1781," *Military Collector and Historian* 55 (2003): 144–54.

11. Medina Rojas, *José de Ezpeleta*, 533–37; Benjamin Baynton, *Authentic Memoirs of William Augustus Bowles, Esquire* (London: R. Faulder, 1791), 28–34; John Campbell, letter to Henry Clinton, Pensacola, 5 January 1781, Sir Guy Carleton Papers, Colonial Office, PRO 30:55/9899, National Archives, Kew, UK; K. G. Davies, ed., *Documents of the American Revolution, 1770–1783*, vol. 20, *Transcripts, 1781* (Dublin: Irish University Press, 1979), 58–60; José de Ezpeleta, letter to Manuel Cabello, Mabila, Enero 1781, Folio 30, Legajo 116, Papeles Procedentes de la Isla de Cuba, Archivo General de Indias, Seville, Spain, and "Una carta . . . al Gobernador de la Luisiana, D. Bernardo de Galvez, Mobila, 20 de Enero de 1781," *Gazeta de Madrid* 28 (April 6, 1781): 291–94.

12. Waselkov and Bunn, "Tale of Two Forts."

Chapter 25

1. Kathrine R. Mickelson, "McLeod Plant Exploitation," in *The Late Woodland Period on the Lower Tombigbee River*, by George W. Shorter, 153–57, Archaeological Monograph 6 (Mobile: Center for Archaeological Studies, University of South Alabama, 1999); Kristen J. Gremillion, "Archaeobotany at Old Mobile," *Historical Archaeology* 36, no. 1 (2002): 117–28; Elizabeth J. Reitz and Gregory A. Waselkov, "Vertebrate Use at Early Colonies on the Southeastern Coasts of Eastern North America," *International Journal of Historical Archaeology* 19, no. 1 (2015): 21–45; Nancy M. Miller Surrey, *The Commerce of Louisiana during the French Régime, 1699–1763*, with an introduction by Gregory A. Waselkov (Tuscaloosa: University of Alabama Press, 2006).

2. Bonnie L. Gums and Gregory A. Waselkov, eds., *Life at the River's Edge: Phase III Archaeological Data Recovery at Sites 1MB510 and 1MB511 for Interstate 10 (I-10) Modifications, ALDOT Project# DPI-AL06(900), City of Mobile, Mobile County Alabama*, Archaeological Monograph 14 (Mobile: Center for Archaeological Studies, University of South Alabama, 2018); Diane E. Silvia and Gregory A. Waselkov, *Roads to the Past: Phase II Archaeological Research and Testing Prior to Interstate-10 Revisions in Mobile, Alabama (Virginia Street Interchange to West Tunnel Interchange)* (Mobile: Center for Archaeological Studies, University of South Alabama, 1993).

3. J. W. Joseph and Mary Beth Reed, *An Increase of the Town: An Archeological and Historical Investigation of the Proposed Mobile Convention Center Site (1MB194)*, Technical Report 13 (Stone Mountain, GA: New South Associates, 1991); Mary Beth Reed and J. W. Joseph, *From Alluvium to Commerce: Waterfront Architecture, Land Reclamation, and Commercial Development in Mobile, Alabama*, Technical Report 126 (Stone Mountain, GA: New South Associates, 1995); see chapters 27, 35, and 42 in this volume.

4. Howard Cyr, "Geoarchaeological Analysis of 1MB510," in Gums and Waselkov, *Life at the River's Edge*, 99–120.

5. David M. Ludlum, *Early American Hurricanes, 1492–1870* (Boston, MA: American Meteorological Society, 1963).

6. Peter H. Wood, *Black Majority: Negroes in Colonial South Carolina from 1670 through the Stono Rebellion* (New York: Alfred K. Knopf, 1974); Ira Berlin and Philip D. Morgan, eds., *Cultivation and Culture: Labor and the Shaping of Slave Life in the Americas* (Charlottesville: University of Virginia Press, 1993); Judith A. Carney, *Black Rice: The African Origins of Rice Cultivation in the Americas* (Cambridge, MA: Harvard University Press, 2001); Gwendolyn Midlo Hall, *Africans in Colonial Louisiana: The Development of Afro-Creole Culture in the Eighteenth Century* (Baton Rouge: Louisiana State University Press, 1992); Daniel C. Littlefield, *Rice and Slaves: Ethnicity and the Slave Trade in Colonial South Carolina* (Baton Rouge: Louisiana State University Press, 1981).

For more on the archaeology and history of rice cultivation in the South, see Andrew Agha, "Standing the Test of Time: Embankment Investigations, Their Implications for African Technology Transfer and Effect on African American Archaeology in South Carolina," *Atlantic Studies* 12, no. 3 (2015): 336–54; Christina Rae Butler, *Lowcountry at High Tide: A History of Flooding, Drainage, and Reclamation in Charleston, South Carolina* (Columbia: University of South Carolina Press, 2020); Richard Dwight Porcher Jr. and William Robert Judd, *The Market Preparation of Carolina Rice: An Illustrated History of Innovations in the Lowcountry Rice Kingdom* (Columbia: University of South Carolina Press, 2014); T. Addison Richards, "The Rice Lands of the South," *Harper's New Monthly Magazine* 19, no. 114 (November 1859): 721–38; Hayden R. Smith, *Carolina's Golden Fields: Inland Rice Cultivation in the South Carolina Lowcountry, 1670–1860* (Cambridge: Cambridge University Press, 2020).

Chapter 26

1. For an earlier effort to confront biased historical maps, see Helen Hornbeck Tanner, "The Land and Water Communication Systems of the Southeastern Indians," in *Powhatan's Mantle: Indians in the Colonial Southeast*, rev. ed., ed. Gregory A. Waselkov, Peter H. Wood, and Tom Hatley, 27–42 (Lincoln: University of Nebraska

Press, 2006). For a detailed place name study of the Alabama River in 1733, see Craig T. Sheldon Jr., Ian Thompson, and Gregory A. Waselkov, "Baron de Crenay's Map of Louisiane in 1733: An Ethnohistoric and Archaeological Voyage into Central Alabama," *Journal of Alabama Archaeology* 68, no. 2 (2022): 95–132.

2. John Stuart, "A Map of West Florida Part of Et: Florida. Georgia Part of So: Carolina . . . & Chactaw Chickasaw & Creek Nations, 1773," known as the Stuart-Gage map, maps 6-E-12, Thomas Gage Papers, Clements Library, University of Michigan, Ann Arbor, and "A Map of the Southern Indian District of North America, 1775," known as the Stuart-Purcell map, Ayer MS map 228 (vault oversize), Edward E. Ayer Collection, Newberry Library, Chicago.

3. John Richard Alden, *John Stuart and the Southern Colonial Frontier: A Study of Indian Relations, War, Trade and Land Problems in the Southern Wilderness, 1754–1775* (Ann Arbor: University of Michigan Press, 1944); William P. Cumming, *The Southeast in Early Maps*, 3rd ed., rev. Louis de Vorsey Jr. (Chapel Hill: University of North Carolina Press, 1998); Louis De Vorsey Jr., "The Colonial Southeast on 'An Accurate General Map,'" *Southeastern Geographer* 6, no. 1 (1966): 20–32, and *The Indian Boundary in the Southern Colonies, 1768–1775* (Chapel Hill: University of North Carolina Press, 1966); Bernard Romans, *A Concise Natural History of East and West Florida*, ed. Kathryn E. Holland Braund (Tuscaloosa: University of Alabama Press, 1999).

Chapter 27

1. Bonnie L. Gums and George W. Shorter Jr., *Archaeology at Mobile's Exploreum: Discovering the Buried Past*, Archaeological Monograph 3 (Mobile: Center for Archaeological Studies, University of South Alabama, 1998); Gregory C. Spies and Michael W. Burchfield, *A Cultural Resource Survey of the Proposed Omnimax Theater and Exhibit Area in the Esplanade and Quay of the French Fort Condé, Mobile, Alabama* (Mobile, AL: Archaeotechnics, Northern Gulf Coast Archaeological Research Consortium, 1995).

2. John T. Powell, "Marked Spanish Colonial Military Buttons of the Gulf Coast Region, Circa 1793–1821," *Military Collector and Historian* 49, no. 1 (1997): 2–11.

3. Gums and Shorter, *Archaeology at Mobile's Exploreum*, 7, 13, 28–31, 34–37.

4. Griffith Morgan Hopkins Jr., "Mobile in 1815," in *City Atlas of Mobile, Alabama: From Actual Surveys and Records* (Philadelphia: G. M. Hopkins, 1878); Work Progress Administration, *Interesting Transcripts of the British, French, and Spanish Records of the City & District of Mobile, State of Alabama, Found in Probate Court in Two Volumes*, trans. Jos. E. Caro (Mobile, AL: Local History and Genealogy Division, Mobile Public Library, 1937), 247–48, 318, 322, 363.

5. Mats Burström, *Ballast: Laden with History* (Lund, Sweden: Nordic Academic Press, 2018).

6. Bonnie L. Gums, *Archaeology at the Old City Hall and Southern Market Courtyard in Mobile, Alabama* (Mobile: Center for Archaeological Studies, University of South Alabama, 1999); George H. Ewert, "Old Times Will Come Again: The Municipal Market System of Mobile, Alabama, 1888–1901," master's thesis, Department of History, University of South Alabama, Mobile, 1993, and "The Politics of Food: Mobile's Public Markets in the Gilded Age," *Gulf Coast Historical Review* 10, no. 2 (1994): 140–50; Nicholas H. Holmes Jr., "Mobile's City Hall," *Alabama Heritage* 6 (1987): 3–15.

7. James M. Goodwin and C. Haire, *Plan and View of the City of Mobile* (New York:

R. Tiller, 1824), Geography and Map Division, 2012593360, Library of Congress, Washington, DC; Elizabeth Barrett Gould, *From Fort to Port: An Architectural History of Mobile, Alabama, 1711–1918* (Tuscaloosa: University of Alabama Press, 1988).

Chapter 28

1. Noel R. Stowe, ed., *An Archaeological-Historical Survey and Test Excavations at the Blakeley Site* (Mobile: Archaeological Research Laboratory, University of South Alabama, 1977).

2. Gregory A. Waselkov and Bonnie L. Gums, *Plantation Archaeology at Rivière aux Chiens, ca. 1725–1848*, Archaeological Monograph 7 (Mobile: Center for Archaeological Studies, University of South Alabama, 2000), 27–30, 53, 92; Francisco de Borja Medina Rojas, *José de Ezpeleta, gobernador de La Mobila, 1780–1781* (Seville, Spain: Escuela de Estudios Hispano-Americanos de Sevilla, 1980), 151, 176–81.

3. Alice A. Ivas, "Caught in the Middle: The Apalachees of Colonial Mobile," master's thesis, Department of Anthropology, University of Alabama, Tuscaloosa, 2005; Patrick Lee Johnson, "Apalachee Identity on the Gulf Coast Frontier," *Native South* 6, no. 2 (2013): 110–41; Michele Marie Piggott, "The Apalachee after San Luis: Exploring Cultural Hybridization through Ceramic Practice," master's thesis, Department of Anthropology, University of West Florida, Pensacola, 2015, and "The Materiality of the Apalachee Diaspora: An Indigenous History of Contact and Colonialism in the Gulf South," *Southeastern Archaeology* 41, no. 1 (2022): 53–73.

4. Clarence B. Moore, "Certain Aboriginal Remains on Mobile Bay and on Mississippi Sound," *Journal of the Academy of Natural Sciences of Philadelphia*, 2nd ser., 13, no. 2 (1905): 284–286; Craig T. Sheldon Jr., ed., *The Southern and Central Alabama Expeditions of Clarence Bloomfield Moore* (Tuscaloosa: University of Alabama Press, 2001), 40–41.

5. Cameron Gill and Bonnie L. Gums, *Summary of Excavations of the "Courthouse Site" (1BA221) at Historic Blakeley State Park, Baldwin County, Alabama* (Mobile: Center for Archaeological Studies, University of South Alabama, 2011); *Mobile Commercial Register*, "Baldwin County Jail," August 15, 1832, 3; James C. Parker, "Blakeley: A Frontier Seaport," *Alabama Review* 27, no. 1 (1974): 39–51.

6. Christopher C. Andrews, *History of the Campaign of Mobile* (New York: D. Van Nostrand, 1867); Arthur W. Bergeron Jr., *Confederate Mobile* (Baton Rouge: Louisiana State University Press, 1991); Mike Bunn, *The Assault on Fort Blakeley* (Charleston, SC: History Press, 2021); Raven Christopher, *Phase I Cultural Resource Assessment of a 103-Acre Tract for the Proposed Location of a Veteran's Cemetery in Spanish Fort, Baldwin County, Alabama* (Mobile: Center for Archaeological Studies, University of South Alabama, 2010).

Chapter 29

1. Gregory A. Waselkov, *A Conquering Spirit: Fort Mims and the Redstick War of 1813–1814* (Tuscaloosa: University of Alabama Press, 2006), 127–35; quotes from Albert James Pickett, "Notes Taken from the Lips of Col. Robert James, 1848," section 12, notes, Pickett Family Papers, LPR185, Alabama Department of Archives and History, Montgomery.

2. Waselkov, *Conquering Spirit*; Claudio Saunt, *Unworthy Republic: The Dispossession of Native Americans and the Road to Indian Territory* (New York: W. W. Norton, 2020).

3. Albert James Pickett, *History of Alabama, and Incidentally of Georgia and Mississippi, from the Earliest Period*, 2 vols. (Charleston, SC: Walker and James, 1851). Also see Theron A. Nunez Jr., ed., "Creek Nativism and the Creek War of 1813–1814," *Ethnohistory* 5, no. 1 (1958): 1–47, no. 2 (1958): 131–75, and no. 3 (1958): 292–301; Kathryn E. Holland Braund, ed., *Tohopeka: Rethinking the Creek War and the War of 1812* (Tuscaloosa: University of Alabama Press, 2012); Howard T. Weir III, *A Paradise of Blood: The Creek War of 1813–14* (Yardley, PA: Westholme Publishing, 2016).

4. Gregory A. Waselkov, Bonnie L. Gums, and James W. Parker, *Archaeology at Fort Mims: Excavation Contexts and Artifact Catalog*, Archaeological Monograph 12 (Mobile: Center for Archaeological Studies, University of South Alabama, 2006), 1–10.

5. Noel R. Stowe and Marvin E. Hoyt, *Archaeological Excavations at Fort Mims: 1973* (Mobile: Archaeological Research Laboratory, University of South Alabama, 1973), and *Archeological Investigation at Fort Mims*, ed. Susan C. Olsen, Archeological Completion Report Series, Number 4 (Washington, DC: National Park Service, 1975); Joseph F. Riccio and Conrad A. Gazzier, "Infrared Color Photography of the Fort Mims Site, Alabama," *Journal of Alabama Archaeology* 20, no. 2 (1974): 217–21.

6. Waselkov, Gums, and Parker, *Archaeology at Fort Mims*.

7. Bryan S. Haley and Jay K. Johnson, *Geophysical Investigations at Fort Mims, Alabama* (Oxford: Center for Archaeological Research, University of Mississippi, 2003); Waselkov, Gums, and Parker, *Archaeology at Fort Mims*, 20–21.

8. Waselkov, Gums, and Parker, *Archaeology at Fort Mims*, 20–24.

9. Wayne Curtis, "Clarifying an Historic Event: Archaeologists Are Working to Uncover the Details of the Massacre at Fort Mims," *American Archaeology* 11, no. 3 (2007): 12–17; Benjamin Salvage, "Map of Fort Mims and Its Environs, 1813," LPR185, Pickett Family Papers, Alabama Department of Archives and History, Montgomery.

10. Lawrence E. Babits and Stephanie Gandulla, eds., *The Archaeology of French and Indian War Frontier Forts* (Gainesville: University Press of Florida, 2013); McDonald Brooms, *Archaeological Investigations at the Kennedy Mill Site, 1BA301, in Baldwin County, Alabama* (Troy, AL: Archaeological Research Center, Troy State University, 1996); Mike Bunn and Clay Williams, *Battle for the Southern Frontier: The Creek War and the War of 1812* (Cheltenham, UK: History Press, 2008); Henry S. Halbert and Timothy H. Ball, *The Creek War of 1813 and 1814* (Chicago: Donohue and Henneberry, 1895); W. Stephen McBride, Kim Arbogast McBride, and Greg Adamson, *Frontier Forts in West Virginia: Historical and Archaeological Explorations* (Charleston: West Virginia Division of Culture and History, 2003); Nancy O'Malley, *Stockading Up: A Study of Pioneer Stations in the Inner Bluegrass Region of Kentucky*, rev. ed. (Lexington: Program for Cultural Resource Assessment, University of Kentucky, 1994), and *Boonesborough Unearthed: Frontier Archaeology at a Revolutionary Fort* (Lexington: University Press of Kentucky, 2019); Dana L. Pertermann and Holly Kathryn Norton, eds., *The Archaeology of Engagement: Conflict and Revolution in the United States* (College Station: Texas A&M University Press, 2015); Gregory A. Waselkov and Raven M. Christopher, *Archeological Identification of Creek War Sites, Part 2: Technical Report on Grant Agreement No. GA-2255–11–025* (Mobile: Center for Archaeological Studies, University of South Alabama, 2012); Gregory A. Waselkov and Brian M. Wood, "The Creek War of 1813–1814: Effects on Creek Society and Settlement Pattern," *Journal of Alabama Archaeology* 32, no. 1 (1986): 1–24.

11. Waselkov, *Conquering Spirit*, and "Formation of the Tensaw Community," in Paredes and Knight, *Red Eagle's Children*, 36–45. Also see Jean Chaudhuri and Joyotpaul Chaudhuri, *A Sacred Path: The Way of the Muscogee Creeks* (Los Angeles: UCLA American Indian Studies Center, University of California, 2001); J. Anthony Paredes and Judith Knight, eds., *Red Eagle's Children: Weatherford vs. Weatherford et al.* (Tuscaloosa: University of Alabama Press, 2012); Claudio Saunt, *A New Order of Things: Property, Power, and the Transformation of the Creek Indians, 1733–1816* (Cambridge: Cambridge University Press, 1999); Thomas S. Woodward, *Woodward's Reminiscences of the Creek, or Muscogee Indians, Contained in Letters to Friends in Georgia and Alabama* (Montgomery, AL: Barrett and Wimbish, 1859).

12. Waselkov, *Conquering Spirit*, 175–76.

Chapter 30

1. Gregory A. Waselkov, *A Conquering Spirit: Fort Mims and the Redstick War of 1813–1814* (Tuscaloosa: University of Alabama Press, 2006), 72–115; Kathryn E. Holland Braund, ed., *Tohopeka: Rethinking the Creek War and the War of 1812* (Tuscaloosa: University of Alabama Press, 2012); John E. Cornelison Jr. et al., *Barricade: Archeological and Geophysical Investigations at the Battle of Horseshoe Bend National Military Park, Alabama*, SEAC Accession 2611 (Tallahassee, FL: Southeast Archeological Center, National Park Service, 2018); Roy S. Dickens Jr., *Archaeological Investigations at Horseshoe Bend National Military Park, Alabama*, Special Publication 3 (Tuscaloosa: Alabama Archaeological Society, 1979); Charles H. Fairbanks, "Excavations at Horseshoe Bend, Alabama," *Florida Anthropologist* 15, no. 1 (1962): 41–56; Henry S. Halbert and Timothy H. Ball, *The Creek War of 1813 and 1814* (Chicago: Donohue and Henneberry, 1895); Theron A. Nunez Jr., ed., "Creek Nativism and the Creek War of 1813–1814," *Ethnohistory* 5, no. 1 (1958): 1–47, no. 2 (1958): 173–74 (quotes), and no. 3 (1958): 292–301.

2. George W. Creagh, "Notes Furnished by Col. G. W. Creagh of Clarke County, Alabama, 1847," section 2, notes, Albert J. Pickett Papers, Pickett Family Papers (1779–1904), LPR185, Alabama Department of Archives and History, Montgomery; Halbert and Ball, *Creek War of 1813 and 1814*, 241–65; Howard T. Weir III, *A Paradise of Blood: The Creek War of 1813–14* (Yardley, PA: Westholme Publishing, 2016).

3. Gregory A. Waselkov, "Return to Holy Ground: The Legendary Battle Site Discovered," *Alabama Heritage* 101 (2011): 28–37.

4. Gregory A. Waselkov, Craig T. Sheldon Jr., and Sarah B. Mattics, "Archaeology at the Site of *Ekvncakv*, Holy Ground," *Journal of Alabama Archaeology* 67, no. 1 (2021): 3–88.

5. Jessica F. Crawford, "The Conservancy to Acquire Its 400th Site," *American Archaeology* 14, no. 3 (2010): 44–45.

6. Dickens, *Archaeological Investigations*, 76; Fairbanks, "Excavations at Horseshoe Bend, Alabama," 48. For earlier forms of Creek domestic architecture, see Craig T. Sheldon Jr., "Persistence and Change in Historic Upper Creek Architecture," in *Native American Log Cabins in the Southeast*, ed. Gregory A. Waselkov, 25–44 (Knoxville: University of Tennessee Press, 2019); Gregory A. Waselkov and Kathryn E. Holland Braund, eds., *William Bartram on the Southeastern Indians* (Lincoln: University of Nebraska Press, 1995), fig. 31.

7. Waselkov, Sheldon, and Mattics, "Archaeology at the Site of *Ekvncakv*, Holy Ground," 19–34.

8. Waselkov, Sheldon, and Mattics, "Archaeology at the Site of *Ekvncakv*," 19–34.
9. Waselkov, Sheldon, and Mattics, "Archaeology at the Site of *Ekvncakv*," 71–75.
10. Waselkov, Sheldon, and Mattics, "Archaeology at the Site of *Ekvncakv*," 75–81.

Chapter 31

1. Louis de Vendel Chaudron, "How We Found the Site of Fort Louis de la Mobile," manuscript, Iberville Historical Society Collections, Mobile History Museum, Mobile, AL, 1902.
2. "Proceedings of the Spanish Evacuation Centennial at St. Stephens, May 6, 1899," in *Transactions of the Alabama Historical Society*, vol. 3, *1898–99* (Tuscaloosa: Alabama Historical Society, 1899), 198–201.
3. Mary Welsh, "Reminiscences of Old Saint Stephens, of More Than Sixty-five Years Ago," in Transactions of the *Alabama Historical Society*, vol. 3, *1898–99* (Tuscaloosa: Alabama Historical Society, 1899), 208, 211.
4. Jack D. L. Holmes, "Notes on the Spanish Fort San Esteban de Tombecbé," *Alabama Review* 18 (October 1965): 281–90.
5. James P. Pate, ed., *The Reminiscences of George Strother Gaines: Pioneer and Statesman of Early Alabama and Mississippi, 1805–1843* (Tuscaloosa: University of Alabama Press, 1998).
6. Thomas Perkins Abernethy, *The Formative Period in Alabama, 1815–1828* (Tuscaloosa: University of Alabama Press, 1965); H. Griffin and C. David, "The Importance of Thomas Freeman's Surveys in the Alabama Territory," *Surveying and Land Information Science* 73, no. 2 (2014): 49–60.
7. Nannetta Rochon, "50 Dollars Reward," *Halcyon and Tombeckbe Public Advertiser*, April 3, 1820, 1. For the first satirical poem published in Alabama, see Lewis Sewell, *The Last Campaign of Sir John Falstaff the II: or, The Hero of the Burnt-Corn Battle, a Heroi-Comic Poem* (St. Stephens, Mississippi Territory: 1815).
8. Tom Bailey, *The Five Capitals of Alabama: The Story of Alabama's Capital Cities from St. Stephens to Montgomery* (Montgomery, AL: New South Books, 2020); William H. Brantley Jr., *Three Capitals, A Book about the First Three Capitals of Alabama: St. Stephens, Huntsville, and Cahawba, 1818–1826* (Tuscaloosa: University of Alabama Press, 1976); Mike Bunn, *Early Alabama: An Illustrated Guide to the Formative Years, 1798–1826* (Tuscaloosa: University of Alabama Press, 2019); Herbert James Lewis, *Lost Capitals of Alabama* (Columbia, SC: History Press, 2014); Jacqueline Anderson Matte, *The History of Washington County: First County in Alabama* (Chatom, AL: Washington County Historical Society, 1982); Jacqueline A. Matte, Doris Brown, and Barbara Waddell, eds., *Old St. Stephens: Historical Records Survey* (Mobile, AL: St. Stephens Historical Commission, 1997).
9. Ernest F. Burchard, *The Cement Industry in Alabama*, Geological Survey of Alabama, Circular 14 (Tuscaloosa: University of Alabama, 1940); Ernest A. Mancini and Charles W. Copeland, "St. Stephens Quarry (Lone Star Cement Company Quarry), St. Stephens, Washington County, Alabama," *Centennial Field Guide, Geological Society of America (Southeastern Section)* 6 (1986): 373–78.
10. Rebecca A. Hawkins and James C. Litfin, *Phase I Survey of 190 Acres of the Citadel Limestone Quarry Property, Washington County, Alabama* (Cincinnati, OH: Algonquin Archaeological Consultants, 1996); Noel R. Stowe and Rebecca N. Stowe, *Summary of Archaeological Investigations at the Site of Old St. Stephens (1995–1996)* (St. Stephens, AL: St. Stephens Historical Commission, 1996); Jack D. Elliott Jr.,

The Streets of Old St. Stephens: An Examination of the Plats of Three Towns—Franklin, Rodney, St. Stephens (St. Stephens, AL: St. Stephens Historical Commission, 1998).

11. Bonnie L. Gums and Gregory A. Waselkov, *Recent Archaeological Investigations at Old St. Stephens* (Mobile: Center for Archaeological Studies, University of South Alabama, 1999), and *Archaeological Investigations on Two Tracts of Land at Old St. Stephens (1WN1)* (Mobile: Center for Archaeological Studies, University of South Alabama, 1999); George W. Shorter Jr., *A Cultural Resources Assessment of a Proposed Boat Launch Facility in Washington County, Alabama* (Mobile: Center for Archaeological Studies, University of South Alabama, 2002); George W. Shorter Jr., Sarah B. Mattics, and James W. Long, *Archaeology at Old St. Stephens (1WN1): Mapping and Testing the Site, Washington County, Alabama* (Mobile: Center for Archaeological Studies, University of South Alabama, 2002); George W. Shorter Jr. and Sarah B. Mattics, *Archaeology at Old St. Stephens (1WN1), River Structures 50 and 51, Washington County, Alabama"* (Mobile: Center for Archaeological Studies, University of South Alabama, 2004); George W. Shorter Jr., "St. Stephens: The Alabama Territory's First Capital," in *Alabama from Territory to Statehood: An Alabama Heritage Bicentennial Collection*, ed. Donna Cox Baker, Susan Reynolds, and Elizabeth Wade, 58–65 (Montgomery, AL: New South Books, 2019).

12. Stowe and Stowe, *Summary of Archaeological Investigations*; Shorter and Mattics, *Archaeology at Old St. Stephens (1WN1)*.

13. Shorter, "St. Stephens."

14. Welsh, "Reminiscences of Old Saint Stephens," 212.

Chapter 32

1. James P. Delgado et al., *Archaeological Investigations of 1BA704, A Nineteenth-Century Shipwreck Site in the Mobile River, Baldwin and Mobile Counties, Alabama*, Report prepared for the Alabama Historical Commission (Orlando: Search Inc., 2019), and *Clotilda: The History and Archaeology of the Last Slave Ship* (Tuscaloosa: University of Alabama Press, 2023); Ben Raines, *The Last Slave Ship: The True Story of How* Clotilda *Was Found, Her Descendants, and an Extraordinary Reckoning* (New York: Simon and Schuster, 2022).

2. Emma Langdon Roche, *Historic Sketches of the South* (New York: Knickerbocker Press, 1914), 120–21; Melanie Thornton, "Emma Langdon Roche's Artistic Legacy," *Alabama Heritage* 126 (Fall 2017): 6–15.

3. Zora Neale Hurston, "Cudjo's Own Story of the Last African Slaver," *Journal of Negro History* 12, no. 4 (1927): 648–63, and *Barracoon: The Story of the Last "Black Cargo,"* ed. Deborah G. Plant (New York: HarperCollins, 2018).

4. Natalie S. Robertson, *The Slave Ship* Clotilda *and the Making of AfricaTown, USA: Spirit of Our Ancestors* (New York: Praeger, 2008); Sylviane A. Diouf, *Dreams of Africa in Alabama: The Slave Ship* Clotilda *and the Story of the Last Africans Brought to America* (Oxford: Oxford University Press, 2009); John S. Sledge, *The Mobile River* (Columbia: University of South Carolina Press, 2015).

5. Neil Norman, *Report on Archaeological Survey and Testing at Peter Lee House Site and Lewis Quarter* (Williamsburg, VA: Department of Anthropology, College of William and Mary, 2010), and *Report on Mapping and Preservation Efforts at Old Plateau Cemetery* (Williamsburg, VA: Department of Anthropology, College of William and Mary, 2010).

6. Justin P. Dunnavant et al., *Phase I Archaeological Testing of the Africatown*

Welcome Center for the City of Mobile, Alabama (Mobile: Center for Archaeological Studies, University of South Alabama, 2021).

7. For more on Africatown, see John E. Land, *Mobile: Her Trade, Commerce and Industries 1883–4* (Mobile, AL: printed by author, 1884); Addie E. Pettaway, *Africatown, U.S.A.: Some Aspects of Folklife and Material Culture of an Historic Landscape* (Madison: Wisconsin Department of Public Instruction, 1985); John Henry Smith, *Africatown, U.S.A.: A Pictorial History of Plateau and Magazine Point, Alabama* (Mobile, AL: American Ethnic Science Society, 1981); Shaun Wilson and Jack Bergstresser, *Africatown Historic District National Register of Historic Places Registration Form* (Washington, DC: U.S. Department of the Interior, National Park Service, 2012).

8. Ayana Omilade Flewellen et al., "'The Future of Archaeology Is Antiracist': Archaeology in the Time of Black Lives Matter," *American Antiquity* 86, no. 2 (2021): 234.

9. Terrence Spivey, *An Ocean in My Bones* (Mobile, AL: Clotilda Descendants Association, 2022); Margaret Brown, dir., *Descendant* (Beverly Hills, CA: Participant, 2022).

Chapter 33

1. Robert N. Scott, ed., *The War of the Rebellion: A Compilation of the Official Records of the Union and Confederate Armies,* ser. I, vol. 35, part 2, *Correspondence* (Washington, DC: Government Printing Office, 1891), 130, 165, 253.

On the archaeology and history of Civil War blockade runners, see J. Barto Arnold III, Thomas J. Oertling, and Andrew W. Hall, "The *Denbigh* Project: Excavation of a Civil War Blockade-Runner," *International Journal of Nautical Archaeology* 30 (2001): 231–49; J. Barto Arnold III, *The Denbigh's Civilian Imports: Customs Records of a Civil War Blockade Runner between Mobile and Havana* (College Station: Texas A&M University, Institute of Nautical Archaeology, 2011); W. Watson, *The Civil War Adventures of a Blockade Runner* (College Station: Texas A&M University Press, 2001).

2. C. P. Watt, letter to his children, from Camp Withers, December 26, 1863, and letter to his wife, Fannie, from Camp Withers, January 13, 1864, C. P. Watt Civil War Letters Collection, SPR167, Alabama Department of Archives and History, Montgomery.

3. Joel Campbell DuBose, "Seventh Alabama Cavalry, Confederate Army," Confederate Regimental History Files, Alabama Department of Archives and History, Montgomery.

4. C. T. Pope, letter to his wife, July 13, 1864, Seventh Alabama Cavalry, CSA, Confederate Regimental History Files, Alabama Department of Archives and History, Montgomery.

5. George W. Shorter Jr., *Phase II Archaeological Testing of a Civil War Camp in Gulf Shores, Baldwin County, Alabama* (Mobile: Center for Archaeological Studies, University of South Alabama, 1995).

Chapter 34

1. Christopher C. Andrews, *History of the Campaign of Mobile* (New York: D. Van Nostrand, 1867); Arthur W. Bergeron Jr., *Confederate Mobile* (Baton Rouge: Louisiana State University Press, 1991); Paul Brueske, *The Last Siege: The Mobile*

Campaign, Alabama 1865 (Havertown, PA: Casemate, 2018); Calvin D. Cowles, comp., *Atlas to Accompany the Official Records of the Union and Confederate Armies*, 3 vols. (Washington, DC: Government Printing Office, 1891–95); George B. Davis, Leslie J. Perry, and Joseph W. Kirkley, eds., *The War of the Rebellion: A Compilation of the Official Records of the Union and Confederate Armies*, ser. 1, vol. 39 (2–3), *Correspondence* (Washington, DC: Government Printing Office, 1892); Major Miles D. McAlester, Major J. C. Palfrey, Captain C. J. Allen, and Captain Patten, *Siege Operations at Spanish Fort, Mobile Bay, by the U.S. Forces under Maj. Gen. Canby* (Philadelphia: Bowen, 1866); Lt. Colonel Victor von Sheliha, *A Treatise on Coast-Defence: Based on the Experience Gained by Officers of the Corps of Engineers of the Army of the Confederate States* (London: E. and F. N. Spon, 1868).

2. Dabney H. Maury, "Defence of Spanish Fort," *Southern Historical Society Papers* 39 (1914): 133; Maxfield Ludlow, *A Map of the State of Louisiana with Part of the State of Mississippi and Alabama Territory* (Philadelphia: W. Charles and J. G. Warnicke, 1817).

3. Lt. Colonel Victor von Sheliha, letter from Chief Engineer to Colonel John H. Gindrat, August 12, 1864, Engineer Office, Mobile. RG 109, War Department Collection of Confederate Archives, Letters Sent, Engineer Office, Department of the Gulf, ch. 3, vol. 16, p. 170, National Archives and Records Administration, Washington, DC (quote), and "Map of Spanish Fort and Vicinity, Drawn under the Direction of Lieut. Col. V. Sheliha, Summer 1864," 276/176, Jeremy Francis Gilmer Papers, Southern Historical Collection, Wilson Library, University of North Carolina, Chapel Hill.

4. Bonnie L. Gums and Gregory A. Waselkov, *Archaeological Investigations at Spanish Fort (1BA336) and the Rochon Plantation Site (1BA337) in Baldwin County, Alabama* (Mobile: Center for Archaeological Studies, University of South Alabama, 1998).

5. Gregory A. Waselkov and Mike Bunn, "A Tale of Two Forts," *Alabama Heritage* 145 (Summer 2022): 32–45.

6. George W. Shorter Jr., *Mapping of Carr's Front* (Mobile: Center for Archaeological Studies, University of South Alabama, 2006).

7. George W. Shorter Jr., *Phase III Archaeological Mitigation at Site 1BA594, Garrison Ridge Development, Spanish Fort, Baldwin County, Alabama* (Mobile: Center for Archaeological Studies, University of South Alabama, 2007).

Chapter 35

1. Peter J. Hamilton, *A Little Boy in Confederate Mobile* (Mobile, AL: Colonial Mobile Book Shop, 1947), 29–30; Charles H. Fondé, *An Account of the Great Explosion of the United States Ordnance Stores, Which Occurred in Mobile, on the 25th Day of May, 1865* (Mobile, AL: Henry Farrow, 1869), 4–5.

2. *Harper's Weekly Magazine*, "The Explosion at Mobile," June 24, 1865, 396–97; Russell W. Blount Jr., "Mobile's Great Magazine Explosion of 1865," *Alabama Review* 74, no. 3 (2021): 240–55; Caldwell Delaney, *The Story of Mobile* (Mobile, AL: Haunted Bookstore, 1981), 29–30; George Schroeter, *The Powder Magazine Explosion* (Mobile, AL: Mobile Public Library, 1993).

3. *Chicago Tribune*, "The Mobile Explosion Attributed to Gross Carelessness," July 25, 1865, 1 (quote); "Record of Proceedings of a Court of Inquiry Convened at the City of Mobile, Alabama, June 3–11, 1865," RG 153, Records of the Office of the Judge Advocate General (Army), National Archives, Washington, DC.

4. Captain William McMicken, letter to his wife Rowena Ostrander McMicken, May 28, 1865, McMicken Family Papers (Accession #0434-001, Box 1/11), Civil War Letters Collection, Special Collections, University of Washington Libraries, Seattle.

5. Fondé, *Account of the Great Explosion*, 4 (quote), 11–12.

6. George W. Shorter Jr., Sarah B. Mattics, and Bonnie L. Gums, *Phase III Archaeological Investigations at Dekle Street (1MB34) for ALDoT Project STPAA-4900(13), in the City of Mobile, Mobile County, Alabama* (Mobile: Center for Archaeological Studies, University of South Alabama, 2006).

Chapter 36

1. Bonnie L. Gums, *Phase II Archaeological Investigation at Site 1MB360 on the University of South Alabama Campus, Mobile, Alabama* (Mobile: Center for Archaeological Studies, University of South Alabama, 2002); Glenn Roberts and Philip J. Carr, *A Cultural Resources Survey for a Proposed Shuttle Transportation System on the University of South Alabama Campus, Mobile, Alabama* (Mobile: Center for Archaeological Studies, University of South Alabama, 2002); Harriet L. Richardson Seacat and Philip J. Carr, *A Cultural Resources Survey of a Proposed Research Park Northeast of the University of South Alabama Campus, Mobile, Alabama* (Mobile: Center for Archaeological Studies, University of South Alabama, 2002); George W. Shorter Jr., Tara L. Potts, and Gregory A. Waselkov, *A Phase I Cultural Resources Assessment of Three Construction Tracts on the Spring Hill College Campus, Mobile, Mobile County, Alabama* (Mobile: Center for Archaeological Studies, University of South Alabama, 2002).

2. R. P. Stephen Davis Jr. and Brett H. Riggs, *An Archaeological Investigation of the South Portico of Gerrard Hall on the University of North Carolina Campus, Chapel Hill, North Carolina*, Research Report no. 24 (Chapel Hill: Research Laboratories of Archaeology, University of North Carolina, 2006); Elizabeth A. Jones, Patricia M. Sanford, R. P. Stephen Davis Jr., and Melissa A. Salvanish, *Archaeological Investigations at the Pettigrew Site on the University of North Carolina, Chapel Hill, North Carolina*, Research Report no. 20 (Chapel Hill: Research Laboratories of Archaeology, University of North Carolina, 1998); Mark Kostro, "Town and Gown Archaeology in Eighteenth-Century Williamsburg," in *Historical Archaeology in the Twenty-first Century: Lessons from Colonial Williamsburg*, ed. Ywone D. Edwards-Ingram and Andrew C. Edwards, 28–41 (Gainesville: University Press of Florida, 2021); Matthew V. Kroot and Lee M. Panich, "Students Are Stakeholders in On-Campus Archaeology," *Advances in Archaeological Practice* 8, no. 2 (2020): 134–50; Russell K. Skowronek and Kenneth E. Lewis, eds., *Beneath the Ivory Tower: The Archaeology of Academia* (Gainesville: University Press of Florida, 2010); John Delano Stubbs Jr., "Underground Harvard: The Archaeology of College Life," PhD diss., Harvard University, Cambridge, MA, 1992.

3. Bonnie L. Gums, *Archaeology at Spring Hill College, Jesuit College of the South, in Mobile, Alabama*, 2 vols. (Mobile: Center for Archaeological Studies, University of South Alabama, 2008).

4. *Spring Hill College, Mobile, Ala. 1830–1905* (Mobile, AL: Commercial Printing, 1905); Everett Larguier, *Jesuit Beginnings at Spring Hill, 1847–1848*, Gautrelet Publications, vol. 3 (Mobile, AL: Spring Hill College Press, 1983).

5. Charles J. Boyle, ed., *Sesquicentennial Lectures: Spring Hill College* (Mobile, AL: Spring Hill College Press, 1982), *Twice Remembered: Moments in the History of Spring Hill College* (Mobile, AL: Friends of the Spring Hill College Library, 1993),

A Pelican's Eye View: History of the Spring Hill College Campus (Mobile, AL: Spring Hill College, 1999), and *Gleanings from the Spring Hill College Archives* (Mobile, AL: Friends of Spring Hill College Library, 2004); Charles J. Boyle and Patrick McGraw, eds., *Sound Mind, Sound Body: A History of Sports at Spring Hill College* (Mobile, AL: Friends of the Spring Hill College Library, 1997).

6. Paul Boudousquie, *Bird's Eye View Drawing of Spring Hill College, ca. 1915*, Spring Hill College Archives and Special Collections, Burke Memorial Library, Mobile, AL.

7. Michael Kenny and James J. Walsh, *Catholic Culture in Alabama: Centenary Story of Spring Hill College, 1830–1930* (New York: America Press, 1931).

Chapter 37

1. Bonnie L. Gums, *Made of Alabama Clay: Historic Potteries on Mobile Bay*, Archaeological Monograph 8 (Mobile: Center for Archaeological Studies, University of South Alabama, 2001), 20–23.

2. Creighton C. "Peco" Forsman, *"She's Bound to Be a Goer!": Fairhope, Alabama and the Steamboats of Mobile Bay, 1894–1934* (Silver Hill, AL: Creekhouse Publishing, 2014).

3. Joey Brackner, *Alabama Folk Pottery* (Tuscaloosa: University of Alabama Press, 2006); Noel R. Stowe, ed., *An Archaeological-Historical Survey and Test Excavations at the Blakeley Site* (Mobile: Archaeological Research Laboratory, University of South Alabama, 1977); Freddy Thuillier, ed., *Les terres cuites architecturales en France du Moyen Âge à l'époque contemporaine: Recherches sur les tuileries et les productions tuilières* (Drémil Lafage, France: Éditions Mergoil, 2019).

Also see Joey Brackner, "Traditional Pottery of Mobile Bay," *Alabama Heritage* 7 (Winter 1988): 30–41, and "Made of Alabama: Alabama Folk Pottery and Its Creators," in *Made in Alabama: A State Legacy*, ed. E. Bryding Adams, 61–82 (Birmingham, AL: Birmingham Museum of Art, 1995); Jerry Brown, *Of Mules and Mud: The Story of Alabama Folk Potter Jerry Brown*, ed. and with an introduction by Joey Brackner (Tuscaloosa: University of Alabama Press, 2022); E. Henry Willett and Joey Brackner, *The Traditional Pottery of Alabama* (Montgomery, AL: Montgomery Museum of Fine Arts, 1983).

4. W. D. Randall and Burton Parker, *A Souvenir of Daphne* (Daphne, AL: Commercial Club of Daphne, 1910); Florence D'Olive Scott, *Montrose as It Was Recorded, Told About, and Lived* (Montrose, AL: Montrose Garden Club, 1959), and *Daphne: A History of Its People and Their Pursuits as Some Saw It and Others Remember It* (Montrose, AL: Montrose Garden Club, 1965); Frederick Simpich, "Smoke over Alabama," *National Geographic Magazine* 60, no. 6 (December 1931): 703–58.

5. Gums, *Made of Alabama Clay*, 44–47; Valerie Webb, "Lost World of Baldwin Potters," *Gulf Coast Newspapers* (Daphne, AL), July 28–29, 1999, B:1, 12.

Chapter 38

1. Kathryn H. Braund, Gregory A. Waselkov, and Raven M. Christopher, *The Old Federal Road in Alabama: An Illustrated Guide* (Tuscaloosa: University of Alabama Press, 2019).

2. Raven M. Christopher and Gregory A. Waselkov, *Archaeological Survey of the Old Federal Road in Alabama* (Mobile: Center for Archaeological Studies, University of South Alabama, 2012); Raven Christopher, Gregory Waselkov, and Tara Potts,

"Archaeological Testing along the Federal Road: Exploring the Site of 'Manack's Store,' Montgomery County, Alabama," *Journal of Alabama Archaeology* 66, no. 1 (2020): 31–55; Braund, Waselkov, and Christopher, *Old Federal Road in Alabama*.

3. Jack D. L. Holmes, "Fort Stoddard in 1799: Seven Letters of Captain Bartholomew Schaumburgh," *Alabama Historical Quarterly* 26 (Fall–Winter 1964): 231–52; Gregory A. Waselkov, *A Conquering Spirit: Fort Mims and the Redstick War of 1813–1814* (Tuscaloosa: University of Alabama Press, 2006), 27.

4. Richard S. Fuller, "An Early Nineteenth-Century Assemblage from Fort Stoddert (1MB100), Southwest Alabama," manuscript on file, University of Alabama, Center for Archaeological Studies, Mobile, 1992; Jacqueline Anderson Matte, *They Say the Wind Is Red: The Alabama Choctaw, Lost in Their Own Land* (Montgomery, AL: New South Books, 2002).

5. *Frank Leslie's Illustrated Newspaper*, "The Mount Vernon Barracks," June 27, 1891, 360, 364; insets on John La Tourette, *Map of the State of Alabama* (New York: J. H. Colton, 1838).

On the Apache incarceration, see Eve Ball, with Nora Henn and Lynda A. Sánchez, *Indeh, An Apache Odyssey* (Norman: University of Oklahoma Press, 1988); Paul Conrad, *The Apache Diaspora: Four Centuries of Displacement and Survival* (Philadelphia: University of Pennsylvania Press, 2021); Jerry A. Davis, "Apache Prisoners of War at Alabama's Mount Vernon Barracks, 1887–1894," *Alabama Review* 52, no. 4 (1999): 243–66; Alicia Delgadillo, with Miriam A. Perrett, eds., *From Fort Marion to Fort Sill: A Documentary History of the Chiricahua Apache Prisoners of War, 1886–1913* (Lincoln: University of Nebraska Press, 2013); Trudy Griffin-Pierce, *Chiricahua Apache Enduring Power: Naiche's Puberty Ceremony Paintings* (Tuscaloosa: University of Alabama Press, 2006).

Also see Angela Pulley Hudson, "Removals and Reminders: Apaches and Choctaws in the Jim Crow South," *Journal of the Civil War Era* 11, no. 1 (2021): 80–102.

6. Conrad, *Apache Diaspora*, 261.

7. Walter Reed, "Geronimo and His Warriors in Captivity," *Illustrated America* 3, no. 26 (August 16, 1890): 231–35.

8. Deborah Jane Belcher, "Minimum Moral Rights: Alabama Mental Health Institutions and the Road to Federal Intervention," master's thesis, Department of History, Auburn University, Auburn, AL, 2008; John S. Hughes, "Labeling and Treating Black Mental Illness in Alabama, 1861–1910," *Journal of Southern History* 58, no. 3 (1993): 435–60.

9. George H. Searcy, "An Epidemic of Acute Pellagra," *Transactions of the Medical Association of the State of Alabama*, April 1907, 387–93.

10. Michael W. Panhorst, *Mount Vernon Arsenal and Searcy Hospital, the State of Alabama's National Treasure at Risk: A White Paper* (Montgomery: Places in Peril, Alabama Trust for Historic Preservation, 2016).

Chapter 39

1. Griffith Morgan Hopkins Jr., *City Atlas of Mobile, Alabama: From Actual Surveys and Records* (Philadelphia: G. M. Hopkins, 1878).

2. Laurie A. Wilkie and George W. Shorter Jr., *Lucrecia's Well: An Archaeological Glimpse of an African-American Midwife's Household*, Archaeological Monograph 11 (Mobile: Center for Archaeological Studies, University of South Alabama, 2001), 10–11.

3. Wilkie and Shorter, *Lucrecia's Well*, 11–14; Marilyn Culpepper, *Mobile Photographs from the William E. Wilson Collection* (Charleston, SC: Arcadia Publishing, 2001), 20.

4. Wilkie and Shorter, *Lucrecia's Well*, 15–43. For more on midwifery in the South, see Gertrude Jacinta Fraser, *African-American Midwifery in the South* (Cambridge, MA: Harvard University Press, 1998); Onnie Lee Logan, as told to Katherine Clark, *Motherwit: An Alabama Midwife's Story* (New York: E. P. Dutton, 1989); Christine McCourt, ed., *Childbirth, Midwifery, and Concepts of Time* (New York: Berghahn, 2009).

5. Laurie A. Wilkie, "Magical Passions: Sexuality and African-American Archaeology," in *Archaeologies of Sexuality*, ed. Robert A. Schmidt and Barbara L. Voss, 129–42 (London: Routledge, 2000), *The Archaeology of Mothering: An African-American Midwife's Tale* (New York: Routledge, 2003), "Granny Midwives: Gender and Generational Mediators of the African American Community," in *Engendering African American Archaeology: A Southern Perspective*, ed. Jillian E. Galle, 73–100 (Knoxville: University of Tennessee Press, 2004), and "Expelling Frogs and Binding Babies: Conception, Gestation and Birth in Nineteenth-Century African-American Midwifery," *World Archaeology* 45, no. 2 (2013): 272–84.

Chapter 40

1. Debbie Elliott, "Double Disasters Leave an Alabama Fishing Village Struggling," August 20, 2015, WFDD Public Radio.

2. Frye Gaillard, Sheila Hagler, and Peggy Denniston, *In the Path of the Storms: Bayou La Batre, Coden, and the Alabama Coast* (Tuscaloosa: University of Alabama Press, 2008); Mai Thi Nguyen and David Salvesen, "Disaster Recovery among Multiethnic Immigrants: A Case Study of Southeast Asians in Bayou La Batre (AL) after Hurricane Katrina," *Journal of the American Planning Association* 80, no. 4 (2014): 385–96.

On the anthropology of Gulf Coast fisheries, see J. Stephen Thomas, *The Shrimp Processing Industry in Bayou La Batre, Alabama* (Mobile: Center for Business and Economic Research, University of South Alabama, 1987); Mark Moberg and J. Stephen Thomas, "Class Segmentation and Divided Labor: Asian Workers in the Gulf of Mexico Seafood Industry," *Ethnology* 32, no. 1 (1993): 1–13, and "Indochinese Resettlement and the Transformation of Identities along the Alabama Gulf Coast," in *Cultural Diversity in the South: Anthropological Contributions to a Region in Transition*, ed. Carole E. Hill and Patricia Beaver, 115–28 (Athens: University of Georgia Press, 1998); Michael Jepson and Lisa L. Colburn, *Development of Social Indicators of Fishing Community Vulnerability and Resilience in the U.S. Southeast and Northeast Regions*, NOAA Technical Memorandum NMFS-F/SPO-129 (St. Petersburg, FL: National Marine Fisheries Service, National Oceanic and Atmospheric Administration, US Department of Commerce, Southeast Regional Office, 2013).

3. Gregory A. Waselkov (principal investigator), "Preserving Oral Histories of Waterfront-Related Pursuits in Bayou La Batre," NOAA Fisheries, Mississippi-Alabama Sea Grant Consortium, interviews by Michael Stieber and Harriet Richardson Seacat, Lynn Rabren, videographer, 2008.

Chapter 41

1. For instance, consider these two diverse perspectives on American history: Roxanne Dunbar-Ortiz, *An Indigenous Peoples' History of the United States* (Boston:

Beacon Press, 2014); Nikole Hannah-Jones et al., *The 1619 Project: A New Origin Story* (New York: One World, 2021).

2. William Graves, "Mobile: Alabama's City in Motion," *National Geographic* 133, no. 3 (March 1968): 368–97. For another community-focused history and archaeology project, see Joel K. Bourne Jr., Sylviane Diouf, and Chelsea Brasted, "The Last Slave Ship," *National Geographic*, February 2020, 42–67.

Epilogue

1. Carey Geiger, "Greenwood Island Coffin Finds," *Mississippi Archaeology* 2, no. 1 (1979): 3–4; Marie Elaine Danforth, J. Lynn Funkhouser, and D. C. Martin, "The United States-Mexican War Soldiers of Greenwood Island, Mississippi: An Historical, Archaeological, and Bioarchaeological Analysis," *Historical Archaeology* 50, no. 4 (2016): 92–114; Carlos Solis and Richard Walling, *Archaeological Survey and Testing of Greenwood Island and Bayou Casotte Proposed Port Facilities, Jackson County, Mississippi* (Moundville: Office of Archaeological Research, University of Alabama, 1982).

2. Tara L. Potts, *Phase III Data Recovery at 1EE639, Wetumpka, Elmore County, Alabama* (Mobile: Center for Archaeological Studies, University of South Alabama, 2010).

3. Gregory A. Waselkov et al., *The Little Market Well at Springhill and Dauphin, Mobile, Alabama*, Archaeological Monograph 2 (Mobile: Center for Archaeological Studies, University of South Alabama, 1996); Lt. Colonel Victor von Sheliha, *A Treatise on Coast-Defence: Based on the Experience Gained by Officers of the Corps of Engineers of the Army of the Confederate States* (London: E. and F. N. Spon, 1868).

4. George W. Shorter Jr. and Sarah B. Mattics, *Excavations at the Retirement Systems of Alabama Tower Site in Downtown Mobile, Alabama: Interim Report* (Mobile: Center for Archaeological Studies, University of South Alabama, 2003).

5. Bonnie L. Gums et al., *Phase I Cultural Resources Assessment of Fort Albert Sidney Johnston, Archaeological Site 1MB369, City of Mobile, Mobile County, Alabama*, with contributions by John E. Ellis and Vonnie S. Zullo (Mobile: Center for Archaeological Studies, University of South Alabama, 2015); Bonnie L. Gums, *Phase II Archaeology at the Site of Fort Albert Sidney Johnston, 1MB369, for the Alabama State Port Authority* (Mobile: Center for Archaeological Studies, University of South Alabama, 2017).

6. Robert L. Kelly, *The Fifth Beginning: What Six Million Years of Human History Can Tell Us about Our Future* (Berkeley: University of California Press, 2019).

Bibliography

Abernethy, Thomas Perkins. *The Formative Period in Alabama, 1815–1828*. Tuscaloosa: University of Alabama Press, 1965.
Ackermann, Brandon Charles. "Archaeological Computer Modeling of Florida's Pre-Columbian Dugout Canoes: Integrating Ground-Penetrating Radar and Geographic Information Science." Master's thesis, Department of Anthropology, University of Denver, Denver, CO, 2019.
Agha, Andrew. "Standing the Test of Time: Embankment Investigations, Their Implications for African Technology Transfer and Effect on African American Archaeology in South Carolina." *Atlantic Studies* 12, no. 3 (2015): 336–54.
Alden, John Richard. *John Stuart and the Southern Colonial Frontier: A Study of Indian Relations, War, Trade and Land Problems in the Southern Wilderness, 1754–1775*. Ann Arbor: University of Michigan Press, 1944.
Anderson, David G. "Archaic Mounds and the Archaeology of Southeastern Tribal Societies." In *Signs of Power: The Rise of Cultural Complexity in the Southeast*, edited by Jon L. Gibson and Philip J. Carr, 270–99. Tuscaloosa: University of Alabama Press, 2004.
Anderson, David G., Thaddeus G. Bissett, Stephen J. Yerka, Joshua J. Wells, Eric C. Kansa, Sarah W. Kansa, Kelsey N. Myers, R. Carl DeMuth, and De vin A. White. "Sea-Level Rise and Archaeological Site Destruction: An Example from the Southeastern United States Using DINAA (Digital Index of North American Archaeology)." *Plos One* 12, no. 11 (2017): e0188142.
Andrews, Christopher C. *History of the Campaign of Mobile*. New York: D. Van Nostrand, 1867.
Andrus, Patrick W. "How to Apply the National Register Criteria for Evaluation." *National Register Bulletin* 15 (1997).
Aptheker, Herbert. "Maroons within the Present Limits of the United States." *Journal of Negro History* 24, no. 2 (1939): 167–84.
Armistead, William R. *Preliminary Underwater Survey of the USS Tecumseh*. Mobile, AL: Gulf Coast Archaeological Society, 1977.
Arnold, J. Barto, III. *The Denbigh's Civilian Imports: Customs Records of a Civil War Blockade Runner between Mobile and Havana*. College Station: Texas A&M University, Institute of Nautical Archaeology, 2011.

Arnold, J. Barto, III, Thomas J. Oertling, and Andrew W. Hall. "The *Denbigh* Project: Excavation of a Civil War Blockade-Runner." *International Journal of Nautical Archaeology* 30 (2001): 231–49.

Azar, Madelaine C. "Making Heads or Tails: An Iconographic Analysis of Late Mississippian Rim-Effigy Bowls in the Central Mississippi River Valley." Master's thesis, Department of Anthropology, University of North Carolina, Chapel Hill, 2020.

Azar, Madelaine C., and Vincas P. Steponaitis. "Modeling the Cosmos: Rim-Effigy Bowl Iconography in the Central Mississippi Valley." In *Archaeologies of Cosmoscapes in the Americas*, edited by J. Grant Stauffer, Bretton T. Giles, and Shawn P. Lambert, 25–45. Oxford, UK: Oxbow Books, 2022.

Babits, Lawrence E., and Stephanie Gandulla, eds. *The Archaeology of French and Indian War Frontier Forts*. Gainesville: University Press of Florida, 2013.

Bache, Alexander D. "Entrance to Mobile Bay, 1851." In *Maps and Charts of the United States Coast Survey, A. D. Bache, Superintendent, to July 1854*. Washington, DC: US Coast Survey, 1854.

Bailey, Tom. *The Five Capitals of Alabama: The Story of Alabama's Capital Cities from St. Stephens to Montgomery*. Montgomery, AL: New South Books, 2020.

Ball, Eve, with Nora Henn and Lynda A. Sánchez. *Indeh, An Apache Odyssey*. Norman: University of Oklahoma Press, 1988.

Barnes Smith, Julie. *Archaeological Investigations of Site 1MB161, Dog River, Mobile County, Alabama*. Report of Investigations 73. Moundville: University of Alabama Museums, Office of Archaeological Services, 1995.

Barney, Howard. *Mister Bell: A Life Story of Walter D. Bellingrath, Founder of Bellingrath Gardens*. Mobile, AL: Bellingrath-Morse Foundation, 1979.

Baynton, Benjamin. *Authentic Memoirs of William Augustus Bowles, Esquire*. London: R. Faulder, 1791.

Belcher, Deborah Jane. "Minimum Moral Rights: Alabama Mental Health Institutions and the Road to Federal Intervention." Master's thesis, Department of History, Auburn University, Auburn, AL, 2008.

Bense, Judith A. *Archeological Investigations at the Dead Lake Site (1MB95), Creola, Alabama*. Pensacola, FL: Heritage Company, 1980.

———, ed. *Presidio Santa María de Galve: A Struggle for Survival in Colonial Spanish Pensacola*. Gainesville: University Press of Florida, 2003.

———. *Presidios of Spanish West Florida*. Gainesville: University Press of Florida, 2022.

Bergeron, Arthur W., Jr. *Confederate Mobile*. Baton Rouge: Louisiana State University Press, 1991.

Berlin, Ira. *Many Thousands Gone: The First Two Centuries of Slavery in North America*. Cambridge, MA: Harvard University Press, 1998.

Berlin, Ira, and Philip D. Morgan, eds. *Cultivation and Culture: Labor and the Shaping of Slave Life in the Americas*. Charlottesville: University of Virginia Press, 1993.

Besch, Edwin W., Shawn Holland, and Dave W. Morgan. "A Bayonet and a Musket Barrel from the 3d Waldeck Regiment at the Museum of Mobile, and Action at 'The Village' on 7 January 1781." *Military Collector and Historian* 55 (2003): 144–54.

Bigelow, Artemas. "Observations on Some Mounds on the Tensaw River." *American Journal of Science and Arts* 15, no. 44 (Article 21, 1853): 186–92.

Billopp, Charles Farmar. *A History of Thomas and Anne Billopp Farmar and Some of Their Descendants in America.* New York: Grafton Press, 1907.

Binford, Lewis. "Behavioral Archaeology and the 'Pompeii Premise.'" *Journal of Anthropological Research* 37, no. 3 (Fall 1981): 195–208.

Blitz, John H., and Lauren E. Downs, eds. *Graveline: A Late Woodland Platform Mound on the Mississippi Gulf Coast.* Archaeological Report No. 34. Jackson: Mississippi Department of Archives and History, 2015.

Blitz, John H., and C. Baxter Mann, eds. *Fisherfolk, Farmers, and Frenchmen: Archaeological Explorations on the Mississippi Gulf Coast.* Archaeological Report No. 30. Jackson: Mississippi Department of Archives and History, 2000.

Blitz, John H., and Grace E. Riehm, eds. "Andrews Place (1MB1): A Late Woodland-Mississippian Shell Midden on the Alabama Gulf Coast." *Journal of Alabama Archaeology* 61, nos. 1–2 (2015): 1–117.

Blount, Russell W., Jr. "Mobile's Great Magazine Explosion of 1865." *Alabama Review* 74, no. 3 (2021): 240–55.

Boles, Steven L. "Earth-Diver and Earth Mother: Ancestral Flint Clay Figures from Cahokia." *Illinois Archaeology* 29 (2017): 127–46.

Boudousquie, Paul. *Bird's Eye View Drawing of Spring Hill College, ca. 1915.* Spring Hill College Archives and Special Collections, Burke Memorial Library, Mobile, AL.

Boudreaux, Edmond A., III. *Archaeological Investigations at Jackson Landing: An Early Late Woodland Mound and Earthwork Site in Coastal Mississippi.* Archaeological Report 36. Jackson: Mississippi Department of Archives and History, 2015.

Bourne, Joel K., Jr., Sylviane Diouf, and Chelsea Brasted. "The Last Slave Ship." *National Geographic*, February 2020, 42–67.

Boyle, Charles J. , ed. *Gleanings from the Spring Hill College Archives.* Mobile, AL: Friends of Spring Hill College Library, 2004.

———. *A Pelican's Eye View: History of the Spring Hill College Campus.* Mobile, AL: Spring Hill College, 1999.

———, ed. *Sesquicentennial Lectures: Spring Hill College.* Mobile, AL: Spring Hill College Press, 1982.

———, ed. *Twice Remembered: Moments in the History of Spring Hill College.* Mobile, AL: Friends of the Spring Hill College Library, 1993.

Boyle, Charles J., and Patrick McGraw, eds. *Sound Mind, Sound Body: A History of Sports at Spring Hill College.* Mobile, AL: Friends of the Spring Hill College Library, 1997.

Brackner, Joey. *Alabama Folk Pottery.* Tuscaloosa: University of Alabama Press, 2006.

———. "Made of Alabama: Alabama Folk Pottery and Its Creators." In *Made in Alabama: A State Legacy*, edited by E. Bryding Adams, 61–82. Birmingham, AL: Birmingham Museum of Art, 1995.

———. "Traditional Pottery of Mobile Bay." *Alabama Heritage* 7 (Winter 1988): 30–41.

Brantley, William H., Jr. *Three Capitals, a Book about the First Three Capitals of Alabama: St. Stephens, Huntsville, and Cahawba, 1818–1826.* Tuscaloosa: University of Alabama Press, 1976.

Brasseaux, Carl A. *France's Forgotten Legion: Service Records of French Military and Administrative Personnel Stationed in the Mississippi Valley and Gulf Coast Region, 1699–1769.* Baton Rouge: Louisiana State University Press, 2000.

Braund, Kathryn E. Holland, ed. *Tohopeka: Rethinking the Creek War and the War of 1812.* Tuscaloosa: University of Alabama Press, 2012.

Braund, Kathryn H., Gregory A. Waselkov, and Raven M. Christopher. *The Old Federal Road in Alabama: An Illustrated Guide.* Tuscaloosa: University of Alabama Press, 2019.

Brooms, McDonald. *Archaeological Investigations at the Kennedy Mill Site, 1BA301, in Baldwin County, Alabama.* Troy, AL: Archaeological Research Center, Troy State University, 1996.

Brown, Ian W. *An Archaeological Survey in Clarke County, Alabama.* Bulletin 26. Tuscaloosa: Alabama Museum of Natural History, 2009.

———, ed. *Bottle Creek: A Pensacola Culture Site in South Alabama.* Tuscaloosa: University of Alabama Press, 2003.

———. *Bottle Creek Reflections: The Personal Side of Archaeology in the Mobile-Tensaw Delta.* Tuscaloosa, AL: Borgo Publishing, 2012.

Brown, Ian W., and Richard S. Fuller, eds. "Bottle Creek Research: Working Papers on the Bottle Creek Site (1BA2), Baldwin County, Alabama." *Journal of Alabama Archaeology* 39, nos. 1–2 (1993): 1–169.

———. *Master Plan for Managing the Bottle Creek Site National Historic Landmark.* Tuscaloosa: Gulf Coast Survey, Alabama Museum of Natural History, University of Alabama, 1999.

———. *Sorting Manual of Pensacola Culture Pottery.* Tuscaloosa: Gulf Coast Survey, Alabama Museum of Natural History, 1992.

Brown, Jerry. *Of Mules and Mud: The Story of Alabama Folk Potter Jerry Brown.* Edited by and with an introduction by Joey Brackner. Tuscaloosa: University of Alabama Press, 2022.

Brown, Margaret, dir. *Descendant.* Beverly Hills, CA: Participant, 2022.

Bruce, Kevin L. "All Rocks Are Not Alike." *Southeastern Archaeology* 20, no. 1 (2001): 78–92.

———. *Supplement to Cultural Resources Survey of Proposed Bridge Replacement on Mississippi Highway 550 at the Homochitto River, Lincoln County, Mississippi.* Jackson: Report to the Mississippi Department of Archives and History, 2002.

Bruce, Kevin L., Bruce J. Gray, and Cliff Jenkins. *Cultural Resources Survey of Proposed Bridge Replacement on Mississippi Highway 550 at the Homochitto River (MDOT Project No. 85–0171–00–009–10/102486201000) Lincoln County, Mississippi.* Jackson: Report to the Mississippi Department of Archives and History, 2000.

Brueske, Paul. *The Last Siege: The Mobile Campaign, Alabama 1865.* Havertown, PA: Casemate, 2018.

Bunn, Mike. *The Assault on Fort Blakeley.* Charleston, SC: History Press, 2021.

———. *Early Alabama: An Illustrated Guide to the Formative Years, 1798–1826.* Tuscaloosa: University of Alabama Press, 2019.

Bunn, Mike, and Clay Williams. *Battle for the Southern Frontier: The Creek War and the War of 1812.* Cheltenham, UK: History Press, 2008.

Burchard, Ernest F. *The Cement Industry in Alabama.* Geological Survey of Alabama, Circular 14. Tuscaloosa: University of Alabama, 1940.

Burgoyne, Bruce E., ed. and trans. *Eighteenth-Century America: A Hessian Report on the People, the Land, the War as Noted in the Diary of Chaplain Philipp Waldeck (1776–1780)*. Bowie, MD: Heritage Books, 1995.

———. *The 3rd English-Waldeck Regiment in the American Revolution*. Bowie, MD: Heritage Books, 1999.

Burström, Mats. *Ballast: Laden with History*. Lund, Sweden: Nordic Academic Press, 2018.

Butler, Christina Rae. *Lowcountry at High Tide: A History of Flooding, Drainage, and Reclamation in Charleston, South Carolina*. Columbia: University of South Carolina Press, 2020.

Butler, Ruth L., ed. and trans. *Journal of Paul du Ru (February 1 to May 8, 1700) Missionary Priest to Louisiana*. Chicago: Caxton Club, 1934.

Cambron, J. W., and D. C. Hulse. *Handbook of Alabama Archaeology: Part One, Point Types*. Huntsville: Alabama Archaeological Society, 1964.

Campbell, John. Letter to Henry Clinton, Pensacola, 5 January 1781. Sir Guy Carleton Papers, Colonial Office, PRO 30:55/9899. National Archives, Kew, UK.

Carney, Judith A. *Black Rice: The African Origins of Rice Cultivation in the Americas*. Cambridge, MA: Harvard University Press, 2001.

Carr, Philip J. *Lithic Use in the Forks: An Archaeological Survey in Choctaw and Clarke Counties*. Mobile: Center for Archaeological Studies, University of South Alabama, 2003.

———. *Phase II Investigations at 22LI504, Lincoln County, Mississippi*. Mobile: Center for Archaeological Studies, University of South Alabama, 2004.

Carr, Philip J., and Andrew P. Bradbury. "Contemporary Lithic Analysis and Southeastern Archaeology." *Southeastern Archaeology* 19, no. 2 (2000): 120–35.

Carr, Philip J., and Alison M. Hadley. "Bifaces, Adzes, and Chert Beads: The Lithic Assemblage from the John Forrest Site (22CB623)." Paper presented at the 58th Annual Meeting of the Southeastern Archaeological Conference, Chattanooga, TN, November 2001.

Carr, Philip J., and Evan Peacock, eds. *Archaeology at Site 22LI504*. Mobile: Center for Archaeological Studies, University of South Alabama, 2006.

Carter, Clarence Edwin, ed. "Daniel E. Burch to the Quartermaster General, Pensacola, March 10th, 1828." In *The Territorial Papers of the United States*. Vol. 23, *The Territory of Florida, 1824–1828*, 1038–43. Washington, DC: National Archives, 1958.

Chartrand, René. *The Forts of New France: The Great Lakes, the Plains, and the Gulf Coast, 1600–1763*. Oxford, UK: Osprey Publishing, 2010.

Chaudhuri, Jean, and Joyotpaul Chaudhuri. *A Sacred Path: The Way of the Muscogee Creeks*. Los Angeles: UCLA American Indian Studies Center, University of California, 2001.

Chaudron, Louis de Vendel. "How We Found the Site of Fort Louis de la Mobile." Manuscript, Iberville Historical Society Collections, Mobile History Museum, Mobile, AL, 1902.

———. "Old Fort and Indian Canal at Bon Secours, from an Essay Read before the Iberville Historical Society." *Lorgnette* 1, no. 1(1902): 1.

Chicago Tribune. "The Mobile Explosion Attributed to Gross Carelessness." July 25, 1865, 1.

Christopher, Raven. *Phase I Cultural Resource Assessment of a 103-Acre Tract for the*

Proposed Location of a Veteran's Cemetery in Spanish Fort, Baldwin County, Alabama. Mobile: Center for Archaeological Studies, University of South Alabama, 2010.

Christopher, Raven M., and Gregory A. Waselkov. *Archaeological Survey of the Old Federal Road in Alabama*. Mobile: Center for Archaeological Studies, University of South Alabama, 2012.

Christopher, Raven, Gregory Waselkov, and Tara Potts. "Archaeological Testing along the Federal Road: Exploring the Site of 'Manack's Store,' Montgomery County, Alabama." *Journal of Alabama Archaeology* 66, no. 1 (2020): 31–55.

Clark, John E., and William J. Parry. "Craft Specialization and Cultural Complexity." *Research in Economic Anthropology* 12 (1990): 289–346.

Coker, William S., ed. *The Military Presence on the Gulf Coast*. Pensacola, FL: Gulf Coast History and Humanities Conference, 1977.

Coker, William S., and Hazel P. Coker. *The Siege of Mobile, 1780, in Maps*. Pensacola, FL: Perdido Bay Press, 1982.

Connaway, John M. *Fishweirs: A World Perspective with Emphasis on the Fishweirs of Mississippi*. Archaeological Report No. 33. Jackson: Mississippi Department of Archives and History, 2007.

———. "The Keenan Bead Cache." *Louisiana Archaeology* 8 (1981): 57–71.

Conrad, Paul. *The Apache Diaspora: Four Centuries of Displacement and Survival*. Philadelphia: University of Pennsylvania Press, 2021.

Cordell, Ann S. *Continuity and Change in Apalachee Pottery Manufacture*. Mobile: Center for Archaeological Studies, University of South Alabama, 2001.

Cornelison, John E., Jr., Guy Prentice, Michael A. Seibert, Rusty Simmons, Cameron Wesson, Jessica McNeil, and Charles Lawson. *Barricade: Archeological and Geophysical Investigations at the Battle of Horseshoe Bend National Military Park, Alabama*. SEAC Accession 2611. Tallahassee, FL: Southeast Archeological Center, National Park Service, 2018.

Cowles, Calvin D., comp. *Atlas to Accompany the Official Records of the Union and Confederate Armies*. 3 vols. Washington, DC: Government Printing Office, 1891–95.

Crabtree, Donald E. *An Introduction to Flintworking*. Occasional Papers 28. Moscow: Idaho Museum of Natural History, 1972.

Crawford, Jessica F. "Archaic Effigy Beads: A New Look at Some Old Beads." Master's thesis, Department of Anthropology, University of Mississippi, Oxford, 2003.

———. "The Conservancy to Acquire Its 400th Site." *American Archaeology* 14, no. 3 (2010): 44–45.

Creagh, George W. "Notes Furnished by Col. G. W. Creagh of Clarke County, Alabama, 1847." Section 2, notes, Albert J. Pickett Papers, Pickett Family Papers (1779–1904), LPR185. Alabama Department of Archives and History, Montgomery.

Culpepper, Marilyn. *Mobile Photographs from the William E. Wilson Collection*. Charleston, SC: Arcadia Publishing, 2001.

Cumming, William P. *The Southeast in Early Maps*. 3rd ed. Revised by Louis de Vorsey Jr. Chapel Hill: University of North Carolina Press, 1998.

Curtis, Wayne. "Clarifying an Historic Event: Archaeologists Are Working to Uncover the Details of the Massacre at Fort Mims." *American Archaeology* 11, no. 3 (2007): 12–17.

Cushing, Frank Hamilton. "Exploration of Ancient Key Dwellers' Remains on the Gulf Coast of Florida." *Proceedings of the American Philosophical Society* 35, no. 153 (1896): 329–448.

Cyr, Howard. "Geoarchaeological Analysis of 1MB510." In Gums and Waselkov, *Life at the River's Edge*, 99–120.

Danforth, Marie Elaine, J. Lynn Funkhouser, and D. C. Martin. "The United States-Mexican War Soldiers of Greenwood Island, Mississippi: An Historical, Archaeological, and Bioarchaeological Analysis." *Historical Archaeology* 50, no. 4 (2016): 92–114.

Daviau, Marie-Hélène, and Roland Tremblay. "Le calumet canadien comme symbole d'un mode de vie fondateur." In *Feu, lueurs et fureurs: Archéologie du Québec*, edited by Christian Gates St.-Pierre and Yves Monette, 146–47. Montréal, Canada: Pointe-à-Callière and Les Éditions de l'Homme, 2022.

Davies, K. G., ed. *Documents of the American Revolution, 1770–1783*. Vol. 18, *Transcripts, 1780*. Dublin: Irish University Press, 1978.

———, ed. *Documents of the American Revolution, 1770–1783*. Vol. 20, *Transcripts, 1781*. Dublin: Irish University Press, 1979.

Davis, Dylan S., Katherine E. Seeber, and Matthew C. Sanger. "Addressing the Problem of Disappearing Cultural Landscapes in Archaeological Research Using Multi-Scalar Survey." *Journal of Island and Coastal Archaeology* 16, nos. 2–4 (2021): 524–40.

Davis, George B., Leslie J. Perry, and Joseph W. Kirkley, eds. *The War of the Rebellion: A Compilation of the Official Records of the Union and Confederate Armies*. Ser. 1, vol. 39 (2–3), *Correspondence*. Washington, DC: Government Printing Office, 1892.

Davis, Hester. "The Future of Archaeology: Dreamtime, Crystal Balls, and Reality." *American Journal of Archaeology* 93, no. 3 (1989): 451–58.

Davis, Jerry A. "Apache Prisoners of War at Alabama's Mount Vernon Barracks, 1887–1894." *Alabama Review* 52, no. 4 (1999): 243–66.

Davis, R. P. Stephen, Jr., and Brett H. Riggs. *An Archaeological Investigation of the South Portico of Gerrard Hall on the University of North Carolina Campus, Chapel Hill, North Carolina*. Research Report no. 24. Chapel Hill: Research Laboratories of Archaeology, University of North Carolina, 2006.

Dawdy, Shannon Lee. *Building the Devil's Empire: French Colonia New Orleans*. Chicago; University of Chicago Press, 2008.

DeJean, Joan. *Mutinous Women: How French Convicts Became Founding Mothers of the Gulf Coast*. New York: Basic Books, 2022.

Delaney, Caldwell. *The Story of Mobile*. Mobile, AL: Haunted Bookstore, 1981.

Delgadillo, Alicia, with Miriam A. Perrett, eds. *From Fort Marion to Fort Sill: A Documentary History of the Chiricahua Apache Prisoners of War, 1886–1913*. Lincoln: University of Nebraska Press, 2013.

Delgado, James P., Deborah E. Marx, Kyle Lent, Joseph Grinnan, and Alexander DeCaro. *Archaeological Investigations of 1BA704, A Nineteenth-Century Shipwreck Site in the Mobile River, Baldwin and Mobile Counties, Alabama*. Report prepared for the Alabama Historical Commission. Orlando, FL: Search Inc., 2019.

———. *Clotilda: The History and Archaeology of the Last Slave Ship*. Tuscaloosa: University of Alabama Press, 2023.

De Vorsey, Louis, Jr. "The Colonial Southeast on 'An Accurate General Map.'" *Southeastern Geographer* 6, no. 1 (1966): 20–32.

———. *The Indian Boundary in the Southern Colonies, 1768–1775*. Chapel Hill: University of North Carolina Press, 1966.

Dickens, Roy S., Jr. *Archaeological Investigations at Horseshoe Bend National Military Park, Alabama*. Special Publication 3. Tuscaloosa: Alabama Archaeological Society, 1979.

Diouf, Sylviane A. "Borderland Maroons." In *Fugitive Slaves and Spaces of Freedom in North America*, edited by Damian Alan Pargas, 168–96. Gainesville: University Press of Florida, 2018.

———. *Dreams of Africa in Alabama: The Slave Ship* Clotilda *and the Story of the Last Africans Brought to America*. Oxford: Oxford University Press, 2009.

———. *Slavery's Exiles: The Story of the American Maroons*. New York: New York University Press, 2014.

Dockry, Michael J., Sophia A. Gutterman, and Mae A. Davenport. "Building Bridges: Perspectives on Partnership and Collaboration from the U.S. Forest Service Tribal Relations Program." *Journal of Forestry* 116, no. 2 (2018): 123–32.

D'Olive, William L., comp. "The D'Olive Family History and Data, 1999." Manuscript on file. Mobile Public Library, Local History and Genealogy Division, Mobile, AL.

Douglass, Andrew E. "Ancient Canals on the South-West Coast of Florida." *American Antiquarian and Oriental Journal* 7 (1885): 277–85.

DuBose, Joel Campbell. "Seventh Alabama Cavalry, Confederate Army." Confederate Regimental History Files. Alabama Department of Archives and History, Montgomery.

Duggins, Julie. "Canoe Caching at Transit Points: Inferring Florida's Ancient Navigation Routes Using Archaeology and Ethnohistory." In *Iconography and Wetsite Archaeology of Florida's Watery Realms*, edited by Ryan J. Wheeler and Joanna Ostapkowicz, 82–110. Gainesville: University Press of Florida, 2019.

Dumont de Montigny, Jean-François-Benjamin. *The Memoir of Lieutenant Dumont, 1715–1747: A Sojourner in the French Atlantic*. Translated by Gordon M. Sayre. Edited by Gordon M. Sayre and Carla Zecher. Chapel Hill: University of North Carolina Press, 2012.

Dunbar-Ortiz, Roxanne. *An Indigenous Peoples' History of the United States*. Boston: Beacon Press, 2014.

Dunnavant, Justin P., Jenny Long, Ginny Newberry, William B. Marriott, Howard Cyr, Claiborne Sea, and Philip J. Carr. *Phase I Archaeological Testing of the Africatown Welcome Center for the City of Mobile, Alabama*. Mobile: Center for Archaeological Studies, University of South Alabama, 2021.

Du Ru, Paul. "Journal d'un voyage fait avec Mr. d'Iberville de la rade de Bilocchis dans le haut du Mississippi," February 1 to May 8, 1700. Vault Ayer MS. 262, f. 64. Edward Ayer Collection, Newberry Library, Chicago.

DuVal, Kathleen. *Independence Lost: Lives on the Edge of the American Revolution*. New York: Random House, 2015.

Dye, David H. "Ceramic Wares and Water Spirits: Identifying Religious Sodalities in the Lower Mississippi Valley." In *Ceramics in Ancient America: Multidisciplinary Approaches*, edited by Yumi Park Huntington, Dean E. Arnold, and Johanna Minich, 29–61. Gainesville: University Press of Florida, 2018.

Elliott, Debbie. "Double Disasters Leave an Alabama Fishing Village Struggling." WFDD Public Radio. August 20, 2015.

Elliott, Jack D., Jr. *The Streets of Old St. Stephens: An Examination of the Plats of Three Towns—Franklin, Rodney, St. Stephens*. St. Stephens, AL: St. Stephens Historical Commission, 1998.

Ellis, Elizabeth N. *The Great Power of Small Nations: Indigenous Diplomacy in the Gulf South*. Philadelphia: University of Pennsylvania Press, 2022.

Ensor, H. Blaine, Eugene M. Wilson, and M. Cassandra Hill. *Historic Resources Assessment: Tennessee-Tombigbee Waterway Wildlife Mitigation Project, Mobile and Tensaw River Deltas, Alabama*. Tuscaloosa, AL: Panamerican Consultants, 1993.

Ewert, George H. "Old Times Will Come Again: The Municipal Market System of Mobile, Alabama, 1888–1901." Master's thesis, Department of History, University of South Alabama, Mobile, 1993.

———. "The Politics of Food: Mobile's Public Markets in the Gilded Age." *Gulf Coast Historical Review* 10, no. 2 (1994): 140–50.

Ezpeleta, José de. Letter to Manuel Cabello, Mabila, Enero 1781. Folio 30, Legajo 116. Papeles Procedentes de la Isla de Cuba, Archivo General de Indias, Seville, Spain.

———. "Una carta . . . al Gobernador de la Luisiana, D. Bernardo de Galvez, Mobila, 20 de Enero de 1781." *Gazeta de Madrid* 28 (April 6, 1781): 291–94.

Fabel, Robin F. A. *The Economy of British West Florida, 1763–1783*. Tuscaloosa: University of Alabama Press, 1988.

Fagan, Brian. "Black Day at Slack Farm." *Archaeology* 41, no. 4 (1988): 15–16, 73.

Fairbanks, Charles H. "Excavations at Horseshoe Bend, Alabama." *Florida Anthropologist* 15, no. 1 (1962): 41–56.

Filion, Barbara, Gregory Waselkov, and Brandon Mitchell. *Jean-Paul's Daring Adventure: Stories from Old Mobile*. Mobile: Archaeology Museum, University of South Alabama, 2014.

Flewellen, Ayana Omilade, Justin P. Dunnavant, Alicia Odewale, Alexandra Jones, Tsione WoldeMichael, Zoë Crossland, and Maria Franklin. "'The Future of Archaeology Is Antiracist': Archaeology in the Time of Black Lives Matter." *American Antiquity* 86, no. 2 (2021): 224–43.

Fondé, Charles H. *An Account of the Great Explosion of the United States Ordnance Stores, Which Occurred in Mobile, on the 25th Day of May, 1865*. Mobile, AL: Henry Farrow, 1869.

Fore, George T. *The La Pointe-Krebs House, Pascagoula, Mississippi: Architectural Development and Interpretation*. Pascagoula, MS: La Pointe-Krebs Foundation, 2017.

Forsman, Creighton C. "Peco." *"She's Bound to Be a Goer!": Fairhope, Alabama and the Steamboats of Mobile Bay, 1894–1934*. Silver Hill, AL: Creekhouse Publishing, 2014.

Foster, Ellen, France Miller, and Gladys Rutan Daw, comps. and eds. *The Krebs Family History*. Pascagoula, MS: printed by author, 1991.

Frank Leslie's Illustrated Newspaper. "The Mount Vernon Barracks." June 27, 1891, 360, 364.

Franzen, John G. *The Archaeology of the Logging Industry*. Gainesville: University Press of Florida, 2020.

Franzen, John G., Terrance J. Martin, and Eric C. Drake. "*Sucreries* and *Züzbaakdokaanan*: Racialization, Indigenous Creolization, and the Archaeology of Maple-Sugar Camps in Northern Michigan." *Historical Archaeology* 52, no. 2 (2018): 164–96.

Fraser, Gertrude Jacinta. *African-American Midwifery in the South*. Cambridge, MA: Harvard University Press, 1998.

French, B. F. *Historical Collections of Louisiana*. Vol. 5, *Historical Memoirs from 1687 to 1770*. New York: Lamport, Blakeman and Law, 1853.

Fuller, Richard S. *An Alternative Rim Effigy Typology for the Pensacola Mississippian Variant*. Tuscaloosa: Gulf Coast Survey, Museum of Natural History, University of Alabama, 1993.

———. "An Analysis of Indian Pottery Recovered during Shovel Testing at the McInnis Site (1BA664), Orange Beach, Alabama." Manuscript on file at the Center for Archaeological Studies, University of South Alabama, Mobile, 2015.

———. "A Ceramic Lingua Franca? The Origins, Attributes, and Dimensions of a Historic Period Indian Pottery Tradition on the Northern Gulf Coastal Plain." Manuscript on file at the Alabama Museum of Natural History, University of Alabama, Tuscaloosa, 1991.

———. "An Early Nineteenth-Century Assemblage from Fort Stoddert (1MB100), Southwest Alabama." Manuscript on file at the Center for Archaeological Studies, University of South Alabama, Mobile, 1992.

———. "Indian Pottery and Cultural Chronology of the Mobile-Tensaw Basin and Alabama Coast." *Journal of Alabama Archaeology* 44, no. 1 (1998): 1–51.

———. "Mississippian Canoes in the Deep South: Examples from Mississippi and Alabama." Paper presented at the 49th Annual Meeting of the Southeastern Archaeological Conference, Little Rock, AR, 1992.

Fuller, Richard S., and Ian W. Brown. *The Mound Island Project: An Archaeological Survey in the Mobile-Tensaw Delta*. Bulletin 19. Tuscaloosa: Alabama Museum of Natural History, 1998.

Fuller, Richard S., and Diane E. Silvia. "Ceramic Rim Effigies in Southwest Alabama." *Journal of Alabama Archaeology* 30, no. 1 (1984): 1–48.

Fuller, Richard S., Diane E. Silvia, and Noel R. Stowe. *The Forks Project: An Investigation of Late Prehistoric–Early Historic Transition in the Alabama-Tombigbee Confluence Basin*. Mobile: Archaeological Research Laboratory, University of South Alabama, 1984.

Fulton, R. B. "Prehistoric Jasper Ornaments in Mississippi." *Publications of the Mississippi Historical Society* 1 (1898): 91–95.

Gaillard, Frye, Sheila Hagler, and Peggy Denniston. *In the Path of the Storms: Bayou La Batre, Coden, and the Alabama Coast*. Tuscaloosa: University of Alabama Press, 2008.

Gaines, A. S., and K. M. Cunningham. "Shell-Heaps on Mobile River." In *Annual Report of the Board of Regents of the Smithsonian Institution for the Year 1877*, 290–91. Washington, DC: Smithsonian Institution, 1878.

Gardner, Jason A., and Clare E. Farrow. "Introduction to the Andrews Place Site (1MB1)." In "Andrews Place (1MB1): A Late Woodland-Mississippian Shell Midden on the Alabama Gulf Coast," edited by John H. Blitz and Grace E. Riehm. *Journal of Alabama Archaeology* 61, no. 1 (2015): 1–11.

Gardner, Jason A., and Julie E. McDuffie. *Phase III Archaeological Data Recovery at Site 1MB414, Thyssenkrupp Steel Mill, Northern Mobile County, Alabama*. Mobile, AL: Barry A. Vittor and Associates, 2010.

Gates, W. D. "Pottery of the Mound Builders." *American Archaeologist* 2, no. 5 (1898): 113–18.

Gazaway, James Austin. "A Comparison and Analysis of the Specie (Coins) Recovered from French Colonial Sites around Old Mobile and Spanish Colonial Sites around Pensacola." Master's thesis, Department of Anthropology, University of West Florida, Pensacola, 2023.

Geiger, Carey. "Greenwood Island Coffin Finds." *Mississippi Archaeology* 2, no. 1 (1979): 3–4.

Gill, Cameron, and Bonnie L. Gums. *Limited Archaeological Survey for Historic-Period Native American Sites in Jackson County, Mississippi*. Mobile: Center for Archaeological Studies, University of South Alabama, 2012.

———. *Summary of Excavations of the "Courthouse Site" (1BA221) at Historic Blakeley State Park, Baldwin County, Alabama*. Mobile: Center for Archaeological Studies, University of South Alabama, 2011.

Giraud, Marcel. *Histoire de la Louisiane française*. Vol. 3, *L'époque de John Law, 1717–1720*. Paris: Presses de Universitaires de France, 1966.

———. *Histoire de la Louisiane française*. Vol. 4, *La Louisiane après le système de Law, 1721–1723*. Paris: Presses de Universitaires de France, 1971.

———. *A History of French Louisiana*. Vol. 1, *The Reign of Louis XIV, 1698–1715*. Translated by Joseph C. Lambert. Baton Rouge: Louisiana State University Press, 1974.

———. *A History of French Louisiana*. Vol. 2, *Years of Transition, 1715–1717*. Translated by Joseph C. Lambert. Baton Rouge: Louisiana State University Press, 1993.

Goddard, Ives, Patricia Galloway, Marvin D. Jeter, Gregory A. Waselkov, and John E. Worth. "Small Tribes of the Western Southeast." In *Handbook of North American Indians*. Vol. 14, *Southeast*, edited by Raymond D. Fogelson, 174–90. Washington, DC: Smithsonian Institution Press, 2004.

Goodwin, James M., and C. Haire. *Plan & View of the City of Mobile*. 1824. Library of Congress, Washington, DC, Geography and Map Division, 2012593360.

Goodwin, R. Christopher, Gregg Brooks, and Martha R. Williams. *Archeological Evaluation of "Feature A," the Wakulla River Fishweir Site (8WA843)*. Frederick, MD: R. Christopher Goodwin and Associates, 2008.

Gould, Elizabeth Barrett. *From Fort to Port: An Architectural History of Mobile, Alabama, 1711–1918*. Tuscaloosa: University of Alabama Press, 1988.

Graeber, David, and David Wengrow. *The Dawn of Everything: A New History of Humanity*. New York: Farrar, Straus and Giroux, 2021.

Graves, William. "Mobile: Alabama's City in Motion." *National Geographic* 133, no. 3 (March 1968): 368–97.

Gremillion, Kristen J. "Archaeobotany at Old Mobile." *Historical Archaeology* 36, no. 1 (2002): 117–28.

Griffin, H., and C. David. "The Importance of Thomas Freeman's Surveys in the Alabama Territory." *Surveying and Land Information Science* 73, no. 2 (2014): 49–60.

Griffin-Pierce, Trudy. *Chiricahua Apache Enduring Power: Naiche's Puberty Ceremony Paintings*. Tuscaloosa: University of Alabama Press, 2006.

Grimes, James W., and Sue Keller. "The Herbarium of Wesleyan University, Middletown, Connecticut." *Brittonia* 34 (1982): 368–75.

Gums, Bonnie L. *Archaeological Investigations on Site 1MB387, the Mobile Country Probate Courthouse Block, Mobile, Alabama*. Mobile: Center for Archaeological Studies, University of South Alabama, 2006.

———. *Archaeological Survey of the D'Olive Plantation (1BA190) and The Village in Daphne, Baldwin County, Alabama*. Mobile: Center for Archaeological Studies, University of South Alabama, 2003.

———. *Archaeology at Lisloy Plantation, Site 1MB312, Bellingrath Gardens and Home, Mobile County, Alabama*. Mobile: Center for Archaeological Studies, University of South Alabama, 2001.

———. *Archaeology at the Old City Hall and Southern Market Courtyard in Mobile, Alabama*. Mobile: Center for Archaeological Studies, University of South Alabama, 1999.

———. *Archaeology at Spring Hill College, Jesuit College of the South, in Mobile, Alabama*. 2 vols. Mobile: Center for Archaeological Studies, University of South Alabama, 2008.

———. *Archaeology Survey of Old Spanish Fort Park, Pascagoula, Mississippi*. Mobile: Center for Archaeological Studies, University of South Alabama, 1996.

———. "Earthfast (*Pieux en Terre*) Structures at Old Mobile." *Historical Archaeology* 36, no. 1 (2002): 13–25.

———. "Eighteenth-Century Plantations in the Northern Gulf Coast Region." *Gulf Coast Historical Review* 14 (1998): 120–42.

———. *Made of Alabama Clay: Historic Potteries on Mobile Bay*. Archaeological Monograph 8. Mobile: Center for Archaeological Studies, University of South Alabama, 2001.

———. *Material Culture of an 18th-Century Gulf Coast Plantation: The Augustin Rochon Plantation, ca. 1750s–1780, Baldwin County, Alabama*. Mobile: Center for Archaeological Studies, University of South Alabama, 2000.

———. *Phase II Archaeological Investigation at Site 1MB360 on the University of South Alabama Campus, Mobile, Alabama*. Mobile: Center for Archaeological Studies, University of South Alabama, 2002.

———. *Phase II Archaeology at the Site of Fort Albert Sidney Johnston, 1MB369, for the Alabama State Port Authority*. Mobile: Center for Archaeological Studies, University of South Alabama, 2017.

———. *Results of Fieldwork for Archaeological Monitoring of Sand and Backfill Removal at La Pointe-Krebs House (22JA526), City of Pascagoula, Jackson County, Mississippi*. Mobile: Center for Archaeological Studies, University of South Alabama, 2015.

———. *Results of Fieldwork for Second Archaeological Monitoring of Restoration Activities at La Pointe-Krebs House (22JA526), City of Pascagoula, Jackson County, Mississippi*. Mobile: Center for Archaeological Studies, University of South Alabama, 2015.

———. *Results of Fieldwork for Third Archaeological Monitoring of Restoration Activities at La Pointe-Krebs House (22JA526), City of Pascagoula, Jackson County, Mississippi*. Mobile: Center for Archaeological Studies, University of South Alabama, 2016.

———. *Summary of Examination of Museum Collections of La Pointe-Krebs House, Pascagoula, Jackson County, Mississippi.* Mobile: Center for Archaeological Studies, University of South Alabama, 2013.

Gums, Bonnie, Karen Leone, Tara Potts, Erin Stacey, Michael Stieber, and Gregory Waselkov. *Phase III Archaeological Data Recovery at Sites 1BA608 and 1BA609 for the Proposed Paradiso Subdivision, Daphne, Baldwin County, Alabama.* Mobile: Center for Archaeological Studies, University of South Alabama, 2009.

Gums, Bonnie L., and George W. Shorter Jr. *Archaeology at Mobile's Exploreum: Discovering the Buried Past.* Archaeological Monograph 3. Mobile: Center for Archaeological Studies, University of South Alabama, 1998.

Gums, Bonnie L., and Gregory A. Waselkov. *Archaeological Investigations at Spanish Fort (1BA336) and the Rochon Plantation Site (1BA337) in Baldwin County, Alabama.* Mobile: Center for Archaeological Studies, University of South Alabama, 1998.

———. *Archaeological Investigations on Two Tracts of Land at Old St. Stephens (1WN1).* Mobile: Center for Archaeological Studies, University of South Alabama, 1999.

———. *Archaeology at La Pointe-Krebs Plantation in Old Spanish Fort Park (22JA526), Pascagoula, Jackson County, Mississippi.* Archaeological Report no. 35. Jackson: Mississippi Department of Archives and History, 2015.

———. *House and Excavation Photos from the La Pointe-Krebs House Site (22JA526), Pascagoula, Mississippi.* Mobile: Center for Archaeological Studies, University of South Alabama, 2010.

———, eds. *Life at the River's Edge: Phase III Archaeological Data Recovery at Sites 1MB510 and 1MB511 for Interstate 10 (I-10) Modifications, ALDOT Project# DPI-AL06(900), City of Mobile, Mobile County Alabama.* Archaeological Monograph 14. Mobile: Center for Archaeological Studies, University of South Alabama, 2018.

———. *Limited Test Excavations at Condé-Charlotte Museum House (1MB470), Mobile, Mobile County, Alabama.* Mobile: Center for Archaeological Studies, University of South Alabama, 2010.

———. *Recent Archaeological Investigations at Old St. Stephens.* Mobile: Center for Archaeological Studies, University of South Alabama, 1999.

Gums, Bonnie, L. Gregory A. Waselkov, Virgil R. Beasley III, and Falicia L. Gordon. *Phase I Cultural Resources Assessment of Fort Albert Sidney Johnston, Archaeological Site 1MB369, City of Mobile, Mobile County, Alabama*, with contributions by John E. Ellis and Vonnie S. Zullo. Mobile: Center for Archaeological Studies, University of South Alabama, 2015.

Gums, Bonnie L., Gregory A. Waselkov, and Sarah B. Mattics. *Planning for the Past: An Archaeological Resource Management Plan for the City of Mobile, Alabama.* Archaeological Monograph 5. Mobile: Center for Archaeological Studies, University of South Alabama, 1999.

Gundersen, James N., Gregory A. Waselkov, and Lillian J. K. Pollock. "Pipestone Argillite Artifacts from Old Mobile and Environs." *Historical Archaeology* 36, no. 1 (2002): 105–16.

Hadden, Carla S., and Alexander Cherkinsky. "Spatiotemporal Variability in ΔR in the Northern Gulf of Mexico, USA." *Radiocarbon* 59, spec. iss. 2 (2017): 343–53.

Hadden, Carla S., Kathy M. Loftis, Alexander Cherkinsky, Brandon T. Ritchison, Isabelle H. Lulewicz, and Victor D. Thompson. "Radiocarbon in Marsh Periwinkle (*Littorina irrorata*) Conchiolin: Applications for Archaeology." *Radiocarbon* 61, no. 5 (2019): 1489–1500.

Hadden, Carla S., Gregory A. Waselkov, Elizabeth J. Reitz, and C. Fred T. Andrus. "Temporality of Fishery Taskscapes on the North-Central Gulf of Mexico Coast (USA) during the Middle/Late Woodland Period (AD 325–1040)." *Journal of Anthropological Archaeology* 67 (September 2022): 101436.

Hadley, Alison M. "Beads, Bifaces, and Blade Cores from the Middle Archaic." Senior Honors thesis, Department of Sociology, Anthropology, and Social Work, University of South Alabama, Mobile, 2003.

Hadley, Alison M., and Philip J. Carr. "Archaic Chert Beads and Craft Specialization: Application of an Organization of Technology Model." In *Exploring Southeastern Archaeology*, edited by Patricia K. Galloway and Evan Peacock, 71–98. Jackson: University Press of Mississippi, 2015.

———. "The Organization of Lithic Technology and Role of Lithic Specialists during the Archaic." Paper presented at the 67th Annual Meeting of the Southeastern Archaeological Conference, Lexington, KY, 2010.

Halbert, Henry S., and Timothy H. Ball. *The Creek War of 1813 and 1814*. Chicago: Donohue and Henneberry, 1895.

Haley, Bryan S., and Jay K. Johnson. *Geophysical Investigations at Fort Mims, Alabama*. Oxford: Center for Archaeological Research, University of Mississippi, 2003.

Hall, Gwendolyn Midlo. *Africans in Colonial Louisiana: The Development of Afro-Creole Culture in the Eighteenth Century*. Baton Rouge: Louisiana State University Press, 1992.

Hamilton, Peter J. *Colonial Mobile*. Edited and annotated by Charles G. Summersell. Tuscaloosa: University of Alabama Press, 1976.

———. *Colonial Mobile: An Historical Study*. 2nd ed. Boston: Houghton Mifflin, 1910.

———. *A Little Boy in Confederate Mobile*. Mobile, AL: Colonial Mobile Book Shop, 1947.

———. *Mobile of the Five Flags*. Mobile, AL: Gill Printing, 1913.

Hannah-Jones, Nikole, Caitlin Roper, Ilena Silverman, and Jake Silverstein, eds. *The 1619 Project: A New Origin Story*. New York: One World, 2021.

Harley, Grant L., Justin T. Maxwell, Joshua S. Oliver, David H. Holt, Joshua Bowman, and Marks Sokolosky-Wixon. "Precision Dating and Cultural History of the La Pointe-Krebs House (22JA526), Pascagoula, Mississippi, USA." *Journal of Archaeological Science: Reports* 20 (August 2018): 87–96.

Harper's Weekly Magazine. "The Explosion at Mobile." June 24, 1865, 396–97.

———. "The Fight Before Mobile—Storming of Fort Blakeley." Saturday, May 27, 1865, 325.

Harriot, Thomas. *A Briefe and True Report of the New Found Land of Virginia*. Edited by Theodor de Bry and Johann Wechel. Frankfurt am Main, Germany: Sigmund Feyerabend, 1590.

Harris, Donald A. "An Archaeological Survey of Fort Louis de la Mobile." Report on file. Mobile Historic Development Commission, Mobile, AL, 1970.

———. "Fort Condé: A Problem in Salvage Archaeology." Master's thesis, Department of Anthropology, University of Florida, Gainesville, 1969.

———. "A French Colonial Well: Its Construction, Excavation and Contents." In *Conference on Historic Site Archaeology Papers 5*, edited by Stanley South, 51–80. Columbia: University of South Carolina, 1970.

Harris, Donald A., and Jerry J. Nielsen. *Archaeological Salvage Investigations at the Site of French Fort Condé, Mobile, Alabama*. Tuscaloosa: Department of Anthropology, University of Alabama, 1972.

Hartmann, Mark Joseph. "The Development of Watercraft in the Prehistoric Southeastern United States." PhD diss., Department of Anthropology, Texas A&M University, College Station, 1996.

Hawkins, Rebecca A., and James C. Litfin. *Phase I Survey of 190 Acres of the Citadel Limestone Quarry Property, Washington County, Alabama*. Cincinnati, OH: Algonquin Archaeological Consultants, 1996.

Hayden, Brian. "Practical and Prestige Technologies: The Evolution of Material Systems." *Journal of Archaeological Method and Theory* 5, no. 1 (1998): 1–55.

Higginbotham, Jay. *Old Mobile: Fort Louis de la Louisiane, 1702–1711*. Mobile, AL: Museum of the City of Mobile, 1977.

Holmes, Jack D. L. "Alabama's Bloodiest Day of the American Revolution: Counterattack at the Village, January 7, 1781." *Alabama Review* 29, no. 3 (1976): 207–19.

———. "Alabama's Forgotten Settlers: Notes on the Spanish Mobile District, 1780–1813." *Alabama Historical Quarterly* 33 (Summer 1971): 87–97.

———, ed. *Documentos inéditos para la historia de la Luisiana, 1792–1810*. Madrid, Spain: Ediciones José Porrúa Turanzas, 1963.

———. "Fort Stoddard in 1799: Seven Letters of Captain Bartholomew Schaumburgh." *Alabama Historical Quarterly* 26 (Fall–Winter 1964): 231–52.

———. "German Troops in Alabama during the American Revolution: The Battle of January 7, 1781." *Alabama Historical Quarterly* 38 (Spring 1976): 5–9.

———. "Notes on the Spanish Fort San Esteban de Tombecbé." *Alabama Review* 18 (October 1965): 281–90.

Holmes, Nicholas H. "Restoration of Mobile's First Court House Jail, Later Known as the Kirkbride House." Manuscript on file, Condé-Charlotte House Museum, Mobile, AL, 1947.

Holmes, Nicholas H., Jr. "Mobile's City Hall." *Alabama Heritage* 6 (1987): 3–15.

Holmes, Nicholas H., Jr., and E. Bruce Trickey. "Late Holocene Sea-Level Oscillations in Mobile Bay." *American Antiquity* 39, no. 1 (1974): 122–24.

Holmes, William H. "Aboriginal Pottery of the Eastern United States." In *Twentieth Annual Report, Bureau of American Ethnology 1898–1899*, 1–201. Washington, DC: Smithsonian Institution, 1903.

———. "Archaeological Collections from Alabama." *American Anthropologist* 2, no. 4 (1889): 350.

Holstein, Harry O. "An Investigation of Parallel Lineal Stone Walls along Alabama Mountain Slopes: Historic Agricultural Terraces or Native American Sacred Stone Monuments?" *Journal of Alabama Archaeology* 65, nos. 1–2 (2019): 87–108.

Hopkins, Griffith Morgan, Jr. *City Atlas of Mobile, Alabama: From Actual Surveys and Records*. Philadelphia: G. M. Hopkins, 1878.

Howard, Milo B., Jr., and Robert R. Rea. "Introduction." In *The Memoire Justificatif of the Chevalier Montault de Monberaut: Indian Diplomacy in British West*

      Florida 1763–1765. Translated and introduced by Milo B. Howard Jr. and Robert R. Rea, 9–58. Tuscaloosa: University of Alabama Press, 1965.

Howell, Mark. "Sonic-Iconic Examination of Adorno Rattles from the Mississippian-era Lake George Site." *Music in Art* 36, nos. 1–2 (2011): 231–44.

Hudson, Angela Pulley. "Removals and Reminders: Apaches and Choctaws in the Jim Crow South." *Journal of the Civil War Era* 11, no. 1 (2021): 80–102.

Hughes, John S. "Labeling and Treating Black Mental Illness in Alabama, 1861–1910." *Journal of Southern History* 58, no. 3 (1993): 435–60.

Hurston, Zora Neale. *Barracoon: The Story of the Last "Black Cargo."* Edited by Deborah G. Plant. New York: HarperCollins, 2018.

———. "Cudjo's Own Story of the Last African Slaver." *Journal of Negro History* 12, no. 4 (1927): 648–63.

Inizian, M. L., H. Roche, and J. Tixier. *Technology of Knapped Stone*. Meudon, France: CREP, 1992.

Irion, Jack B. *Underwater Archaeological Investigations, Mobile Bay Ship Channel, Mobile Harbor, Alabama*. Austin, TX: Espey, Huston and Associates, 1986.

Ivas, Alice A. "Caught in the Middle: The Apalachees of Colonial Mobile." Master's thesis, Department of Anthropology, University of Alabama, Tuscaloosa, 2005.

Jackson, H. Edwin, ed. *Archaeological Investigations of Coastal Shell Middens in the Grand Bay Estuary, Mississippi*. Archaeological Report no. 37. Jackson: Mississippi Department of Archives and History, 2015.

Jenkins, Ned J., and Richard A. Krause. *The Tombigbee Watershed in Southeastern Prehistory*. Tuscaloosa: University of Alabama Press, 1986.

Jepson, Michael, and Lisa L. Colburn. *Development of Social Indicators of Fishing Community Vulnerability and Resilience in the U.S. Southeast and Northeast Regions*. NOAA Technical Memorandum NMFSF/SPO-129. St. Petersburg, FL: National Marine Fisheries Service, National Oceanic and Atmospheric Administration, US Department of Commerce, Southeast Regional Office, 2013.

Johnson, Jay K. "Beads, Microdrills, Bifaces, and Blades from Watson Brake." *Southeastern Archaeology* 19, no. 1 (2000): 95–104.

Johnson, Patrick Lee. "Apalachee Identity on the Gulf Coast Frontier." *Native South* 6, no. 2 (2013): 110–41.

Jones, Elizabeth A., Patricia M. Sanford, R. P. Stephen Davis Jr., and Melissa A. Salvanish. *Archaeological Investigations at the Pettigrew Site on the University of North Carolina, Chapel Hill, North Carolina*. Research Report no. 20. Chapel Hill: Research Laboratories of Archaeology, University of North Carolina, 1998.

Jones, Walter B. "Alabama." In "Archaeological Field Work in North America during 1934: Part 1," edited by Carl E. Guthe. *American Antiquity* 1, no. 1 (1935): 47–48.

———. "Archaeological Survey of Baldwin County." Manuscript on file at the Center for Archaeological Studies, University of South Alabama, Mobile, 1933.

Joseph, J. W., and Mary Beth Reed. *An Increase of the Town: An Archeological and Historical Investigation of the Proposed Mobile Convention Center Site (1MB194)*. Technical Report 13. Stone Mountain, GA: New South Associates, 1991.

Justice, Noel D. *Stone Age Spear and Arrow Points of the Midcontinental and Eastern*

United States: A Modern Survey and Reference. Bloomington: Indiana University Press, 1987.

Kandare, Richard P. "A Contextual Study of Mississippian Dugout Canoes: A Research Design for the Moundville Phase." Master's thesis, Department of Anthropology, University of Arkansas, Fayetteville, 1983.

Kelly, Robert L. *The Fifth Beginning: What Six Million Years of Human History Can Tell Us about Our Future*. Berkeley: University of California Press, 2019.

———. "The Three Sides of a Biface." *American Antiquity* 53, no. 4 (1988): 717–34.

Kenny, Michael, and James J. Walsh. *Catholic Culture in Alabama: Centenary Story of Spring Hill College, 1830–1930*. New York: America Press, 1931.

Key, Watt. *Among the Swamp People: Life in Alabama's Mobile-Tensaw River Delta*. Tuscaloosa: University of Alabama Press, 2015.

Klippel, Walter E., and Bonnie E. Price. "Bone Disc Manufacturing Debris from Newfoundland to Antigua during the Historic Period." In *Bones as Tools: Current Methods and Interpretations in Worked Bone Studies*, edited by Christian Gates StPierre and Renee B. Walker, 133–42. International Series 1622. Oxford, UK: BAR, 2007.

Knight, Vernon J., Jr. *Archaeological Investigations on Dauphin Island, Mobile County, Alabama*. Tuscaloosa: Department of Anthropology, University of Alabama, 1976.

———. "Professionalization of Archaeology in the Alabama Museum of Natural History: 1929–1950." *Alabama Review* 75, no. 1 (2022): 14–49.

Kocis, James J. "Geoarchaeology of Site 1RU142." In Price, *Phase III Archaeological Testing*, 25–61.

Konstam, Angus. *Confederate Submarines and Torpedo Vessels, 1861–65*. Oxford, UK: Osprey, 2004.

Kostro, Mark. "Town and Gown Archaeology in Eighteenth-Century Williamsburg." In *Historical Archaeology in the Twenty-First Century: Lessons from Colonial Williamsburg*, edited by Ywone D. Edwards-Ingram and Andrew C. Edwards, 28–41. Gainesville: University Press of Florida, 2021.

Kroot, Matthew V., and Lee M. Panich. "Students Are Stakeholders in On-Campus Archaeology." *Advances in Archaeological Practice* 8, no. 2 (2020): 134–50.

Lackey, Richard S., comp. *Frontier Claims in the Lower South*. New Orleans, LA: Polyanthos, 1977.

Land, John E. *Mobile: Her Trade, Commerce and Industries 1883–4*. Mobile, AL: printed by author, 1884.

Langlois, Gilles-Antoine. *Des villes pour la Louisiane française: Théorie et pratique de l'urbanistique coloniale au 18e siècle*. Paris: L'Harmattan, 2003.

Lankford, George E. "Chacato, Pensacola, Tohomé, Naniaba, and Mobila." In *Handbook of North American Indians*. Vol. 14, *Southeast*, edited by Raymond D. Fogelson, 664–68. Washington, DC: Smithsonian Institution Press, 2004.

Lankford, George E., and David H. Dye. "Conehead Effigies: A Distinctive Art Form of the Mississippi Valley." *Arkansas Archeologist* 53 (2014): 37–50.

Lapham, Heather A., and Gregory A. Waselkov, eds. *Bears: Archaeological and Ethnohistorical Perspectives in Native Eastern North America*. Gainesville: University Press of Florida, 2020.

Larguier, Everett. *Jesuit Beginnings at Spring Hill, 1847–1848*. Gautrelet Publications, vol. 3. Mobile, AL: Spring Hill College Press, 1983.

La Tourette, John. *Map of the State of Alabama*. New York: J. H. Colton, 1838.

Lau, Stephen, and Oscar W. Brock Jr. *An Archaeological Survey and Test Excavations at Ideal Basic Industries, Inc., Theodore Park Plant Site, Mobile County, Alabama*. Mobile: Archaeological Research Laboratory, University of South Alabama, 1978.

Le Moyne, Joseph, Sieur de Serigny, and Valentin Devin. "Carte de l'entrée de la Baye de la Mobile et de L'Isle, 1719." Département des cartes et plans, Ge SH 18, portefeuille 138, division 10, p 12 D. Bibliothèque Nationale de France, Paris.

Lewis, Herbert James. *Lost Capitals of Alabama*. Columbia, SC: History Press, 2014.

Lewis, R. Barry. "Sea-Level Rise and Subsidence Effects on Gulf Coast Archaeological Site Distributions." *American Antiquity* 65, no. 3 (2000): 525–41.

Littlefield, Daniel C. *Rice and Slaves: Ethnicity and the Slave Trade in Colonial South Carolina*. Baton Rouge: Louisiana State University Press, 1981.

Logan, Onnie Lee, as told to Katherine Clark. *Motherwit: An Alabama Midwife's Story*. New York: E. P. Dutton, 1989.

Lolley, Terry L. "Weeden Island Occupation in the Borderland: An Example from South Alabama." *Southeastern Archaeology*. 22, no. 1 (2003): 63–76.

Lowrie, Walter. *American State Papers, Public Lands*. Vol. 3. Washington, DC: Duff Green, 1984.

Ludlow, Maxfield. *A Map of the State of Louisiana with Part of the State of Mississippi and Alabama Territory*. Philadelphia: W. Charles and J. G. Warnicke, 1817.

Ludlum, David M. *Early American Hurricanes, 1492–1870*. Boston: American Meteorological Society, 1963.

Luer, George M. "Calusa Canals in Southwestern Florida: Routes of Tribute and Exchange." *Florida Anthropologist* 42, no. 2 (1989): 89–130.

———. "The Naples Canal." *Florida Anthropologist* 51, no. 1 (1998): 15–24.

Luer, George M., and Ryan J. Wheeler. "How the Pine Island Canal Worked: Topography, Hydraulics, and Engineering." *Florida Anthropologist* 50, no. 2 (1997): 115–31.

Mancini, Ernest A., and Charles W. Copeland. "St. Stephens Quarry (Lone Star Cement Company Quarry), St. Stephens, Washington County, Alabama." *Centennial Field Guide, Geological Society of America (Southeastern Section)* 6 (1986): 373–78.

Matte, Jacqueline Anderson. *The History of Washington County: First County in Alabama*. Chatom, AL: Washington County Historical Society, 1982.

———. *They Say the Wind Is Red: The Alabama Choctaw, Lost in Their Own Land*. Montgomery, AL: New South Books, 2002.

Matte, Jacqueline A., Doris Brown, and Barbara Waddell, eds. *Old St. Stephens: Historical Records Survey*. Mobile, AL: St. Stephens Historical Commission, 1997.

Maury, Dabney H. "Defence of Spanish Fort." *Southern Historical Society Papers* 39 (1914): 130–36.

McAlester, Major Miles D., Major J. C. Palfrey, Captain C. J. Allen, and Captain Patten. *Siege Operations at Spanish Fort, Mobile Bay, by the U.S. Forces under Maj. Gen. Canby*. Philadelphia: Bowen, 1866.

McBride, W. Stephen, Kim Arbogast McBride, and Greg Adamson. *Frontier Forts in West Virginia: Historical and Archaeological Explorations*. Charleston: West Virginia Division of Culture and History, 2003.

McCourt, Christine, ed. *Childbirth, Midwifery, and Concepts of Time*. New York: Berghahn, 2009.

McGahey, Samuel O. *Mississippi Projectile Point Guide*. Rev. ed. Archaeological Report no. 31. Jackson: Mississippi Department of Archives and History, 2004.

———. "Prehistoric Stone Bead Manufacture: The Loosa Yokena Site, Warren County, Mississippi." *Mississippi Archaeology* 40, no. 1 (2005): 3–29.

McMicken, Captain William. Letter to his wife Rowena Ostrander McMicken, May 28, 1865. McMicken Family Papers (Accession #0434–001, Box 1/11), Civil War Letters Collection. Special Collections, University of Washington Libraries, Seattle.

McWilliams, Richebourg G., ed. and trans. *Fleur de Lys and Calumet: Being the Pénicault Narrative of French Adventure in Louisiana*. Tuscaloosa: University of Alabama Press, 1988.

———, ed. and trans. *Iberville's Gulf Journals*. Tuscaloosa: University of Alabama Press, 1981.

Medina Rojas, Francisco de Borja. *José de Ezpeleta, gobernador de La Mobila, 1780–1781*. Seville, Spain: Escuela de Estudios Hispano-Americanos de Sevilla, 1980.

Meredith, Steven M. "Culture History of the Middle Cahaba River Drainage in Alabama before AD 1800." *Journal of Alabama Archaeology* 63, nos. 1–2 (2017): 13–93.

Mickelson, Kathrine R. "McLeod Plant Exploitation." In *The Late Woodland Period on the Lower Tombigbee River*, by George W. Shorter, 153–57. Archaeological Monograph 6. Mobile: Center for Archaeological Studies, University of South Alabama, 1999.

Milanich, Jerald, Ann Cordell, Vernon Knight, Timothy Kohler, and Brenda Sigler-Lavelle. *Archaeology of Northern Florida AD 200–900: The McKeithen Weeden Island Culture*. Rev. ed. New York: Academic Press, 1997.

Miller Surrey, Nancy M. *The Commerce of Louisiana during the French Régime, 1699–1763*, with an introduction by Gregory A. Waselkov. Tuscaloosa: University of Alabama Press, 2006.

Millett, Nathaniel. *The Maroons of Prospect Bluff and Their Quest for Freedom in the Atlantic World*. Gainesville: University Press of Florida, 2013.

Mistovich, Tim S., and Vernon James Knight Jr. *Cultural Resources Survey of Mobile Harbor, Alabama*. Moundville, AL: OSM Archaeological Consultants, 1983.

Moberg, Mark, and J. Stephen Thomas. "Class Segmentation and Divided Labor: Asian Workers in the Gulf of Mexico Seafood Industry." *Ethnology* 32, no. 1 (1993): 1–13.

———. "Indochinese Resettlement and the Transformation of Identities along the Alabama Gulf Coast." In *Cultural Diversity in the South: Anthropological Contributions to a Region in Transition*, edited by Carole E. Hill and Patricia Beaver, 115–28. Athens: University of Georgia Press, 1998.

Mobile Commercial Register. "Baldwin County Jail." August 15, 1832, 3.

Moore, Clarence B. "Certain Aboriginal Remains of the Northwest Florida Coast, Part I." *Journal of the Academy of Natural Sciences of Philadelphia*, 2nd ser., 11, no. 4 (1901): 421–97.

———. "Certain Aboriginal Remains on Mobile Bay and on Mississippi Sound." *Journal of the Academy of Natural Sciences of Philadelphia*, 2nd ser., 13, no. 2 (1905): 279–97.

Morgan, David W. "Archeology—Arrival to AD 1550." In Waselkov, Andrus, and Plumb, *State of Knowledge*, 131–39.

———. "Mississippian Heritage: Late Woodland Subsistence and Settlement Patterns in the Mobile-Tensaw Delta, Alabama." PhD diss., Department of Anthropology, Tulane University, New Orleans, 2003.

———. *The Tensaw Bluffs Project: An Archaeological Survey of the Eastern Upland Margin of the Mobile-Tensaw Delta, Alabama*. Tuscaloosa: Alabama Museum of Natural History, University of Alabama, 1997.

Morris, J. Brent. *Dismal Freedom: A History of the Maroons of the Great Dismal Swamp*. Chapel Hill: University of North Carolina Press, 2022.

Moussette, Marcel, and Gregory A. Waselkov. *Archéologie de l'Amérique Coloniale Française*. Montréal, Canada: Lévesque Éditeur, 2013.

Muntz, Alice Eileen. "Interpreting Ritual in Ceramics of Late Mississippian Southern Illinois." Master's thesis, Department of Anthropology, Southern Illinois University, Carbondale, 2018.

Nevius, Marcus P. *City of Refuge: Slavery and Petit Marronage in the Great Dismal Swamp, 1765–1856*. Athens: University of Georgia Press, 2020.

Newsom, Lee Ann, and Barbara A. Purdy. "Florida Canoes: A Maritime Heritage from the Past." *Florida Anthropologist* 43, no. 3 (1990): 164–80.

New-York Spectator. "Mobile, June 21st." July 17, 1827, 2.

Nguyen, Mai Thi, and David Salvesen. "Disaster Recovery among Multiethnic Immigrants: A Case Study of Southeast Asians in Bayou La Batre (AL) after Hurricane Katrina." *Journal of the American Planning Association* 80, no. 4 (2014): 385–96.

Nicolson, Frank W., ed. *Alumni Record of Wesleyan University, Middletown, Conn*. 4th ed. New Haven, CT: Tuttle, Morehouse, and Taylor, 1911.

Norman, Neil. *Report on Archaeological Survey and Testing at Peter Lee House Site and Lewis Quarter*. Williamsburg, VA: Department of Anthropology, College of William and Mary, 2010.

———. *Report on Mapping and Preservation Efforts at Old Plateau Cemetery*. Williamsburg, VA: Department of Anthropology, College of William and Mary, 2010.

Norton, Holly K., and Christopher T. Espenshade. "The Challenge of Locating Maroon Refuge Sites at Maroon Ridge, St. Croix." *Journal of Caribbean Archaeology* 7 (2007): 1–17.

Nunez, Theron A., Jr., ed. "Creek Nativism and the Creek War of 1813–1814." *Ethnohistory* 5, no. 1 (1958): 1–47.

———. "Creek Nativism and the Creek War of 1813–1814, Part 2." *Ethnohistory* 5, no. 2 (1958): 131–75.

———. "Creek Nativism and the Creek War of 1813–1814, Part 3." *Ethnohistory* 5, no. 3 (1958): 292–301.

Nuzum, Kay. "Bon Secour." *Baldwin County Historical Society Quarterly* 1 (1973): 10–14.

O'Malley, Nancy. *Boonesborough Unearthed: Frontier Archaeology at a Revolutionary Fort*. Lexington: University Press of Kentucky, 2019.

———. *Stockading Up: A Study of Pioneer Stations in the Inner Bluegrass Region of Kentucky*. Rev. ed. Lexington: Program for Cultural Resource Assessment, University of Kentucky, 1994.

Orr, Kelly L. "Coastal Weeden Island Subsistence Adaptations: Zooarchaeological

Evidence from Bayou St. John (1BA21), Alabama." PhD diss., Department of Anthropology, University of Georgia, Athens, 2007.

Ostahowski, Brian, and Alison Hanlon. *Archaeological Investigations in Support of the MC252 (Deepwater Horizon) Oil Spill Response in the State of Alabama*. New Orleans: HDR Environmental, Operations and Construction, 2014.

Owen, Thomas M. "Mounds and Prehistoric Works in Alabama." In *Handbook of the Alabama Anthropological Society, 1910*, edited by Thomas M. Owen, 36–58. Montgomery, AL: Brown Printing, 1910.

———. "Prehistoric Works." In *Report of the Alabama History Commission*. Vol. 1, edited by Thomas M. Owen, 357–69. Montgomery, AL: Brown Printing, 1901.

———. "Some Notes on the Shell Banks of the Alabama Coast." *Arrow Points* 4, no. 1 (1922): 2–10.

Padgett, Thomas J. *Archaeological Testing at the Old Spanish Fort, Pascagoula*. Hattiesburg: Department of Sociology and Anthropology, University of Southern Mississippi, 1979.

Panhorst, Michael W. *Mount Vernon Arsenal and Searcy Hospital, the State of Alabama's National Treasure at Risk: A White Paper*. Montgomery: Places in Peril, Alabama Trust for Historic Preservation, 2016.

Paredes, J. Anthony, and Judith Knight, eds. *Red Eagle's Children: Weatherford vs. Weatherford et al*. Tuscaloosa: University of Alabama Press, 2012.

Parker, James C. "Blakeley: A Frontier Seaport." *Alabama Review* 27, no. 1 (1974): 39–51.

Parker, Prescott A. *Story of the Tensaw: Blakely; Spanish Fort; Jacksons Oak; Fort Mims*. Montrose, AL: P. A. Parker, 1922.

Pate, James P., ed. *The Reminiscences of George Strother Gaines: Pioneer and Statesman of Early Alabama and Mississippi, 1805–1843*. Tuscaloosa: University of Alabama Press, 1998.

Pertermann, Dana L., and Holly Kathryn Norton, eds. *The Archaeology of Engagement: Conflict and Revolution in the United States*. College Station: Texas A&M University Press, 2015.

Pettaway, Addie E. *Africatown, U.S.A.: Some Aspects of Folklife and Material Culture of an Historic Landscape*. Madison: Wisconsin Department of Public Instruction, 1985.

Phelps, David Sutton. *Ancient Pots and Dugout Canoes: Indian Life as Revealed by Archaeology at Lake Phelps*. Creswell, NC: Pettigrew State Park, 1989.

Pickett, Albert James. *History of Alabama, and Incidentally of Georgia and Mississippi, from the Earliest Period*. 2 vols. Charleston, SC: Walker and James, 1851.

———. "Notes Taken from the Lips of Col. Robert James, 1848." Section 12, notes, Pickett Family Papers, LPR185. Alabama Department of Archives and History, Montgomery.

Piggott, Michele Marie. "The Apalachee after San Luis: Exploring Cultural Hybridization through Ceramic Practice." Master's thesis, Department of Anthropology, University of West Florida, Pensacola, 2015.

———. "The Materiality of the Apalachee Diaspora: An Indigenous History of Contact and Colonialism in the Gulf South." *Southeastern Archaeology* 41, no. 1 (2022): 53–73.

Pintado, Sebastian. "Plan no. 1815." Pintado Papers, volume 7, page 38. Special Collections, Louisiana State University, Baton Rouge.

"Plan de la ville et du Fort Louis sur La Mobile" (1704). Louisiane, III 6 PFB 120, Dépôt des Fortifications des Colonies. Archives Nationales, Aix-en-Provence, France.

"Plan no. 1815, Luis Dolive, Mobile, 1808." Pintado Papers. Special Collections, Louisiana State University Libraries, Baton Rouge.

Pluckhahn, Thomas J. *Kolomoki: Settlement, Ceremony, and Status in the Deep South, A.D. 350–750.* Tuscaloosa: University of Alabama Press, 2003.

Plumb, Glenn E. "A Brief History of the Mobile-Tensaw River Bottomlands National Natural Landmark." In Waselkov, Andrus, and Plumb, *State of Knowledge*, 5–9.

Pope, C. T. Letter to his wife, July 13, 1864. Seventh Alabama Cavalry, CSA, Confederate Regimental History Files. Alabama Department of Archives and History, Montgomery.

Porcher, Richard Dwight, Jr., and William Robert Judd. *The Market Preparation of Carolina Rice: An Illustrated History of Innovations in the Lowcountry Rice Kingdom.* Columbia: University of South Carolina Press, 2014.

Potts, Tara L. *Phase III Data Recovery at 1EE639, Wetumpka, Elmore County, Alabama.* Mobile: Center for Archaeological Studies, University of South Alabama, 2010.

Potts, Tara, and Cameron Gill. *Coastal Survey, Site Assessment, and Testing in Mobile and Baldwin Counties, Alabama.* Mobile: Center for Archaeological Studies, University of South Alabama, 2011.

Powell, John T. "Marked Spanish Colonial Military Buttons of the Gulf Coast Region, Circa 1793–1821." *Military Collector and Historian* 49, no. 1 (1997): 2–11.

Price, Sarah E., ed. *Archaeology at Orange Beach: Phase III Data Recovery at 1BA21, the Bayou St. John Site, Orange Beach, Baldwin County, Alabama.* Mobile: Center for Archaeological Studies, University of South Alabama, 2009.

———, ed. *Archaeology on the Tombigbee River: Phase III Data Recovery at 1CK56, the Corps Site, Clarke County, Alabama.* Mobile: Center for Archaeological Studies, University of South Alabama, 2009.

———, ed. *Phase III Archaeological Testing at the Silver Run Site, Archaeological Site 1RU142, Russell County, Alabama, Associated with Adding Lanes to US 431.* Mobile: Center for Archaeological Studies, University of South Alabama, 2008.

———, ed. *Phase III Archaeology at Plash Island, Archaeological Site 1BA134, in Baldwin County, Alabama.* Mobile: Center for Archaeological Studies, University of South Alabama, 2008.

Price, Sarah E., and Justin Stickler. *The McInnis Site, Orange Beach, Alabama*, with photographs by Lyle Ratliff. Orange Beach, AL: printed by author, 2015.

"Proceedings of the Spanish Evacuation Centennial at St. Stephens, May 6, 1899." In *Transactions of the Alabama Historical Society*. Vol. 3, 1898–99. Tuscaloosa: Alabama Historical Society, 1899, 198–201.

Raines, Ben. *The Last Slave Ship: The True Story of How* Clotilda *Was Found, Her Descendants, and an Extraordinary Reckoning.* New York: Simon and Schuster, 2022.

———. "Modern Cultures of the Mobile-Tensaw Delta." In Waselkov, Andrus, and Plumb, *State of Knowledge*, 151–54.

———. *Saving America's Amazon: The Threat to Our Nation's Most Diverse River System.* Montgomery, AL: New South Books, 2020.

Randall, W. D., and Burton Parker. *A Souvenir of Daphne.* Daphne, AL: Commercial Club of Daphne, 1910.

Rau, Charles. "The Stock-in-Trade of an Aboriginal Lapidary." *Smithsonian Institution, Annual Report for 1877*, 1–4. Washington, DC: Smithsonian Institution, 1878.

"Record of Proceedings of a Court of Inquiry Convened at the City of Mobile, Alabama, June 3–11, 1865." RG 153, Records of the Office of the Judge Advocate General (Army). National Archives, Washington, DC.

Reed, Mary Beth, and J. W. Joseph. *From Alluvium to Commerce: Waterfront Architecture, Land Reclamation, and Commercial Development in Mobile, Alabama.* Technical Report 126. Stone Mountain, GA: New South Associates, 1995.

Reed, Walter. "Geronimo and His Warriors in Captivity." *Illustrated America* 3, no. 26 (August 16, 1890): 231–35.

Reitz, Elizabeth J., Carla S. Hadden, Maran E. Little, Gregory A. Waselkov, C. Fred T. Andrus, and Evan Peacock. *Final Project Report: Woodland Seasonality on the Northern Coast of the Gulf of Mexico.* Report on Awards BCS-1026166, BCS-1026168, and BCS-1026169. Washington, DC: National Science Foundation, 2013.

Reitz, Elizabeth J., Carla S. Hadden, Gregory A. Waselkov, and C. Fred T. Andrus. "Woodland-Period Fisheries on the North-Central Coast of the Gulf of Mexico." *Southeastern Archaeology* 40, no. 2 (2021): 135–55.

Reitz, Elizabeth J., and Gregory A. Waselkov. "Vertebrate Use at Early Colonies on the Southeastern Coasts of Eastern North America." *International Journal of Historical Archaeology* 19, no. 1 (2015): 21–45.

Rezek, Zeljko, Simon J. Holdaway, Deborah I. Olszewski, Sam C. Lin, Matthew Douglass, Shannon P. McPherron, Radu Iovita, David R. Braun, and Dennis Sandgathe. "Aggregates, Formational Emergence, and the Focus on Practice in Stone Artifact Archaeology." *Journal of Archaeological Method and Theory* 27, no. 4 (2020): 887–928.

Riccio, Joseph F., and Conrad A. Gazzier. "Infrared Color Photography of the Fort Mims Site, Alabama." *Journal of Alabama Archaeology* 20, no. 2 (1974): 217–21.

Richards, T. Addison. "The Rice Lands of the South." *Harper's New Monthly Magazine* 19, no. 114 (November 1859): 721–38.

Riley, B. F. "Hal's Lake." *Watson's Magazine* 4, no. 3 (May 1906): 391–93.

Ritchie, William A. "The Lamoka Lake Site." *Researches and Transactions of the New York State Archeological Association* 7, no. 4 (1932): 79–134.

Roberts, Glenn, and Philip J. Carr. *A Cultural Resources Survey for a Proposed Shuttle Transportation System on the University of South Alabama Campus, Mobile, Alabama.* Mobile: Center for Archaeological Studies, University of South Alabama, 2002.

Robertson, Natalie S. *The Slave Ship* Clotilda *and the Making of AfricaTown, USA: Spirit of Our Ancestors.* New York: Praeger, 2008.

Roche, Emma Langdon. *Historic Sketches of the South.* New York: Knickerbocker Press, 1914.

Rochon, Nannetta. "50 Dollars Reward." *Halcyon and Tombeckbe Public Advertiser* 5, no. 48 (April 3, 1820): 1.

Rodning, Christopher B. "Water Travel and Mississippian Settlement at Bottle Creek." In Brown, *Bottle Creek*, 194–204.

Romans, Bernard. *A Concise Natural History of East and West Florida*, edited with an introduction by Kathryn E. Holland Braund. Tuscaloosa: University of Alabama Press, 1999.

Rowland, Dunbar, ed. *Peter Chester: Third Governor of the Province of British West Florida under British Domination 1770–1781*. Vol. 5, centenary ser. Jackson: Mississippi Historical Society, 1925.

Rushforth, Brett. *Bonds of Alliance: Indigenous and Atlantic Slaveries in New France*. Chapel Hill: University of North Carolina Press, 2012.

Russo, Michael. "Southeastern Archaic Mounds." In *Archaeology of the Mid-Holocene Southeast*, edited by Kenneth E. Sassaman and David G. Anderson, 259–87. Gainesville: University Press of Florida, 1996.

Ryan, Kevin C., Ann Trinkle Jones, Cassandra L. Koerner, and Kristine M. Lee. *Wildland Fire in Ecosystems: Effects of Fire on Cultural Resources and Archaeology*. General Technical Report RMRSGTR-42-vol. 3. Fort Collins, CO: US Department of Agriculture, 2012.

Salvage, Benjamin. "Map of Fort Mims and Its Environs, 1813." LPR185, Pickett Family Papers. Alabama Department of Archives and History, Montgomery.

Saunders, Joe W., Rolfe D. Mandel, C. Garth Sampson, Charles M. Allen, E. Thurman Allen, Daniel A. Bush, James K. Feathers, et al. "Watson Brake: A Middle Archaic Mound Complex in Northeast Louisiana." *American Antiquity* 70, no. 4 (2005): 631–68.

Saunt, Claudio. *A New Order of Things: Property, Power, and the Transformation of the Creek Indians, 1733–1816*. Cambridge: Cambridge University Press, 1999.

———. *Unworthy Republic: The Dispossession of Native Americans and the Road to Indian Territory*. New York: W. W. Norton, 2020.

Sayers, Daniel O. *A Desolate Place for a Defiant People: The Archaeology of Maroons, Indigenous Americans, and Enslaved Laborers in the Great Dismal Swamp*. Gainesville: University Press of Florida, 2014.

Schneider, David B., Bonnie L. Gums, Gregory A. Waselkov, George W. Shorter Jr., and Richard S. Fuller. "National Historic Landmarks." In Waselkov, Andrus, and Plumb, *State of Knowledge*, 155–66.

Schroeder, William W., and N. Read Stowe. *Archaeological Survey of a Portion of Mobile Bay*. Technical Report 74–001. Dauphin Island, AL: Dauphin Island Sea Lab, 1974.

Schroeter, George. *The Powder Magazine Explosion*. Mobile, AL: Mobile Public Library, 1993.

Scott, Florence D'Olive. *Daphne: A History of Its People and Their Pursuits as Some Saw It and Others Remember It*. Montrose, AL: Montrose Garden Club, 1965.

———. *Montrose as It Was Recorded, Told about, and Lived*. Montrose, AL: Montrose Garden Club, 1959.

Scott, Florence D'Olive, and Frank Laraway. "D'Olive Cemetery." *Quarterly* 5 (1977): 21–22. Bay Minette, AL: Baldwin County Historical Society.

Scott, Robert N., ed. *The War of the Rebellion: A Compilation of the Official Records of the Union and Confederate Armies*. Ser. 1, vol. 35, part 2, *Correspondence*. Washington, DC: Government Printing Office, 1891.

Seacat, Harriet L. Richardson, and Philip J. Carr. *A Cultural Resources Survey of a*

    Proposed Research Park Northeast of the University of South Alabama Campus, Mobile, Alabama. Mobile: Center for Archaeological Studies, University of South Alabama, 2002.

Searcy, George H. "An Epidemic of Acute Pellagra." *Transactions of the Medical Association of the State of Alabama*, April 1907, 387–93.

Sewell, Lewis. *The Last Campaign of Sir John Falstaff the II: or, The Hero of the Burnt-Corn Battle, a Heroi-Comic Poem.* St. Stephens, Mississippi Territory: 1815.

Sheldon, Craig T., Jr. "Persistence and Change in Historic Upper Creek Architecture." In *Native American Log Cabins in the Southeast*, edited by Gregory A. Waselkov, 25–44. Knoxville: University of Tennessee Press, 2019.

———, ed. *The Southern and Central Alabama Expeditions of Clarence Bloomfield Moore.* Tuscaloosa: University of Alabama Press, 2001.

Sheldon, Craig T., and John W. Cottier. *Origins of Mobile: Archaeological Investigations at the Courthouse Site, Mobile, Alabama.* Archaeological Monograph 5. Auburn, AL: Department of Sociology and Anthropology, Auburn University, 1983.

Sheldon, Craig T., Ned J. Jenkins, and Gregory A. Waselkov. "French Habitations at the Alabama Post, ca. 1720–1763." *Archéologiques, Collection Hors Série* 2 (2008): 112–26. L'Association des Archéologues du Québec.

Sheldon, Craig T., Jr., Ian Thompson, and Gregory A. Waselkov. "Baron de Crenay's Map of Louisiane in 1733: An Ethnohistoric and Archaeological Voyage into Central Alabama." *Journal of Alabama Archaeology* 68, no. 2 (2022): 95–132.

Sheliha, Lt. Colonel Victor von. Letter from Chief Engineer to Colonel John H. Gindrat, August 12, 1864. Engineer Office, Mobile. RG 109, War Department Collection of Confederate Archives, Letters Sent, Engineer Office, Department of the Gulf, ch. 3, vol. 16, p. 170. National Archives and Records Administration, Washington, DC.

———. "Map of Spanish Fort and Vicinity, Drawn under the Direction of Lieut. Col. V. Sheliha, Summer 1864." 276/176, Jeremy Francis Gilmer Papers. Wilson Library, Southern Historical Collection, University of North Carolina, Chapel Hill.

———. *A Treatise on Coast-Defence: Based on the Experience Gained by Officers of the Corps of Engineers of the Army of the Confederate States.* London: E. and F. N. Spon, 1868.

Sherwood, Sarah C., and Tristram R. Kidder. "The DaVincis of Dirt: Geoarchaeological Perspectives on Native American Mound Building in the Mississippi River Basin." *Journal of Anthropological Archaeology* 30, no. 1 (2011): 69–87.

Shorter, George W., Jr. "The Archaeological Site of Port Dauphin (1MB61): Its Role in the French Colony on Mobile Bay." Master's thesis, Department of Geography and Anthropology, Louisiana State University, Baton Rouge, 1995.

———. *A Cultural Resources Assessment of a Proposed Boat Launch Facility in Washington County, Alabama.* Mobile: Center for Archaeological Studies, University of South Alabama, 2002.

———, ed. *The Late Woodland Period on the Lower Tombigbee River.* Archaeological Monograph 6. Mobile: Center for Archaeological Studies, University of South Alabama, 1999.

———. *Mapping of Carr's Front.* Mobile: Center for Archaeological Studies, University of South Alabama, 2006.

———. *Phase II Archaeological Testing of a Civil War Camp in Gulf Shores, Baldwin County, Alabama.* Mobile: Center for Archaeological Studies, University of South Alabama, 1995.

———. *Phase III Archaeological Mitigation at Site 1BA594, Garrison Ridge Development, Spanish Fort, Baldwin County, Alabama.* Mobile: Center for Archaeological Studies, University of South Alabama, 2007.

———. "Status and Trade at Port Dauphin." *Historical Archaeology* 36, no. 1 (2002): 135–42.

———. "St. Stephens: The Alabama Territory's First Capital." In *Alabama from Territory to Statehood: An Alabama Heritage Bicentennial Collection.* edited by Donna Cox Baker, Susan Reynolds, and Elizabeth Wade, 58–65. Montgomery, AL: New South Books, 2019.

Shorter, George W., Jr., Sonja Kaderly Axsmith, Sarah B. Mattics, Tara L. Potts, and Gregory A. Waselkov. *Phase I and II Archaeological Investigations in Fort Condé Village (1MB132), Mobile, Alabama.* Mobile: Center for Archaeological Studies, University of South Alabama, 2001.

Shorter, George W., Jr., and Sarah B. Mattics. *Archaeology at Old St. Stephens (1WN1), River Structures 50 and 51, Washington County, Alabama.* Mobile: Center for Archaeological Studies, University of South Alabama, 2004.

———. *Excavations at the Retirement Systems of Alabama Tower Site in Downtown Mobile, Alabama: Interim Report.* Mobile: Center for Archaeological Studies, University of South Alabama, 2003.

Shorter, George W., Jr., Sarah B. Mattics, and Bonnie L. Gums. *Phase III Archaeological Investigations at Dekle Street (1MB34) for ALDoT Project STPAA-4900(13), in the City of Mobile, Mobile County, Alabama.* Mobile: Center for Archaeological Studies, University of South Alabama, 2006.

Shorter, George W., Jr., Sarah B. Mattics, and James W. Long. *Archaeology at Old St. Stephens (1WN1): Mapping and Testing the Site, Washington County, Alabama.* Mobile: Center for Archaeological Studies, University of South Alabama, 2002.

Shorter, George W., Jr., Tara L. Potts, and Gregory A. Waselkov. *A Phase I Cultural Resources Assessment of Three Construction Tracts on the Spring Hill College Campus, Mobile, Mobile County, Alabama.* Mobile: Center for Archaeological Studies, University of South Alabama, 2002.

Shulsky, Linda R. "Chinese Porcelain at Old Mobile." *Historical Archaeology* 36, no. 1 (2002): 97–104.

Shulsky, Linda Rosenfeld. "Chinese Porcelain in Old Mobile." *Antiques* 150, no. 1 (July 1996): 80–89.

Silvia, Diane. "Indian and French Interaction in Colonial Louisiana during the Early Eighteenth Century." PhD diss., Department of Anthropology, Tulane University, New Orleans, 2000.

———. "Native American and French Cultural Dynamics on the Gulf Coast." *Historical Archaeology* 36, no. 1 (2002): 26–35.

Silvia, Diane E., and Gregory A. Waselkov. *Roads to the Past: Phase II Archaeological Research and Testing Prior to Interstate-10 Revisions in Mobile, Alabama (Virginia Street Interchange to West Tunnel Interchange).* Mobile: Center for Archaeological Studies, University of South Alabama, 1993.

Simek, Jan F., Beau Duke Carroll, Julie Reed, Alan Cressler, Tom Belt, Wayna Adams, and Mary White. "The Red Bird River Shelter (15CY52) Revisited:

Simpich, Frederick. "Smoke over Alabama." *National Geographic Magazine* 60, no. 6 (December 1931): 703–58.

Skowronek, Russell K., and Kenneth E. Lewis, eds. *Beneath the Ivory Tower: The Archaeology of Academia*. Gainesville: University Press of Florida, 2010.

Sledge, John S. *The Gulf of Mexico: A Maritime History*. Columbia: University of South Carolina Press, 2019.

———. *The Mobile River*. Columbia: University of South Carolina Press, 2015.

Smith, Hayden R. *Carolina's Golden Fields: Inland Rice Cultivation in the South Carolina Lowcountry, 1670–1860*. Cambridge: Cambridge University Press, 2020.

Smith, John Henry. *Africatown, U.S.A.: A Pictorial History of Plateau and Magazine Point, Alabama*. Mobile, AL: American Ethnic Science Society, 1981.

Smith, Marvin T. "Eighteenth-Century Glass Beads in the French Colonial Trade." *Historical Archaeology* 36, no. 1 (2002): 55–61.

Smith, Robert Leslie. *Gone to the Swamp: Raw Materials for the Good Life in the Mobile-Tensaw Delta*. Tuscaloosa: University of Alabama Press, 2008.

Smith, Roger C., ed. *Submerged History: Underwater Archaeology in Florida,*. Sarasota, FL: Pineapple Press, 2018.

Smithweck, David. *Historic Cannons of Mobile, Alabama: An Illustrated Guide*. Mobile, AL: printed by author, 2014.

———. *In Search of the CSS* Huntsville *and CSS* Tuscaloosa*: Confederate Ironclads*. Mobile, AL: printed by author, 2016.

———. *The USS* Tecumseh *in Mobile Bay*. Charleston, SC: History Press, 2021.

Snitker, Grant, Christopher I. Roos, Alan P. Sullivan III, S. Yoshi Maezumi, Douglas W. Bird, Michael R. Coughlan, Kelly M. Derr, Linn Gassaway, Anna Klimaszewski-Patterson, and Rachel A. Loehman. "A Collaborative Agenda for Archaeology and Fire Science." *Nature Ecology and Evolution* 6, no. 7 (2022): 835–39.

Snow, Amy, and Jennie Trimble. *Archaeological Excavation of the Ginhouse Island Site, 1WN86*. Mobile: Archaeological Research Laboratory, University of South Alabama, 1983.

Solis, Carlos, and Richard Walling. *Archaeological Survey and Testing of Greenwood Island and Bayou Casotte Proposed Port Facilities, Jackson County, Mississippi*. Moundville: Office of Archaeological Research, University of Alabama, 1982.

Spalding, Thomas. "On the Mode of Constructing Tabby Buildings, and the Propriety of Improving Our Plantations in a Permanent Manner." *Southern Agriculturalist* 3, no. 12 (December 1830): 617–24.

Spies, Gregory C., and Michael W. Burchfield. *A Cultural Resource Survey of the Proposed Omnimax Theater and Exhibit Area in the Esplanade and Quay of the French Fort Condé, Mobile, Alabama*. Mobile, AL: Archaeotechnics, Northern Gulf Coast Archaeological Research Consortium, 1995.

Spies, Gregory C., and Michael T. Rushing. *Archaeological Investigations at the Bay Oaks Site on Dog River, Mobile County, Alabama*. Mobile, AL: Northern Gulf Coast Archaeological Research Consortium, 1983.

Spivey, Terrence. *An Ocean in My Bones*. Mobile, AL: Clotilda Descendants Association, 2022.

Spring Hill College, Mobile, Ala. 1830–1905. Mobile, AL: Commercial Printing, 1905.

Steponaitis, Vincas P. *Ceramics, Chronology, and Community Patterns: An Archaeological Study of Moundville.* New York: Academic Press, 1983.

Sternberg, G. M. "Indian Burial Mounds and Shellheaps near Pensacola, Florida." *Proceedings of the American Association for the Advancement of Science* 24 (1876): 282–92.

Stowe, Noel R. *Archaeological Excavations at Port Dauphin.* Mobile: Archaeological Research Laboratory, University of South Alabama, 1977.

———, ed. *An Archaeological-Historical Survey and Test Excavations at the Blakeley Site.* Mobile: Archaeological Research Laboratory, University of South Alabama, 1977.

———, ed. *A Cultural Resources Assessment of the Mobile-Tensaw Bottomlands: Phase II.* Mobile: Archaeological Research Laboratory, University of South Alabama, 1981.

———. "Pot Sherds and a Brass Kettle: Continuity and Change at 1MB82." *Journal of Alabama Archaeology* 21, no. 1 (1975): 68–78.

———, ed. *A Preliminary Cultural Resource Literature Search of the Mobile-Tensaw Bottomlands.* Mobile: Archaeological Research Laboratory, University of South Alabama, 1978.

———. "A Preliminary Report on Four Dugout Canoes from the Gulf Coast." *Journal of Alabama Archaeology* 20, no. 2 (1974): 194–203.

Stowe, Noel R., Richard S. Fuller, Amy Snow, and Jennie Trimble. *A Preliminary Report on the Pine Log Creek Site (1BA462).* Mobile: Archaeological Research Laboratory, University of South Alabama, 1982.

Stowe, Noel R., and Marvin E. Hoyt. *Archaeological Excavations at Fort Mims: 1973.* Mobile: Archaeological Research Laboratory, University of South Alabama, 1973.

———. *Archeological Investigation at Fort Mims.* Edited by Susan C. Olsen. Archeological Completion Report Series, Number 4. Washington, DC: National Park Service, 1975.

Stowe, Noel R., and Diane E. Silvia. *Report of the Preliminary Archaeological Testing of the Alabama Highway Department's Proposed New Dog River Bridge.* Mobile: Archaeological Research Laboratory, University of South Alabama, 1988.

Stowe, Noel R., and Rebecca N. Stowe. *Summary of Archaeological Investigations at the Site of Old St. Stephens (1995–1996).* St. Stephens, AL: St. Stephens Historical Commission, 1996.

Stuart, John. "A Map of West Florida Part of Et: Florida. Georgia Part of So: Carolina . . . & Chactaw Chickasaw & Creek Nations, 1773," known as the Stuart-Gage map. Maps 6-E-12, Thomas Gage Papers. Clements Library, University of Michigan, Ann Arbor.

———. "A Map of the Southern Indian District of North America, 1775," known as the Stuart-Purcell map. Ayer MS map 228 (vault oversize), Edward E. Ayer Collection. Newberry Library, Chicago.

Stubbs, John Delano, Jr. "Underground Harvard: The Archaeology of College Life." PhD diss., Harvard University, Cambridge, MA, 1992.

"Survey of the Bay and River Mobile, 1775." CO 700/Florida 51, 1775, Colonial Office. National Archives, Kew, UK.

Taitt, David. "A Plan of Part of the Rivers Tombecbe, Alabama, Perdido, & Scambia in the Province of West Florida, 1771." Geography and Map Division. Library of Congress, Washington, DC.

Tanner, Helen Hornbeck. "The Land and Water Communication Systems of the Southeastern Indians." In *Powhatan's Mantle: Indians in the Colonial Southeast*, rev. ed., edited by Gregory A. Waselkov, Peter H. Wood, and Tom Hatley, 27–42. Lincoln: University of Nebraska Press, 2006.

Thomas, J. Stephen. *The Shrimp Processing Industry in Bayou La Batre, Alabama*. Mobile: Center for Business and Economic Research, University of South Alabama, 1987.

Thompson, Victor D., William H. Marquardt, Michael Savarese, Karen J. Walker, Lee A. Newsom, Isabelle Lulewicz, Nathan R. Lawres, Amanda D. Roberts Thompson, Allan R. Bacon, and Christoph A. Walser. "Ancient Engineering of Fish Capture and Storage in Southwest Florida." *Proceedings of the National Academy of Sciences* 117, no. 15 (2020): 8374–81.

Thornton, Melanie. "Emma Langdon Roche's Artistic Legacy." *Alabama Heritage* 126 (Fall 2017): 6–15.

Thuillier, Freddy, ed. *Les terres cuites architecturales en France du Moyen Âge à l'époque contemporaine: Recherches sur les tuileries et les productions tuilières*. Drémil Lafage, France: Éditions Mergoil, 2019.

Torch Light and Public Advertiser (Hagers-Town, MD). "Mobile Register." July 12, 1827, 2.

Trickey, E. Bruce. "A Chronological Framework for the Mobile Bay Region." *American Antiquity* 23, no. 4 (1958): 388–96.

Trickey, E. Bruce, Nicholas H. Holmes Jr., and Janet R. Clute. "Archaeological and Historical Investigations at Pinto Battery or Battery Gladden, Site 1MB17, Mobile Bay, Alabama." *Journal of Alabama Archaeology* 32, no. 1 (1986): 39–62.

Trigger, Bruce G. *A History of Archaeological Thought*. 2nd ed. Cambridge: Cambridge University Press, 2006.

Usner, Daniel H., Jr. *Indians, Settlers, and Slaves in a Frontier Exchange Economy: The Lower Mississippi Valley before 1783*. Chapel Hill: University of North Carolina Press, 1992.

———. "'A Prospect of the Grand Sublime': An Atlantic World Borderland Seen and Unseen by William Bartram." In *The Attention of a Traveller: Essays on William Bartram's Travels and Legacy*, edited by Kathryn H. Braund, 19–36. Tuscaloosa: University of Alabama Press, 2022.

Vidrine, Jacqueline Oliver. *Love's Legacy: The Mobile Marriages Recorded in French, Transcribed and Annotated Abstracts in English, 1724–1786*. Lafayette: Center for Louisiana Studies, University of Southwestern Louisiana, 1985.

Villamil, Luciano. "Round Bon Secours Bay." *Spring Hill Review* 1, no. 1 (1899): 71–73.

Wakeford, Charley, and Meme Wakeford. *Food, Fun, and Fable: Recipes and Tales of the River Country*. Bon Secour, AL: printed by author, 1965.

Walker, S. T. "Mounds and Shell Heaps of the West Coast of Florida." *Annual Report of the Board of Regents of the Smithsonian Institution for the Year 1883*, 854–68. Washington, DC: Smithsonian Institution, 1885.

Waselkov, Gregory A. "Archeology and History, AD 1550 to 1950." In Waselkov, Andrus, and Plumb, *State of Knowledge*, 141–49.

———. *Archaeology at the French Colonial Site of Old Mobile (Phase I: 1989–1991)*. Mobile: University of South Alabama, 1991.

———. *The Archaeology of French Colonial North America, English-French Edition*. Guides to Historical Archaeological Literature, no. 5. Uniontown, PA: Society for Historical Archaeology, 1997.

———. *A Conquering Spirit: Fort Mims and the Redstick War of 1813–1814*. Tuscaloosa: University of Alabama Press, 2006.

———. "A Contour Map of the Bottle Creek Site." *Journal of Alabama Archaeology* 39, no. 1 (1993): 30–35.

———. "Formation of the Tensaw Community." In Paredes and Knight, *Red Eagle's Children*, 36–45.

———. "French Colonial Archaeology at Old Mobile: An Introduction." *Historical Archaeology* 36, no. 1 (2002): 3–12.

———. "Gulf Shores' Ancient Canoe Canal." *Mobile Bay* 39, no. 7 (2023): 72–75.

———. "Old Mobile: Archaeological Treasures in Louisiana's First Capital." *64 Parishes* (Fall 2022): 44–52.

———. *Old Mobile Archaeology*. Tuscaloosa: University of Alabama Press, 2005.

———. "Preserving Oral Histories of Waterfront-Related Pursuits in Bayou La Batre." NOAA Fisheries, Mississippi-Alabama Sea Grant Consortium, interviews by Michael Stieber and Harriet Richardson Seacat; Lynn Rabren, videographer; 2008. NOAA website.

———. "Return to Holy Ground: The Legendary Battle Site Discovered." *Alabama Heritage* 101 (2011): 28–37.

——— "Shellfish Gathering and Shell Midden Archaeology." *Advances in Archaeological Method and Theory* 10 (1987): 93–210.

———. "Smoking Pipes as Signifiers of French Creole Identity." In *Tu Sais Mon Vieux Jean-Pierre: Essays on the Archaeology and History of New France and Canadian Culture in Honour of Jean-Pierre Chrestien*, edited by John Willis, 137–59. Mercury Series, Archaeology Paper 178. Ottawa, Canada: Canadian Museum of History and University of Ottawa Press, 2017.

Waselkov, Gregory A., C. Fred Andrus, and Glenn E. Plumb, eds. *A State of Knowledge of the Natural, Cultural, and Economic Resources of the Greater Mobile-Tensaw River Area*. Natural Resource Report NPS/NRSS/BRD/ NRR—2016/1243. Fort Collins, CO: Biological Resources Division, National Park Service, 2016.

Waselkov, Gregory A., Donald A. Beebe, Howard Cyr, Elizabeth L. Chamberlain, Jayur Madhusudan Mehta, and Erin S. Nelson. "History and Hydrology: Engineering Canoe Canals in the Estuaries of the Gulf of Mexico." *Journal of Field Archaeology* 47, no. 7 (2022): 486–500.

Waselkov, Gregory A., and Kathryn E. Holland Braund, eds. *William Bartram on the Southeastern Indians*. Lincoln: University of Nebraska Press, 1995.

Waselkov, Gregory A., and Mike Bunn. "A Tale of Two Forts." *Alabama Heritage* 145 (Summer 2022): 32–45.

Waselkov, Gregory A., and Philip J. Carr. "Avoidance Strategies of a Displaced Post-Mississippian Society on the Northern Gulf Coast, circa 1710." In *Contact, Colonialism, and Native Communities in the Southeastern United States*, edited by Edmond A. Boudreaux III, Maureen Meyers, and Jay K. Johnson, 126–39. Gainesville: University Press of Florida, 2020.

Waselkov, Gregory A., and Raven M. Christopher. *Archeological Identification of Creek War Sites, Part 2: Technical Report on Grant Agreement No. GA-2255–11–025*. Mobile: Center for Archaeological Studies, University of South Alabama, 2012.

Waselkov, Gregory A., and Bonnie L. Gums. *Plantation Archaeology at Rivière aux Chiens, ca. 1725–1848*. Archaeological Monograph 7. Mobile: Center for Archaeological Studies, University of South Alabama, 2000.

Waselkov, Gregory A., Bonnie L. Gums, and James W. Parker. *Archaeology at Fort Mims: Excavation Contexts and Artifact Catalog*. Archaeological Monograph 12. Mobile: Center for Archaeological Studies, University of South Alabama, 2006.

Waselkov, Gregory A., David W. Morgan, and Billie Coleman. "Ceramics and Glass Beads as Symbolic Mixed Media in Colonial Native North America." *Beads: Journal of the Society of Bead Researchers* 27 (2015): 3–15.

Waselkov, Gregory A., Tara L. Potts, and Raven M. Christopher. *Archeological Identification of Creek War Sites on the Alabama River: Technical Report on Grant Agreement No. GA-2255–09–032*. Mobile: Center for Archaeological Studies, University of South Alabama, 2011.

Waselkov, Gregory A., Sarah E. Price, Alexandra Stenson, Carla Hadden, and Long Dinh. "A Woodland-Period Bone Tool Industry on the Northern Gulf of Mexico Coastal Plain." In *Bones at a Crossroads: Integrating Worked Bone Research with Archaeometry and Social Zooarchaeology*, edited by Markus Wild, Beverly A. Thurber, Stephen Rhodes, and Christian Gates StPierre, 259–88. Leiden, Netherlands: Sidestone Press, 2021.

Waselkov, Gregory A., and Craig T. Sheldon Jr. "Redstick Creek Log Cabins at Holy Ground." In *Native American Log Cabins in the Southeast*, edited by Gregory A. Waselkov, 45–66. Knoxville: University of Tennessee Press, 2019.

Waselkov, Gregory A., Craig T. Sheldon Jr., and Sarah B. Mattics. "Archaeology at the Site of *Ekvncakv*, Holy Ground." *Journal of Alabama Archaeology* 67, no. 1 (2021): 3–88.

Waselkov, Gregory A., George W. Shorter Jr., Amy S. Carruth, and Catherine M. Henderson. *The Little Market Well at Springhill and Dauphin, Mobile, Alabama*. Archaeological Monograph 2. Mobile: Center for Archaeological Studies, University of South Alabama, 1996.

Waselkov, Gregory A., and Diane E. Silvia. *Archaeology at the Krebs House (Old Spanish Fort), Pascagoula, Mississippi*. Archaeological Monograph 1. Mobile: Center for Archaeological Studies, University of South Alabama, 1995.

Waselkov, Gregory A., and Brian M. Wood. "The Creek War of 1813–1814: Effects on Creek Society and Settlement Pattern." *Journal of Alabama Archaeology* 32, no. 1 (1986): 1–24.

Watson, W. *The Civil War Adventures of a Blockade Runner*. College Station: Texas A&M University Press, 2001.

Watt, C. P. Letter to his children, from Camp Withers, December 26, 1863. C. P. Watt Civil War Letters Collection, SPR167. Alabama Department of Archives and History, Montgomery.

———. Letter to his wife, Fannie, from Camp Withers, January 13, 1864. C. P. Watt Civil War Letters Collection, SPR167. Alabama Department of Archives and History, Montgomery.

Webb, Valerie. "Lost World of Baldwin Potters." *Gulf Coast Newspapers* (Daphne, AL), July 28–29, 1999, B:1, 12.

Weir, Howard T., III. *A Paradise of Blood: The Creek War of 1813–14*. Yardley, PA: Westholme Publishing, 2016.

Welsh, Mary. "Reminiscences of Old Saint Stephens, of More Than Sixty-five Years Ago." In *Alabama Historical Society Transactions*. Vol. 3, 1898–99, 208–26. Tuscaloosa: Alabama Historical Society, 1899.

West, W. Wilson, Jr. *USS* Tecumseh *Shipwreck Management Plan*. Washington, DC: Naval Historical Center, 1997.

Wettstaed, James R. "Cutting It Back and Burning It Back: Archaeological Investigations of Charcoal Production in the Missouri Ozarks." *Journal of the Society for Industrial Archaeology* 29, no. 2 (2003): 29–46.

Whatley, John S. "An Overview of Georgia Projectile Points and Selected Cutting Tools." *Early Georgia* 30, no. 1 (2002): 7–133.

Wheeler, Ryan J. "Aboriginal Canoe Canals of Cape Sable." *Florida Anthropologist* 51, no. 1 (1998): 15–24.

———. "The Ortona Canals: Aboriginal Canal Hydraulics and Engineering." *Florida Anthropologist* 48, no. 4 (1995): 265–81.

———. "Walker's Canal: An Aboriginal Canal in the Florida Panhandle." *Southeastern Archaeology* 17, no. 2 (1998): 174–81.

White, David M. "The 'Mystery Fort' Site in Bon Secour, Alabama: Excavations, 1964–65." Manuscript on file. Center for Archaeological Studies, University of South Alabama, Mobile, 1965.

White, David M., and Susan M. Guyette. *Zen Birding*. Ropley, UK: O-Books, 2009.

White, Sarah E. *Phase II Investigations at 1BA55: Midden, Mounds, and Chungke Stones on the Bon Secour River*. Mobile: Center for Archaeological Studies, University of South Alabama, 2006.

Widerquist, Karl, and Grant S. McCall. *Prehistoric Myths in Modern Political Philosophy*. Edinburgh, Scotland: Edinburgh University Press, 2018.

Wilkie, Laurie A. *The Archaeology of Mothering: An African-American Midwife's Tale*. New York: Routledge, 2003.

———. "Expelling Frogs and Binding Babies: Conception, Gestation and Birth in Nineteenth-Century African-American Midwifery." *World Archaeology* 45, no. 2 (2013): 272–84.

———. "Granny Midwives: Gender and Generational Mediators of the African American Community." In *Engendering African American Archaeology: A Southern Perspective*, edited by Jillian E. Galle, 73–100. Knoxville: University of Tennessee Press, 2004.

———. "Magical Passions: Sexuality and African-American Archaeology." In *Archaeologies of Sexuality*, edited by Robert A. Schmidt and Barbara L. Voss, 129–42. London: Routledge, 2000.

Wilkie, Laurie A., and George W. Shorter Jr. *Lucrecia's Well: An Archaeological Glimpse of an African-American Midwife's Household*. Archaeological Monograph 11. Mobile: Center for Archaeological Studies, University of South Alabama, 2001.

Willett, E. Henry, and Joey Brackner. *The Traditional Pottery of Alabama*. Montgomery, AL: Montgomery Museum of Fine Arts, 1983.

Willey, Gordon R. *Archeology of the Florida Gulf Coast*. Smithsonian Miscellaneous Collections, vol. 113. Washington, DC: Smithsonian Institution, 1949.

———. "The Weeden Island Culture: A Preliminary Definition." *American Antiquity* 10, no. 3 (1945): 225–54.

Williams, Scott S., and Roberto Junco, eds. *The Archaeology of Manila Galleons in the American Continent: The Wrecks of Baja California, San Agustín, and Santo Cristo de Burgos (Oregon)*. Cham, Switzerland: Springer, 2021.

Wilson, Edward O. "Foreword." In Waselkov, Andrus, and Plumb, *State of Knowledge*, xix–xx.

Wilson, Shaun, and Jack Bergstresser. *Africatown Historic District National Register of Historic Places Registration Form*. Washington, DC: US Department of the Interior, National Park Service, 2012.

Wimberly, Steve B. *Indian Pottery from Clarke County and Mobile County, Southern Alabama*. Museum Paper 19. Tuscaloosa: Alabama Museum of Natural History, University of Alabama, 1960.

———. "Indian Pottery Human Effigy Heads from the Mobile Bay Region of Alabama." *Journal of Alabama Archaeology* 14, no. 1 (1968): 30–37.

Wood, Peter H. *Black Majority: Negroes in Colonial South Carolina from 1670 through the Stono Rebellion*. New York: Alfred K. Knopf, 1974.

———. "Missing the Boat: Ancient Dugout Canoes in the Mississippi-Missouri Watershed." *Early American Studies* 16, no. 2 (2018): 197–254.

Woodward, Thomas S. *Woodward's Reminiscences of the Creek, or Muscogee Indians, Contained in Letters to Friends in Georgia and Alabama*. Montgomery, AL: Barrett and Wimbish, 1859.

Work Progress Administration. *Interesting Transcripts of the British, French, and Spanish Records of the City & District of Mobile, State of Alabama, Found in Probate Court in Two Volumes*, translated by Jos. E. Caro. Mobile, AL: Local History and Genealogy Division, Mobile Public Library, 1937.

Index

Page numbers in italics refer to figures and maps.

Abaché (Clara Turner), 225–26
Africa, 177
African Americans, 19, 151–53, 181, 189, 199, 216–18, 225–31, 237; houses, 151, 173, 181, 227, 270–71, 273–78, 297
Africatown, 6, 225–31; Visitor Center site (1MB592), 227–30
agate, 79
agriculture, 18–19, 74, 175–78, 199, 209
Alabama (steamboat), 217
Alabama Archaeological Society, Southwest Chapter, 68
Alabama Department of Archives and History, 6, 109, 181–85
Alabama Department of Conservation and Natural Resources, 89; archaeology, 200; Marine Resources Division, 90; State Lands Division, 89
Alabama Department of Mental Health, 270–71
Alabama Department of Transportation (ALDOT), 54, 129, 155, 172, 186, 246, 267, 287, 292
Alabama Historical Commission (AHC), 23, 27, 31, 75, 85, 116, 125, 156, 161, 166, 193, 200, 205, 218, 261, 272, 292; Places in Peril, 272
Alabama Historic Cemetery Register, 229
Alabama Museum of Natural History, 25, 31–32, 73, 85, 89, 144, 218; Museum Expedition program, 218–19
Alabama River, 110–11, 208–9; place names, 321n1
Alabamas, 208
Alabama School of Mathematics and Science, 124
Alabama State Docks, 246, 292
Alabama Territory, 214, 217, 266
Aldea. *See* The Village
Allegri, Doris, 32
American Diver, 33–34
American Historical Association, 288
American Revolution, 130, 167–70, 275
Andrews Place site (1MB1), 25–27
Andrus, Fred, 18, 71
antiracist archaeology, 231
Antona (blockade runner), 232
Apaches, 268–70; village site, 271
Apalachees, 151, 194, 196
Archaeological Conservancy, The (TAC), 123, 209
Archaeological Research Laboratory, 109, 111
Archaic period, 51–52: Early, 44, 54–58; Middle, 44–52; Late, 49–50, 240, 290
Archeological Resource Protection Act (ARPA), 24
architecture, 116–22, 137–40, 126, 145–46, 158–59, 161–62, 166, 173–75, 188, 196, 209–13, 246–48, 291
Armistead, William, 33

arrowpoints: brass, *201*; stone, 151
Arts and Crafts Movement, 265
ashes, 211, 270
atlatl weight, 45
Auburn University—Montgomery, 131
Axsmith, Sonja, *16*

Badillo, Jody, 234
Badon, Joseph, 195–96
Badon plantation site (1BA221), 195–96
Baldin County, Alabama, 85, 171, 197, 232
Barker, Amy, *203*
Barnhill, William and Paula, 156, 239
Barracoon, 227
barrels, 155; well, 173
Barrett, Donnie, 238, *241*, *264*
Bartram, William, 213
Bartram Canoe Trails, 89
Bates, Avery, 283, 285
Battle House Hotel, 246, 292
bayberry, southern (wax myrtle), 143
Bayou La Batre, Alabama, *6*, 281–85
Bayou La Batre period (ca. 700–200 BC), 149, 253
Bayou St. John site (1BA21), 68–72
beach patrols, 232–33
beads: glass, 88, 213, 218; glass, inset into pottery, 140; stone, 43–48, 50
Beane, Tammy, 15
Bear Point peninsula, 68, 97–98
Bear Point site (1BA1), 99–101
bears, 84, 104, 143
Beebe, Donald Alex, 63–64
Bellingrath Gardens and Home, *6*, 160–62
Bellingrath-Morse Foundation, 161
Benchley, Elizabeth, 147
Bennett, Joe, 283
Bense, Judith, 116
berchas (barges or lighters), 170
Bienville Square, 294
Bigelow, Artemas, 84–85
Big Sandy points, 56–57
Biloxi Bay, 115
Binford, Lewis, 53
Biot storage jar, *256*
bioturbation, 55

birds, 84, 104–5
bitumen, 27, 69
blacksmith's forge, 118, *121*, 122
Black Warrior River, 86
blade cores, 50
Blakeley battlefield, 197–98
Blakeley town site (1BA221), 193–97, 216, 296; courthouse, 196–97; pottery kiln, 262
Blakeley Shell Mounds site (1BA229), 193, 197, 296
blockade runners, 232–33
Blue, Uriah, 207
Boas, Franz, 226–27
boatbuilding, 281, 283
Boatyard Lake, 110
bone tools, 69, *71*, *77*, *79*
Bon Secour Bay, 65; saltworks, 233
Bon Secour mound site (1BA55), 148
Bon Secour River, 65
Bon Secour tabby house site (1BA53), 139, 144–48
Bosarge, Stephanie Nelson, 281
Bottle Creek site (1BA2), *6*, 13–14, 18–19, 83–89, 171, 296
bottles, glass, 126–27, 189, 202, 234, 258, 276–77; collecting, 195, 218, 273, 278, 297
Boudousquie, Paul, 61, 255, 258
bousillage, 139
Boy Scouts, 97
Brackner, Joey, 262
Bradbury, Andrew, 12
Braund, Kathryn, 183, 267
braziers, 265, *285*
bricks, 196–97, *220*, 234, 249
Brookley Field, 109–10
Brown, Ian, 32, 73, 85–87
Brown, Margaret, 231
Bruce, Kevin, 58
Bryant's Landing sites (1BA175), *31*,
Burch, Daniel, 61
Burks, Mary Ivy, 17
Burns, Kara, 15
Butler, Katheryn and Marshall, 275
Butler, Wiley, Jr., 275
buttons: bone, 131–32; brass, *163*, 234–35, 259

Cahokia, 91
Camp Jefferson Davis, 291
Camp Powell, 233
Camp Withers, 232–35
canals, *6*, 61–67, 85, 289, 298
canebrakes, 199
cannonballs, 116, *118*, 249
cannons, 130–131, 169, 313n3
canoes, dugout, 63–64, 66, 83, 107–12
Carr, Philip, 38–46, 49–52, 54, 68, 75, 103, 229, 253, 287, 289
Carruth, Amy, 85
Carruth, Warren, 234
catlinite, *142*, *159*, *163*
cattle, 34, 131–32, 154–55, 158, 161, 164, 169, 171, 195
Cedar Point, 92
cemetery, 228–30, 271–72
charcoal production, 19, 38
Chamberlain, Reuben, 218
chamber pot, 203
charpente construction, 139–40
Chatos, 149–53
Chaudron, Louis de Vendel, 144
Chauvin family, 121–22
Cherokees, 182–85
Cherokee syllabary, 39
chert: Bangor, 57; Knox, 57; Ocala, 57
Chickasawhay River, 110
Chickasaws, 184–85, 207
Chihuahua, Eugene, 269
Choctaw Point, 294
Choctaws, 2, 157, 161, 169–70, 184–85, 207, 208, 210, 215, 218, 267
Choctaw Trading House, 215, 218–19
Christopher, Raven, 4, *30*, 267
church, 218–19
Citronelle Formation, 45
Civil War, 197–98, 232–49, 273
Clarke County, Alabama, 73–80, 237
Clay, Berle, *119*
Cleveland Museum of Natural History, 296
Clotilda shipwreck (1BA704), *30*, 32, 225, 227–28, 231, 289
Coastal Plain chert, 56–58
Coe, Joffre, 295
cofferdam, 154

coins, *168*
Col. Cowles (steamboat), 246
College of William and Mary, 228
Colon (Rochon), Henriette, 149, 157
colonialism: British, 130–31, 138–39, 156–59; French, 115–28, 130–31, 137–43, 146–47; Spanish, 147, 188–89, 215, 236, 240
Condé-Charlotte (Jonathan Kirkbride) House (1MB470), 131–32, 137
Conecuh National Forest, *6*, 36, 38–40
Confederate fortifications, 32, 92, 197–98, 236–42, 292, 294–95
Connell, Timmy, 292
context, 296–97
Cooper, Matthew, *191*
Coosa River, 208
corks, 189
Cornells, Levitia (Vicey), 207
Corps site (1CK56), 74–80
cosmology, 104
cotton, 155, 171; warehouses, 189–91, 193, 246–49
Courtaulds Fibers, 116
crabs, 281, 283–84
craft specialization, 46
Crampton Trust, 12
crawfish, 91–92
Crawford, Jessica, 209
Crawford Park, 273–75
Creeks. *See* Muscogee Creeks
Creek War (1813–1814), 199–213
crockery store, 292
cultural resource management (CRM), 3, 36–38
Cunningham, Traci, *195*, *211*
Cyr, Howard, 63, 173, 230

Daniel Foundation of Alabama, 12
Daphne, Alabama, 164–65
Daphne Pottery Company, 264–65, *285*
daub, 211
Dauphin Island, 124, 294
Dauphin Island Shell Mounds site (1MB72), *6*, 90–96, *103*
Davis, Hester, 75
Davis, Walter, 74–76, 80
De Crenay, Baron, map, *151*

INDEX 371

Deepwater Horizon oil spill, 23, 25, 27, 283
deerskins, 101
DeJarnette, David, 85, 130
DeJean, Joan, 314n3–4
Delchamps Archaeology Building, 11, 12,
Delta Explorer, 89
Demassimo, Faye, 186
dementia, 270
dendrochronology, 139
De Soto National Forest, 6, 36, 38
De Tonti Square, 294
Dinh, Long, 69
Diouf, Sylvaine, 227
Dog River, 149–51; plantation site (1MB161), 149–55
D'Olive, Dominique, 164
D'Olive plantation site (1BA190), 165–66
domesticated animals, 143
Douglas Hotel, 220
drills, 45, 50
ducks, 104
Dumas, Ashley, 4, *191*, 238, 282
Dumont de Montigny, Jean-François-Benjamin, 90, 137, 139
Dungan, Brett, 283, 285
Dunnavant, Justin, 228–30
Du Ru, Paul, 105
Dye, David, 104
dysentery, 269

ear spool, 290
Earth Diver, 90–91
earthworks, 170, 197–98, 236–42, 273
Eastern Shore of Mobile Bay, 164, 169, 260–65
Eastin, Thomas, 215
education, 252–59
effigies: anthropomorphic, 84, 88, 99–106; zoomorphic, 84, 91–92, 97, 99–102, 104–6
Eight Mile Creek, 195
España regiment, 169
Espejo, Antonio, 187–89
Espejo, Catalina, 188
ethnomedicine, 277
Exipakinoea, Catherine, 153, 157

Exploreum Science Center site (1MB189), 6, 14, 172, 186–90
Ezpeleta, José de, 169

Fagan, Brian, 76
faience, 146–47
feasting, 105
Federal Emergency Management Agency (FEMA), 23–24
Federal Highway Administration. *See* Alabama Department of Transportation
Federal Road. *See* Old Federal Road
fences, palisade, 159, 161, 166, 170, 174, 202–3, 205–6, 320n5
Fievre, Louise, 156–58
Fifty-first US Colored Troops, 244
Fillion, Barbara, 12
Finch, Bill, 18
firearms, 84, 88, 146–47
fire ecology, 40
fishhooks, 72, 77
fishing, 66, 71–72, 79, 143, 281–85, 333n2
Fish River, pottery kilns, 263
Fixed Cuba Regiment, 188
flakes (stone), 55–58, 79–80
Flirt, Jo Ann, 194
Florida Anthropological Society, Emerald Coast Chapter, 68
Florida State University, 144
Fly Creek, pottery kiln, 263
Folch, Juan Vincente, 34, 215
Fondé, Charles, 244
food remains, 71–72, 143, 171
footprints, 175–78
Fore, George, 139
Forrest, John, 45
Forrest Gump, 281
Fort Albert Sidney Johnston site (1MB369), 292, 294–95
Fort Condé (*aka* Charlotte, Carlota) site (1MB262), 6, 116, 129–33, *151*, *173*; fraising timbers, 189, *192*; moat, 131, 133; 1780 siege, 130
Fort Condé Village site (1MB132), 131, *133*
Fort Gaines, 232
Fort Louis de la Louisiane, 115–23

Fort Maurepas, 115
Fort McDermott, 237
Fort Mims Restoration Association (FMRA), 205–6
Fort Mims site (1BA218), 6, 199–207; latrine, 203; palisade, 202–3; reconstruction, 202, 204–5
Fort Morgan, 32, 61, 109, 232–33
Fort Payne chert, 57
Fort Sill, Oklahoma, 270
Fort Stoddert, 215, 266–68
Fort Toulouse, 116, 160
Fowl River, 27, 160–61
France, influence of, 259, 262
Friend, John (Jack), 33, 116, 260, 298
Friends of Old Mobile, 118
Fuerte San Esteban de Tombecbé, 215, 217
Fuller, Richard, 3, 31–32, 73, 85, 100, 103, 105, 109–10, *194*, 267

Gage, Thomas, 183
Gaines, George Strother, 215, 218
Gálvez, Bernardo de, 156, 169, 195
Geiger, Carey, *51*, 290–91
geoarchaeology, 63, 173
geophysical survey, 119, 202, 228–29, 296
Geronimo, 269
Giliberti, Joe, 75
Gill, Cameron, 23, *26*
Girard, Caroline, 68
Girl Scouts, 124, 201
Globe Hotel, 218, 220–21
gneiss, Auburn Formation, 56–57
Goode, Harriet, 275
Gopher, 91
Grace, Ed, *265*
Grand Bay National Wildlife Refuge, 23
Grand Bay shell middens, 24, *26*
grave markers, 271–72
Great Dismal Swamp, 35
Green Corn Ceremony (*poskita*), 211
Greenwood Island site (22JA516), 290–91
Grimes, Robert L., 109–10
Grise, Marie Anne, 158
Gulf of Mexico, 2, 23, 69, 281

Gulf Shores canal site (1BA709), *6*, 61–67, 289, 296, 298
Gums, Bonnie L., 4, 63, 68, 89, 97, 118, 139, 156, 161, 165–66, 187, *191*, 194, 201, 203, 237–38, 248, 254, 261, 271, 291, 294
Guyette, Susan, 147
Guynes, Jason, 12–13

Hadley, Alison, 45–46
Halcyon and Tombeckbe Public Advertiser, 215–17
Hall, John, 218
Hall's Landing, 85
Hal's Lake, 34–35
Hamilton, Peter J., 116, 214–15, 243–44
Hamilton points, 78
hammerstones, 45
Hampton Inn, Mobile, 296
Harris, Donald, 116, 130
Harvard University, 254
Harwell, Edith, 265
Havana regiment, 169
Hayden, Brian, 46
HDR, 24, 27
Hearin-Chandler Foundation, 12
hearths, 211–12
heat treatment, 45
Henry, Thomas, 292
Hickory Ground (Oce Vpofv), 207, 291–92
Higginbotham, Jay, 116, 119, 123
Hillabee greenstone, 57
Historic American Buildings Survey (HABS), 138–39
Historic Blakeley Foundation, 193
Historic Blakeley State Park, *6*, 89, 193–98
History Museum of Mobile site (1MB189), *6*, 110, 131, 172, 189–92
Hitchcock's Row, 188
Hite, Sid, 13
H. L. Hunley, 33–34, 134
Hobbes, Thomas, 43
Holland, Shawn, 156, 238
Hollis quartzite, 57
Holmes, Nancy N., and Nicholas H., Jr. 129

INDEX   373

Holmes, William Henry, 99, 103
Holy Ground (Ekvncakv) site (1LO210), 208–13, 296, 298
Homochitto River, 49–51
Horn, Teresa, 105
Horne, Verda, 17
horses, 161
Huntsville (CSS), 33
hurricanes, 24, 124–25, 138–39, 175–78, 281; Danny, 125; Ivan, 197; Katrina, 139, 281
Hurston, Zora Neale, 226–27
hydrology, 63–65

Iberville Historical Society, 214
Indian Meeting House, 296
Indian Removal, 200, 288
indigo, 155, 171
inkwells, 257
Innerarity Point, 99
Intermodal Surface Transportation Efficiency Act, 186
Interstate-10, 129; Bayway, 286; Mobile River Bridge, 286–88
Isle aux Statues, 84
Isle Dauphine, 90
Isle Massacre, 90, 128

Jackson, Andrew, 164, 199
Jackson, H. Edwin, 85
Jackson, Kern, 229, 231, 286
Jackson County Historical Society, 139
Jackson Oak, 165–66
Jamaica, 275
Jefferson, Thomas, 266–67
Jenkins, Dan, 193
Jessup, Thomas, 61
Jesuits, 254–59
J. L. Bedsole Foundation, 12
John Forrest site (22CB623), 43–48
Johnson, David, 11
Johnson, James Lawrence, 283
Johnson, Jay, 202
Johnstone, George, 161
Jones, Walter B., 25, 28, 31, 144, 148

Kaskaskias, 153, 157
Kate Dale (steamboat), 246

Kazoola (Cudjoe Lewis), 225–27
Keenan Cache, 44–45
Keene, Ray, 234
Kelly, Robert, 299
Ketchum Warehouse, 247–49
Kidder, T. R., 83
kiln sites, 194
King, Harry, 63–64, 298
King's Wharf, 130
Klotz, Joy, 118
Knutson, Jennifer, 15
Koasatis, 208
Kocis, James, 54
Krebs, Hugo Ernestus, 138

La Bellone, 128
LaCoste, Augustin and Francis, 260–61
land cessions, 199–200, 215
land survey, 215
Lankford, George, 104
lapidary technology, 43–48
La Pointe, Joseph Simon de, 137–38
La Pointe, Marie Jeanne Simon de, 153, 156
La Pointe, Marie Josephine Simon de, 138
La Pointe-Krebs plantation site (22JA526): *6*, 24, 137–43, 153; house, 137–39
La Salle, René-Robert Cavelier, Sieur de, 115
latrine. *See* privy
Lawrence, Deborah, 253
Le, Minh Van, 283
lead balls, 200–203
Le Moyne de Bienville, Jean-Baptiste, 84, 89, 128
Le Moyne d'Iberville, Pierre, 83–84, 90, 115
Les Oignonets, 149–50
Levasseur, Charles, 121–22
LeVert family, 131
LiDAR, 29–30, *62*, 198
Lightning-boy, 104
limestone quarry, 215, 217
Lincoln County Mound site (22LI504), 49–52
Lisloy plantation (1MB313), 160–63

Little Lagoon, 61–62, 233
Little Lagoon site (1BA61), 61–62, 66
Little Market well (1MB193), 292–93
livestock, 155, 161
log cabins, 209–13, 269
logging, 19, 38, 164
Lone Star Cement Company, 217
Long, Jim, Cherokee matmaker, 12
Long, Jim, St. Stephens Historical Commission director, 217–18
Loosa Yokena site (22WR691), 44–45
Louisiana State University (LSU), 273–74
Louisiane, French colonial, 115–28, 137–38, 149
Lowndes County, Alabama, 208
Loyalists, 169, 275
loyalty oaths, 156
Ludlow, Maxfield, 236
Luisiana, Spanish colonial, 169
Luna y Arellano, Tristán de, 115
Lyons, Rodney, 283, 285

Magnolia Warehouse, 246–48
maize (corn), 18, 74, 87, 98, 101, 155, 164, 171, 188, 233, 270
malaria, 269
maple syrup processing, 38
Marguerite, 137
Marianne [Rochon], 153–54
markets, 189, 262, 283, 292–93
maroons, 34–35, 216
Marshall, Jim, 283
marshes, 172–77, 188, 249
Marx, Isaac and Amelia: house, 132
Mason, J. J., 109–10
Mattics, Sarah, 4, 12, 183, 191, 220
Matt Sloan Building, 188
Maury, Dabney, 236
McAdam, John and Peter, 261
McGahey, Sam, 44–45, 110
McGirth, Zachariah, 199, 207
McGrew's Shoals, 215
McInnis, John M, III, 97
McInnis site (1BA664), 97–106, 298
McLeod phase, 73–80
McMicken, William, 244
McMillan family, 89
Mease, Edward, 164

medicine, 276–77
metal detecting, 195, 218, 234, 236, 249, 294
métis, 206–7
midwifery, 275–78, 297
Miller, Abraham, 263
millstones, 189
Mims, Samuel, 199
minié balls, 234–35, 240, 249
Mississippi-Alabama Sea Grant Consortium, 282
Mississippian iconography, 104
Mississippian period, 83–112, 148, 291
Mississippi Department of Archives and History, 24, 110
Mississippi Department of Transportation, 49
Mississippi River, 91
Mississippi Territorial Volunteers, 199, 204
Mississippi Territory, 215–17, 266
Mobile, Alabama, 115–16, 171–72, 186–92, 206, 273–78, 288, 291–92
Mobile & Birmingham Railroad, 214
Mobile & Ohio Railroad, 246
Mobile Bay, 32, 65, 149, 160, 164, 236; battle of, 32, 232, 237
Mobile Centinel, 215, 267
Mobile City Hall and Southern Market, 189–92
Mobile City Police building, 187–88
Mobile Convention Center, 172, 186
Mobile County Probate Courthouse site (1MB387), 131
Mobile Historical Commission, 129
Mobile Historic Development Commission, 292
Mobile Insurance Company, 244
Mobile Main Library, 294
Mobile Medical Museum, 137
Mobile River, 130, 161, 214, 246, 249; I-10 Bridge project, 286–88
Mobile-Tensaw delta. 17–20, 29–35, 83–84, 171, 193, 216, 268
Mobile-Washington County Choctaws (MOWA), 267
Mobilian house site (1MB147), 88–89, 118

Mobilians, 84, 90, 151, 166, 171
Montault de Monberaut, Henri, 160–63
Montault de Monberaut, Louis Augustin, 161
Montelimar, Catherine, 195
Montrose, Alabama, 260, 262
Montuse, Sylvain, 188
Montuse's Tavern and Wharf, 188–89, 190
Moore, Clarence B., 68, 91, 99–100, 103, 165
Morgan, David, 18
Morphy, Paul, 255
Mosher, Dean, 12
mosquitoes, 101, 188, 269
motherhood, 275–78
Moulton, Gordon, 11
Mound Island, 18–19, 84, 89
Mound Island Trail, 89
mounds, 49–52, 68, 83–86, 88–89
Moundville, 85–86
Mount, Robert, 17
Mount Vernon Arsenal, 268, 271
Mount Vernon Barracks, 268–71, 296; archaeological site (1MB509), 271–72
Mount Vernon Cantonment, 268, 271
Mount Vernon Insane Hospital, 270
Murray, Steve, 183
Muscogee (Creek) Nation, 207, 215, 266
Muscogee Creeks, 2, 150, 160–61, 164, 182–85; domestic dwellings, 291–92
Museum of Alabama, 6, 109, 181–85

National Center for Preservation Technology, 116
National Commercial Bank, 292
National Endowment for the Humanities, 85, 116
National Geographic magazine, 288
National Historic Landmarks, 20, 89, 123, 189
National Historic Preservation Act (NHPA), 36–37, 129
National Oceanic and Atmospheric Administration (NOAA), Voices Oral History Archives, 282
National Park Service, 18, 31, 90, 147, 201, 210; American Battlefield Protection Program, 209, 267
National Register of Historic Places, 37, 54, 123
National Science Foundation, 92, 116
National Trust for Historic Preservation, Most Endangered Historic Places, 272
Native Americans. *See* names of specific nations
naval stores, 155, 158
Navarra regiment, 169
Nell, Carlton, 156
Nelson, Erin, 103
netmaking, 281, 283–84
Newberry, Ginny, 4, 38
New Orleans, 161, 217, 275
New Orleans Colored Militia, 169
New South Associates, 172
newspapers, 215–16
Nguyen Overstreet, Sheila, 12
Nielsen, Jerry, 130
Norman, Neil, 228
Notasulga, Alabama, 226
nutting stones, 45

O'Donnell-Rosales, John, 234
Old Federal Road, 266–67
Old Mobile site (1MB94), 19, 89, 115–23, 149, 289, 296, 298, 313n3; barracks, 121–22; bicentennial, 214; residential structures, 117–21; town plan, 120–21
Old Plateau Cemetery, 228–30
Old St. Stephens site (1WN1), 6, 214–21, 296; centennial, 214; bicentennial, 217
oral history, 229, 282–25, 286–28
Orange Beach, 68, 97
ordnance explosion, 243–29
organization of technology, 55
Outlaw, Maury, 76
owls, 84, 104
Oyster Bay (Bay John), 61–62, 65
oysters, 66, 90, 98, 285; tonging, 281, 283

Paradiso sites (1BA608, 1BA609), 166–17
Parnell, James "Buddy," 116, 298
Parsons, Francis H., 99–101
Pascagoula, Mississippi, 137–13, 290–21
Pascagoulas, 140–12
Paux, Catherine, 153
Peavy's Landing, 109–11
Pélican, 137
pellagra, 270
Pénigault, André-Joseph, 90
Pensacola, Florida 115, 157, 165, 169–70, 195, 206, 217
Pensacolas, 166
peppermint, 277
Perdido Bay, 97, 99
Perdido River, 233
Perkins, Eric, *191*
Perryman, Lucrecia, 14, 273–78; archaeological site (1MB99), 273–78, 297
Perryman, Marshall, 273, 275
pestle, 154
petites nations, 151
Pfeifer, Marian, 187
Phasadvona, Souksavanh, 283
Pickett, Albert James, 200, 206
piece plotting, 55
pigs, 161
Pintlala Historical Society, 267
Pioneer II, 33–34, 303n8
pipes, 91–92
pitch, 155, 158
Pitchlynn, John, 169
Plash Island site (1BA134), 65–67
Pleistocene, 1
Plumb, Glenn, 18
plummet, 45
Poarch Band of Creek Indians (PBCI), 4, 6, 38–40, 207; Museum (Kerretv Cuko), 38, 40
Pocahontas, USS, *232*
Poe, Michael, 32–33
Pomeroy and Marshall's Warehouse, 244, 246
Pope, C. T., 233
portages, 107–8
Port Dauphin site (1MB61, 1MB221), 124–28, 314n4; tabby, 140

Porter phase (ca. AD 300–650), 149
Portier, Michael, 254
Potter, Catherine, *86*
pottery: African American, 153, 196; Apalachee, 196; Bayou La Batre-Tchefuncte, 90; Bottle Creek I, 100–101; Bottle Creek II, 101; British/American, *168*, 213, 230, 240, 257; Chato, 153; Chickachae Combed, 267; Chinese porcelain, 121, *123*; Choctaw, 196, 218, 267; colonowares, 153, 196; discs, 147–48; effigies, 88; fiber-tempered, 32, 261; French, *168*, *256*, *258*; inset with glass beads, 140; kilns, 194; McLeod, 73–74; Mound Place Incised, *var. Walton's Camp*, 103; Muscogee Creek, 207, 209, 212–13, 292; porcelain, 277; Porter-Marksville, 90; salt-glazed stoneware, 260–65; Spanish, 188; Weeden Island, 68, 70, 90
pottery kilns, 260–65, 298; clay sources, 262–63; furniture, 262, 264
Potts, Tara, 292
Poverty Point site, 50
preservation, xvi, 7, 28, 36, 74–76, 123, 129–31, 139, 147, 209, 236, 242, 271, 296–97
Presidio Santa María de Galve, 115
Price, Sarah, 4, 51, 54, 68, 75, 148, 287
Principe regiment, 169
privy, 203, 255, 257–58
Public Archaeology Day, 267

quartz, 79

Rabren, Lynn, 282
racial equity, 230
radial breaks, 55–58
raw materials, 55–57, 79–80
Reams, Robert, 38
Redstick Creeks, 164, 199–207, 208–13, 267
Reed, Walter, 270
religious medallions, 143, 258–59
resin, 155

Retirement System of Alabama (RSA) Tower site (1MB475), 172, 292–93
Revolutionary War battle sites, 156, 167, 169–70
rice, 155, 171; field, 171, 175–78
Rice Creek Landing, 89
Richardson Seacat, Harriet, 4, *256*, 282–83
Ritchie, William, 51–52
Rivière aux Chiens. *See* Dog River
Roche, Emma Langdon, 225–26
Rochon, Augustin, 153, 156–57, 240; plantation site (1BA337), 140, 153, 156–59, 170, 240–41
Rochon, Charles, 149
Rochon, Madame. *See* Louise Fievre
Rochon, Pierre, 151, 153–54; plantation site (1MB161), 149–56
rock art, 39
rock mounds, 40
Roman Catholicism, 254–59
Romans, Bernard, 138–39
Rousseau, Jean-Jacques, 43
Royal Artillery Corps, 169
Royal Forester mounted militia, 169

salt processing, 19–20, 27, 75, 233, 237
Saltus, Allen, 33
Salvage, Benjamin, 203–4
Sanborn Fire Insurance Company maps, 173
sassafras, 277
Sawyer, Lori, *98*, *211*
Sayers, David, 35
Schell, Sidney, 33
Schneider, David, 20
Scott Paper Company, 89
sculptures, 258
sea level, 1–2, 28, 282
Seaman's Bethel, 132, 134
Searcy, George, 270
Searcy, James, 270
Searcy Hospital, 270–71, 296; cemetery, 271–72
seasonality, 71–72
Seminoles, 210
Seventh Alabama Cavalry Regiment, 232–33

Seymour's Bluff site (1BA72), *19*
Shaw, Doug, *33*
sheep, 161
Sheldon, Craig T., Jr., 85, 209, *211*, 294
Sheliha, Victor von, 237, 239–40, 292
shellfish, 71–72
shell middens, 25–27, 31, 66, 90–100, 189, 197
Sherwood, Sarah, 83
Shores, Janie and Jim, 260, 298; archaeological site (1BA276), 260–61
Shorter, George, 4, 12, 68, 73–74, 124, 146, 187, *191*, 218–20, 234, 238, 241–42, 248
shovel tests, 29–30, 37–38, 45, 54, 101, 116, 139, 273–75, 278
Shrestha, Sangita, 30
shrimp trawling, 281, 283–84
signet, carnelian, 127–28
Silver Run site (1RU142), 53–58
Silvia, Diane, 3, 31–32, 85–86, 88, 92, 105, 116, 118, 139
Sixth Alabama Cavalry Regiment, 232–33
Sixtieth Infantry Regiment, 169
slavery, 19, 34, 138, 149–54, 157, 159, 161, 164, 171, 177–78, 181, 188–89, 199, 215–16, 218, 225, 237, 254, 275, 318n6
Smith, Davis, 205–6
Smith, Dawn, *191*
Smith, Hale G., 144
Smithsonian Institution, 99
Smithweck, David, 32–33, 303n8, 313n3
smoking pipes: African style, 212; Canadian style, 142–43, 159, 162–63; white clay, 235
Smoot, Benjamin, 218
smudge pits, 188
sofke, 211
Spanish Fort battlefield: Carr's Front, 241; Garrison Ridge, Union batteries, 242
Spanish Fort earthwork (1BA336), 170, 233, 236–42; postern, 237, 239–40
Spanish Fort, Alabama, 156, 236
Spanish Fort Estates, 236
Spanish Fort Historical Society, 238

Spanos, Mary, 12
Spring Hill community, 254
Spring Hill College site (1MB356), 6, 61, 254–59
Sprinkle, George Henry and Bonnie, 283
Stacey, Erin, 23, 26
stages of production, 45–47, 79
Star Ice Company, 173
statues, 84
St. Augustine, Florida, 269
steamboats, 217
Stenson, Alexandra, 69
Sternberg, George, 97–100, 103
Stickler, Justin, 97, 287
Stieber, Michael, 282
Stiggins, George, 208
St. Joseph's Chapel, 255, 257
St. Joseph's College, 254
Stockton, 85
stone tools, 44–45, 49–50, 51–52, 55–58, 78–80, 151, 240, 290
Stowe, Noel Read, 3, 31–33, 73, 109–10, 124, 130, 165, 193, 201, 218, 262, 267
Stowe (née Lumpkin), Rebecca, 124, 218
stratigraphy, 292
Strong's Bayou site (1BA81), 27
St. Stephens. *See* Old St. Stephens
St. Stephens Historical Commission, 217–18
St. Stephens Historical Park, 217, 220
Stuart, John, 183
Stuart-Gage map, 182–85
Stuart-Purcell map, 182–83
student life, 254–59
StudioEIS, 12
sugarcane, 155
superposition, 292
survey, archaeological, 23–40, 193–94, 209, 218, 228–30, 254, 271, 296
Sybil H. Smith Charitable Trust, 12
Sykes point, 44

tabby (oyster shell concrete), 138–40, 144–47, 161, 240
Taensas, 105
Taitt, David, map, 157, 164

Talladega National Forest, 40
Tallahatta sandstone, 56–57, 78, 79–80
Tallapoosa River, 208
Tangipahoa points, 52
Tankersley, Richard, 189
tanning vats, 154
tar, 38, 155, 158, 161: balls, 69
Tate, Bryan, 256
Tates Hammock phase, 68, 253
taverns, 126–27
Taylor, Robert, 23, 26
Tecumseh, 208
Tecumseh, USS, 32, 296
tenant houses, 253
Tensaw district, 200, 206
Tensaw River, 34
Tenskwatawa, 208
Tenth Minnesota Infantry Volunteer Regiment, 244
Teste de mort, 91
Third Infantry Regiment, 266
Thirteenth US Army Corps, 233–34, 242
Thomas, David Hurst, 38
Thompson, B. G., 283, 285
Thompson, Mary, 12
Thompson, Sarah, 12
Three Mile Creek, 253
Till family, 200, 205
timber, 155
tobacco, 155, 158, 171
Tohopeka, 208, 210
Tombigbee River, 73–74, 109–10, 214–15, 217–18
Tomés, 171
Tonti, Henri, 149
Towasas, 103, 166
trade, with Spain, 122–23, 128
trails, 107, 183
Troupes de la Marine, 121, 160
tuberculosis, 275
Turner, William, 287
turpentine, 19, 38, 155
Tuscaloosa (CSS), 33
Twenty-first Alabama Infantry Regiment (reenactors), 238
Twenty-seven Mile Bluff, 115–16, 149, 214

Twenty-third Wisconsin Volunteer Regiment, 244
Twenty-ninth Illinois Volunteer Regiment, 244

underwater archaeology, 32
Université Laval, 68
University of Alabama, 90, 130, 131, 254
University of North Carolina, 295
University of South Alabama: Archaeology Museum, 5, *6*, 11–16, 97, 292, 295, 299; archaeology program, 2–5, 31, 33, 253–54, 289, 295, 298–99; archaeological sites, 253–254; Center for Archaeological Studies, 3–4; students, 298
University of West Florida, 116
Upper Bryant's Landing, 18
urban archaeology, 286–88
US Army Corps of Engineers, 74, 110, 116
US Army Ordnance Department, 244
US Coast and Geodetic Survey, 99
US Department of Defense, 270
US Fish and Wildlife Service, 24
US Forest Service, 36–40; Tribal Relations Program, 38

View Point site (1BA281), 32
Village, The, 164–70; battle at, 167, 169–70
Village Point, *6*, 164
Village Point Preserve, 165
volunteers, 28, 63, 97, 195, 202–3, 209, 238, 220, 260–61, 263, 271, 289, 291, 298–99

Waldeck Regiment, Third, 169
Walkingstick, Geraldine, 12
Wallace Tunnel, 129–31
warehouses, 189–91, 244–49
Waselkov, Greg, 63–64, 68, 85–86, 89, 92, 97, 100, 103, 116, 118, 124, 139, 146–47, 156, 161, 166, 183, 194, 201–3, 206, 209, 237–38, 261, 267, 271, 282, 292
Waselkov, Kate, *264*

Waselkov, Nick, 12
Waselkov, Peter, *64*
Washington County, Alabama, 214
Washington County Courthouse Museum, 109
Water Street site (1MB510), 171–78, 287
Watson Brake site (16OU175), 44–45, 50
Watt, C. P., 233
Weatherford, William (Opunvkv Fvccetv), 209
Weatherford's plantation site (1MN112), 30
Weeden Island culture, *19*, 68–80
weirs, 72, 79
Welch, Kevin, 12
wells: barrel, 125, 173–75; Fort Mims, 200; Little Market, 292; Lucrecia Perryman's, 273–74, 297; stone-lined, 130, 218
Welsh, Mary, 215, 217, 220
West Florida: British colonial, 138–39, 147, 161, 164, 195; Spanish colonial, 34, 215, 267
White, David, 144–48
White, Sarah. *See* Sarah Price
white-tailed deer, 69, 71, 79, 143
Wilkerson, Dillard, 283
Wilkie, Laurie, 274–78
Wilson, E. O., 18
Wimberly, Steve, 105
Winona, USS, 214
Wiregrass Archaeological Consulting, 97, 100, 287
Woodland period: Early, 253; Middle, 61–67, 148, 149, 290; Late, 68–80, 253, 290
woodpeckers, 104
Wood, Peter, 177
Woodward, Thomas, 209
Works Progress Administration, 109
Wraight, Sarah, 271

Yancey Branch, 164
yellow fever, 193, 254

Zirlott, Milton and Midge, 283